ADVANCED TEXTS IN ECONOMETRICS

General Editors

C. W. J. Granger   G. E. Mizon

D1561776

LIKELIHOOD-BASED INFERENCE IN COINTEGRATED VECTOR AUTOREGRESSIVE MODELS

SØREN JOHANSEN

OXFORD
UNIVERSITY PRESS

*This book has been printed digitally and produced in a standard specification
in order to ensure its continuing availability*

OXFORD
UNIVERSITY PRESS

Great Clarendon Street, Oxford OX2 6DP

Oxford University Press is a department of the University of Oxford.
It furthers the University's objective of excellence in research, scholarship,
and education by publishing worldwide in

Oxford New York

Auckland Cape Town Dar es Salaam Hong Kong Karachi
Kuala Lumpur Madrid Melbourne Mexico City Nairobi
New Delhi Shanghai Taipei Toronto
With offices in
Argentina Austria Brazil Chile Czech Republic France Greece
Guatemala Hungary Italy Japan South Korea Poland Portugal
Singapore Switzerland Thailand Turkey Ukraine Vietnam

Oxford is a registered trade mark of Oxford University Press
in the UK and in certain other countries

Published in the United States
by Oxford University Press Inc., New York

ISBN 978-0-19-877450-1

Preface

THROUGHOUT the period of preparing this monograph I have had the pleasure of collaborating with Katarina Juselius, who introduced me to the topic of cointegration by asking me to give some lectures on the basic paper by Clive Granger (1983). Since then we have worked on developing the theory in close contact with the applications, and the results we have obtained have been driven by the need to understand the variation of economic data. Thus the theory has been forced upon us by the applications, and the theory has suggested new questions that could be asked in practice. I feel fortunate in having had the opportunity for this type of collaboration, and would like to use this opportunity to thank Katarina for being so inspiring.

The monograph is on the mathematical statistical analysis of models that have turned out to be helpful in the analysis of economic data. I have used two economic examples that have been analysed in the literature, so that the statistical concepts can be illustrated by some economic concepts, but the main emphasis is on the statistical analysis. If the reader is more interested in the applications of the techniques, I must refer to the many publications on the modelling of economic data using cointegration that have been published.

It is my hope that there is still room for a thorough exposition of the details of this theory even if the method has already found its way into textbooks in econometrics, see for instance Reinsel (1991), Banerjee *et al.* (1993), Hamilton (1994), and Lütkepohl (1991). There are a number of collections of papers that deal almost exclusively with cointegration, see Engle and Granger (1991), and special issues of *Oxford Bulletin of Economics and Statistics* (1990, 1992) and *Journal of Policy Modelling* (1993).

The monograph does not cover all aspects of cointegration but it is my hope that by studying some topics in detail one can understand the further developments. Thus I have left out the important work by Phillips (1991), Park (1992), Stock (1987) Stock and Watson (1988, 1993) to mention a few. These papers deal with cointegration from a different perspective which one can summarize as cointegrating regressions, that is, they study how the usual regression estimator can be improved in view of the underlying stochastic model. Phillips (1991) also gives a statistical theory for a semiparametric model for cointegration, but the approach taken here is entirely parametric.

In 1989 we were invited by Domenico Sartore to present the theory and application of cointegration at a summer school in Bagni di Lucca organized by Centro Interuniversitario di Econometria.

I would like to thank Domenico Sartore for inviting us, thereby creating the need for the preparation of lecture notes, Johansen (1989). Since then the theory has expanded and the notes have been used for teaching in Copenhagen at an advanced course in mathematical statistics in the Institute of Mathematical Statistics, as well as an advanced course on econometrics at the Economics Institute. We usually managed to go through Part I, that is, Chapters 1-9 in a course of two to four lectures plus two hours of exercises per week for fifteen weeks. The rest of the material, that is, the asymptotic theory would require a similar amount of time. A good background in statistics is recommended, although strictly speaking what is being used in the first part of the monograph is only the idea of analysing the likelihood function and a few mathematical techniques, which are explained in some detail. The second part requires some familiarity with probability theory and the theory of weak convergence. The program CATS in RATS was developed by Henrik Hansen in collaboration with Katarina Juselius and myself at the same time as the book was in preparation and the program is a great help in analysing economic data. The calculations in this book are performed using this package.

Many have helped me with the notes at various stages. They were originally written in T3 and later translated into Scientific Word, and I would like to thank Vivi Arp for helping me with this task, and Jurgen Doornik for an excellent file T3TEXTEX, which saves a lot of work in the translation.

I would also like to thank my many students for reading the various versions of the notes and listening and commenting carefully.

In particular I would like to thank Henrik Hansen, Bent Nielsen, Lene Pedersen, Anders Rahbek, Peter Reinhard Hansen, and Dennis Nilsson. Bent Nielsen performed the simulations, Henrik Hansen helped with the layout of the tables in Chapter 14, and Peter Reinhard Hansen helped me with the graphs. Dennis Nilsson read the entire manuscript very carefully and found numerous unfortunate formulations and many misprints.

Peter Boswijk and David Hendry have given me many very useful comments that have led to improvements in the presentation.

During the period of time in which the notes have been prepared I have enjoyed continual support from the Danish Social Science Research Foundation, which has made it possible for me to travel and discuss the ideas with many econometricians.

S. J.
Copenhagen
June 1995

Preface to second printing

Many misprints have been found and I would like to thank Peter Boswijk, Peter Reinhard Hansen, Katarina Juselius, Hans Christian Kongsted, Paolo Paruolo, Anders Rahbek and my students in Copenhagen for carefully reading the book and communicating the misprints and some improvements to the formulations.

S. J.
Copenhagen
June 1996

Models are, for the most part, caricatures of reality, but if they are good, then, like good caricatures, they portray, though perhaps in a distorted manner, some of the features of the real world. The main role of models is not so much to explain and to predict—though ultimately these are the main functions of science—as to polarize thinking and to pose sharp questions.

Mark Kac, Some mathematical models in science.

Contents

PART II

THE PROBABILITY ANALYSIS OF COINTEGRATION

PART III

APPENDICES

Part I

The Statistical Analysis of Cointegration

1

Introduction

THIS monograph is concerned with the statistical analysis of multivariate systems of a special class of non-stationary time series using the concepts of cointegration and common trends in the framework of the autoregressive model with Gaussian errors. The methodology is to formulate economic hypotheses as parametric restrictions on the Gaussian vector autoregressive model and analyse these submodels using the likelihood function.

A statistical model is a parametrized family of probability measures. The main emphasis will be put on the analysis of the statistical model. The reason for this is that by carefully constructing a statistical model where the economic concepts can be defined precisely, and the hypotheses of interest can be tested, one would hope that the analysis of the model would lead to relevant methods that have better properties than methods that are suggested on more intuitive grounds. Although some authors emphasize models and others emphasize methods, the two concepts complement one another, in the sense that a prime goal of the analysis of a model is to produce a method, and the properties of a method can only be discussed with some sort of model in the background.

Once the method has been derived by an analysis of a statistical model one can of course use it under all sorts of different circumstances, provided one can prove that it has reasonable properties under these other circumstances, that is, under some other probability model. Thus one can think of the statistical model as a method-generating tool, but my conviction is that it is much more than that, and I hope to demonstrate this claim in the following.

From my experience with economic data I find that formulating the interrelations between economic variables as a system is a useful activity. Certainly the ideal is to have a serious economic theory for the variables actually observed. Since opinions on what a serious economic theory is seem to diverge, it would be good to have some way of checking which of two rival economic theories is better. Statistics offers such a possibility using the ideas of hypothesis testing, and in econometrics this is developed as the concept of encompassing, see Mizon and Richard (1986). Unfortunately all tests rest on precise assumptions on the underlying statistical model and it is therefore important to have methods that can check if such assumptions are satisfied.

Thus the methodology is to build a statistical model that describes the fluctuations of the data, and express the economic theory in terms of the parameters of the statistical model as hypotheses on these parameters or submodels. Once this has been done an analysis of the models will reveal how the interesting economic parameters can be estimated, and how the hypotheses of economic interest can be tested.

1.1 The Vector Autoregressive Model

The basic model considered here is a vector autoregressive model (VAR) possibly including constant and linear terms or seasonal dummies, and with independent Gaussian errors. We formulate the hypothesis of reduced rank, or the hypothesis of the existence of cointegration vectors, in a simple parametric form which allows the application of the method of maximum likelihood and likelihood ratio tests. In this way we can derive estimators and test statistics for the hypothesis of a given number of cointegration vectors, as well as estimators and tests for a number of hypotheses about the cointegration vectors and their adjustment coefficients.

The VAR model formulation has been applied in econometrics in the last decade, and many of the estimation problems in the unrestricted VAR have been solved by Sims *et al.* (1990). The reduced rank regression technique, which originally was proposed by an analysis of the likelihood function for regression analysis by Anderson (1951) was applied by Velu and Reinsel (1987) for stationary processes, and by Johansen (1988*b*) for non-stationary processes. The corresponding asymptotic theory was given in Johansen (1988*b*) and was also developed by Ahn and Reinsel (1990) and Reinsel and Ahn (1992), and the results are generalized by Phillips (1991).

In my opinion the flexibility of the autoregressive formulation allows not only the statistical description of a large number of real data sets, but it also allows the embedding of interesting economic hypotheses in a general statistical framework, in which one can define the concepts of interest and actually prove results about them. In particular we can define the notions of integration, cointegration and common trends, see Chapter 3.

Such models do not represent the truth about economic phenomena, but should be considered a useful tool in describing the statistical variation of the data, such that insight can be gained on the interrelations between economic variables.

Our experience with analysing macro economic data is that the models quite often provide an adequate fit of the data, especially after we have been thinking hard about which variables we should include in the analysis. It is an empirical finding that we have usually been able to do so with two lags for seasonally unadjusted data.

1.2   Building Statistical Models

First of all it must be emphasized that the purpose of constructing a statistical model is not to replace serious economic models with arbitrary statistical descriptions, but rather to provide a framework in which one can compare the economic theories with reality, as measured by the data series. It seems that a proper statistical treatment of systems of economic variables should include the formulation of a statistical model where one can

- describe the stochastic variation of the data, such that inferences concerning the various economic questions are valid;
- define the economic concepts in terms of the statistical concepts, like long-run relations which become cointegrating relations;
- formulate the interesting economic theories and questions in terms of the parameters of the model;
- derive estimators and test statistics as well as their (asymptotic) distribution such that useful inferences can be drawn.

If we have such a statistical model describing a relevant set of economic variables, the first task is to check for model specification, to make sure that the first point is satisfied, or at least not completely false. If it turns out that the model is a valid description from a statistical point of view, one can proceed to test that the formulated economic theory is consistent with the data. The reason that this point is important is that often the economic theory is developed for rather abstract concepts, whereas when it comes to the observations, one has to put up with actual data series that are not observations of the abstract concepts, but carefully selected proxies. Thus although one's economic theory may be fine, the data chosen may not illustrate this. Hence a careful statistical analysis helps to support the economic conclusions.

In the case of cointegration and common trends there are a number of questions that need a statistical formulation and treatment. First of all, the number of the cointegrating relations or common trends has to be determined and compared with the number prescribed by the theory. Next, economic hypotheses about the cointegrating relations or common trends have to be formulated and tested, and here the interpretation of the concepts becomes very important.

An economic theory is often formulated as a set of behavioural relations or structural equations between the levels of the variables, possibly allowing for lags as well. If the variables are $I(1)$, that is, non-stationary with stationary differences, it is convenient to reformulate them in terms of levels and differences, such that if a structural relation is modelled by a stationary relation then we are led to considering stationary relations between levels, that is, cointegrating relations.

It is well known that structural results are difficult to extract from the reduced form equations, but the property of stationarity and non-stationarity can be deduced from the reduced form since they are basically statistical concepts, rather than economic notions, see section 5.5.

Thus the reason that cointegration is interesting is that the cointegrating relation captures the economic notion of a long-run economic relation. And the reason that a statistical theory for the estimation and testing of cointegrating relations can be constructed rests on the fact that the reduced form suffices for the determination of the basic cointegrating relations. On the other hand a mindless attempt at finding cointegrating relations without knowing what they mean is not going to be fruitful, so I believe that the econometrician has to carefully choose the variables that should enter the study, and carefully discuss the economic theory that motivates this.

The reason for this discussion of the statistical model is that one often finds the opinion expressed that the purpose of a statistical analysis is to find the estimates of the parameters that one knows are the interesting ones. What I want to point out is that the statistical model offers a much richer basis for discussion of the relation between economic theory and economic reality.

In the above discussion we have focused entirely on statistical models that describe full systems, that is, the joint stochastic behaviour of all the processes observed. In situations where one has twenty-five, or even 100, variables, this may not be feasible, since the interrelations between so many variables are extremely difficult to understand. It is customary to fix certain variables, which it is felt influence the main variables without being influenced by the variables of main concern. Thus assuming some sort of exogeneity one can construct a partial model. It is obvious that if we do not specify the stochastic properties of the exogenous variables it is impossible to make statistical inference for the parameters that we have been estimating. A compromise is to model some variables carefully and some variables less carefully, that is, one can try to develop methods for the parameters of interest that are valid under a wide range of assumptions on the exogenous variables.

A main point of view in the development of the likelihood-based theory of cointegration has been to find models that can be handled analytically.

A very general procedure for the analysis of statistical data is to formulate a family of densities $\{f(x,\theta), \theta \in \Theta\}$ for the data $X = x$, and then postulate the existence of the maximum likelihood estimator $\hat{\theta}$, which is then calculated by some general optimizing algorithm. The theory of weak convergence of probability measures gives the possibility to make asymptotic inference.

This general scheme can always be followed but it is worthwhile to pay special attention to situations where models exist, like the general linear regression model with Gaussian errors, where $\hat{\theta}$ can be proved to exist, and conditions are known for it to be unique. The algorithms for solving linear equations are well understood, and we even have the possibility to make exact inference.

In the autoregressive model with Gaussian errors one is immediately led to ordinary regression as the maximum likelihood estimator of the unrestricted VAR and, as will be shown below, to reduced rank regression for the cointegrated VAR. We then describe a number of models by parametric restrictions and for each model analyse the likelihood function to see how the maximum likelihood estimator has to be modified in view of the imposed restrictions. The models chosen have the property that reduced rank regression, or some simple modification of it, can be used for the analysis since these models are also models where the existence and uniqueness of the maximum likelihood estimator can be checked.

One can of course impose all sorts of restrictions on the parameters, for instance different lag lengths in different equations, non-linear restrictions on the long-run parameters, identities between long-run and short-run parameters, but it is hard to obtain any exact results for such models.

The models we have chosen to discuss in this book have the property that one can discuss existence and uniqueness of maximum likelihood estimators and describe algorithms for their calculation. This is not possible for general hypotheses, but of course general optimization algorithms can be used if the model formulated is very complex. Thus the models we are discussing are relatively simple, not because all models are but because those are the models for which we have results. It is my basic conviction that in order to analyse statistical data one has to understand simple models well.

1.3   Illustrative Examples

As illustrative examples to serve as motivation for the analysis given here we have chosen two sets of data, which illustrate different types of economic questions. The first example is chosen with the purpose of finding a money relation expressing a relation between real money, real income, and the cost of holding money as proxied by the difference between the long and short interest rate. Since multiplicative effects are assumed we use logs of money and income. Thus the data consist of observations from 1974: 1 to 1987: 3 of log real money ($m2$), log real income (y) the bank deposit rate i^d for interest-bearing deposits, and the bond rate i^b which plays an important role in the Danish economy.

The data are analysed in detail in Johansen and Juselius (1990) and Juselius (1994).

The other example is an investigation of the purchasing power parity and uncovered interest parity between Australia and the United States. The data were supplied by Tony Hall and analysed in Johansen (1992c) and consist of quarterly observations for the period 1972: 1 to 1991: 1.

The variables measured are the consumer price index in logarithms for Australia, p^{au}, the United States, p^{us}, the exchange rate, $exch$, measured as the log of the price of US dollars in Australian dollars, and the five-year treasury bond rate in both countries i^{au} and i^{us}.

The reason for choosing these examples is that we can illustrate the procedures for finding cointegrating relations and formulate simple economic hypotheses in terms of the parameters.

It must be emphasized that a cointegration analysis cannot be the final aim of an econometric investigation, but it is our impression that as an intermediate step a cointegration analysis is a useful tool in the process of gaining understanding of the relation between data and theory, which should help in building a relevant econometric model.

1.4   An Outline of the Contents

I have chosen to split the book into two parts and two appendices.

Part I consists of the first nine chapters, and gives the basic results around Granger's theorem, the model formulation, and the derivation of estimators and test statistics. We briefly indicate the asymptotic theory for the test statistics and the estimators.

In Part II, which consists of Chapters 10 to 15, I then give the theory for the asymptotic analysis using the weak convergence of probability measures. Whereas Part I mainly assumes the Gaussian error distribution in order to work with the likelihood methods, I relax this assumption in Part II, since the asymptotic analysis is valid under more general circumstances. One can prove very general results, but I have chosen to assume independent identically distributed errors with finite second moments. Then the solution of the autoregressive model is a linear process, and the theory for such processes is quite simple. I have collected some algebraic and analytic results in Appendix A, and in Appendix B a brief introduction to weak convergence on $C[0,1]$ is given. This is by no means a crash course in weak convergence, but a gentle reminder of some of the basic concepts.

The contents of the chapters are as follows.

In Chapter 2 the statistical analysis of the unrestricted vector autoregressive model is discussed in some detail. These results are of course classical and can be found in Anderson (1971). For completeness and to establish the notation they are given here. Chapter 3 gives the definitions of integrated variables, cointegration and common trends. Examples are given and it is shown that moving average models in terms of common trends and the autoregressive error correction model give rise to integrated and cointegrated variables.

In Chapter 4 the representation theorems for integrated variables are given. The basic idea throughout is to give necessary and sufficient conditions for a process to be $I(0)$, $I(1)$, and $I(2)$ respectively. These conditions, see Theorems 2.3, 4.2, and 4.4, are rather complicated but are necessary for a full understanding of the statistical models as well as the probability results that follow in later chapters.

In Chapter 5 we spend most of the space on a discussion of what the $I(1)$ model for cointegration can be used for, that is, which economic hypotheses can be conveniently investigated in the framework described. The question of identification is discussed, and various models described by restrictions on the deterministic terms are considered.

Chapter 6 contains the statistical analysis of the $I(1)$ model, where it is shown that estimation of the unrestricted cointegrating space can be performed using reduced rank regression, and that the same analysis can be used for models with restrictions on the deterministic terms. Estimators and likelihood ratio tests are derived and the asymptotic distribution is given. Finally it is shown how the asymptotic distributions can be applied to determine the rank of the cointegrating space.

In Chapter 7 hypotheses on β are discussed, and it is shown how to estimate β under various linear restrictions. The theory is illustrated by some examples. The partial models and hypothesis testing on the adjustment parameters α are discussed and analysed in Chapter 8. Finally Chapter 9 contains a brief analysis of the $I(2)$ model with the purpose of deriving a misspecification test for the $I(1)$ model.

In Chapter 10 the properties of the process and the sample moments are given and the asymptotic properties of the test statistic for cointegration rank are given in Chapter 11. Chapter 12 then applies these results to test hypotheses on the cointegrating rank and to estimate it in case it is not known a priori. In Chapter 13 the asymptotic distribution of the estimator for the cointegrating vector is shown to be mixed Gaussian. Only the estimator in the unrestricted model is discussed in detail, but results are also given for the case of identified vectors. The asymptotic properties of the estimators for the other parameters are also given and the asymptotic distributions of test statistics for hypotheses on β are given. In Chapter 14 we derive some results for the power function of the test for cointegrating rank for local alternatives and in Chapter 15 tables are given of the asymptotic distributions derived in previous chapters. In Appendix A, I have collected some useful results about eigenvalues and eigenvectors and some general results from multivariate statistics and regression that are needed in the analysis of the statistical models.

The main emphasis in this monograph is on the derivation of test statistics and estimators, but for the derivation of the asymptotic properties, knowledge of the Brownian motion is necessary, and Appendix B contains a brief reminder of the theory of weak convergence and the construction of Brownian motion as given in Billingsley (1968).

1.5   Some Further Problems

The theory presented in the monograph is the beginning of a systematic investigation of the structure of autoregressive models for non-stationary processes. Many problems remain open, even in this simple framework.

In my opinion the most important is the development of improved finite sample approximations to the distributions of the test statistics, which can supplement the asymptotic results presented here. It is important to develop Bartlett corrections or Edgeworth expansions, as is known from the theory of stationary processes.

The analysis of models for $I(2)$ processes is mentioned in Chapter 9, but much needs to be worked out in detail, and the methods need the constant input from applications to make sure that the theory is kept on the right track.

There is one topic that is not mentioned in this monograph, and that is seasonal cointegration. Seasonal cointegration seems to be a useful concept for the analysis of some time series, and the mathematical and statistical analysis has been worked out, see Hylleberg, *et al.* (1990), Lee (1992), and Johansen and Schaumburg (1996). Since seasonal cointegration can occur at different frequencies and with different ranks and cointegrating vectors, the theory becomes somewhat more complicated, and I have chosen only to give the basic version of the representation theorem as exercise 4.8.

2
The Vector Autoregressive Model

THIS chapter deals with the statistical analysis of the unrestricted vector autoregressive model (VAR) but first a result is given which is a necessary and sufficient condition that the autoregressive process defined by the equations is stationary. This condition is an important diagnostic tool in the applications of the models and should routinely be checked in the applications. We first formulate a general expression for the solution of the equation defining the process and then give conditions on the parameters such that the initial values can be chosen such that the process becomes stationary. In section 2.2 we derive the ordinary least squares estimators as the maximum likelihood estimators and deal briefly with the asymptotic properties of the estimators in case the process is stationary. This is of course standard knowledge, see Anderson (1971), but the results are given here in order to contrast them with the results that are valid for non-stationary processes. Finally in section 2.3 we give a brief description of some misspecification tests for the VAR.

2.1 The Vector Autoregressive Process

Consider the p-dimensional autoregressive process X_t defined by the equations

$$X_t = \Pi_1 X_{t-1} + \cdots + \Pi_k X_{t-k} + \Phi D_t + \epsilon_t, \, t = 1, \ldots, T, \qquad (2.1)$$

for fixed values of $X_{-k+1}, \ldots, X_0$, and independent identically distributed errors ϵ_t that are $N_p(0, \Omega)$.

The deterministic terms D_t can contain a constant, a linear term, seasonal dummies, intervention dummies, or other regressors that we consider fixed and non-stochastic. The results and conditions are conveniently expressed in terms of the characteristic polynomial:

$$A(z) = I - \sum_{i=1}^{k} \Pi_i z^i,$$

with determinant $|A(z)|$.

The first result gives the solution X_t of equation (2.1) as a function of the initial values and the ϵ and hence determines the properties of X_t given its initial values. Note that the result does not impose any conditions on the parameters .

THEOREM 2.1 *The solution of equation (2.1) as a function of initial values and ϵ is given by*

$$X_t = \sum_{s=1}^{k} C_{t-s}(\Pi_s X_0 + \cdots + \Pi_k X_{-k+s}) + \sum_{j=0}^{t-1} C_j(\epsilon_{t-j} + \Phi D_{t-j}), \quad (2.2)$$

where $C_0 = I$ and C_n is defined recursively by

$$C_n = \sum_{j=1}^{\min(k,n)} C_{n-j}\Pi_j, \, n = 1, 2, \ldots \qquad (2.3)$$

The generating function $C(z) = \sum_{n=0}^{\infty} z^n C_n$ is convergent for $|z| < \delta$ for some $\delta > 0$. For these values of z it satisfies $C(z)A(z) = I$ such that $C(z) = A(z)^{-1}$.

PROOF There is no loss of generality in setting $\Phi = 0$, since the result is a purely algebraic result which does not depend on the nature of the ϵ. Consider first the case $k = 2$, where the equations defining C_n give

$$C_0 = I, C_1 = \Pi_1, C_2 = C_1\Pi_1 + \Pi_2, C_3 = C_2\Pi_1 + C_1\Pi_2, \ldots$$

The equations defining X_t can be written as

$$\begin{aligned} X_t &= \Pi_1 X_{t-1} + \Pi_2 X_{t-2} + \epsilon_t, \\ X_{t-1} &= \Pi_1 X_{t-2} + \Pi_2 X_{t-3} + \epsilon_{t-1}, \\ &\vdots \\ X_2 &= \Pi_1 X_1 + \Pi_2 X_0 + \epsilon_2, \\ X_1 &= \Pi_1 X_0 + \Pi_2 X_{-1} + \epsilon_1. \end{aligned}$$

If these equations are multiplied by C_0, C_1, ..., C_{t-1} respectively, and then summed it is seen that the recursive definition of C_n implies that X_{t-1}, X_{t-2}, ..., X_1 are eliminated and that what remains is

$$X_t = \sum_{j=0}^{t-1} C_j \epsilon_{t-j} + (C_{t-2}\Pi_2 + C_{t-1}\Pi_1)X_0 + C_{t-1}\Pi_2 X_{-1}.$$

This is a special case ($k = 2$) of the general result (2.2).

The general case is proved as follows. We multiply by C_n in (2.1) with t replaced by $t - n$ and sum from 0 to $t - 1$

$$\sum_{n=0}^{t-1} C_n X_{t-n} = \sum_{n=0}^{t-1} C_n \sum_{i=1}^{k} \Pi_i X_{t-n-i} + \sum_{n=0}^{t-1} C_n \epsilon_{t-n}.$$

Introducing $m = n + i$ we get

$$\sum_{m=1}^{t-1} \left[\sum_{i=1}^{\min(m,k)} C_{m-i} \Pi_i \right] X_{t-m}$$

$$+ \sum_{m=t}^{t+k-1} \left[\sum_{j=m-t+1}^{k} C_{m-j} \Pi_j \right] X_{t-m} + \sum_{n=0}^{t-1} C_n \epsilon_{t-n}.$$

The recursive definition of C_m shows that X_{t-m}, $m = 1, \ldots, t - 1$ has the same coefficient on both sides such that X_{t-m} cancels. What is left is

$$X_t = \sum_{m=t}^{t+k-1} \left[\sum_{i=m-t+1}^{k} C_{m-i} \Pi_i \right] X_{t-m} + \sum_{n=0}^{t-1} C_n \epsilon_{t-n}.$$

Introducing $s = m - t$ we find

$$X_t = \sum_{s=0}^{k-1} [\sum_{i=s+1}^{k} C_{s+t-i} \Pi_i] X_{-s} + \sum_{n=0}^{t-1} C_n \epsilon_{t-n},$$

which proves the representation (2.2).

If we define $\Pi_0 = -I$, then we can write the recursion for C_n as

$$\sum_{j=0}^{\min(k,n)} C_{n-j} \Pi_j = -\delta_{n0}, \quad n = 0, 1, \ldots,$$

where δ_{n0} is zero for $n = 1, 2, \ldots$, and I for $n = 0$. This implies a relation for the generating functions

$$-I = \sum_{n=0}^{\infty} (-\delta_{n0}) z^n = \sum_{n=0}^{\infty} \sum_{j=0}^{\min(k,n)} z^{n-j} C_{n-j} z^j \Pi_j = C(z)(-A(z)).$$

Note that the determinant $|A(z)|$ is a polynomial such that it has only finitely many roots $z_1, \ldots, z_p$, say. Let $\delta = \min_i |z_i|$ then since $A(0) = I$ it is seen that $\delta > 0$ and $A(z)^{-1}$ is convergent for $|z| < \delta$. $\square$

As a simple special case consider $k = 1$, where the representation (2.2) reduces to

$$X_t = \Pi_1^t X_0 + \epsilon_t + \Pi_1 \epsilon_{t-1} + \cdots + \Pi_1^{t-1} \epsilon_1.$$

In this case $A(z) = I - z\Pi_1$ and $C(z) = \sum_{n=0}^{\infty} z^n \Pi_1^n = (I - z\Pi_1)^{-1}$.

The solution given in Theorem 2.1 is valid for any set of parameters. In the following we show how the parameters must be restricted in order for equation (2.1) to define a stationary process. By a stationary process we mean a process for which the distribution of $X_{t_1}, \ldots, X_{t_m}$ is the same as the distribution of $X_{t_1+h}, \ldots, X_{t_m+h}$ for any $h = 1, 2, \ldots$

The only stationary processes that we need here are the linear processes generated by i.i.d. errors, as discussed in Appendix B.

The basic assumption which will be used throughout is

ASSUMPTION 1 *The characteristic polynomial satisfies the condition that if $|A(z)| = 0$, then either $|z| > 1$ or $z = 1$.*

The assumption excludes explosive roots with $|z| < 1$, and seasonal roots, with $|z| = 1$, other than $z = 1$. If $z = 1$ is a root we say that the process has a unit root. The following result is well known, see Anderson (1971).

THEOREM 2.2 *Under Assumption 1 and if D_t is bounded by a polynomial in t, a necessary and sufficient condition that the initial values of X_t can be given a distribution such that the process $X_t - E(X_t)$ becomes stationary, is that $|A(1)| \neq 0$. In this case the process has the representation*

$$X_t = \sum_{n=0}^{\infty} C_n(\epsilon_{t-n} + \Phi D_{t-n}), \qquad (2.4)$$

where $C_0(z) = \sum_{n=0}^{\infty} C_n z^n = A(z)^{-1}$ is convergent for $|z| < 1 + \delta$ for some $\delta > 0$.

PROOF We will give the proof for $k = 1$ first and then apply the usual trick of writing the process in companion form, that is, consider the process $X_t, \ldots, X_{t-k}$ as an $AR(1)$ process. In case $k = 1$, where $A(z) = I - z\Pi_1$, the roots of $|A(z)|$ are just the reciprocal of the non-zero eigenvalues of Π_1. In this case the solution of equation (2.1) is given by

$$X_t = \Pi_1^t X_0 + \sum_{i=0}^{t-1} \Pi_1^i(\epsilon_{t-i} + \Phi D_{t-i}). \qquad (2.5)$$

Since the roots of $|A(z)| = |I - z\Pi_1|$ are assumed to be outside the unit disk, the eigenvalues of Π_1 are all inside the unit disk, which means that the coefficients Π_1^i tend to zero exponentially fast, and hence that the linear process

$$X_t^* = \sum_{i=0}^{\infty} \Pi_1^i \epsilon_{t-i}$$

is well defined as a stationary and ergodic process. In order to see this we use Kolmogorov's three series criterion or Breiman (1992, Corollary 3.22).

It follows from these results that since the variance

$$\text{Var}(X_t^*) = \sum_{i=0}^{\infty} \Pi_1^i \Omega \Pi_1^{i\prime}$$

is finite, see (A.4), the series defining X_t^* is convergent almost surely.
Similarly it is seen that

$$\sum_{i=0}^{\infty} \Pi_1^i \Phi D_{t-i}$$

is convergent for all t by the assumption on D_t. If in (2.5) we choose the initial values as fixed quantities, that is, condition on the initial values, then clearly the process $X_t - E(X_t)$ is not stationary, although in some sense it is asymptotically stationary. In order to make the process stationary we need to choose the initial values to have the invariant distribution which in this case is Gaussian with mean zero and variance given by $\text{Var}(X_0^*)$. We can also obtain a representation of the process as expressed by the infinite past, by choosing the initial values to have the representation given by X_0^*. Thus the condition on the eigenvalues is not enough to make the process stationary but enough to make the process stationary for a suitable choice of the initial values.   We therefore choose the initial value X_0 to have the invariant distribution given by $X_0^* = \sum_{i=0}^{\infty} \Pi_1^i \epsilon_{-i} + \sum_{i=0}^{\infty} \Pi_1^i \Phi D_{-i}$ and find the representation

$$X_t = \Pi_1^t \sum_{i=0}^{\infty} \Pi_1^i (\epsilon_{-i} + \Phi D_{-i}) + \sum_{i=0}^{t-1} \Pi_1^i (\epsilon_{t-i} + \Phi D_{t-i}) = \sum_{i=0}^{\infty} \Pi_1^i (\epsilon_{t-i} + \Phi D_{t-i}),$$

such that $X_t - E(X_t)$ is a stationary process. Note that $C_0(z) = \sum_{i=0}^{\infty} \Pi_1^i z^i$ is related to the polynomial $A(z) = I - z\Pi_1$ by the relation $A(z)C_0(z) = I$.
Next consider the general case, $k > 1$, and define the companion form

$$\tilde{X}_t = (X_t', X_{t-1}', \ldots, X_{t-k+1}')',$$
$$\tilde{\epsilon}_t = (D_t'\Phi' + \epsilon_t', 0, \ldots, 0)',$$

$$\tilde{\Pi}_1 = \begin{pmatrix} \Pi_1 & \Pi_2 & \cdots & \Pi_{k-1} & \Pi_k \\ I & 0 & \cdots & 0 & 0 \\ \vdots & \vdots & & \vdots & \vdots \\ 0 & 0 & \cdots & I & 0 \end{pmatrix},$$

such that

$$\tilde{X}_t = \tilde{\Pi}_1 \tilde{X}_{t-1} + \tilde{\epsilon}_t = \tilde{\Pi}_1^t \tilde{X}_0 + \tilde{\epsilon}_t + \tilde{\Pi}_1 \tilde{\epsilon}_{t-1} + \cdots + \tilde{\Pi}_1^{t-1} \tilde{\epsilon}_1.$$

We can recover X_t as a function of the initial values X_0 and $\epsilon_1, \ldots, \epsilon_t$ by multiplying by the matrix $(I, 0, \ldots, 0)$.

The process $\tilde{X}_t - E(\tilde{X}_t)$ is an $AR(1)$ process with a singular variance matrix for the errors $\tilde{\epsilon}_t$ which by the above result for $k = 1$ is stationary if the roots of $\tilde{\Pi}_1$ are inside the unit disk.

We now want to show that the conditions on the roots of the matrix polynomial $A(z)$ can be converted to a condition on the non-zero eigenvalues of $\tilde{\Pi}_1$.

Consider therefore an eigenvector $v = (v_1', \ldots, v_k')'$ for $\tilde{\Pi}_1$ which satisfies the equation $\lambda v = \tilde{\Pi}_1 v$ for $\lambda \neq 0$, or

$$\begin{aligned} \lambda v_1 &= \Pi_1 v_1 + \cdots + \Pi_k v_k \\ \lambda v_{i+1} &= v_i, \qquad\qquad\qquad i = 1, \ldots, k-1. \end{aligned} \qquad (2.6)$$

Thus v_i has the form

$$v_i = \lambda^{-i+1} v_1, \, i = 1, \ldots, k.$$

Inserting this into (2.6) we find that (λ, v_1) satisfies

$$\lambda v_1 = \Pi_1 v_1 + \cdots + \lambda^{-k+1} \Pi_k v_1,$$

or

$$(I - \lambda^{-1}\Pi_1 - \cdots - \lambda^{-k}\Pi_k)v_1 = 0,$$

which shows that λ^{-1} is a root of $|A(z)| = |I - z\Pi_1 - \cdots - z^k\Pi_k| = 0$. This gives a convenient way to calculate the roots of a matrix polynomial $A(z)$ as the eigenvalues of a square but non-symmetric matrix $\tilde{\Pi}_1$.

The condition that the roots of $A(z)$ are greater than 1 in modulus implies that the reciprocal values, which are the eigenvalues of $\tilde{\Pi}_1$, are all less than 1 in absolute value, hence inside the unit circle. Thus under Assumption 1 and $|A(1)| \neq 0$ we can define the process

$$\tilde{X}_t^* = \sum_{n=0}^{\infty} \tilde{\Pi}_1^n \tilde{\epsilon}_{t-n}$$

as above and we find that $\tilde{X}_t - E(\tilde{X}_t)$ becomes stationary if we choose the initial values $\tilde{X}_0 = (X_0', X_{-1}', \ldots, X_{-k+1}')'$ to have the distribution of $\tilde{X}_0^*$, and then $\tilde{X}_t = \tilde{X}_t^*$.

The representation for X_t is found by premultiplying by $(I, 0, \ldots, 0)$ and we find

$$X_t = \sum_{n=0}^{\infty} C_n(\epsilon_{t-n} + \Phi D_{t-n}).$$

This proves that the condition that $A(1)$ has full rank is sufficient.

To prove that it is necessary assume that $A(1)$ has reduced rank. Since all entries of $A(z) - A(1)$ have a root at $z = 1$ they can each be factorized into $(1 - z)$ times a polynomial. Hence we can define a polynomial

$$A^*(z) = \frac{A(z) - A(1)}{1 - z}, \; z \neq 1,$$

such that

$$A(z) = A(1) + A^*(z)(1 - z).$$

See Lemma 4.1 for a general formulation of this result. We define the lag operator L by the property that $LX_t = X_{t-1}$, and the difference operator $\Delta = 1 - L$ or $\Delta X_t = X_t - X_{t-1}$. In this notation we write equation (2.1) as

$$A(L)X_s = A(1)X_s + A^*(L)(1 - L)X_s = \Phi D_s + \epsilon_s, \; s = 1, \ldots, T, \quad (2.7)$$

Now the reduced rank of $A(1)$ implies that there exists a vector $\xi \in R^p$ such that $\xi' A(1) = 0$ and $\xi \neq 0$. Multiplying in (2.7) by ξ' and summing over s from 1 to t we find that

$$\xi' A^*(L)(X_t - X_0) = \xi' \sum_{s=1}^{t} (\Phi D_s + \epsilon_s).$$

We shall now argue that $X_t - E(X_t)$ is non-stationary. This follows since if it were stationary, then clearly the left-hand side would be stationary, which contradicts that there is a non-stationary random walk on the right-hand side. This proves the necessity.

That $C(z)$ is convergent for $|z| < 1 + \delta$ for some $\delta > 0$ follows from the fact that if the roots of $|A(z)|$, $z_1, \ldots, z_p$, say, satisfy the condition that $\min_i |z_i| = 1 + \delta > 1$, then the power series for $A(z)^{-1}$ will be convergent for $|z| < 1 + \delta$. $\qquad \square$

2.2 The Statistical Analysis of the VAR

The unrestricted autoregressive model (VAR) with Gaussian errors and deterministic terms D_t is defined by

$$X_t = \Pi_1 X_{t-1} + \cdots + \Pi_k X_{t-k} + \Phi D_t + \epsilon_t, \; t = 1, \ldots, T, \quad (2.8)$$

where the errors ϵ_t are independent Gaussian with mean zero and variance Ω. The initial values $X_{-k+1}, \ldots, X_0$ are fixed and the parameters are

$$(\Pi_1, \ldots, \Pi_k, \Phi, \Omega),$$

which are unrestricted.

We introduce the notation $Z_t' = (X_{t-1}', \ldots, X_{t-k}', D_t')$, for the stacked vector and $B' = (\Pi_1, \ldots, \Pi_k, \Phi)$ for the corresponding parameters. Thus

Z_t is a vector of dimension $pk + m$ and B' is a matrix of dimension $p \times (pk + m)$.

The model expressed in these variables becomes

$$X_t = B'Z_t + \epsilon_t, \ t = 1, \ldots, T. \qquad (2.9)$$

The Gaussian errors allow us to analyse the log likelihood function

$$\log L(B, \Omega) = -\frac{1}{2}T\log(2\pi) - \frac{1}{2}T\log|\Omega| - \frac{1}{2}\sum_{t=1}^{T}(X_t - B'Z_t)'\,\Omega^{-1}(X_t - B'Z_t),$$

which leads to the equations for estimating B

$$\sum_{t=1}^{T} X_t Z_t' = \hat{B}' \sum_{t=1}^{T} Z_t Z_t',$$

and the usual regression estimators

$$\hat{B} = (\sum_{t=1}^{T} Z_t Z_t')^{-1}(\sum_{t=1}^{T} Z_t X_t') = S_{zz}^{-1} S_{zx}, \qquad (2.10)$$

$$\hat{\Omega} = T^{-1} \sum_{t=1}^{T}(X_t - \hat{B}'Z_t)(X_t - \hat{B}'Z_t)' = S_{xx.z} = S_{xx} - S_{xz}S_{zz}^{-1}S_{zx}. \quad (2.11)$$

The maximal value is apart from a constant given by

$$L_{\max}^{-2/T} = |\hat{\Omega}|.$$

Here we use for any two processes X_t and Z_t the notation

$$S_{zx} = T^{-1} \sum_{t=1}^{T} Z_t X_t'.$$

The next result describes the asymptotic properties of the estimators in the VAR model under the assumption of stationarity for the case where $D_t = 1$. The asymptotic distributions are formulated by means of the Kronecker product.

If U and V are independent multivariate Gaussian with variances Σ_u and Σ_v respectively we let $M = UV'$ and use the notation

$$\text{Var}(M) = \text{Var}(UV') = \Sigma_u \otimes \Sigma_v,$$

such that for any two vectors ξ and η we have

$$\mathrm{Var}(\xi' M \eta) = \xi' \Sigma_u \xi \eta' \Sigma_v \eta.$$

This formula allows us to calculate the variances and covariances of the elements of M by choosing ξ and η as suitable combinations of unit vectors. Then

$$\mathrm{Var}(M_{ij}, M_{km}) = \Sigma_{u.ik} \Sigma_{v.jm}.$$

One can think of $\Sigma_u \otimes \Sigma_v$ as a matrix of a large dimension, but that requires that the matrix M is vectorized first. This will not be done here. I prefer the notation as above rather than the notation $\Sigma_v \otimes \Sigma_u$, as is usually applied, but this should cause no confusion.

THEOREM 2.3 *Under the assumptions that the ϵ are independent and identically distributed with mean zero and variance Ω, that X_t is stationary, and that $\Phi D_t = \mu$ it holds that the asymptotic distribution of the maximum likelihood estimators of the parameters $B' = (\Pi_1, \Pi_2, \ldots, \Pi_k, \mu)$ is Gaussian and given by*

$$T^{\frac{1}{2}} (\hat{B} - B) \overset{w}{\to} N(0, \Sigma^{-1} \otimes \Omega),$$

where

$$\hat{\Sigma} = T^{-1} \sum_{t=1}^{T} Z_t Z_t' \overset{P}{\to} \Sigma, \;\; and \;\; \hat{\Omega} \overset{P}{\to} \Omega.$$

Here $Z_t' = (X_{t-1}', \ldots, X_{t-k}', 1)$. Thus for any vectors ξ and η it holds that

$$\frac{T^{\frac{1}{2}} \xi' (\hat{B} - B) \eta}{\sqrt{\xi' \hat{\Sigma}^{-1} \xi \eta' \hat{\Omega} \eta}} \overset{w}{\to} N(0, 1).$$

PROOF From the expressions for the estimators (2.10) and (2.11) we find

$$\hat{B} - B = (T^{-1} \sum_{t=1}^{T} Z_t Z_t')^{-1} (T^{-1} \sum_{t=1}^{T} Z_t \epsilon_t'),$$

$$\hat{\Omega} - \Omega = T^{-1} \sum_{t=1}^{T} \epsilon_t \epsilon_t' - \Omega - (\hat{B} - B)' T^{-1} \sum_{t=1}^{T} Z_t \epsilon_t'$$

$$- T^{-1} \sum_{t=1}^{T} \epsilon_t Z_t' (\hat{B} - B) + (\hat{B} - B)' T^{-1} \sum_{t=1}^{T} Z_t Z_t' (\hat{B} - B).$$

We first prove that all quantities on the right-hand side tend to zero. Under the assumption that the errors are independent identically distributed with mean zero and finite variance, the processes $\epsilon_t \epsilon_t'$, $\epsilon_t Z_t'$, and $Z_t Z_t'$ are ergodic with finite mean, such that

$$T^{-1} \sum_{t=1}^{T} \epsilon_t \epsilon_t' \overset{P}{\to} \Omega,$$

$$T^{-1} \sum_{t=1}^{T} \epsilon_t Z_t' \overset{P}{\to} 0,$$

$$T^{-1} \sum_{t=1}^{T} Z_t Z_t' \overset{P}{\to} E Z_t Z_t' = \Sigma.$$

This shows the consistency of $\hat{B}$ and hence $\hat{\Omega}$. To find the asymptotic distribution we normalize as follows:

$$T^{\frac{1}{2}}(\hat{B}-B) = (T^{-1}\sum_{t=1}^{T} Z_t Z_t')^{-1}(T^{-\frac{1}{2}}\sum_{t=1}^{T} Z_t\epsilon_t') = \Sigma^{-1}(T^{-\frac{1}{2}}\sum_{t=1}^{T} Z_t\epsilon_t')+o_P(1).$$

Thus we only have to find the asymptotic distribution of $T^{-\frac{1}{2}}\sum_{t=1}^{T} Z_t\epsilon_t'$. But this is given in Theorem B.13 as Gaussian with mean zero and variance $\Sigma \otimes \Omega$.

We have here used the familiar concepts of weak convergence of probability measures and convergence in probability of random variables. These concepts are discussed in more detail in Appendix B. The notation $o_P(1)$ denotes a term that tends to zero in probability.   □

The above is the analysis of the unrestricted vector autoregressive model, where the statistical calculations are given by ordinary least squares. Before we finish this section we just note that the same type of analysis can be made of a number of different models given by restrictions on the parameters. Thus for instance we can leave out certain lags: if we have quarterly data, we may want to fit only lags 1, 2, 4, and 5. The maximum likelihood estimation of such a model is again ordinary least squares. The same holds for any model where the variation of the coefficients is restricted as $\Pi_i = \xi_i H_i'$, since then the variable Z_t in the above analysis should contain the transformed variables $H_i'X_{t-i}$. Still more complicated models are possible, like the model defined by $(\Pi_1, \ldots, \Pi_k) = \xi H'$. It is also easily seen how the analysis can be modified if other variables are included as regressors. Thus the statistical calculations are easily modified if for instance time or the world oil price is included as a regressor. The simplicity gained by leaving the parameters unrestricted should be clear, but one can of course estimate the parameters under any restriction one wishes, at the price of a more complicated numerical technique, but then the existence and uniqueness of the likelihood estimators are no longer easy to discuss. In fact the remaining part of this monograph deals with a very special non-linear restriction where many results can be obtained.

2.3   Misspecification Tests

Fitting the unrestricted VAR model with k lags can easily be accomplished by usual regression programs, but it is of course important to check that the assumptions underlying the model are satisfied, since otherwise the procedures derived may not be valid. In particular we have to determine the lag length k and check that the estimated residuals $\hat{\epsilon}_t$ have no serial correlation, no conditional heteroscedasticity, and do not deviate too much from Gaussian white noise.

We give here a brief discussion of a few of the many misspecification tests that are being applied in practice. We do not give proofs of these results but refer to Doornik and Hendry (1994) for a discussion of how these test are implemented in PcFiml, and to the manual for CATS in RATS by Hansen and Juselius (1995). References and a more thorough discussion can be found in these texts, see also Godfrey (1988). There are two types of results that one can prove. One can find asymptotic distributions of the test statistics and in some cases give improved approximations to these.

Many of the asymptotic distributions are derived only for stationary processes even if the results are probably valid also for the non-stationary processes that we are interested in. The small sample approximations are most often given by analogy with the i.i.d. case and are therefore less satisfactory.

2.3.1   Lag length determination

The lag length can be determined by some of the many information criteria procedures, see Lütkepohl (1991) for an excellent comparison of the criteria. It is important to avoid too many lags, since the number of parameters grows very fast with the lag length and the information criteria strike a compromise between lag length and number of parameters by minimizing a linear combination of the residual sum of squares and the number of parameters.

It is our experience that if a long lag length is required to get white noise residuals then it often pays to reconsider the choice of variables, and look around for another important explanatory variable to include in the information set. That is, rather than automatically increase the lag length, it is more fruitful in a multivariate context to increase the information set.

The methods that will be derived in the subsequent chapters are based upon the time independence of the residuals, hence an important criterion for the choice of lag length is that the residuals are uncorrelated. The first thing to do is to plot the autocorrelation and cross-correlation functions for the individual residual series to see if there is any obvious autocorrelation left in the residuals. This graphical inspection can then be followed by summary test statistics.

Another strategy for determining the lag length is to start with a sufficiently large lag length and test successively that the coefficient to the largest lag is zero. It is a good idea to use a rather small size of these tests since the type one error cumulates, see Teräsvirta and Mellin (1986) for a comparison of procedures based on information criteria and sequences of tests. As a test statistic one can apply the likelihood ratio test in model (2.1) for the hypothesis $\Pi_k = 0$, which is asymptotically distributed as χ^2 with p^2 degrees of freedom.

A summary test statistic that measures the magnitude of the residual autocorrelations is given by the Portmanteau test

$$LB(s) = T(T+2) \sum_{j=1}^{s} \frac{1}{T-j} tr\{\hat{C}_{0j}\hat{C}_{00}^{-1}\hat{C}_{0j}'\hat{C}_{00}^{-1}\},$$

where

$$\hat{C}_{0j} = T^{-1} \sum_{t=j+1}^{T} \hat{\epsilon}_t \hat{\epsilon}_{t-j}'.$$

Under the assumptions of the model the asymptotic distribution of this test statistic can be approximated for large T and large s by a χ^2 distribution with $f = p^2(s-k)$ where k is the lag length of the model.

A test that gives the proper weighting to the residual autocorrelations is a Lagrange multiplier test for residual autocorrelation. This is calculated by regressing the estimated residuals from (2.1) on the residual lagged s as well as the regressors in model (2.1). The corresponding test statistic

$$LM(s) = (T - pk - m - p - \frac{1}{2}) \log \frac{|\hat{\Omega}|}{|\tilde{\Omega}|}$$

is asymptotically distributed as χ^2 with degrees of freedom given by $f = p^2$. Here $\hat{\Omega}$ is the variance estimate from (2.1) and $\tilde{\Omega}$ is the estimate from the auxiliary regression.

2.3.2   Autoregressive conditional heteroscedasticity

For each of the individual series a test for ARCH effects can be calculated by regressing the squared residuals $\hat{\epsilon}_{it}^2$ on a constant and lagged values of the squared residuals. The asymptotic distribution of such a test is also χ^2 with f equal to the number of lags in the auxiliary regression.

2.3.3   Test for Gaussian distribution

The marginal distribution of the residuals should be checked by histograms, and by calculating skewness and kurtosis. A test can be based on the central moments

$$m_i = T^{-1} \sum_{t=1}^{T} (\hat{\epsilon}_t - \bar{\epsilon})^i, \; i = 2, 3, 4,$$

through skewness and kurtosis

$$b_1^{\frac{1}{2}} = \frac{m_3}{m_2^{\frac{3}{2}}}, \; b_2 = \frac{m_4}{m_2^2}.$$

The test statistic is

$$JB = (T - pk - m)(\frac{b_1}{6} + \frac{(b_2-3)^2}{24}),$$

which is asymptotically $\chi^2(2)$ if the underlying distribution of the errors is Gaussian. This test is known as the Jarque–Bera test, but is given by Shenton and Bowman (1977) in a version that has better small sample properties for i.i.d. variables. We have chosen here a simple correction for degrees of freedom. A multivariate version of this test is developed in Doornik and Hansen (1994).

Autoregressive models do not necessarily always describe the data, but they provide a flexible statistical tool. It often happens that if a VAR model does not fit the data, it is because of the information set, that is, the choice of variables should be reconsidered. Thus it is important to extend the information set to contain the right explanatory variables for the relation that one is really interested in. Another technique for constructing a modified VAR model is to consider a partial or conditional model. This will be discussed in Chapter 8. The choice of the correct economic variables to investigate is an art which requires economic insight, and no final answers can be given on how to do it.

2.4   The Illustrative Examples

2.4.1   The Danish Data

As a first example of an analysis of a data set consider the Danish data discussed in section 1.3 consisting of (m_t, y_t, i_t^b, i_t^d), $t = 1974 : 1, \ldots, 1987 : 3$. We use two lags and let $k = 2$ and keep the first two observations from 1974: 1 and 1974: 2 for initial values. This leaves $T = 53$ observations, and $p = 4$ dimensions fitted with 2 lags ($k = 2$) and seasonal dummies ($m = 4$). The seasonal dummies are orthogonalized to the constant term. The data are plotted in levels and differences in Fig. 2.1. All four variables appear non-stationary with stationary differences. We write the model in the error correction form as

$$\Delta X_t = \Pi X_{t-1} + \Gamma_1 \Delta X_{t-1} + \Phi D_t + \epsilon_t.$$

Thus we have 4×53 observations and condition on the initial values corresponding to the data for 1974: 1 and 1974: 2. Each equation is fitted with $kp + m = 12$ parameters, leaving $41 = 53 - 12$ degrees of freedom for the variance. The estimated coefficient matrices are given in Tables 2.1, 2.2, and 2.3, and the correlation matrix and standard deviations of the errors are given in Table 2.4.

In Fig. 2.2 the standardized residuals and their histograms are given for each of the four series.

We first investigate the residual autocorrelations in order to check that we have found a description of the data consistent with the assumption of white noise errors. The residual correlations and cross-correlations are given in Fig. 2.3. The large correlations ($\geq 2T^{-\frac{1}{2}}$) are indicated with vertical bars.

TABLE 2.1 The estimates of Π for the Danish data

	m	y	i^b	i^d
Δm	−0.181	0.110	−1.042	0.638
Δy	0.186	−0.309	0.658	−0.648
Δi^b	0.014	−0.018	0.082	−0.167
Δi^d	−0.004	0.020	0.143	−0.314

TABLE 2.2 The estimates of Γ_1 for the Danish data

	Δm	Δy	Δi^b	Δi^d
Δm	0.195	−0.096	−0.138	−0.462
Δy	0.504	−0.045	−0.377	0.060
Δi^b	0.051	0.136	0.301	0.253
Δi^d	0.069	−0.022	0.227	0.265

TABLE 2.3 The estimates of the constant and seasonal dummies for the Danish data

	season(1)	season(2)	season(3)	constant
Δm	−0.023	0.016	−0.039	1.583
Δy	−0.019	−0.007	−0.032	−0.390
Δi^b	−0.003	−0.007	−0.007	−0.064
Δi^d	−0.002	0.001	−0.003	−0.071

TABLE 2.4 Standard deviations (σ_{ii}) and correlations (ρ_{ij}) for the Danish data

$10^2\sigma_{ii}$	1.90	1.95	0.76	0.48
ρ_{ij}	1.00			
	0.53	1.00		
	−0.45	−0.08	1.00	
	−0.31	−0.24	0.25	1.00

We calculated $LM(1) = 18.62$, which is distributed as χ^2 with 16 degrees of freedom (p-value $= 0.29$), and $LM(4) = 17.55$ which gives a p-value of 0.35. An overall evaluation of correlations up to thirteenth order is given by the multivariate Ljung–Box test $LB(13) = 197.63$ with $p^2(s - k) = 16 \times (13 - 2) = 176$ degrees of freedom corresponding to a p-value of 0.13. Finally we test the hypothesis $k = 2$ in the model with $k = 3$ lags and find the likelihood ratio test $LR = (T - kp - m)\log(|\hat{\Omega}_2|/|\hat{\Omega}_3|) = 16.42$. This is again asymptotically distributed as χ^2 with 16 degrees of freedom and does

TABLE 2.5 The univariate diagnostic statistics for
the Danish data

	ARCH(2)	Skewness	Kurtosis	JB
m	0.655	0.552	−0.075	2.09
y	0.875	0.524	−0.087	1.89
i^b	0.148	−0.297	0.576	1.17
i^d	1.292	0.415	0.562	1.72

not give any hint of misspecification. Next we investigate the individual
series by the ARCH test for residual conditional heteroscedasticity (of order
2). We calculate the Jarque–Bera test which is asymptotically χ^2 with 2
degrees of freedom. The results are given in Table 2.5. None of these tests
seems to indicate that there are serious deviations from the assumptions
underlying the model. For an AR(2) model the properties are given by the
roots of the characteristic polynomial, or equivalently the eigenvalues of
the coefficient matrix in companion form, which we next calculate, and the
results are give in Table 2.6. It is seen that the eigenvalues are all inside the
unit circle but that some are very close to the unit root $z = 1$. Note also
that there is no indication that the roots are close to any other value on the
unit circle indicating that the type of non-stationarity is the one that can
be removed by differencing. That is, an inspection of the roots indicates
that we can focus on integrated variables and the subsequent chapters deal
with how to handle this issue in the framework that has been established,
that is, the vector autoregressive model.

TABLE 2.6 The eigenvalues (ρ_i) of the companion
matrix for the Danish data

Root	Real	Complex	Modulus
ρ_1	0.9725	0.0000	0.9725
ρ_2	0.7552	−0.1571	0.7713
ρ_3	0.7552	0.1571	0.7713
ρ_4	0.6051	−0.0000	0.6051
ρ_5	0.5955	−0.3143	0.6734
ρ_6	0.5955	0.3143	0.6734
ρ_7	−0.1425	−0.2312	0.2716
ρ_8	−0.1425	0.2312	0.2716

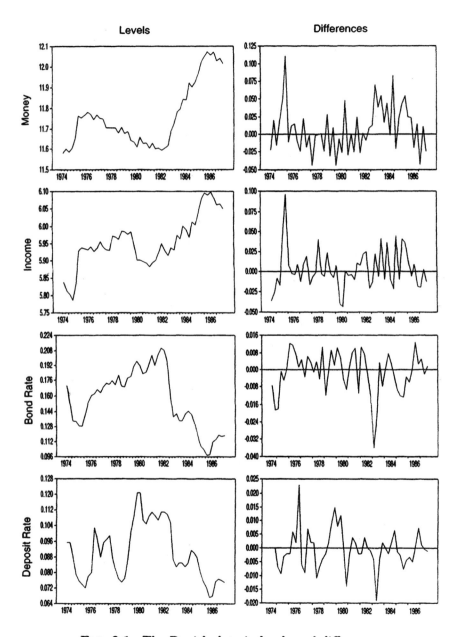

FIG. 2.1. The Danish data in levels and differences

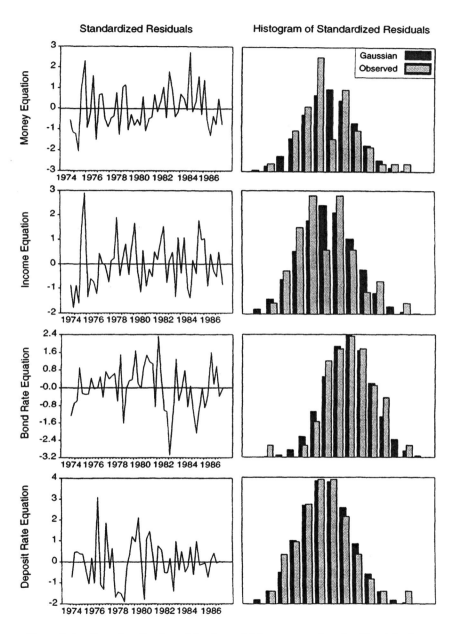

FIG. 2.2. Standardized residuals and histograms for the Danish data

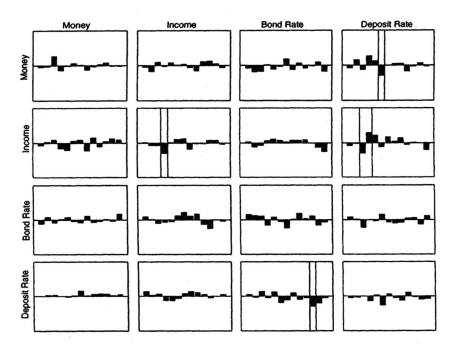

FIG. 2.3. Autocorrelation and cross-correlation functions for the residuals of a VAR(2) for the Danish data

2.4.2   The Australian Data

As the other example consider the Australian data. We have here chosen the five-variable system discussed in Section 1.3 consisting of log prices in Australia and United States, the exchange rate, and a bond rate from each country. This time we have data from 1972: 1 to 1991: 1 giving a total of $T = 75$ observations, if we fix the first two for initial values. Subtracting $2 \times 5 + 4 = 14$ we get 61 effective observations for the variance.

The data are plotted in Fig. 2.4 in levels and differences. It is seen that the prices are clearly non-stationary due to the trend, but that the differences look more stationary. One notices that the interest rates move in much the same way for the first part of the period, but then the US interest rate decreases while the Australian interest rate stays up. Notice also the sudden fluctuation in the US interest rate around 1980. This fluctuation will show up in the test statistic for the individual series below, see Table 2.11.

The estimates of the autoregressive model with two lags written in error correction form are given in Tables 2.7-2.10. The graphs of the standardized residuals and their histograms are given in Fig. 2.5, and Fig. 2.6 gives the autocorrelation function and cross-correlation functions.

TABLE 2.7 Estimated coefficient matrix Π for the Australian data

	p^{au}	p^{us}	$exch$	i^{au}	i^{us}
Δp^{au}	−0.056	0.061	−0.008	0.308	−0.280
Δp^{us}	0.004	0.011	−0.022	−0.142	−0.016
$\Delta exch$	−0.020	0.093	−0.210	0.814	−0.257
Δi^{au}	−0.036	0.084	−0.016	−0.462	0.073
Δi^{us}	−0.069	0.137	−0.052	−0.080	−0.388

TABLE 2.8 Estimated coefficient matrix Γ_1 for the Australian data

	Δp^{au}	Δp^{us}	$\Delta exch$	Δi^{au}	Δi^{us}
Δp^{au}	−0.007	0.418	0.017	0.030	0.040
Δp^{us}	0.113	0.307	0.005	0.126	0.241
$\Delta exch$	−0.896	−1.457	0.038	−0.256	−0.181
Δi^{au}	0.294	−0.318	−0.014	0.250	0.031
Δi^{us}	−0.110	−0.210	−0.011	0.050	−0.017

The test for residual autocorrelation of order 1 is LM(1) = 29.26 and for order 4 LM(4) = 16.86, each with $p^2 = 25$ degrees of freedom. These correspond to the p-values 0.25 and 0.89 respectively. The Ljung–Box statistic becomes LB(18) = 442.197 with $f = 25 \times (18-2) = 400$ degrees of freedom corresponding to a p-value of 0.07. The univariate diagnostic statistics are given in Table 2.11.

It is seen that the US interest rate has a very strong ARCH effect probably due to the very large residual around 1980, see Baba $et\ al.$ (1992). The normality tests and the histograms indicate that there are some very large observations especially in the Australian prices and the US interest rate, whereas the exchange rate has a slightly skew distribution. The methods derived are based upon the Gaussian likelihood but the asymptotic properties of the methods only depend on the i.i.d. assumption of the errors. Thus the normality assumption is not so serious for the conclusion, but the ARCH effect may be. Fortunately it turns out the US interest is weakly

TABLE 2.9 The estimates of the constant and seasonal dummies for the Australian data

	season(1)	season(2)	season(3)	constant
Δp^{au}	−0.001	0.006	−0.003	0.001
Δp^{us}	−0.000	−0.001	0.002	−0.041
$\Delta exch$	0.004	−0.007	0.009	−0.329
Δi^{au}	−0.002	−0.003	−0.003	−0.154
Δi^{us}	0.003	−0.003	0.003	−0.221

TABLE 2.10 Standard deviations (σ_{ii}) and correlations (ρ_{ij}) for the Australian data

$10^2\sigma_{ii}$	0.73	0.57	4.44	0.66	0.88
ρ_{ij}	1.00				
	−0.14	1.00			
	0.33	0.01	1.00		
	0.26	0.26	0.21	1.00	
	−0.41	0.50	−0.14	0.17	1.00

TABLE 2.11 Univariate diagnostic statistics for the Australian data

	ARCH(2)	Skewness	Kurtosis	JB
p^{au}	1.134	0.214	1.470	5.96
p^{us}	0.850	0.322	0.499	1.69
$exch$	0.528	0.755	0.969	8.18
i^{au}	5.279	0.359	0.351	1.62
i^{us}	18.357	0.200	1.439	5.67

exogenous for the cointegrating relations and in Chapter 7 we analyse the conditional model, where we have conditioned on the US interest rate as well as the past of all the variables. Obviously for a serious modelling of the data we need to find out what happens to the US interest rate around the period with the large deviation. This will not be attempted here.

We proceed to calculate the eigenvalues in Table 2.12, and see that there are roots very close to 1, but that none of them is close to other points on the unit circle. Thus we conclude that we can continue with the analysis of the VAR with two lags, as the starting-point of a cointegration analysis.

TABLE 2.12 The eigenvalues (ρ_i) of the companion matrix for the Australian data

Root	Real	Complex	Modulus
ρ_1	0.9894	−0.0000	0.9894
ρ_2	0.9128	0.1192	0.9205
ρ_3	0.9128	−0.1192	0.9205
ρ_4	0.7303	0.0529	0.7322
ρ_5	0.7303	−0.0529	0.7322
ρ_6	0.1975	0.0000	0.1975
ρ_7	0.1295	0.0000	0.1295
ρ_8	0.0600	0.3718	0.3767
ρ_9	0.0600	−0.3718	0.3767
ρ_{10}	−0.2561	0.0000	0.2561

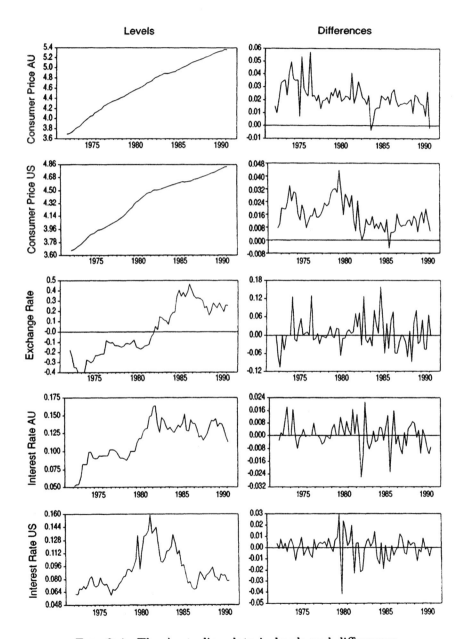

FIG. 2.4. The Australian data in levels and differences

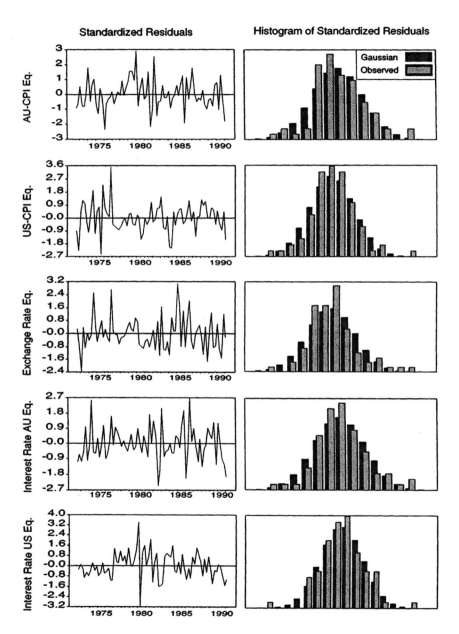

FIG. 2.5. Standardized residuals and histograms for the Australian data

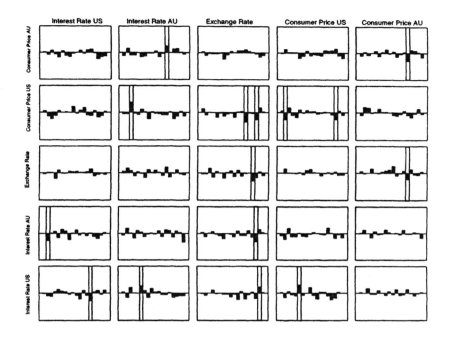

FIG. 2.6. Autocorrelation and cross-correlation functions for the residuals of a VAR(2) for the Australian data

3

Basic Definitions and Concepts

IN this chapter we give the basic definitions of integration, cointegration and common trends, which will be applied in the following. The definitions are essentially those given in Engle and Granger (1987) but have been modified slightly to accommodate the simpler framework that we are working in. It is important that we allow the components of a vector process to be integrated of different orders. The reason for this is that when analysing economic data the variables are chosen for their economic importance and not for their statistical properties. Hence we should be able to analyse for instance stationary as well as non-stationary variables in the same model, in order to be able to describe the long-run relations as well as the short-term adjustments.

3.1   Cointegration and Common Trends

Many economic variables are not stationary, and we consider the type of non-stationarity that can be removed by differencing. When modelling this phenomenon one can focus on two aspects of the economy, either the 'stable' economic relations between variables that show less variability than the original variables, or the cumulated disturbances, which create the non-stationarity. The purpose of this section is to give these concepts a precise statistical definition in order to be able to discuss them in detail in a statistical model.

   It turns out that it is difficult to give a general definition of the concept of an integrated process without including processes with unwanted properties, and we therefore give a definition that is not so general but which covers exactly the processes that we want. Let in the following ϵ_t be a sequence of independent identically distributed p-dimensional random variables with mean zero and variance matrix Ω.

DEFINITION 3.1 *A linear process is defined by* $Y_t = \sum_{i=0}^{\infty} C_i \epsilon_{t-i}$, $t = 0, 1, \ldots$ *where* $C(z) = \sum_{i=0}^{\infty} C_i z^i$ *is convergent for* $|z| \leq 1 + \delta$ *for some* $\delta > 0$.

   Note that the coefficients decrease exponentially fast. In Appendix B some results are given for linear processes, which we need for the probability analysis in Part II.

DEFINITION 3.2 *A stochastic process Y_t which satisfies that $Y_t - E(Y_t) = \sum_{i=0}^{\infty} C_i \epsilon_{t-i}$ is called $I(0)$ if $C = \sum_{i=0}^{\infty} C_i \neq 0$.*

Note that the matrix C can be singular, and in fact it is this property that gives rise to cointegration in the following. As a simple example of a univariate linear process consider the AR(1) process for $|\rho| < 1$,

$$X_{1t} = \sum_{i=0}^{\infty} \rho^i \epsilon_{1t-i}.$$

The sum of the coefficients is $\sum_{i=0}^{\infty} \rho^i = \frac{1}{1-\rho}$, such that the process is $I(0)$. The process

$$X_{2t} = \epsilon_{2t} - \theta \epsilon_{2t-1},$$

is stationary for all θ, but for $\theta \neq 1$ it is an $I(0)$ process. The process $X_t = (X_{1t}, X_{2t})'$ is called an $I(0)$ process even if $\theta = 1$ since the C-matrix is

$$\begin{bmatrix} \frac{1}{1-\rho} & 0 \\ 0 & 1-\theta \end{bmatrix} \neq 0, \text{ for all } \theta.$$

The process X_t given in the representation (2.4) has the property that $X_t - E(X_t)$ is an $I(0)$ process, since $C(1) = A(1)^{-1}$ is non-zero and in fact has full rank.

DEFINITION 3.3 *A stochastic process X_t is called integrated of order d, $I(d)$, $d = 0, 1, 2, \ldots$ if $\Delta^d (X_t - E(X_t))$ is $I(0)$.*

We only deal with integrated processes that are $I(0)$, $I(1)$, and $I(2)$ in the following. Note that the property of being integrated is related to the stochastic part of the process since we have subtracted the expectation in the definition. The concept of $I(0)$ is defined without regard to deterministic terms like a mean or a trend. Note also that there are no restrictions on the levels of an integrated process, only the differences.

Another aspect of the definition is that we want to describe the two-dimensional process consisting of a random walk and a stationary sequence as an $I(1)$ process thus allowing the component processes to be integrated of different orders. Definition 3.3 has the property that it is invariant to non-singular linear transformations of the process. That is, if X_t is $I(1)$ and A is a $p \times p$ matrix of full rank then AX_t is also $I(1)$.

A consequence of the definition is that the stochastic part of an $I(1)$ process X_t is non-stationary, since if

$$X_t = X_0 + \sum_{i=1}^{t} Y_i,$$

for some $I(0)$ process $Y_t = \sum_{i=0}^{\infty} C_i \epsilon_{t-i}$, we can show that $\sum_{i=0}^{\infty} C_i \neq 0$ implies that X_t is non-stationary. Let $C(z) = \sum_{i=0}^{\infty} C_i z^i$. We define the function $C^*(z)$ by the expression

$$C^*(z) = \frac{C(z) - C(1)}{1 - z} = \sum_{i=0}^{\infty} C_i^* z^i, \ C_i^* = -\sum_{j=i+1}^{\infty} C_j.$$

It is shown in Lemma 4.1 that the power series for $C^*(z)$ is convergent for $|z| < 1 + \delta$. Thus we have the representation

$$C(z) = \sum_{i=0}^{\infty} C_i + C^*(z)(1 - z) = C + C^*(z)(1 - z),$$

with $C = C(1) = \sum_{i=0}^{\infty} C_i$. Next we define the stationary process $Y_t^* = \sum_{i=0}^{\infty} C_i^* \epsilon_{t-i}$ and interpret the relation as a relation for the lag operator L and replace z^i by L^i and find

$$Y_t = \sum_{i=0}^{\infty} C_i \epsilon_{t-i} = C\epsilon_t + Y_t^* - Y_{t-1}^*, \ Y_t^* = \sum_{i=0}^{\infty} C_i^* \epsilon_{t-i} = C^*(L)\epsilon_t.$$

Hence

$$X_t = X_0 + \sum_{i=1}^{t} Y_i = X_0 + C\sum_{i=1}^{t} \epsilon_i + Y_t^* - Y_0^*.$$

This process is non-stationary since $Y_t = \Delta X_t$ is an $I(0)$ process, such that $C \neq 0$. We next discuss stationary linear combinations of the process X_t. Let therefore β be any vector in R^p, then we have

$$\beta' X_t = \beta' X_0 + \beta' C\sum_{i=1}^{t} \epsilon_i + \beta' Y_t^* - \beta' Y_0^*,$$

which shows that if we want $\beta' X_t$ to be stationary we must have $\beta' C = 0$, and then

$$\beta' X_t = \beta' Y_t^* + \beta' X_0 - \beta' Y_0^*.$$

This is stationary only if we choose the initial values of the process $\beta' X_t$ properly, that is, if we take $\beta' X_0 = \beta' Y_0^*$, in which case we get

$$\beta' X_t = \beta' Y_t^*.$$

The definition of $I(1)$ gives no condition on the initial values or the levels of the process, thus if we want to consider the stationarity of linear combinations of levels we need the extra condition that the initial values can be chosen as indicated.

We apply this idea in the definition of cointegration.

DEFINITION 3.4 *Let X_t be integrated of order 1. We call X_t cointegrated with cointegrating vector $\beta \neq 0$ if $\beta' X_t$ can be made stationary by a suitable choice of its initial distribution. The cointegrating rank is the number of linearly independent cointegrating relations, and the space spanned by the cointegrating relations is the cointegrating space.*

Note that $\beta' X_t$ need not be $I(0)$, but for AR processes the cointegrating relations we find are in fact $I(0)$, as we shall see in Theorem 4.2. We give some elementary examples which illustrate the notion of integration and cointegration.

EXAMPLE 3.1 We define the two-dimensional process X_t, $t = 1, \ldots, T$ by

$$X_{1t} = \sum_{i=1}^{t} \epsilon_{1i} + \epsilon_{2t},$$

$$X_{2t} = a \sum_{i=1}^{t} \epsilon_{1i} + \epsilon_{3t},$$

Clearly X_{1t}, X_{2t}, and also X_t are $I(1)$ processes. They cointegrate with cointegrating vector $\beta' = (a, -1)$ since the linear combination $\beta' X_t = aX_{1t} - X_{2t} = a\epsilon_{2t} - \epsilon_{3t}$ is stationary. If further

$$X_{3t} = \epsilon_{4t},$$

then clearly X_{3t} is $I(0)$ but the vector process $X_t' = (X_{1t}, X_{2t}, X_{3t})$ is an $I(1)$ process now with two cointegrating vectors given by $(a, -1, 0)$ and $(0, 0, 1)$. Thus we allow, with a slight abuse of language, for unit vectors as cointegrating vectors, and see that by including a stationary variable in the process we increase the dimension of the cointegrating space by one.

EXAMPLE 3.2 Let us define the three-dimensional process

$$X_{1t} = \sum_{i=1}^{t} \sum_{j=1}^{i} \epsilon_{1j} + \sum_{i=1}^{t} \epsilon_{2i},$$

$$X_{2t} = a \sum_{i=1}^{t} \sum_{j=1}^{i} \epsilon_{1j} + b \sum_{i=1}^{t} \epsilon_{2i} + \epsilon_{3t},$$

$$X_{3t} = c \sum_{i=1}^{t} \epsilon_{2i} + \epsilon_{4t}.$$

In this case X_1 and X_2 are $I(2)$ processes, whereas X_3 is an $I(1)$ process. Hence the process $X' = (X_1, X_2, X_3)$ is $I(2)$, and cointegrates since

$$aX_{1t} - X_{2t} = (a - b) \sum_{i=1}^{t} \epsilon_{2i} - \epsilon_{3t}$$

is $I(1)$, and

$$acX_{1t} - cX_{2t} - (a - b) X_{3t} = -c\epsilon_{3t} - (a - b) \epsilon_{4t}$$

is $I(0)$. Thus $(a, -1, 0)$ is a cointegrating vector that changes the order of the process from two to one, whereas $[ac, -c, -(a - b)]$ changes the order from two to zero. Another possibility is to define the process as follows

$$X_{3t} = c \sum_{i=1}^{t} \sum_{j=1}^{i} \epsilon_{2j} + \epsilon_{4t}.$$

In this case a different phenomenon appears since while $aX_{1t} - X_{2t}$ is still $I(1)$, stationarity can be achieved by calculating

$$c(aX_{1t} - X_{2t}) - (a - b)\,\Delta X_{3t} = -c\epsilon_{3t} - (a - b)\,\Delta\epsilon_{4t}.$$

Thus differences of X_{3t} are needed to remove the non-stationarity from the process $aX_{1t} - X_{2t}$. This phenomenon is called polynomial cointegration and will be discussed briefly below.

Consider the following general process that illustrates the various possibilities in p dimensions for $d = 2$:

$$X_t = C_2 \sum_{s=1}^{t} \sum_{i=1}^{s} \epsilon_i + C_1 \sum_{i=1}^{t} \epsilon_i + \tau_0 + \tau_1 t + \frac{1}{2}\tau_2 t^2 + Y_t, \ t = 1, 2, \ldots \quad (3.1)$$

Here ϵ_t are as above and Y_t is a linear process. Clearly X_t is $I(2)$ if $C_2 \neq 0$, since it is non-stationary and differencing it twice makes it $I(0)$. Note, however, that if $C_2 = 0$, then the presence of the quadratic trend implies that we still need to difference it twice to make it $I(0)$. We prefer to call such a process an $I(1)$ process with a quadratic trend, since the stochastic trend needs only one differencing.

The moving average representation (3.1) is a useful way of modelling the variation of the economic data through the matrices C_1 and C_2 as the results of the influence of its unobserved common trends given by the cumulated sums of ϵ. It is furthermore very convenient for describing the properties of the process, the mean and covariance functions can be calculated and the cointegration properties are easily illustrated, as will now be discussed. The asymptotic properties too are simple consequences of (3.1).

Granger (1981) used this representation to note that if we take linear combinations β, such that $\beta'C_2 = 0$, then the order of integration of the process is reduced from 2 to 1. He coined the phrase cointegration and denoted it $CI(2, 1)$ in this case. The idea is to describe the 'stable' relations in the economy by linear relations that are more stationary than the original variables.

DEFINITION 3.5 *The $I(d)$ process X_t is called cointegrated $CI(d, b)$ with cointegrating vector $\beta \neq 0$ if $\beta'X_t$ is $I(d - b)$, $b = 1, \ldots, d$, $d = 1, \ldots$*

Thus the class CI(1,1) are the integrated processes that are $I(1)$ and which cointegrate to $I(0)$. In general we can have cointegration to stationarity but we mainly meet processes that are CI(1,1) when working with autoregressive processes. If in (3.1) we can find β such that $\beta'C_1 = \beta'C_2 = 0$, then clearly $\beta'X_t$ is stationary apart from its quadratic trend. Thus the stochastic variation has been reduced to stationarity. We call $\beta'X_t$ trend stationary (with a quadratic trend). Thus cointegration is a consequence of reduced rank of the matrices C_1 and C_2. If we find two vectors β_0 and β_1, such that $\beta_0'C_2 = 0$, and such that $\beta_0'C_1 + \beta_1'C_2 = 0$, then, disregarding the deterministic terms,

$$
\beta_0'X_t + \beta_1'\Delta X_t
$$
$$
= \beta_0'C_2 \sum_{s=1}^{t}\sum_{i=1}^{s} \epsilon_i + (\beta_0'C_1 + \beta_1'C_2) \sum_{s=1}^{t} \epsilon_s + \beta_0'Y_t + \beta_1'C_1\epsilon_t + \beta_1'\Delta Y_t,
$$

which is stationary by the choice of β_0 and β_1. Thus the levels X_t are reduced to $I(1)$ by the coefficients β_0, and these linear combinations then cointegrate with the differences through the linear combinations $\beta_1'\Delta X_t$ which also form an $I(1)$ process. This phenomenon is called polynomial cointegration, see Engle and Yoo (1991), Granger and Lee (1989), Gregoir and Laroque (1993), and Johansen (1988a,1992a). This will be exemplified for $I(2)$ processes in Chapter 4.

DEFINITION 3.6 *The $I(2)$ process X_t is called polynomially cointegrated if there exist $\beta_0 \neq 0$, and $\beta_1 \neq 0$, such that $\beta_0'X_t + \beta_1'\Delta X_t$ is stationary.*

The representation (3.1) models the variables by common trends, and the reduced rank of the coefficient matrices C_1 and C_2 ensures that the variables cointegrate, since by suitable linear combinations the common trends can be eliminated, thereby creating the 'stable' economic relations. Another way of modelling cointegrating variables is through the error correction models.

An example of a reduced form error correction model is given by the equations

$$
\Delta X_t = \alpha\beta'X_{t-1} + \mu + \epsilon_t, \ t = 1, \ldots, T, \tag{3.2}
$$

with initial value X_0, where α and β are $p \times r$ matrices. One motivation for this model is to consider the relation $\beta'X_t = E(\beta'X_t) = c$ as defining the underlying economic relations, and assume that the agents react to the disequilibrium error $\beta'X_{t-1} - c$ through the adjustment coefficient α, to bring back the variables on the right track, that is, such that they satisfy the economic relations.

Together with a matrix α of dimension $p \times r$ and full rank we consider another matrix $\alpha_\perp$ of full rank and dimension $p \times (p-r)$ such that $\alpha'\alpha_\perp = 0$. Then rank$(\alpha, \alpha_\perp) = p$. The matrix $\alpha_\perp$ is not uniquely defined, but whenever we use it the conclusions do not depend on which version we choose. Note the beautiful relation

$$\beta_\perp \left(\alpha'_\perp \beta_\perp\right)^{-1} \alpha'_\perp + \alpha \left(\beta'\alpha\right)^{-1} \beta' = I,$$

which expresses that if $\beta'\alpha$ has full rank then any vector v in R^p can be decomposed into a vector in $v_1 \in sp(\beta_\perp)$ and a vector in $v_2 \in sp(\alpha)$:

$$v = v_1 + v_2 = \beta_\perp \left(\alpha'_\perp \beta_\perp\right)^{-1} \alpha'_\perp v + \alpha \left(\beta'\alpha\right)^{-1} \beta'v.$$

It is not difficult to show, see also Theorem 4.2, that if $\alpha'_\perp \beta_\perp$ has full rank then one can solve (3.2) and find a representation of the form (3.1):

$$X_t = C \sum_{i=1}^{t} \epsilon_i + \tau_0 + \tau_1 t + Y_t,$$

where

$$C = \beta_\perp \left(\alpha'_\perp \beta_\perp\right)^{-1} \alpha'_\perp \quad \text{and} \quad \tau_1 = C\mu, \qquad (3.3)$$

whereas the value of τ_0 depends on initial conditions. To see this multiply equation (3.2) by β' and let $U_t = \beta' X_t$. Then we get the equation

$$U_t = (I + \beta'\alpha) U_{t-1} + \beta'\mu + \beta'\epsilon_t,$$

such that the r-dimensional process U_t is stationary if the matrix $(I + \beta'\alpha)$ has its eigenvalues inside the unit circle. In this case we find the stationary representation from Theorem 2.2

$$\beta' X_t = \sum_{i=0}^{\infty} (I + \beta'\alpha)^i \beta' \left(\epsilon_{t-i} + \mu\right).$$

Multiplying (3.2) by $\alpha'_\perp$ we get the equation

$$\alpha'_\perp \Delta X_t = \alpha'_\perp \epsilon_t + \alpha'_\perp \mu,$$

which has solution $\alpha'_\perp X_t = \alpha'_\perp X_0 + \sum_{i=1}^{t} \alpha'_\perp \left(\epsilon_i + \mu\right)$. Combining these results we find

$$X_t = (\beta_\perp(\alpha'_\perp \beta_\perp)^{-1}\alpha'_\perp + \alpha(\beta'\alpha)^{-1}\beta')X_t$$

$$= CX_0 + C\sum_{i=1}^{t} \left(\epsilon_i + \mu\right) + \alpha \left(\beta'\alpha\right)^{-1} \sum_{i=0}^{\infty} (I + \beta'\alpha)^i \beta' \left(\epsilon_{t-i} + \mu\right).$$

This is an instance of the celebrated representation theorem by Granger, see Engle and Granger (1987), which is just a way of finding the moving average representation from the autoregressive representation, and vice versa, when there are $I(1)$ variables in the system.

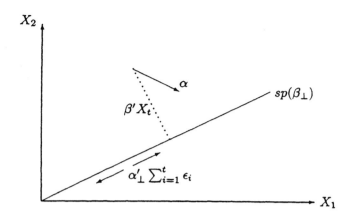

FIG. 3.1. The process X_t is pushed along the attractor set by the common trends and pulled towards it by the adjustment coefficients

It is seen from this representation that the non-stationarity in the process X_t is created by the cumulative sum of the ϵ, but from the expression for C it is seen that only the combinations $\alpha'_\perp \Sigma_{i=1}^t \epsilon_i$ enter the processes. This gives rise to the following definition:

DEFINITION 3.7 *The common trends in (3.2) are the variables* $\alpha'_\perp \Sigma_{i=1}^t \epsilon_i$.

The error correction model (3.2), which is constructed around the disequilibrium errors as error correction terms, and the moving average model (3.1) that is constructed in terms of unobserved common trends, are of course complementary, in the sense that the two approaches are mathematically equivalent, but they may appeal to different types of intuition.

The picture that one should have in mind is that the cumulated disturbances, $\alpha'_\perp \Sigma_{i=1}^t \epsilon_i$, push the economic variables around in the space spanned by $\beta_\perp$, the attractor set. The agents react to these forces and create economic variables that move around the common trends following the economic 'laws' or structural relations $\beta' X_t = E(\beta' X_t)$ in the sense that the variables react to the disequilibrium errors $\beta' X_t - E(\beta' X_t)$ through the adjustment coefficients α and are forced back towards the attractor set.

Thus the long-run relations $\beta' X_t = E(\beta' X_t)$ are not relations that are satisfied in the limit as $t \dashrightarrow \infty$, or relations between levels of variables in equilibrium, but they are relations between the variables in the economy, as described by the statistical model, which show themselves in the adjustment behaviour of the agents in the sense that the agents try to force the variables back towards the attractor set defined by the relations.

There are many ways of interpreting the attractor set. It is a consequence of the equations, that the system, if left to itself by letting $\epsilon_{t+h} = 0$,

$h = 1, 2, \ldots$, will converge to a point on the attractor set. Another way of thinking about the attractor set is that again if the noise is shot off and we place X_t in the attractor set, then X_{t+h} stays there, hence there is no inherent tendency to move away once the attractor is reached.

It must be emphasized that the picture above is only valid for model (3.2) where the short-term dynamics have been left out. See Example 4.3 for an example where none of the variables reacts with a coefficient with a reasonable sign, despite the fact that the process is actually cointegrating, and exercise 4.3 for an example where $\alpha'_\perp X_t$ is stationary, which shows that we cannot replace the common trends $\alpha'_\perp \Sigma_{i=1}^t \epsilon_i$ by $\alpha'_\perp X_t$. We return to the problem of how to choose linear combinations of the levels to represent common trends after the representation given in Theorem 4.2.

The notion of common trend and cointegrating relation appear side by side and are of course two sides of the same coin. This will be apparent in the following, where β and $\alpha_\perp$ can always be treated in a similar manner. There is, however, one aspect in which the two concepts are radically different. The cointegrating relations enjoy the property that if the information set is increased by adding new variables, then the cointegrating relations that we found for the smaller information set correspond naturally to cointegrating relations in the larger set where the new variables have a zero coefficient. An unanticipated shock in a small system which forms the basis of the common trend need not be unanticipated in a larger system, since the unobserved shock in the small system could depend on the added variable, in which case it would not be an unanticipated shock anymore, and hence the definition of the common trend has changed, see Hendry (1995).

3.2   Exercises

3.1

Let

$$X_{1t} = \sum_{i=1}^t \epsilon_{1i} + \epsilon_{2t},$$

$$X_{2t} = \tfrac{1}{2} \sum_{i=1}^t \epsilon_{1i} + \epsilon_{3t},$$

$$X_{3t} = \epsilon_{2t}.$$

Show that $(1, -2, 0)$ and $(0, 0, 1)$ are cointegrating vectors for the $I(1)$ process X_t.

3.2

Let

$$X_{1t} = \sum_{i=1}^{t} \sum_{j=1}^{i} \epsilon_{1j} + \sum_{i=1}^{t} \epsilon_{2i} + \epsilon_{3t},$$

$$X_{2t} = \sum_{i=1}^{t} \sum_{j=1}^{i} \epsilon_{1j} - \sum_{i=1}^{t} \epsilon_{2i} + \epsilon_{3t},$$

$$X_{3t} = \sum_{i=1}^{t} \epsilon_{1i} + \sum_{i=1}^{t} \epsilon_{2i} + \epsilon_{3t}.$$

Show that X_t is $I(2)$ and that $X_{1t} - X_{2t}$ is $I(1)$, $X_{1t} - X_{2t} - 2X_{3t}$ is $I(1)$ while $X_{1t} - X_{2t} - 2X_{3t} + 2\Delta X_{1t}$ is stationary.

3.3

Consider the simple process $X_t = \epsilon_t$.
1. Show that X_t is $I(0)$.
Define $Y_t = \Delta X_t$.
2. Show that Y_t is stationary but that it is not $I(0)$.
3. Show now in general that if X_t is $I(0)$, then ΔX_t is not $I(0)$, and neither is $\Delta^d X_t$, $d = 1, 2, \ldots$
One could in this case call $\Delta^d X_t$ an $I(-d)$ process.
Note that we have shown that if X_t is $I(d_1)$ and $I(d_2)$ then $d_1 = d_2$, and further that $I(0)$ does not include all the stationary processes. The processes in the union of $I(-d)$, $d = 1, 2, \ldots$ are also stationary.

3.4

Let $Z_{1t} = \sum_{i=1}^{t} \epsilon_{1i}$, and $Z_{2t} = \epsilon_{2t}$.
1. Show that Z_{2t} is $I(0)$, and that Z_{1t} and $Z_t = Z_{1t} + Z_{2t}$ are $I(1)$.
2. Show now in general that if X_t is $I(d_1)$ and Y_t is $I(d_2)$, where $d_1 = 0, 1, \ldots$, $d_2 = 0, 1, \ldots$, and $d_1 \neq d_2$, then $X_t + Y_t$ is $I(d)$ where

$$d = \max(d_1, d_2).$$

3.5

Consider the autoregressive process X_t defined by

$$\Delta X_{1t} = -\tfrac{1}{2}(X_{1t-1} - X_{2t-1}) + \epsilon_{1t},$$

$$\Delta X_{2t} = \epsilon_{2t}.$$

Find an expression for X_t as a function of $X_0, \epsilon_1, \ldots, \epsilon_t$. Show that $X_{1t} - X_{2t}$ can be given an initial distribution such that it becomes stationary.

3.6

Consider the equations

$$\Delta X_{1t} = -\tfrac{1}{2}\left(X_{1t-1} - X_{2t-1}\right) + \epsilon_{1t},$$

$$\Delta X_{2t} = \tfrac{1}{4}\left(X_{1t-1} - X_{2t-1}\right) + \epsilon_{2t}.$$

Solve the equations for X_{1t} and X_{2t}, and show by direct calculation that $X_{1t} - X_{2t}$ is stationary, while the processes X_{1t} and X_{2t} are non-stationary. (Hint: find an equation for $X_{1t} - X_{2t}$ and another for $X_{1t} + 2X_{2t}$.)
    What happens if you replace $\tfrac{1}{4}$ by $-\tfrac{1}{4}$?

3.7

Under the assumption that $\beta'\alpha$ has full rank show that
    1. $(\alpha, \beta_\perp)$ and $(\beta, \alpha_\perp)$ has full rank.
    2. $\alpha'_\perp \beta_\perp$ has full rank.
    Let $x = \alpha x_1 + \beta_\perp x_2$.
    3. Show that

$$x_1 = (\beta'\alpha)^{-1}\beta'x,$$

$$x_2 = (\alpha'_\perp \beta_\perp)^{-1}\alpha'_\perp x,$$

and hence

$$I = \alpha\,(\beta'\alpha)^{-1}\beta' + \beta_\perp\,(\alpha'_\perp\beta_\perp)^{-1}\alpha'_\perp.$$

3.8

Consider the model

$$\Delta X_t = \alpha\beta' X_{t-1} + \mu + \epsilon_t\,, t = 1, \ldots, T. \qquad (3.4)$$

Show that if $|\mathrm{eig}(I + \beta'\alpha)| < 1$, then X_t has the representation

$$X_t = (I - \alpha\,(\beta'\alpha)^{-1}\beta')(X_0 + \sum_{i=1}^{t}\epsilon_i + \mu t) + Y_t,$$

where Y_t is a stationary process. [Hint: multiply (3.4) by β' and solve for $\beta' X_t$, then insert it into (3.4) and sum over t.]

4

Cointegration and Representation of Integrated Variables

THIS chapter contains the mathematical and algebraic results needed to understand the properties of $I(1)$ and $I(2)$ processes generated by autoregressive and moving average models. The basic result which is applied throughout is Theorem 4.2, which solves the problem of giving necessary and sufficient conditions on the coefficients of the autoregressive model for the process to be integrated of order 1. For this purpose we reparametrize the VAR model as an error correction model and introduce the matrices (Π, Γ, C) which will be important for the subsequent discussion of the models. In section 4.1 we give the conditions for the solution of the autoregressive equations to be an $I(1)$ process and derive its moving average representation. In section 4.2 we show the opposite result that a process defined by its moving average representation as an $I(1)$ process with cointegration can be represented as the solution of an (infinite order) autoregressive set of equations. In section 4.3 we give the representation theorem for $I(2)$ variables.

4.1 From AR to MA Representation for $I(1)$ Variables

We consider again the p-dimensional autoregressive process X_t defined by the equations (2.1) but written in error correction form

$$\Delta X_t = \Pi X_{t-1} + \sum_{i=1}^{k-1} \Gamma_i \Delta X_{t-i} + \Phi D_t + \epsilon_t, \ t = 1, \ldots, T, \qquad (4.1)$$

for fixed values of $X_{-k+1}, \ldots, X_0$, and independent identically distributed errors ϵ_t. Here $\Pi = \sum_{i=1}^{k} \Pi_i - I$ and $\Gamma_i = -\sum_{j=i+1}^{k} \Pi_j$ and for later use we define $\Gamma = I - \sum_{i=1}^{k-1} \Gamma_i$.

This way of reparametrizing the model is convenient for the following. For a process with two lags the explicit calculation is

$$X_t - X_{t-1} = (\Pi_1 - I)X_{t-1} + \Pi_2 X_{t-2} + \Phi D_t + \epsilon_t$$

$$= (\Pi_1 + \Pi_2 - I)X_{t-1} - \Pi_2(X_{t-1} - X_{t-2}) + \Phi D_t + \epsilon_t.$$

This is a special case of the general form (4.1). From now on only the form (4.1) will be applied for the analysis of $I(1)$ processes.

Before formulating the main result we consider two examples.

EXAMPLE 4.1 Let the process X_t, $t = 1, \ldots, T$, be defined by the error correction model

$$\Delta X_{1t} = \alpha_1(X_{1t-1} - X_{2t-1}) + \epsilon_{1t},$$

$$\Delta X_{2t} = \epsilon_{2t}.$$

Subtracting these equations we find

$$X_{1t} - X_{2t} = (1 + \alpha_1)(X_{1t-1} - X_{2t-1}) + \epsilon_{1t} - \epsilon_{2t},$$

and hence by Theorem 2.1 it follows that

$$X_{1t} - X_{2t} = \sum_{i=0}^{t-1}(1 + \alpha_1)^i(\epsilon_{1t-i} - \epsilon_{2t-i}) + (1 + \alpha_1)^t(X_{10} - X_{20}),$$

and

$$X_{2t} = X_{20} + \sum_{i=1}^{t} \epsilon_{2i}.$$

If $-2 < \alpha_1 < 0$ we can choose $X_{1t} - X_{2t}$ to be stationary by choosing the initial values $X_{10} - X_{20}$ to have their invariant distribution. If this is expressed as

$$X_{10} - X_{20} = \sum_{i=0}^{\infty}(1 + \alpha_1)^i(\epsilon_{1.-i} - \epsilon_{2.-i})$$

we find

$$X_{1t} - X_{2t} = \sum_{i=0}^{\infty}(1 + \alpha_1)^i(\epsilon_{1t-i} - \epsilon_{2t-i}).$$

Thus X_{1t} and X_{2t} and hence X_t are $I(1)$ with cointegrating vector $(1, -1)$ if and only if $-2 < \alpha_1 < 0$. If $\alpha_1 = 0$ we get an $I(1)$ process consisting of two random walks that do not cointegrate, and if $|1 + \alpha_1| > 1$ then the process becomes explosive. If $\alpha_1 = -2$ we get a non-stationary process which is not $I(1)$. Thus the properties of the process depend on the choice of parameter values.

EXAMPLE 4.2 Let X_t, $t = 1, \ldots, T$, be defined by

$$\Delta X_{1t} = \epsilon_{1t},$$

$$\Delta X_{2t} = X_{1t-1} + \epsilon_{2t}.$$

These equations can be solved for

$$X_{1t} = \sum_{i=1}^{t} \epsilon_{1i} + X_{10},$$

and

$$X_{2t} = X_{20} + \sum_{i=1}^{t}(X_{1i-1} + \epsilon_{2i}) = X_{20} + \sum_{i=1}^{t} \epsilon_{2i} + \sum_{i=1}^{t}\sum_{j=1}^{i-1} \epsilon_{1j} + tX_{10}.$$

Thus this simple autoregressive model with only one lag can generate an $I(2)$ process. Note that the initial value X_{10} generates a linear trend in the process.

The conclusion that can be drawn from these examples is that some conditions are needed on the coefficients to determine what are the properties of a process generated by an autoregressive model.

In the following we apply an expansion of a power series at the point 1 given in

LEMMA 4.1 *Let* $C(z) = \sum_{i=0}^{\infty} z^i C_i$ *be convergent for* $|z| < 1 + \delta$ *for some* $\delta > 0$, *and define* $C_i^* = -\sum_{j=i+1}^{\infty} C_j$, $i = 0, 1, \ldots$ *and* $C^*(z) = \sum_{i=0}^{\infty} z^i C_i^*$. *Then* $C^*(z)$ *is convergent for* $|z| < 1 + \delta$ *and*

$$C(z) = C(1) + (1 - z)C^*(z). \tag{4.2}$$

Further it holds that $C^*(1) = -\frac{dC(z)}{dz}|_{z=1} = -\sum_{i=1}^{\infty} iC_i$. *If* $C(z)$ *is a polynomial, then so is* $C^*(z)$.

PROOF Since the coefficients C_i are exponentially decreasing the same holds for C_i^*, such that $C^*(z)$ has (at least) the same radius of convergence. Identifying coefficients in (4.2) we find

$$C_0 = C(1) + C_0^*,$$
$$C_i = C_i^* - C_{i-1}^*, \ i = 1, 2, \ldots$$

which has solution $C_i^* = -\sum_{j=i+1}^{\infty} C_j$. It follows from (4.2) that

$$C^*(1) = -\frac{dC(z)}{dz}|_{z=1} = -\sum_{i=0}^{\infty} iC_i = \sum_{i=0}^{\infty} C_i^*.$$

Note that if $C(z)$ is a polynomial then the entries in the matrix polynomial $C(z) - C(1)$ are polynomials too, with the property that they have a zero at $z = 1$. Hence each can be factorized as $(1 - z)$ times a polynomial. Thus if $C(z)$ is a polynomial then so is $C^*(z)$, see (2.7). □

Below we formulate the main result in this chapter, but first we need some notation. The characteristic polynomial for the process X_t given in (4.1) is

$$A(z) = (1 - z)I - \Pi z - \sum_{i=1}^{k-1} \Gamma_i(1 - z)z^i.$$

Note that $A(1) = -\Pi$ and that

$$\dot{A}(1) = \frac{d}{dz}A(z)|_{z=1} = -\Pi - I + \sum_{i=1}^{k-1} \Gamma_i = -\Pi - \Gamma.$$

Expanding the polynomial around $z = 1$, we apply Lemma 4.1 twice and find that we can define

$$A^{**}(z) = \frac{A(z) - A(1) - \dot{A}(1)(z - 1)}{(1 - z)^2}$$

such that

$$A(z) = -\Pi + (\Gamma + \Pi)(1 - z) + A^{**}(z)(1 - z)^2,$$

where $A^{**}(z)$ is a polynomial. If in this expression we replace z^i by L^i and $1 - z$ by $\Delta = 1 - L$ we can write the equation for X_t as

$$A(L)X_t = -\Pi X_t + (\Gamma + \Pi)\Delta X_t + A^{**}(L)\Delta^2 X_t = \epsilon_t + \Phi D_t. \qquad (4.3)$$

The conditions of Theorem 4.2 below (known as Granger's representation theorem), are expressed in terms of the parameters Π and Γ, that is, the value of $A(\cdot)$ at $z = 1$ and the derivative of $A(\cdot)$ at $z = 1$.

If $A(z)$ has no roots with modulus ≤ 1 the process X_t becomes stationary, and since we here want to describe $I(1)$ processes, we allow roots at the point $z = 1$, see Assumption 1, p. 14.

If we allow for unit roots, then $\Pi = -A(1)$ has to be singular. A singular matrix of rank r, say, has the representation $\Pi = \alpha\beta'$ for some $p \times r$ matrices α and β. To see this let β' denote r linearly independent rows of Π and let α denote the coefficients that are needed to write the rows of Π as linear combinations of the rows β', then $\Pi = \alpha\beta'$. Recall that if β is any $p \times r$ matrix of full rank, we define $\beta_\perp$ as a $p \times (p - r)$ matrix of full rank, such that $\beta'\beta_\perp = 0$. An explicit construction of $\beta_\perp$ can be given as follows: let c be the $p \times r$ matrix $c = (I_r, 0)'$, where I_r is an $r \times r$ identity matrix, and choose $c_\perp = (0, I_{p-r})'$. Then one can take

$$\beta_\perp = (I_p - c(\beta'c)^{-1}\beta')c_\perp.$$

This definition works for any matrix c for which $\beta'c$ has full rank. For mathematical convenience we define $\beta_\perp = 0$ if β has full rank p, and define

$\beta_\perp = I_p$ if β has rank 0. Further we define $\bar\beta = \beta(\beta'\beta)^{-1}$, such that the projection on the space spanned by the columns of β is $P_\beta = \beta(\beta'\beta)^{-1}\beta' = \beta\bar\beta' = \bar\beta\beta'$, and $\beta'\bar\beta = \bar\beta'\beta = I_r$. These normalizations will be discussed in more detail in section 13.2.

THEOREM 4.2 *If $|A(z)| = 0$ implies that $|z| > 1$ or $z = 1$, and $rank(\Pi) = r < p$, then there exist $p \times r$ matrices α and β of rank r such that*

$$\Pi = \alpha\beta'. \tag{4.4}$$

A necessary and sufficient condition that $\Delta X_t - E(\Delta X_t)$ and $\beta' X_t - E(\beta' X_t)$ can be given initial distributions such that they become $I(0)$ is that

$$\left| -\alpha'_\perp \dot A(1)\beta_\perp \right| = |\alpha'_\perp \Gamma \beta_\perp| \neq 0. \tag{4.5}$$

In this case the solution of (4.1), X_t, has the representation

$$X_t = C \sum_{i=1}^{t}(\epsilon_i + \Phi D_i) + C_1(L)(\epsilon_t + \Phi D_t) + A, \tag{4.6}$$

where A depends on initial values, such that $\beta' A = 0$, and where $C = \beta_\perp(\alpha'_\perp \Gamma \beta_\perp)^{-1}\alpha'_\perp$. It follows that X_t is a cointegrated $I(1)$ process with cointegrating vectors β. The function $C_1(z)$ satisfies

$$A^{-1}(z) = C\frac{1}{1-z} + C_1(z), \; z \neq 1, \tag{4.7}$$

where the power series for $C_1(z)$ is convergent for $|z| < 1 + \delta$ for some $\delta > 0$.

The solution of equation (4.1) contains contributions from the ϵ and from the initial values. Since some linear combinations of the X_t as well as ΔX_t can be made stationary by suitable choices of the initial distribution the representation (4.6) only contains part of the initial values. Thus for instance if the process has one random walk component and one stationary component, then the representation (4.6) only contains the initial value of the random walk. Instead of all the initial values $X_{-k+1}, \ldots, X_0$ only X_0 is present because ΔX_t has been represented as a stationary process. Thus it is not a representation of the process given the initial value X_0, but a representation that includes as little as possible of the initial values.

It is an immediate consequence of the representation (4.6) that $\beta' X_t - E(\beta' X_t)$ is stationary, since $\beta' C = 0$, and in fact $\beta' C_1(L)(\epsilon_t + \Phi D_t)$ is a representation of the disequilibrium error $\beta' X_t$. The matrix C plays an important role for the understanding of the $I(1)$ models. For large t the random walk dominates the stochastic component of X_t and the variance is given by the so-called long-run variance $C\Omega C'$. This matrix is singular, and in fact the null space is the directions determined by β, the stationary components. One can interpret the matrix C as indicating how the common trends $\alpha'_\perp \Sigma^t_{i=1} \epsilon_i$ contribute to the various variables through the matrix $\beta_\perp$. Another interpretation is that a random shock to the first equation, say, at time $t = 1$ gives rise to short-run random effects as represented by the coefficients of $C_1(L)$ which die out over time, and a long-run effect given by $C\epsilon_{11}$. This permanent effect is orthogonal to β such that the process is shifted to another position on the attractor. Thus the coefficients of the cointegrating relation cannot usually be interpreted as elasticities, even if the variables are in logs, since a shock to one variable implies a shock to all variables in the long run, and hence the coefficients do not in general allow a *ceteris paribus* interpretation, see Lütkepohl (1994).

PROOF   There is no loss of generality in setting $\Phi = 0$. The idea of the proof is to apply Theorem 2.2 for stationary processes to $Z_t = \beta' X_t$ and $U_t = \beta'_\perp \Delta X_t$, which, if the theorem is correct, will be stationary. We find the expressions

$$\Delta X_i = (P_{\beta_\perp} + P_\beta)\Delta X_i = \bar{\beta}_\perp U_i + \bar{\beta}\Delta Z_i.$$

Summing from $i = 1, \ldots, t$ we get

$$X_t = \bar{\beta}_\perp \sum_{i=1}^t U_i + \bar{\beta} Z_t + X_0 - \bar{\beta} Z_0 = \bar{\beta}_\perp \sum_{i=1}^t U_i + \bar{\beta} Z_t + P_{\beta_\perp} X_0. \quad (4.8)$$

This shows that if the process $\tilde{X}_t = (Z'_t, U'_t)'$ is stationary the results will follow. Note that Z_t is r-dimensional and U_t is $(p - r)$-dimensional, and that

$$\tilde{X}'_t = (X'_t\beta, \Delta X'_t\beta_\perp).$$

We want to show that $\tilde{X}_t$ is an autoregressive process and therefore want to show how (4.1) or (4.3) can be rewritten in terms of $\tilde{X}_t$. We multiply equation (4.3) by $\bar{\alpha}'$ and $\bar{\alpha}'_\perp$ and get

$$-\beta' X_t + \bar{\alpha}'(\Gamma + \alpha\beta')\Delta X_t + \bar{\alpha}' A^*(L)\Delta^2 X_t = \bar{\alpha}'\epsilon_t, \quad (4.9)$$

$$\bar{\alpha}'_\perp \Gamma \Delta X_t + \bar{\alpha}'_\perp A^*(L)\Delta^2 X_t = \bar{\alpha}'_\perp \epsilon_t. \quad (4.10)$$

These equations define the process X_t, $t = 1, \ldots, T$, as function of the initial values and $\epsilon_1, \ldots, \epsilon_t$. Note that multiplication by $\bar{\alpha}'_\perp$ cancels the term involving the levels.

Next inserting the expression for $\beta' X_t$ and ΔX_t in terms of Z_t and U_t we obtain equations for the new variables

$$-Z_t + \bar{\alpha}'(\Gamma + \alpha\beta')\bar{\beta}\Delta Z_t + \bar{\alpha}'\Gamma\bar{\beta}_\perp U_t + \bar{\alpha}' A^*(L)\Delta^2 X_t = \bar{\alpha}'\epsilon_t, \quad (4.11)$$

$$\bar{\alpha}'_{\perp}\Gamma\bar{\beta}\Delta Z_t + \bar{\alpha}'_{\perp}\Gamma\bar{\beta}_{\perp}U_t + \bar{\alpha}'_{\perp}A^*(L)\Delta^2 X_t = \bar{\alpha}'_{\perp}\epsilon_t. \quad (4.12)$$

Since $\Delta^2 X_t$ is a function of $\Delta\tilde{X}_t$ and $\Delta^2\tilde{X}_t$, equations (4.11) and (4.12) can be written

$$\tilde{A}(L)\tilde{X}_t = \begin{bmatrix} -I & \bar{\alpha}'\Gamma\bar{\beta}_{\perp} \\ 0 & \bar{\alpha}'_{\perp}\Gamma\bar{\beta}_{\perp} \end{bmatrix} \begin{bmatrix} Z_t \\ U_t \end{bmatrix} + A^{**}(L)\Delta\tilde{X}_t = (\bar{\alpha}, \bar{\alpha}_{\perp})'\epsilon_t.$$

Here $A^{**}(L)$ is a polynomial in the lag operator L which collects the remaining terms. Thus the process $\tilde{X}_t$ is an autoregressive process with a lag polynomial $\tilde{A}(z)$ that satisfies the relation

$$\begin{aligned}(\bar{\alpha}, \bar{\alpha}_{\perp})'A(z) &= (\bar{\alpha}, \bar{\alpha}_{\perp})'A(z)(\bar{\beta}, \bar{\beta}_{\perp}(1-z)^{-1})(\beta, \beta_{\perp}(1-z))' \\ &= \tilde{A}(z)(\beta, \beta_{\perp}(1-z))', \; z \neq 1.\end{aligned} \quad (4.13)$$

It follows that

$$|\tilde{A}(z)| = |(\bar{\alpha}, \bar{\alpha}_{\perp})'A(z)(\bar{\beta}, \bar{\beta}_{\perp}(1-z)^{-1})|, \; z \neq 1$$

has the same roots as $|A(z)|$ except for $z = 1$. Note also that

$$\tilde{A}(1) = \begin{bmatrix} -I & \bar{\alpha}'\Gamma\bar{\beta}_{\perp} \\ 0 & \bar{\alpha}'_{\perp}\Gamma\bar{\beta}_{\perp} \end{bmatrix} \quad (4.14)$$

has full rank if and only if assumption (4.5) holds since

$$|\tilde{A}(1)| = |\bar{\alpha}'_{\perp}\Gamma\bar{\beta}_{\perp}| \neq 0. \quad (4.15)$$

Thus $\tilde{A}(z)$ has no unit roots and all other roots are outside the unit circle by Assumption 1. Hence the processes Z_t and U_t are given by the autoregressive equations

$$\tilde{A}(L)\tilde{X}_t = \tilde{A}(L)\begin{bmatrix} Z_t \\ U_t \end{bmatrix} = (\bar{\alpha}, \bar{\alpha}_{\perp})'\epsilon_t, \quad (4.16)$$

which are invertible if and only if condition (4.5) holds, as we have removed the unit roots from the process by the transformation from X_t to the process $\tilde{X}_t$.

Thus U_t and Z_t can, by Theorem 2.2, be given initial distributions such that they become stationary and in fact $I(0)$.

This proves the main results of Theorem 4.2, but we want to get an explicit expression for the leading term in the representation of X_t in terms of the ϵ_i, that is, the matrix C. From (4.16) we find

$$\tilde{X}_t = \tilde{C}(L)(\bar{\alpha}, \bar{\alpha}_{\perp})'\epsilon_t,$$

where $\tilde{C}(z) = \tilde{A}(z)^{-1} = \tilde{A}(1)^{-1} + (1-z)\tilde{C}^*(z)$, see (4.2), since $\tilde{C}(1) = \tilde{A}(1)^{-1}$, such that

$$\tilde{X}_t = \tilde{A}(1)^{-1}(\bar{\alpha}, \bar{\alpha}_\perp)'\epsilon_t + \tilde{C}^*(L)(\bar{\alpha}, \bar{\alpha}_\perp)'\Delta\epsilon_t,$$

which implies that

$$(0, I_{p-r})\tilde{X}_t = U_t = (0, I_{p-r})\tilde{A}(1)^{-1}(\bar{\alpha}, \bar{\alpha}_\perp)'\epsilon_t + \Delta Y_t,$$

where $Y_t = (0, I_{p-r})\tilde{C}^*(L)(\bar{\alpha}, \bar{\alpha}_\perp)'\epsilon_t$. Summing we find

$$\bar{\beta}_\perp \sum_{i=1}^t U_i = (0, \bar{\beta}_\perp)\tilde{A}(1)^{-1}(\bar{\alpha}, \bar{\alpha}_\perp)' \sum_{i=1}^t \epsilon_i + \bar{\beta}_\perp(Y_t - Y_0).$$

The coefficient to the random walk is found to be:

$$C = (0, \bar{\beta}_\perp)\tilde{A}(1)^{-1}(\bar{\alpha}, \bar{\alpha}_\perp)'$$

$$= (0, \bar{\beta}_\perp) \begin{bmatrix} -I & \bar{\alpha}'\Gamma\bar{\beta}_\perp \\ 0 & \bar{\alpha}'_\perp\Gamma\bar{\beta}_\perp \end{bmatrix}^{-1} (\bar{\alpha}, \bar{\alpha}_\perp)'$$

$$= \bar{\beta}_\perp(\bar{\alpha}'_\perp\Gamma\bar{\beta}_\perp)^{-1}\bar{\alpha}'_\perp = \beta_\perp(\alpha'_\perp\Gamma\beta_\perp)^{-1}\alpha'_\perp.$$

Next insert these results into (4.8) and we get

$$X_t = C\sum_{i=1}^t \epsilon_i + \bar{\beta}_\perp(Y_t - Y_0) + \bar{\beta}Z_t + P_{\beta_\perp}X_0.$$

We let $A = -\bar{\beta}_\perp Y_0 + P_{\beta_\perp}X_0$, which shows that $\beta'A = 0$. Finally we define $C_1(L)$ by

$$C_1(L)\epsilon_t = \bar{\beta}_\perp Y_t + \bar{\beta}Z_t.$$

The representation (4.6) implies, for $\Phi = 0$, that

$$\Delta X_t = C\epsilon_t + C_1(L)\Delta\epsilon_t,$$

or equivalently

$$(1 - z)A^{-1}(z) = C + C_1(z)(1 - z),$$

which shows (4.7).

$$\square$$

COROLLARY 4.3 *Under the assumption that* $|A(z)| = 0$ *implies* $|z| > 1$ *or* $z = 1$, *the number of unit roots is greater than or equal to* $p - r$ *where* $r = \text{rank}(\Pi)$. *Equality holds if and only if* X_t *is* $I(0)$, $(r = p)$, *or* $I(1)$, $(r < p)$.

PROOF The first statement follows from the representation (4.13) which shows that the number of unit roots is at least $p - r$ since the matrix $(\beta, \beta_\perp(1 - z))$ has $p - r$ unit roots. Equality holds if and only if $\bar{A}(L)$ has no unit roots, that is, if and only if the process $\tilde{X}_t$ is $I(0)$. If this is the case then X_t is also $I(0)$ if $r = p$, otherwise X_t is $I(1)$. □

The corollary shows that the number of unit roots of a system cannot be decided by inspection of the matrix Π alone, that is, the value of the polynomial at $z = 1$. Just like for univariate polynomials a condition on the derivative is needed, see (4.5). The result is a special case of a general result for higher order integrated systems, see Johansen (1988a) or Boswijk (1993).

This result gives a useful diagnostic tool to see if a fitted $I(1)$ model contains processes that are $I(2)$, since if the processes are $I(2)$ then the unit roots of the polynomial $A(z)$ cannot be removed by changing the rank of Π, that is, by changing the cointegrating rank.

COROLLARY 4.4 *The process $\beta'_\perp X_t$ is not cointegrating, and the same holds for $\alpha'_\perp \Gamma X_t$ and they can both be used as common trends.*

PROOF It follows from the expression for the matrix $C = \beta_\perp(\alpha'_\perp \Gamma \beta_\perp)^{-1}\alpha'_\perp$ that if $\beta_\perp$ has full rank $p - r$ then so does $\beta'_\perp \beta_\perp$ and hence $\beta'_\perp C$ has full rank $p - r$ which shows that $\beta'_\perp X_t$ does not cointegrate. Next note that

$$\alpha'_\perp \Gamma C = \alpha'_\perp \Gamma \beta_\perp (\alpha'_\perp \Gamma \beta_\perp)^{-1}\alpha'_\perp = \alpha'_\perp,$$

such that

$$\alpha'_\perp \Gamma X_t = \alpha'_\perp \Sigma_{i=1}^t (\epsilon_i + \Phi D_i) + \alpha'_\perp \Gamma C_0(L)(\epsilon_t + \Phi D_t) + \alpha'_\perp \Gamma P_{\beta_\perp} X_0.$$

Thus the linear combinations $\alpha'_\perp \Gamma X_t$ almost capture the common trends as defined in Definition 3.7. □

The representation in Theorem 4.2 is known as Granger's representation theorem, see Engle and Granger (1987), even though they state a slightly different version, see Theorem 4.5. Thus they arrive at cointegration from an assumption that X_t is at most $I(1)$, and an assumption that the moving average representation is of reduced rank. We have chosen in Theorem 4.2 to go the other way and start with the autoregressive model since that is what is usually fitted to the data, and then express in terms of conditions on the parameters when we get $I(1)$ variables and cointegration. The importance of this result is first of all that it shows the equivalence between the notion of error correction models and cointegration. Thus the process that satisfies an error correction model must exhibit cointegration and a cointegrated process can be considered a solution of an error correction model. Another important aspect of the representation (4.6) is that it immediately gives the asymptotic properties of the process X_t defined by the error correction model.

Perhaps the most important consequence of condition (4.5) is that it allows to formulate a corresponding result for $I(2)$ processes, see Theorem 4.6.

EXAMPLE 4.1 continued. For this case we find

$$\Pi = \begin{bmatrix} \alpha_1 & -\alpha_1 \\ 0 & 0 \end{bmatrix}, \Gamma = \begin{bmatrix} 1 & 0 \\ 0 & 1 \end{bmatrix},$$

such that $\beta = (1, -1)'$, $\alpha = (\alpha_1, 0)'$, $\beta_\perp = (1, 1)'$, $\alpha_\perp = (0, 1)'$ and finally condition (4.5) becomes

$$\alpha'_\perp \Gamma \beta_\perp = (0, 1) \begin{bmatrix} 1 & 0 \\ 0 & 1 \end{bmatrix} \begin{bmatrix} 1 \\ 1 \end{bmatrix} = 1,$$

which has full rank consistent with the solution being $I(1)$.

EXAMPLE 4.2 continued. We find

$$\Pi = \begin{bmatrix} 0 & 0 \\ 1 & 0 \end{bmatrix}, \Gamma = \begin{bmatrix} 1 & 0 \\ 0 & 1 \end{bmatrix}$$

giving $|A(z)| = (1 - z)^2$, such that Assumption 1 is satisfied. We also find that $\alpha = (0, 1)'$, $\beta = (1, 0)'$, $\alpha_\perp = (1, 0)'$ $\beta_\perp = (0, 1)'$ and $\alpha'_\perp \Gamma \beta_\perp = 0$. Thus in this situation condition (4.5) is not satisfied, corresponding to the process being $I(2)$. Note that Γ has full rank despite the property that $\alpha'_\perp \Gamma \beta_\perp = 0$.

EXAMPLE 4.3 We define the process X_t by the equations

$$\Delta X_{1t} = \tfrac{1}{4}(X_{1t-1} - X_{2t-1}) + \gamma \Delta X_{2t-1} + \epsilon_{1t},$$

$$\Delta X_{2t} = -\tfrac{1}{4}(X_{1t-1} - X_{2t-1}) + \epsilon_{2t}.$$

If $\gamma = 0$ these equations are easily solved to give

$$X_{1t} - X_{2t} = \frac{3}{2}(X_{1t-1} - X_{2t-1}) + \epsilon_{1t} - \epsilon_{2t},$$

which shows that $X_{1t} - X_{2t}$, and hence also X_{1t} and X_{2t} are explosive, simply because the error correction coefficients have the wrong sign, such that X_t is pushed away from the relation $X_1 - X_2 = 0$. We now want to show that if we choose $\gamma = 9/4$ then the process becomes $I(1)$. For $\gamma = 9/4$ we find

$$\Pi = \begin{bmatrix} 1/4 & -1/4 \\ -1/4 & 1/4 \end{bmatrix}, \Gamma = \begin{bmatrix} 1 & -9/4 \\ 0 & 1 \end{bmatrix}.$$

This gives

$$|A(z)| = \det \begin{bmatrix} 1 - 5z/4 & -8z/4 + 9z^2/4 \\ z/4 & 1 - 5z/4 \end{bmatrix}$$

$$= -9z^3/16 + 33z^2/16 - 10z/4 + 1$$

$$= (1 - z)(3z/4 - 1)^2,$$

which has roots 1 and 4/3 which are outside the unit disk or at 1. Further

$$\alpha = \frac{1}{4}(1, -1)', \beta = (1, -1)', \alpha_\perp = (1, 1)', \beta_\perp = (1, 1)', \alpha'_\perp \Gamma \beta_\perp = -\frac{1}{4}.$$

This shows that the process is $I(1)$ since condition (4.5) holds with $(1, -1)'$ as a cointegrating vector despite the fact that the adjustment coefficients have the wrong sign. Thus the effect of the adjustment coefficients is not so easy to assess without taking into account all the parameters of the model.

4.2 From MA to AR Representation for $I(1)$ Variables

In this section we want to find out when an $I(1)$ process given by its moving average representation can be shown to satisfy an autoregressive equation.

Thus let $C(z) = \sum_{i=0}^{\infty} C_i z^i$ be convergent for $|z| < 1 + \delta$, $C(1) \neq 0$, and assume that Assumption 1 is satisfied for $C(z)$. We further assume that the $I(1)$ process X_t satisfies

$$\Delta X_t = C(L)(\epsilon_t + \Phi D_t), \tag{4.17}$$

such that ΔX_t is an $I(0)$ process. We let $C = C(1)$ and introduce $C^* = -dC(z)/dz|_{z=1}$, then the following result holds

THEOREM 4.5 *If* $rank(C) = p - r < p$, *then* $C = \xi\eta'$ *for* ξ *and* η $(p \times (p-r))$ *of full rank. If furthermore* $\xi'_\perp C^* \eta_\perp$ *has full rank then* $\xi'_\perp(X_t - E(X_t))$ *can be given an initial distribution such that it is stationary, and* X_t *satisfies an (infinite order) error correction model of the form*

$$A(L)X_t = \eta_\perp(\xi'_\perp C^* \eta_\perp)^{-1}\xi'_\perp X_{\cdot} + A^*(L)\Delta X_t = \epsilon_t + \Phi D_t. \tag{4.18}$$

PROOF We assume again without loss of generality that $\Phi = 0$. The proof runs roughly as that for Theorem 4.2. We write (4.17) as

$$\Delta X_t = C\epsilon_t + C^*(L)\Delta \epsilon_t = \xi\eta'\epsilon_t + C^*(L)\Delta \epsilon_t,$$

and multiply by $\bar{\xi}'$ and $\bar{\xi}'_\perp$ and introduce the variables $u_t = \eta'\epsilon_t$ and $v_t = \eta'_\perp \epsilon_t$ such that $\epsilon_t = \bar{\eta}u_t + \bar{\eta}_\perp v_t$. Then

$$\begin{aligned} \bar{\xi}'\Delta X_t &= \eta'\epsilon_t + \bar{\xi}'C^*(L)\Delta\epsilon_t \\ &= u_t + \bar{\xi}'C^*(L)\Delta(\bar{\eta}u_t + \bar{\eta}_\perp v_t), \end{aligned} \tag{4.19}$$

and

$$\bar{\xi}'_\perp \Delta X_t = \bar{\xi}'_\perp C^*(L)\Delta \epsilon_t. \tag{4.20}$$

Summing (4.20) we find

$$\bar{\xi}'_\perp X_t - \bar{\xi}'_\perp X_0 = \bar{\xi}'_\perp C^*(L)(\epsilon_t - \epsilon_0). \tag{4.21}$$

This shows that if we choose $\bar{\xi}'_\perp X_t$ to have initial distribution $\bar{\xi}'_\perp C^*(L)\epsilon_0$, then $\bar{\xi}'_\perp X_t$ has the representation

$$\bar{\xi}'_\perp X_t = \bar{\xi}'_\perp C^*(L)\epsilon_t = \bar{\xi}'_\perp C^*(L)(\bar{\eta} u_t + \bar{\eta}_\perp v_t), \tag{4.22}$$

such that $\bar{\xi}'_\perp X_t$ is stationary. We then find from (4.19) and (4.22), since $C^*(1) = C^*$, that in terms of the errors u_t and v_t we find

$$\begin{bmatrix} \bar{\xi}' \Delta X_t \\ \bar{\xi}'_\perp X_t \end{bmatrix} = \tilde{C}(L) \begin{bmatrix} u_t \\ v_t \end{bmatrix} = \begin{bmatrix} I & 0 \\ \bar{\xi}'_\perp C^* \bar{\eta} & \bar{\xi}'_\perp C^* \bar{\eta}_\perp \end{bmatrix} \begin{bmatrix} u_t \\ v_t \end{bmatrix} + C^{**}(L)\Delta \begin{bmatrix} u_t \\ v_t \end{bmatrix}, \tag{4.23}$$

for suitable functions $\tilde{C}(z)$ and C^{**}. The matrix $\tilde{C}(1)$ given by

$$\tilde{C}(1) = \begin{bmatrix} I & 0 \\ \bar{\xi}'_\perp C^* \bar{\eta} & \bar{\xi}'_\perp C^* \bar{\eta}_\perp \end{bmatrix}$$

has full rank by the assumptions made. Thus $z = 1$ is not a root in $\tilde{C}(z)$. Just as before we can check that the remaining roots of $C(z)$ are outside the unit disk, such that $\tilde{C}(z)$ can be inverted. Let $\tilde{A}(z) = \tilde{C}(z)^{-1}$. Then (4.23) can be solved for u_t and v_t :

$$\begin{bmatrix} u_t \\ v_t \end{bmatrix} = \tilde{A}(L) \begin{bmatrix} \bar{\xi}' \Delta X_t \\ \bar{\xi}'_\perp X_t \end{bmatrix} = \tilde{A}(1) \begin{bmatrix} \bar{\xi}' \Delta X_t \\ \bar{\xi}'_\perp X_t \end{bmatrix} + \tilde{A}^*(L)\Delta \begin{bmatrix} \bar{\xi}' \Delta X_t \\ \bar{\xi}'_\perp X_t \end{bmatrix}.$$

The only term that involves the levels is

$$\tilde{A}(1) \begin{bmatrix} 0 \\ \bar{\xi}'_\perp X_t. \end{bmatrix}$$

all remaining terms involve only ΔX_t and can be collected in a term $\tilde{A}^{**}(L)\Delta X_t$. Thus

$$\begin{bmatrix} u_t \\ v_t \end{bmatrix} = \tilde{A}(1) \begin{bmatrix} 0 \\ \bar{\xi}'_\perp X_t \end{bmatrix} + \tilde{A}^{**}(L)\Delta X_t.$$

Hence

$$\epsilon_t = (\bar{\eta}, \bar{\eta}_\perp) \begin{bmatrix} I & 0 \\ \bar{\xi}'_\perp C^* \bar{\eta} & \bar{\xi}'_\perp C^* \bar{\eta}_\perp \end{bmatrix}^{-1} \begin{bmatrix} 0 \\ \bar{\xi}'_\perp X_t \end{bmatrix} + (\bar{\eta}, \bar{\eta}_\perp)\tilde{A}^{**}(L)\Delta X_t,$$

which can be written

$$\bar\eta_\perp(\bar\xi'_\perp C^* \bar\eta_\perp)^{-1}\bar\xi'_\perp X_t + (\bar\eta,\, \bar\eta_\perp)\tilde{A}^{**}(L)\Delta X_t = \epsilon_t,$$

which is the required result if we define $A^*(z) = (\bar\eta,\, \bar\eta_\perp)\tilde{A}^{**}(z)$.   □

4.3   The MA Representation of $I(2)$ Variables

We consider again the equation

$$\Delta X_t = \Pi X_{t-1} + \sum_{i=1}^{k-1}\Gamma_i \Delta X_{t-i} + \Phi D_t + \epsilon_t,\; t = 1,\dots, T. \qquad (4.24)$$

The result of Theorem 4.2 shows that in order to find solutions of (4.24) that are $I(1)$ we need condition (4.5) that $\alpha'_\perp\Gamma\beta_\perp$ has full rank. If this matrix has reduced rank we get the possibility of finding processes that are integrated of order higher than one. We here focus on $I(2)$ since it seems that higher orders of integration than two are not so important for the type of macro economic data that we have in mind. The result is taken from Johansen (1992a).

We have seen that for $I(2)$ processes we can have vectors that reduce the order of integration of the process from two to one, and linear combinations that cointegrate with the differences of the process. These linear combinations can be expressed in terms of the parameters α, β, and Γ, but in order to do so we need some notation. If $\alpha'_\perp\Gamma\beta_\perp$ has reduced rank s it holds that

$$\alpha'_\perp\Gamma\beta_\perp = \xi\eta'$$

for some ξ and η of dimension $(p-r) \times s$, and rank s, with $s < p - r$. We then decompose $\alpha_\perp$ and $\beta_\perp$ as follows

$$\alpha_1 = \bar\alpha_\perp\xi,\; \alpha_2 = \alpha_\perp\xi_\perp,$$

$$\beta_1 = \bar\beta_\perp\eta,\; \beta_2 = \beta_\perp\eta_\perp.$$

Thus $(\alpha,\, \alpha_1,\, \alpha_2)$ is of full rank p and α, α_1, and α_2 are mutually orthogonal. The same holds for $(\beta,\, \beta_1,\, \beta_2)$. The directions given by $(\beta,\, \beta_1,\, \beta_2)$ express the different types of cointegration that are possible for $I(2)$ variables. The following relations can easily be verified since $\bar\alpha'_\perp\bar\alpha_\perp = (\alpha'_\perp\alpha_\perp)^{-1}$

$$\alpha'_1\Gamma\beta_2 = \xi'(\alpha'_\perp\alpha_\perp)^{-1}\alpha'_\perp\Gamma\beta_\perp\eta_\perp = \xi'(\alpha'_\perp\alpha_\perp)^{-1}\xi\eta'\eta_\perp = 0,$$

$$\alpha'_2\Gamma\beta_2 = \xi'_\perp\alpha'_\perp\Gamma\beta_\perp\eta_\perp \qquad = \xi'_\perp\xi\eta'\eta_\perp \qquad = 0,$$

$$\alpha'_2\Gamma\beta_1 = \xi'_\perp\alpha'_\perp\Gamma\beta_\perp(\beta'_\perp\beta_\perp)^{-1}\eta = \xi'_\perp\xi\eta'(\beta'_\perp\beta_\perp)^{-1}\eta = 0.$$

We also find

$$\bar{\alpha}'_1 \Gamma \bar{\beta}_1 = (\xi'(\alpha'_\perp \alpha_\perp)^{-1}\xi)^{-1}\xi'(\alpha'_\perp \alpha_\perp)^{-1}\xi \eta'(\beta'_\perp \beta_\perp)^{-1}\eta(\eta'(\beta'_\perp \beta_\perp)^{-1}\eta)^{-1} = I.$$

We need a special notation for the matrix

$$\theta = \Gamma \bar{\beta}\bar{\alpha}'\Gamma + \sum_{i=1}^{k-1} i\Gamma_i,$$

since it will appear in the conditions below. With this notation we then formulate a representation theorem for $I(2)$ variables which is an analogue of Theorem 4.2 for $I(1)$ variables.

THEOREM 4.6 *Assume that $|A(z)| = 0$ implies that $|z| > 1$ or $z = 1$, and that*

$$\Pi = \alpha\beta', \ \alpha, \ \beta \ (p \times r) \ of \ full \ rank \ r < p, \qquad (4.25)$$

$$\alpha'_\perp \Gamma \beta_\perp = \xi\eta', \ \xi, \ \eta \ ((p-r) \times s) \ of \ full \ rank \ s < p - r. \qquad (4.26)$$

Then a necessary and sufficient condition that the processes $\Delta^2 X_t, \beta'_1 \Delta X_t$ and $\beta'X_t - \bar{\alpha}'\Gamma\bar{\beta}_2\beta'_2\Delta X_t$ corrected for their means can be made $I(0)$ is that

$$\alpha'_2 \theta \beta_2 = \alpha'_2 \{\Gamma\bar{\beta}\bar{\alpha}'\Gamma + \sum_{i=1}^{k-1} i\Gamma_i\}\beta_2 \qquad (4.27)$$

has full rank. In this case the process X_t has the representation

$$X_t = C_2 \sum_{s=1}^{t} \sum_{i=1}^{s}(\epsilon_i + \Phi D_i) + C_1 \sum_{i=1}^{t}(\epsilon_i + \Phi D_i) + C_2(L)(\epsilon_t + \Phi D_t) + A + Bt,$$

$$(4.28)$$

where

$$C_2 = \beta_2(\alpha'_2 \theta \beta_2)^{-1}\alpha'_2,$$

$$\beta'C_1 = \bar{\alpha}'\Gamma\bar{\beta}_2(\bar{\alpha}'_2 \theta \bar{\beta}_2)^{-1}\bar{\alpha}'_2 = \bar{\alpha}'\Gamma C_2,$$

$$\beta'_1 C_1 = \bar{\alpha}'_1 - \bar{\alpha}'_1 \theta \bar{\beta}_2(\bar{\alpha}'_2 \theta \bar{\beta}_2)^{-1}\bar{\alpha}'_2 = \bar{\alpha}'_1(I - \theta C_2).$$

The coefficients A and B depend on the initial conditions and satisfies $(\beta, \beta_1)'B = 0$ and $\beta'A - \bar{\alpha}'\Gamma\bar{\beta}_2\beta'_2B = 0$.

   Thus X_t is an $I(2)$ process and the vectors (β, β_1) are cointegrating vectors that reduce the order from 2 to 1. Finally X_t allows polynomial cointegration since $\beta'X_t - \bar{\alpha}'\Gamma\bar{\beta}_2\beta'_2\Delta X_t$ corrected for its mean can be made $I(0)$. The function $C_2(z)$ satisfies

$$A^{-1}(z) = C_2 \frac{1}{(1-z)^2} + C_1 \frac{1}{1-z} + C_2(z), \tag{4.29}$$

and has a convergent power series for $|z| < 1 + \delta$ for some $\delta > 0$.

PROOF We set $\Phi = 0$ without loss of generality. The idea is to apply Theorem 4.2 to the variables

$$Z_t = \beta' X_t, \ V_t = \beta_1' X_t, \ U_t = \beta_2' \Delta X_t, \tag{4.30}$$

which, if the theorem is correct, will be $I(1)$. Thus we want to show that the process $\tilde{X}_t = (Z_t', V_t', U_t')'$ is an $I(1)$ process under the conditions stated, and we therefore want to derive the autoregressive representation for this process from (4.24). Just as for the proof of Theorem 4.2 we expand the polynomial $A(z)$ around the point $z = 1$ and find the derivatives

$$dA(z)/dz|_{z=1} \quad = -I - \Pi + \sum_{i=1}^{k-1} \Gamma_i = -\alpha\beta' - \Gamma,$$

$$\tfrac{1}{2} d^2 A(z)/dz^2|_{z=1} = \sum_{i=1}^{k-1} i\Gamma_i = \Psi.$$

Then

$$A(z) = -\alpha\beta' + (\Gamma + \alpha\beta')(1-z) + \Psi(1-z)^2 + A^*(z)(1-z)^3,$$

where $A^*(z)$ is a suitable polynomial. From (4.30) we find

$$\Delta^2 X = \bar{\beta}\Delta^2 Z_t + \bar{\beta}_1 \Delta^2 V_t + \bar{\beta}_2 \Delta U_t,$$

$$\Delta X_t = \bar{\beta}\Delta Z_t + \bar{\beta}_1 \Delta V_t + \bar{\beta}_2 U_t,$$

$$X_t = \bar{\beta} Z_t + \bar{\beta}_1 V_t + \bar{\beta}_2 \sum_{i=1}^{t} U_i + P_{\beta_2} X_0.$$

Equation (4.24) can be expressed as

$$A(L)X_t = -\alpha\beta' X_t + (\Gamma + \alpha\beta')\Delta X_t + \Psi\Delta^2 X_t + A^*(L)\Delta^3 X_t = \epsilon_t.$$

If we multiply by $(\bar{\alpha}, \bar{\alpha}_1, \bar{\alpha}_2)'$ and insert the expressions for ΔX_t and $\Delta^2 X_t$ in terms of Z_t, V_t, and U_t we find

$$- \begin{bmatrix} I & 0 & -\bar{\alpha}'\Gamma\bar{\beta}_2 \\ 0 & 0 & 0 \\ 0 & 0 & 0 \end{bmatrix} \begin{bmatrix} Z_t \\ V_t \\ U_t \end{bmatrix} + \begin{bmatrix} \bar{\alpha}'(\Gamma + \alpha\beta')\bar{\beta} & \bar{\alpha}'\Gamma\bar{\beta}_1 & \bar{\alpha}'\Psi\bar{\beta}_2 \\ \bar{\alpha}_1'\Gamma\bar{\beta} & I & \bar{\alpha}_1'\Psi\bar{\beta}_2 \\ \bar{\alpha}_2'\Gamma\bar{\beta} & 0 & \bar{\alpha}_2'\Psi\bar{\beta}_2 \end{bmatrix} \begin{bmatrix} \Delta Z_t \\ \Delta V_t \\ \Delta U_t \end{bmatrix}$$

$$+ A^{**}(L) \begin{bmatrix} \Delta^2 Z_t \\ \Delta^2 V_t \\ \Delta^2 U_t \end{bmatrix} = \tilde{\epsilon}_t. \tag{4.31}$$

Here $A^{**}(L)$ is a polynomial which collects the remaining terms. In a different notation this is written

$$\tilde{A}(L)\tilde{X}_t = -\tilde{\Pi}\tilde{X}_t + (\tilde{\Gamma} + \tilde{\Pi})\Delta\tilde{X}_t + A^{**}(L)\Delta^2\tilde{X}_t = \tilde{\epsilon}_t.$$

Notice that the coefficient $\bar{\alpha}'\Gamma\bar{\beta}_2$ now appears as a coefficient to levels, and $\bar{\alpha}'\Psi\bar{\beta}_2$ is a coefficient to differences since U_t is defined in terms of differences of X_t. In order to discuss $\tilde{X}_t$ as an $I(1)$ system we note that the levels matrix, $\tilde{\Pi}$, is of reduced rank and hence can be written as $\tilde{\Pi} = \tilde{\alpha}\tilde{\beta}'$, where

$$\tilde{\alpha} = \begin{bmatrix} I \\ 0 \\ 0 \end{bmatrix}, \tilde{\beta} = \begin{bmatrix} I \\ 0 \\ -\bar{\beta}_2'\Gamma'\bar{\alpha} \end{bmatrix}, \tilde{\alpha}_\perp = \begin{bmatrix} 0 & 0 \\ I & 0 \\ 0 & I \end{bmatrix}, \tilde{\beta}_\perp = \begin{bmatrix} 0 & \bar{\alpha}'\Gamma\bar{\beta}_2 \\ I & 0 \\ 0 & I \end{bmatrix}.$$

Next we want to check the conditions for the application of Theorem 4.2. The transformation from X_t to $\tilde{X}_t$ involves a matrix of the form $(\beta, \beta_1, (1-L)\beta_2)$, which has only unit roots. Thus $\tilde{X}_t$ has the same roots outside the unit circle as the process X_t. What remains is to see that condition (4.5) is satisfied for $\tilde{X}_t$. We find

$$\tilde{\alpha}_\perp'\tilde{\Gamma}\tilde{\beta}_\perp = \begin{bmatrix} I & \bar{\alpha}_1'\Gamma\bar{\beta}\bar{\alpha}'\Gamma\bar{\beta}_2 + \bar{\alpha}_1'\Psi\bar{\beta}_2 \\ 0 & \bar{\alpha}_2'\Gamma\bar{\beta}\bar{\alpha}'\Gamma\bar{\beta}_2 + \bar{\alpha}_2'\Psi\bar{\beta}_2 \end{bmatrix} = \begin{bmatrix} I & \bar{\alpha}_1'\theta\bar{\beta}_2 \\ 0 & \bar{\alpha}_2'\theta\bar{\beta}_2 \end{bmatrix}.$$

This has full rank if and only if the matrix $\bar{\alpha}_2'\theta\bar{\beta}_2 = \bar{\alpha}_2'\Gamma\bar{\beta}\bar{\alpha}'\Gamma\bar{\beta}_2 + \bar{\alpha}_2'\Psi\bar{\beta}_2$ has full rank. Thus condition (4.27) is a necessary and sufficient condition for $\tilde{X}_t$ to be $I(1)$ and hence X_t to be $I(2)$. Note that a consequence of applying Theorem 4.2 is that $\tilde{X}_t$ cointegrates in the sense that $Z_t - \bar{\alpha}'\Gamma\bar{\beta}_2 U_t = \beta'X_t - \bar{\alpha}'\Gamma\bar{\beta}_2\bar{\beta}_2'\Delta X_t$ is stationary. That is, what is polynomial cointegration for X_t is usual cointegration for $\tilde{X}_t$. The process $\tilde{X}_t$ has a representation of the form (4.6)

$$\tilde{X}_t = \tilde{C}\sum_{i=1}^{t}\tilde{\epsilon}_t + \tilde{C}(L)\tilde{\epsilon}_t + \tilde{A},$$

with

$$\tilde{C} = \tilde{\beta}_\perp(\tilde{\alpha}_\perp'\tilde{\Gamma}\tilde{\beta}_\perp)^{-1}\tilde{\alpha}_\perp' = \begin{bmatrix} 0 & 0 & \bar{\alpha}'\Gamma\bar{\beta}_2(\bar{\alpha}_2'\theta\bar{\beta}_2)^{-1} \\ 0 & I & -\bar{\alpha}_1'\theta\bar{\beta}_2(\bar{\alpha}_2'\theta\bar{\beta}_2)^{-1} \\ 0 & 0 & (\bar{\alpha}_2'\theta\bar{\beta}_2)^{-1} \end{bmatrix}, \tilde{\beta}'\tilde{A} = 0.$$

Thus we find the representations

$$Z_t = \bar{\alpha}'\Gamma\bar{\beta}_2(\bar{\alpha}_2'\theta\bar{\beta}_2)^{-1}\sum_{i=1}^{t}\bar{\alpha}_2'\epsilon_i + C_z(L)\epsilon_t + \tilde{A}_z,$$

$$V_t = \sum_{i=1}^{t}\bar{\alpha}_1'\epsilon_i - \bar{\alpha}_1'\theta\bar{\beta}_2(\bar{\alpha}_2'\theta\bar{\beta}_2)^{-1}\sum_{i=1}^{t}\bar{\alpha}_2'\epsilon_i + C_v(L)\epsilon_t + \tilde{A}_v,$$

$$U_t = (\bar{\alpha}_2'\theta\bar{\beta}_2)^{-1}\sum_{i=1}^{t}\bar{\alpha}_2'\epsilon_i + C_u(L)\epsilon_t + \tilde{A}_u,$$

where $\tilde{A}_z$, $\tilde{A}_v$, and $\tilde{A}_u$ depend on the initial conditions, such that $\bar{\beta}'\tilde{A} = \tilde{A}_z - \bar{\alpha}'\Gamma\bar{\beta}_2\tilde{A}_u = 0$. Notice that the expression for X_t in terms of (Z_t, V_t, U_t) involves the cumulated values of U_t. This means that the initial value $\tilde{A}_u$ is multiplied by t, and we find $B = \bar{\beta}_2\tilde{A}_u$ and $A = \bar{\beta}\tilde{A}_z + \bar{\beta}_1\tilde{A}_v + P_{\bar{\beta}_2}X_0$ such that $(\beta, \beta_1)'B = 0$ and

$$\beta'A - \bar{\alpha}'\Gamma\bar{\beta}_2\beta_2'B = \tilde{A}_z - \bar{\alpha}'\Gamma\bar{\beta}_2\tilde{A}_u = \bar{\beta}'\tilde{A} = 0.$$

We now want to find the properties of the matrices C_1 and C_2 as indicated in the theorem. The matrix C_2 is found as the coefficient to $\sum_{i=1}^{t}\epsilon_i$ in U_t, that is,

$$C_2 = \bar{\beta}_2(\bar{\alpha}_2'\theta\bar{\beta}_2)^{-1}\bar{\alpha}_2' = \bar{\beta}_2(\alpha_2'(\Gamma\bar{\beta}\bar{\alpha}'\Gamma + \Psi)\beta_2)^{-1}\alpha_2'.$$

The matrix C_1 is more complicated. In the direction β_2 the process is dominated by the cumulated random walk from the ϵ and the next term involving C_1 times a random walk plays little role. In the directions β, and β_1, however, the term involving the cumulated random walk cancels since $(\beta, \beta_1)'C_2 = 0$, and the process is dominated by the next term, which is found from the expressions for Z_t and V_t. We find

$$\beta'C_1 = \bar{\alpha}'\Gamma\bar{\beta}_2(\bar{\alpha}_2'\theta\bar{\beta}_2)^{-1}\bar{\alpha}_2' = \bar{\alpha}'\Gamma C_2,$$

$$\beta_1'C_1 = \bar{\alpha}_1' - \bar{\alpha}_1'\theta\bar{\beta}_2(\bar{\alpha}_2'\theta\bar{\beta}_2)^{-1}\bar{\alpha}_2' = \bar{\alpha}_1'(I - \theta C_2).$$

From the representation (4.28) we find that, for $\Phi = 0$,

$$\Delta^2 X_t = C_2\epsilon_t + C_1\Delta\epsilon_t + C_2(L)\Delta^2\epsilon_t,$$

and hence

$$(1 - z)^2 A(z) = C_2 + C_1(1 - z) + C_2(z)(1 - z)^2,$$

which implies (4.29). □

COROLLARY 4.7 *Under the assumption that $|A(z)| = 0$ implies that $|z| > 1$ or $z = 1$, the number of unit roots is greater than or equal to $2(p - r) - s$ where $r = rank(\Pi)$, which defines α and β, and $s = rank(\alpha_{\perp}'\Gamma\beta_{\perp})$. Equality holds if and only if the process is $I(0)$, $I(1)$, or $I(2)$. If equality holds then X_t is $I(0)$ if $r = p$, $I(1)$ if $r < p$ and $s = p - r$, and finally X_t is $I(2)$ if $r < p$ and $s < p - r$.*

PROOF The construction of $\tilde{X}_t = (\beta, \beta_1, \beta_2\Delta)'X_t$ removes $p - r - s$ unit roots from X_t. The AR process $\tilde{X}_t$ has by Corollary 4.5 at least $p - rank(\tilde{\Pi}) = p - r$ unit roots. Thus the total number of unit roots of X_t is $p - r - s + p - r = 2(p - r) - s$.

If equality holds then $\tilde{X}_t$ has $p - r$ unit roots and hence is an $I(0)$ process if $r = p$, in which case $s \leq p - r = 0$, such that $\beta_1 = \beta_2 = 0$ and also $X_t = \tilde{X}_t$ is $I(0)$. If $r < p$ then $\tilde{X}_t$ is an $I(1)$ process and so is X_t if $s = p - r$ which implies $\beta_2 = 0$. Finally if $r < p$ and $s < p - r$ then $\tilde{X}_t$ is $I(1)$ and X_t is $I(2)$. $\square$

4.4   Exercises

4.1

Consider the system

$$\Delta X_{1t} = \alpha_1 \left(X_{1t-1} - \beta_2 X_{2t-1} \right) + \mu_1 + \epsilon_{1t}, \tag{4.32}$$

$$\Delta X_{2t} = \mu_2 + \epsilon_{2t}. \tag{4.33}$$

1. Find the matrices α, β, Π, C, and Γ expressed in terms of the new parameters α_1, β_2, and μ. Note the two cases, $\alpha_1 = 0$ and $\alpha_1 \neq 0$.

2. Find the representation of X_t in terms of ϵ_i, $i = 1, \ldots, t$ and find $E(X_t|X_0)$ and $\mathrm{Var}(X_t|X_0)$.

3. Calculate the roots of the characteristic polynomial. Under what condition on the parameters is the process X_t an $I(1)$ process? If the process is not $I(1)$ what is it then?

4. Show explicitly from (4.32) and (4.33) without using Granger's representation that $\beta' X_t$ is stationary if $-2 < \alpha_1 < 0$.

5. Under what condition on the parameters is there no linear trend.

6. If we add a linear term $\eta_1 t$ and $\eta_2 t$ to (4.32) and (4.33) respectively, show that X_t has a quadratic trend.

7. Under what condition does the quadratic trend disappear?

4.2

Granger's theorem is formulated for a characteristic polynomial $A(z)$ with $A(0) = I$.

Find the conditions for the process to be $I(1)$ as expressed by $A(0)$, $A(1)$, and $\dot{A}(1)$ when $A(0)$ has full rank even if $A(0) \neq I$.

4.3

Under the assumptions of Theorem 4.2 show that for the model

$$\Delta X_t = \alpha \beta' X_{t-1} + \epsilon_t,$$

the matrix $\beta' \alpha$ has full rank, and has eigenvalues in $\{z : |z + 1| < 1$. Show that $\alpha'_{\perp} X_t$ is non-stationary. Next consider the example

$$\Delta X_{1t} = -\tfrac{1}{4} \left(X_{1t-1} - X_{2t-1} \right) + \Delta X_{2t-1} + \epsilon_{1t},$$

$$\Delta X_{2t} = -\tfrac{1}{4} \left(X_{1t-1} - X_{2t-1} \right) + \epsilon_{2t}.$$

Show that in this case $\alpha_\perp = \beta$, such that $\alpha'_\perp X_t$ is stationary.

4.4

Consider the equations

$$\begin{bmatrix} 1 & 2 \\ 2 & 4 \end{bmatrix} X_t + \begin{bmatrix} 0 & \frac{1}{2} \\ \frac{1}{2} & 2 \end{bmatrix} \Delta X_t + \begin{bmatrix} 0 & -\frac{1}{2} \\ -\frac{1}{2} & -1 \end{bmatrix} \Delta^2 X_t = \epsilon_t, \ t = 0, 1, \ldots$$

1. Define in this case the characteristic polynomial $A(z)$ as

$$A(z) = \begin{bmatrix} 1 & 2 \\ 2 & 4 \end{bmatrix} + \begin{bmatrix} 0 & \frac{1}{2} \\ \frac{1}{2} & 2 \end{bmatrix} (1 - z) + \begin{bmatrix} 0 & -\frac{1}{2} \\ -\frac{1}{2} & -1 \end{bmatrix} (1 - z)^2,$$

and note that $A(0)$ is not the identity (see exercise 4.2), and show that

$$|A(z)| = (1 - z)^2 \left(1 - \tfrac{1}{4} z^2\right).$$

2. Show that $\Pi = -A(1)$ has reduced rank and find α and β such that $\Pi = \alpha\beta'$. Find the matrix Γ.

3. Show that $\alpha'_\perp \Gamma \beta_\perp = 0$, such that the process X_t is not $I(1)$.

4. Show that if we define

$$Y_{1t} = X_{1t} + 2X_{2t},$$

$$Y_{2t} = \Delta X_{2t},$$

then Y_t is $I(1)$.

5. Find the cointegrating relations between Y_1 and Y_2. What are they expressed in terms of X_{1t} and X_{2t}?

4.5

1. In the context of Granger's theorem show that for the process

$$\Delta X_t = \alpha\beta' X_{t-1} + \sum_{i=1}^{k-1} \Gamma_i \Delta X_{t-i} + \mu + \epsilon_t,$$

the stationary process $\beta' X_t$ has mean given by

$$E(\beta' X_t) = \bar{\alpha}'(\Gamma C - I)\mu, \tag{4.34}$$

where $C = \beta_\perp (\alpha'_\perp \Gamma \beta_\perp)^{-1} \alpha'_\perp$ and $\bar{\alpha} = \alpha (\alpha'\alpha)^{-1}$.

2. Calculate $E(\beta' X_t)$ in the case where $\Gamma_1 = \Gamma_2 = \cdots = \Gamma_{k-1} = 0$. Consider in the following the process

$$\Delta X_t = \begin{bmatrix} -\frac{1}{2} \\ \frac{1}{2} \end{bmatrix} (1, -1) X_{t-1} + \begin{bmatrix} \mu_1 \\ \mu_2 \end{bmatrix} + \epsilon_t.$$

3. Find $E(\beta' X_t)$ as a function of μ_1 and μ_2.

4. Draw in a two-dimensional coordinate system (X_{1t}, X_{2t}) a typical example of the behaviour of the process in each of the cases $\mu' = (0, 0)$, $\mu' = (-1, 1)$ and $\mu' = (1, 1)$.

Comment: the decomposition

$$\alpha\beta' X_t + \mu = \alpha(\beta' X_t + (\alpha'\alpha)^{-1}\alpha'\mu) + \alpha_\perp(\alpha'_\perp\alpha_\perp)^{-1}\alpha'_\perp\mu,$$

decomposes μ into two components, the first can be given the following interpretation: the agents react to a disequilibrium as measured by the deviation of

$$\beta' X_t + (\alpha'\alpha)^{-1}\alpha'\mu,$$

from zero. One could call the relation

$$\beta' X_t + (\alpha'\alpha)^{-1}\alpha'\mu = 0$$

the revealed target. The strength of the reaction is measured by the coefficients α. The actual process $\beta' X_t$ fluctuates around its mean as given above in (4.34). Thus the actual behaviour results in a path that deviates from the target relation. The difference is given by $\bar{\alpha}'\Gamma C\mu$.

4.6

Consider the processes defined by the equations

$$\Delta Y_t = \gamma_1 Y_{t-1} + \gamma_2 X_{t-1} + \mu_1 + \epsilon_{1t},$$

$$\Delta X_t = \mu_2 + \epsilon_{2t}.$$

1. Find the characteristic polynomial and its roots.
2. Find the matrices Π, Γ, α, β, $\alpha_\perp$, and $\beta_\perp$.
3. Check that Π has reduced rank and find the condition for $\alpha'_\perp\Gamma\beta_\perp$ to have reduced rank.
4. Find in this case $(\alpha, \alpha_1, \alpha_2)$ and $(\beta, \beta_1, \beta_2)$ and show that

$$C_2 = \begin{bmatrix} 0 & \gamma_2 \\ 0 & 0 \end{bmatrix}$$

What is C_1? When does the quadratic trend disappear ?

4.7

Consider the model

$$X_t = \Pi_1 X_{t-1} + \epsilon_t.$$

1. Show that the conditions from Granger's Theorem, (4.4) and (4.5), are given by

$$\Pi_1 = I + \alpha\beta',$$

$$\alpha'_\perp \beta_\perp \text{ full rank.} \tag{4.35}$$

2. Consider next the model

$$X_t = \Pi_1 X_{t-1} + \Pi_2 X_{t-2} + \epsilon_t,$$

and define $\Pi = -I + \Pi_1 + \Pi_2$ and $\Gamma = I + \Pi_2$. The conditions are now

$$\Pi_1 + \Pi_2 = I + \alpha\beta',$$

$$\alpha'_\perp (I + \Pi_2) \beta_\perp \text{ full rank.} \tag{4.36}$$

Now rewrite the model as

$$\Delta \begin{bmatrix} X_t \\ X_{t-1} \end{bmatrix} = \begin{bmatrix} \Pi_1 - I & \Pi_2 \\ I & -I \end{bmatrix} \begin{bmatrix} X_{t-1} \\ X_{t-2} \end{bmatrix} + \begin{bmatrix} \epsilon_t \\ 0 \end{bmatrix} = \tilde{\Pi}\tilde{X}_{t-1} + \tilde{\epsilon}_t.$$

Show that the matrix $\tilde{\Pi}$ has reduced rank $\tilde{\Pi} = \tilde{\alpha}\tilde{\beta}'$ and that

$$\tilde{\beta}_\perp = \begin{bmatrix} \beta_\perp \\ \beta_\perp \end{bmatrix}, \tilde{\alpha}_\perp = \begin{bmatrix} \alpha_\perp \\ \Pi'_2\alpha_\perp \end{bmatrix},$$

such that condition (4.36) reduces to condition (4.35) for the companion matrix.

4.8

An extension of Granger's Theorem.

Let $A(z) = I - \sum_{i=1}^k \Pi_i z^i$ be the characteristic polynomial of the p-dimensional autoregressive process X_t. We assume that $|A(z)| = 0$ implies that $|z| > 1$ except for s distinct points $z = (z_1, \ldots, z_s)$, where $|z_i| \le 1$, $i = 1, \ldots, s$ and want to find an expression for $A^{-1}(z)$. We define $z_0 = 0$ and the polynomials

$$P(z) = \prod_{m=0}^s (z - z_m),$$

$$P_i(z) = \prod_{m=0,m\neq i}^s (z - z_m),$$

$$P_{ij}(z) = \prod_{m=0,m\neq i,j}^s (z - z_m).$$

1. Show that

$$dP(z)/dz = \sum_{i=0}^s P_i(z),$$

$$d^2P(z)/dz^2 = \sum_{i\neq j}^s P_{ij}(z).$$

EXERCISE 4.1 2. Prove the representation

$$A(z) = \sum_{i=0}^s A(z_i) \frac{P_i(z)}{P_i(z_i)} + P(z)A^*(z), \tag{4.37}$$

where $A^*(z)$ is a polynomial, and show how this representation gives rise to an error correction formulation of the model for X_t. [Hint: consider the polynomial

$$A(z) - \sum_{i=0}^{s} A(z_i) \frac{P_i(z)}{P_i(z_i)},$$

and check the values for $z = z_0, z_1, \ldots, z_s$.]

3. Show that for $m = 0, \ldots, s$

$$\Gamma_m = \frac{dA(z)}{dz}\Big|_{z=z_m}$$

$$= \sum_{i \neq m}^{s} A(z_i) \frac{P_{im}(z_m)}{P_i(z_i)} + \frac{A(z_m)}{P_m(z_m)} \sum_{j \neq m} P_{mj}(z_m) + P_m(z_m) A^*(z_m).$$

4. Consider the special case where $z = 1$ is the only root with absolute value ≤ 1, and define $z_0 = 0$, $z_1 = 1$ and let $A(1) = \alpha\beta'$, and note that $A(0) = I$. Find the error correction model for this case.

5. Consider next the case where $z = 1$ and $z = -1$ are roots and choose $z_0 = 0$, $z_1 = 1$, $z_2 = -1$ and define $A(1) = -\alpha_1\beta_1'$, $A(z_2) = -\alpha_2\beta_2'$ and find the corresponding error correction model, and Granger's representation.

Consider again the general situation. Since $z_1, \ldots, z_s$ are roots of the equation $|A(z)| = 0$ it follows that $A(z_i) = -\alpha_i\beta_i'$ for some $p \times r_i$ matrices of full rank, $0 \leq r_i < p$, $i = 1, \ldots, s$. Assume further that for $i = 1, \ldots, s$, $\alpha_{i\perp}'\Gamma_i\beta_{i\perp}$ has full rank and define

$$C_i = \beta_{i\perp}[\alpha_{i\perp}'\Gamma_i\beta_{i\perp}]^{-1}\alpha_{i\perp}'.$$

6. Show that

$$C(z) = \sum_{i=1}^{s} C_i \frac{1}{z - z_i} + C^*(z),$$

where $C^*(z) = \sum_{i=0}^{\infty} C_i^* z^i$, can be chosen such that $C(z)A(z) = I$.

[Hint: the function $A^{-1}(z)$ is well defined for all points $|z| \leq 1$, apart from the points in $z_1, \ldots, z_s$}. Show that in a neighbourhood of z_i

$$A^{-1}(z) - C_i \frac{1}{z - z_i}$$

$$= (\beta_i, \frac{1}{z - z_i}\beta_{i\perp})\{(\alpha_i, \alpha_{i\perp})'A(z)(\beta_i, \frac{1}{z - z_i}\beta_{i\perp})\}^{-1}(\alpha_i, \alpha_{i\perp})' - C_i \frac{1}{z - z_i}$$

has no pole at $z = z_i$, and hence that

$$A^{-1}(z) - \sum_{i=1}^{s} C_i \frac{1}{z - z_i}$$

has a convergent power series.] (Hylleberg *et al.*(1990), Johansen and Schaumburg (1996).)

4.9

Let the univariate process be defined by the equations

$$\Delta X_t = \pi X_{t-1} + \epsilon_t,$$

for some π in the interval $-2 < \pi < 0$, and define the correlation

$$\lambda^2 = \mathrm{Cov}\left(\Delta X_t, X_{t-1}\right)^2 / \mathrm{Var}\left(\Delta X_t\right) \mathrm{Var}\left(X_{t-1}\right).$$

Show that $\lambda^2 = -\frac{1}{2}\pi$.

4.10

Consider the usual model

$$\Delta X_t = \alpha\beta' X_{t-1} + \epsilon_t,$$

where ϵ_t have variance Ω, and define the matrices

$$\Sigma_{00} = \mathrm{Var}\left(\Delta X_t\right),$$

$$\Sigma_{\beta\beta} = \mathrm{Var}\left(\beta' X_t\right),$$

$$\Sigma_{\beta 0} = \mathrm{Cov}\left(\beta' X_{t-1}, \Delta X_t\right).$$

1. Show that

$$\Sigma_{00} = \alpha\Sigma_{\beta 0} + \Omega,$$

$$\Sigma_{\beta 0} = \Sigma_{\beta\beta}\alpha',$$

such that

$$\Sigma_{00} = \alpha\Sigma_{\beta\beta}\alpha' + \Omega.$$

2. Use these results to show that

$$(\alpha'\Sigma_{00}^{-1}\alpha)^{-1}\alpha'\Sigma_{00}^{-1} = (\alpha'\Omega^{-1}\alpha)^{-1}\alpha'\Omega^{-1},$$

$$\begin{aligned}
\Sigma_{00}^{-1} - \Sigma_{00}^{-1}\alpha(\alpha'\Sigma_{00}^{-1}\alpha)^{-1}\alpha'\Sigma_{00}^{-1} &= \alpha_\perp(\alpha'_\perp\Sigma_{00}\alpha_\perp)^{-1}\alpha'_\perp \\
&= \alpha_\perp(\alpha'_\perp\Omega\alpha_\perp)^{-1}\alpha'_\perp \\
&= \Omega^{-1} - \Omega^{-1}\alpha(\alpha'\Omega^{-1}\alpha)^{-1}\alpha'\Omega^{-1},
\end{aligned}$$

$$\Sigma_{\beta\beta}(\Sigma_{\beta 0}\Sigma_{00}^{-1}\Sigma_{0\beta})^{-1}\Sigma_{\beta\beta} - \Sigma_{\beta\beta} = (\alpha'\Omega^{-1}\alpha)^{-1}.$$

4.11

Consider the equation

$$|\lambda\Sigma_{\beta\beta} - \Sigma_{\beta0}\Sigma_{00}^{-1}\Sigma_{0\beta}| = 0. \tag{4.38}$$

1. Introduce $\alpha = \Sigma_{0\beta}\Sigma_{\beta\beta}^{-1}$ and use $\Sigma_{00} = \alpha\Sigma_{\beta\beta}\alpha' + \Omega$ to reduce (4.38) to

$$|\lambda\Sigma_{\beta\beta}^{-1} - \alpha'(\alpha\Sigma_{\beta\beta}\alpha' + \Omega)^{-1}\alpha| = 0.$$

2. Show that if ρ solves

$$|\rho\Sigma_{\beta\beta}^{-1} - \alpha'\Omega^{-1}\alpha| = 0,$$

then

$$\lambda = \rho/(1+\rho).$$

4.12

Consider the model

$$\Delta X_t = \alpha\beta' X_{t-1} + \epsilon_t.$$

1. Show that

$$\beta' X_t = \sum_{i=0}^{t-1}(I + \beta'\alpha)^i \beta'\epsilon_{t-i} + (I + \beta'\alpha)^t \beta' X_0.$$

2. Show that if the roots of the characteristic polynomial are either greater than 1 in absolute value or equal to 1, and if $\alpha'_\perp\beta_\perp$ has full rank then $I + \beta'\alpha$ has eigenvalues in the unit circle and we can define

$$\beta' X_0 = \sum_{i=0}^{\infty}(I + \beta'\alpha)^i \beta'\epsilon_{0-i},$$

which makes $\beta' X_t$ a stationary process.

3. Show that this relation implies that $\Delta X_t = C(L)\epsilon_t$, where

$$C(0) = I \text{ and } C_n = \alpha(I + \beta'\alpha)^{n-1}\beta', n = 1, 2, \ldots$$

and show that

$$C = C(1) = \beta_\perp(\alpha'_\perp\beta_\perp)^{-1}\alpha'_\perp.$$

4. Define $\Sigma_{\beta\beta} = \text{Var}(\beta' X_t)$ and show that

$$\Sigma_{\beta\beta} = \sum_{i=0}^{\infty}(I + \beta'\alpha)^i \beta'\Omega\beta(I + \alpha'\beta)^i$$

$$= \beta'\Omega\beta + (I + \beta'\alpha)\Sigma_{\beta\beta}(I + \alpha'\beta).$$

Show that

$$\Sigma_{00} = \text{Var}\,(\Delta X_t) = \alpha \Sigma_{\beta\beta}\alpha' + \Omega,$$

and that

$$\Sigma_1 = \lim_{T\to\infty} T^{-1} \sum_{t=1}^{T} E(\sum_{i=1}^{t-1} \Delta X_i)\Delta X_t'$$

$$= -\alpha \Sigma_{\beta\beta}\,(I + \alpha'\beta)^{-1}\,(\alpha'\beta)^{-1}\,\alpha' - \Omega\beta\,(\alpha'\beta)^{-1}\,\alpha',$$

and

$$\Sigma = \lim_{T\to\infty} T^{-1}E(\sum_{i=1}^{T}\Delta X_i)(\sum_{i=1}^{T}\Delta X_i)' = C\Omega C'.$$

5. Next show that

$$\Sigma = \Sigma_{00} + \Sigma_1 + \Sigma_1'.$$

[Hint: it pays to show that

$$(\beta'\alpha)^{-1}\,\beta'\Omega\beta\,(\alpha'\beta)^{-1} = -\Sigma_{\beta\beta} - \Sigma_{\beta\beta}\,(\alpha'\beta)^{-1} - (\beta'\alpha)^{-1}\,\Sigma_{\beta\beta}.]$$

4.13

Let

$$Y_t = B'X_t + \epsilon_{1t},$$

$$\Delta^2 X_t = \epsilon_{2t}.$$

1. Find the characteristic polynomial and its roots. Find Π, Γ, $\alpha, \beta, \alpha_\perp$, $\beta_\perp$ and check the rank condition for $I(2)$.
2. Find $(\alpha, \alpha_1, \alpha_2)$ and $(\beta, \beta_1, \beta_2)$ and the representation of (Y_t, X_t) as a function of the initial values and the ϵ.

5

The $I(1)$ Models and their Interpretation

IN this chapter we consider model (4.1) with deterministic terms D_t

$$\Delta X_t = \Pi X_{t-1} + \sum_{i=1}^{k-1} \Gamma_i \Delta X_{t-i} + \Phi D_t + \epsilon_t. \qquad (5.1)$$

We define in section 5.1 the basic reduced form error correction model for cointegration in terms of a reduced rank hypothesis on the matrix $\Pi = \alpha \beta'$ which defines the cointegrating vectors β and adjustment coefficients α. The parameters α and β are not identified and this is discussed in section 5.2, where a convenient normalization is suggested. In section 5.3 we discuss the hypotheses that can be formulated in terms of linear restrictions on β and formulate the identification problem for cointegrating relations. In section 5.4 similar hypotheses are formulated in terms of the adjustment coefficients. One can formulate quite general hypotheses about the coefficients, and we give in section 5.6 a formulation of the hypothesis of Granger non-causality. In section 5.7 we show how the deterministic terms can give rise to a number of different models describing different properties of the process, depending on restrictions on the deterministic terms like constant and linear drift terms. Finally the role of intervention dummies is discussed in section 5.8.

5.1 The $I(1)$ Models for Cointegration

DEFINITION 5.1 *The $I(1)$ model $H(r)$ is defined as the submodel of the VAR we obtain under the reduced rank condition*

$$\Pi = \alpha \beta'$$

where α and β are $p \times r$ matrices. The reduced form error correction model is

$$\Delta X_t = \alpha \beta' X_{t-1} + \sum_{i=1}^{k-1} \Gamma_i \Delta X_{t-i} + \Phi D_t + \epsilon_t, \qquad (5.2)$$

where the parameters $(\alpha, \beta, \Gamma_1, \ldots, \Gamma_{k-1}, \Phi, \Omega)$ vary freely.

Note that the parameter space allows for all kinds of non-stationarity, and that the full rank condition (4.5) for $I(1)$ is satisfied for all but a set of Lebesgue measure zero. Thus in this sense 'most' of the parameter values in the $I(1)$ model correspond to $I(1)$ variables. This means that the estimates derived without the restrictions (4.5) will automatically satisfy the condition. We also leave out the assumption that the roots should be outside the unit circle or at 1, since this condition is difficult to handle analytically. Fortunately it happens most often that the estimates of the roots have the proper position, and if they do not it is an important piece of information to get.

The $I(1)$ model $H(r)$ can be formulated as the condition that the rank of Π is less than or equal to r. This formulation shows that $I(1)$ models form a nested sequence of models

$$H(0) \subset \cdots \subset H(r) \subset \cdots \subset H(p),$$

where $H(p)$ is the unrestricted VAR model or the $I(0)$ model, and $H(0)$ corresponds to the restriction $\Pi = 0$, which is just the VAR model for the process in differences. The models in between, $H(1)$, ..., $H(p-1)$, ensure cointegration and are the models of primary interest to us here. Note that a different formulation would be to define $H^0(r)$ as the hypothesis that rank $(\Pi) = r$. In this way the models $H^0(r)$, $r = 0, 1, \ldots, p$ are no longer nested. We prefer the formulation in terms of nested hypotheses but the problem reappears in Chapter 12, where the rank is being determined.

The formulation allows us to derive likelihood ratio tests for the hypothesis $H(r)$ in $H(r+1)$ and $H(r)$ in the unrestricted model $H(p)$. These procedures can then be applied to check if ones prior knowledge of the number of cointegrating relations is consistent with the data, or alternatively to construct an estimator of the cointegrating rank.

Vector autoregressive models in levels have been applied to describe stationary processes and for $I(1)$ variables the VAR model in differences was often applied. The cointegration models give a nested sequence of models between the VAR in levels and the VAR in differences and give the possibility to investigate the coefficient matrix Π as to the information it may convey concerning long-run information in the data.

5.2   The Parametrization of the $I(1)$ Model

The β vectors are the cointegrating vectors and $\beta' X_t$ is the disequilibrium error. The coefficients α measure the adjustment to past equilibrium errors once these have been uniquely defined.

The parameters α and β in (5.2) are not uniquely identified in the sense that given any choice of α and β and any non-singular matrix ξ $(r \times r)$ the choice $\alpha\xi$ and $\beta(\xi')^{-1}$ will give the same matrix Π and hence determine the same probability distribution for the variables. One way of expressing this is to say that what the data can determine is the space spanned by the columns in β, the cointegrating space, and the space spanned by α, the adjustment space.

In general the only functions of α and β that can be estimated are those that can be expressed as functions of the matrix Π. If Π has rank r, then the space spanned by the rows, the cointegrating space, is r-dimensional. Any two coordinate systems in this space, i.e. any two choices of β are related by a non-singular transformation ξ $(r \times r)$, i.e. $\beta_1 = \beta_2 \xi$. In order that $f(\beta)$ be estimable it must take the same value for all choices of the coordinate system in the row space spanned by Π. Hence the functions that can be estimated must satisfy

$$f(\beta) = f(\beta\xi) \text{ for all } \xi \ (r \times r).$$

If we choose a matrix c $(p \times r)$ and assume that $c'\beta$ has full rank we define $\beta_c = \beta(c'\beta)^{-1}$ such that β has been normalized by c, i.e. $c'\beta_c = I$. It is easily checked that

$$\beta(c'\beta)^{-1} = \beta\xi(c'\beta\xi)^{-1}, \text{ for all } \xi \ (r \times r) \text{ of full rank,}$$

such that the function $f(\beta) = \beta_c$ is estimable. Hence β_c is one way of identifying the coefficients using zero restrictions and normalizations as specified by the columns of c. If in particular $X_t = (X'_{1t}, X'_{2t})'$, $c = (I, 0)'$ and $\beta = (-\beta'_1, \beta'_2)'$, then $\beta_c = (I, -(\beta'_1)^{-1}\beta'_2)' = (I, -B)'$ corresponding to solving the relations $\beta'X_t$ for the first r components of X_t, that is, $X_{1t} = BX_{2t}$. Another way of uniquely identifying β would be to impose different restrictions on the individual relations, see (5.6), or even cross-equation restrictions.

It is important to emphasize that one cannot estimate the individual coefficients of β unless one specifies a normalization or identification. This is obvious for $r = 1$, where estimation of a single coefficient has no meaning, but where the estimation of the ratio of two coefficients is what one is interested in. For $r > 1$ the situation is somewhat more difficult. It must be emphasized too that even though one cannot estimate individual coefficients without identifying the system, it is nevertheless possible to test some hypotheses on the parameters without necessarily identifying the system first. This is discussed in the next section.

5.3   Hypotheses on the Long-run Coefficients β

We here formulate some natural questions concerning the cointegrating vectors β, and show how they can be formulated in terms of linear restrictions on β.

In order to formulate the relevant questions it is useful to have an example and we consider the first illustrative example with the variables: m_t, log real money, y_t, log real income, and two interest rates: a deposit rate i_t^d and a bond rate i_t^b.

It seems a natural hypothesis that in the long-run relation the velocity of money is a function of the interest rates. This can be formulated as the hypothesis that the cointegrating relation only contains m_t and y_t through $m_t - y_t$, or in other words that the coefficients to money and income add to zero. For $R' = (1, 1, 0, 0)$ the restriction that the coefficients to m and y are equal with opposite sign can be expressed as the indirect parametrization $R'\beta = 0$. For the analysis that follows in later sections it is convenient to express these restrictions in the direct parametrization in terms of $H = R_\perp$:

$$\beta = H\varphi, \tag{5.3}$$

where $H(p \times s)$ is known and $\varphi(s \times r)$ is the parameter to be estimated. For $R = (1, 1, 0, 0)'$ the matrix H is given by

$$H = \begin{bmatrix} 1 & 0 & 0 \\ -1 & 0 & 0 \\ 0 & 1 & 0 \\ 0 & 0 & 1 \end{bmatrix},$$

such that $H\varphi = (\varphi_1, -\varphi_1, \varphi_2, \varphi_3)'$. The condition can also be expressed geometrically as a restriction on the cointegrating space $sp(\beta)$:

$$sp\,(\beta) \subset sp\,(H).$$

In other words, whereas the restriction $\Pi = \alpha\beta'$ gives rise to estimation of an r-dimensional subspace chosen in R^p, then the restriction (5.3) restricts the subspace to lie in the given subspace $sp\,(H)$ of R^p.

Note that this hypothesis about the coefficients can be formulated without first identifying the cointegrating relations, since it is formulated as a restriction that holds for all vectors in $sp(\beta)$.

The hypothesis that only the interest differential $i_t^b - i_t^d$ enters the long-run relation can be expressed as (5.3) with the choice

$$R = \begin{bmatrix} 0 \\ 0 \\ 1 \\ 1 \end{bmatrix}, \quad R_\perp = H = \begin{bmatrix} 1 & 0 & 0 \\ 0 & 1 & 0 \\ 0 & 0 & 1 \\ 0 & 0 & -1 \end{bmatrix}.$$

If our hypothesis is that, say, the long bond rate is excluded from the cointegrating relations this can be formulated as (5.3) using

$$R = \begin{bmatrix} 0 \\ 0 \\ 0 \\ 1 \end{bmatrix}, \quad R_\perp = H = \begin{bmatrix} 1 & 0 & 0 \\ 0 & 1 & 0 \\ 0 & 0 & 1 \\ 0 & 0 & 0 \end{bmatrix}.$$

Another question of interest is whether velocity, as measured by $m_t - y_t$ is stationary, that is, if the vector $b' = (1, -1, 0, 0)$ is a cointegrating vector. More generally one can consider a given set of s vectors b $(p \times s)$ and ask if they belong to the cointegrating space. This can be expressed as

$$\beta = (b, \phi), \qquad\qquad (5.4)$$

where the $p \times (r - s)$ matrix ϕ, containing the remaining $r - s$ cointegrating vectors, is to be estimated.

This hypothesis can also be expressed as

$$sp\,(b) \subset sp\,(\beta).$$

Thus natural economic questions can be formulated as simple linear restrictions on the cointegrating space.

Note that (5.4) can be used to formulate the hypothesis that one of the components of the vector X_t is in fact stationary. If for instance we take $b' = (0, 0, 1, 0)$, then hypothesis (5.4) specifies that the short-term interest rate is stationary. Thus the question of stationarity of individual series can be formulated in a natural way in terms of parameters in the multivariate system, and is a hypothesis that is conveniently checked inside the model rather than a question that has to be determined before the analysis starts. Thus one can include in the cointegration analysis the variables that are considered economically meaningful as long as they are $I(1)$ or $I(0)$. By including a stationary variable in the vector X_t we add an extra cointegrating vector, that is, an extra dimension to the cointegrating space. It is this possibility to have unit vectors as cointegrating vectors that forces us to have a definition of $I(1)$ that allows both $I(1)$ and $I(0)$ components.

Finally we consider a general hypothesis of the form

$$\beta = (H_1 \varphi_1, H_2 \varphi_2), \qquad\qquad (5.5)$$

where for $i = 1, 2$, H_i is $p \times s_i$, and φ_i is $s_i \times r_i$, with $r_i \leq s_i \leq p$ and $r_1 + r_2 = r$. In other words we impose $p - s_1$ restrictions on one set of cointegrating vectors and $p - s_2$ on the remaining vectors.

This hypothesis contains the previous ones as special cases. First let $r_2 = s_2 = 0$, and $H_1 = H$, then (5.5) reduces to (5.3). Next let $H_1 = b$, and choose $s_1 = r_1 = s$, and $s_2 = p$, and $H_2 = I$. Then the first set of vectors, $H_1 \varphi_1$, will just give the vectors in b, and the second set is unrestricted.

The geometric formulation of the hypothesis is that

$$sp\,(\beta) \cap sp\,(H_i)$$

is of dimension at least r_i, $i = 1, 2$, or in other words that there are at least r_i of the cointegrating relations that satisfy the restrictions expressed by H_i or rather $(H_i)_\perp$. As an example of such a hypothesis consider the case $r = 2$, and the hypotheses that m_t and y_t cointegrate. This hypothesis can be formulated as the existence of a cointegrating vector of the form $(\varphi_1, \varphi_2, 0, 0)$ for some φ_1 and φ_2. For this case we would take

$$H_1 = \begin{bmatrix} 1 & 0 \\ 0 & 1 \\ 0 & 0 \\ 0 & 0 \end{bmatrix}, \quad H_2 = \begin{bmatrix} 1 & 0 & 0 & 0 \\ 0 & 1 & 0 & 0 \\ 0 & 0 & 1 & 0 \\ 0 & 0 & 0 & 1 \end{bmatrix}$$

such that $r_1 = 1$, $s_1 = 2$, $r_2 = 1$, and $s_2 = 4$.

Note that (5.5) can be used to formulate linear restrictions on the various cointegrating relations, and is thus a formulation of the general problem of specifying identifying and over-identifying restrictions in structural equations. To be specific let $r = 2$ and define the identifying restrictions on the cointegrating vectors by the restrictions $R_1'\beta_1 = 0$ and $R_2'\beta_2 = 0$. Then we define $H_i = R_{i\perp}$, $i = 1, 2$, and formulate the estimation problem as that of estimating β_1 and β_2 under the constraint (5.5). This then is the estimation problem for structural long-run relations with individual linear restrictions.

In the second illustrative example we can consider the hypothesis that the real exchange rate $p_t^{au} - p_t^{us} - exch_t$ is a stationary relation. This can clearly be formulated as (5.4) with $sp(1, -1, -1, 0, 0) \in sp(\beta)$. If this fails we can ask another question, namely whether there is a cointegrating relation between p_t^{au}, p_t^{us}, and $exch_t$, and another between the interest rates. This can be formulated as (5.5) with

$$H_1 = \begin{bmatrix} 1 & 0 & 0 \\ 0 & 1 & 0 \\ 0 & 0 & 1 \\ 0 & 0 & 0 \\ 0 & 0 & 0 \end{bmatrix}, \quad H_2 = \begin{bmatrix} 0 & 0 \\ 0 & 0 \\ 0 & 0 \\ 1 & 0 \\ 0 & 1 \end{bmatrix}.$$

One can of course generalize the above hypothesis to involve more than two types of restrictions, see (5.6). If we have r cointegrating relations we naturally want to identify them as economically meaningful relations. This is usually formulated by restricting the coefficients in each relation by linear restrictions. Thus let R_i be the restrictions on the ith cointegrating relation, i.e. $R_i'\beta_i = 0$. With $H_i = R_{i\perp}$ one can write this hypothesis as

$$\beta = (H_1\varphi_1, \ldots, H_r\varphi_r), \tag{5.6}$$

where each φ_i is $s_i \times 1$.

The rank condition applied to this problem states that as long as there are no further identifying conditions on the parameters of the model then β_i is identified if and only if the parameters satisfy the conditions

$$\text{rank}\,(R'_i\beta) = \text{rank}\,(R'_i\,(H_1\varphi_1, \ldots, H_r\varphi_r)) = r - 1, \; i = 1, \ldots, r.$$

Since the true parameter value is unknown this condition is usually interpreted as follows, see Fisher (1966): for each i we define a polynomial, which for $i = 1$, say, becomes

$$P_1\,(\varphi) = |\,(H_2\varphi_2, \ldots, H_r\varphi_r)'\,R_1R'_1\,(H_2\varphi_2, \ldots, H_r\varphi_r)\,|.$$

A polynomial is either identically equal to zero, in which case the rank condition fails for any parameter value, or is zero on a very small set (of Lebesgue measure zero). In this case 'most' parameter values are identified. One can say that in this case the cointegrating relations are generically identified. Note that the property of being generically identifying is a property of the restrictions, not the parameter value, and is hence a property of the statistical model, as specified by (5.1) with the restrictions imposed. An algebraic condition for generic identification is given in Johansen (1995b), expressed as a set of necessary and sufficient conditions for the restrictions $R_1, \ldots, R_r$ to be identifying. The conditions involve checking the rank of certain matrices, depending on R and H. Thus in particular for $r = 3$ the conditions become

$$\text{rank}(R'_i H_j) \geq 1, \, i \neq j, \; \text{and rank}(R'_i(H_j, H_k)) \geq 2, \, i \neq j \neq k.$$

The parametrization (5.6) only determines the parameters $\varphi_1, \ldots, \varphi_r$ up to a constant factor, and it is customary to normalize β_i as follows:

$$\beta_i = h_i + H^i\psi_i,$$

where ψ_i is now $(s_i - 1) \times 1$, h_i is a vector in $sp\,(H_i)$, and $sp\,(h_i, H^i) = sp\,(H_i)$. Usually h_i is a unit vector and H^i has zeroes in the corresponding row, such that β_i is normalized on one of the coefficients. Thus for instance if we consider the above example with prices, exchange rate and interest rates, and we want to normalize on the coefficient to p^{au} and i^{au} then we choose

$$h_1 = \begin{bmatrix} 1 \\ 0 \\ 0 \\ 0 \\ 0 \end{bmatrix}, \; H^1 = \begin{bmatrix} 0\,0 \\ 1\,0 \\ 0\,1 \\ 0\,0 \\ 0\,0 \end{bmatrix}, \; h_2 = \begin{bmatrix} 0 \\ 0 \\ 0 \\ 1 \\ 0 \end{bmatrix}, \; H^2 = \begin{bmatrix} 0 \\ 0 \\ 0 \\ 0 \\ 1 \end{bmatrix}.$$

Even though the classical rank condition solves the problem of identification there still remains the empirical problem of testing that the true parameter does not actually correspond to one of the exceptional points where the rank condition fails to hold. As an example consider the following situation, where $p = 4$ and $r = 2$ and β is given by

$$\beta = \begin{bmatrix} \varphi_1 & \varphi_3 \\ 0 & \varphi_4 \\ \varphi_2 & 0 \\ 0 & \varphi_5 \end{bmatrix} = \left\{ \begin{bmatrix} 1 & 0 \\ 0 & 0 \\ 0 & 1 \\ 0 & 0 \end{bmatrix} \begin{bmatrix} \varphi_1 \\ \varphi_2 \end{bmatrix}, \begin{bmatrix} 1 & 0 & 0 \\ 0 & 1 & 0 \\ 0 & 0 & 0 \\ 0 & 0 & 1 \end{bmatrix} \begin{bmatrix} \varphi_3 \\ \varphi_4 \\ \varphi_5 \end{bmatrix} \right\}.$$

The rank condition is satisfied if $R_1'\beta_2 = (\varphi_4, \varphi_5)' \neq (0, 0)'$ and $R_2'\beta_1 = \varphi_2 \neq 0$. This condition holds in general, that is, in the five-dimensional parameter space for $(\varphi_1, \varphi_2, \ldots, \varphi_5)$. The set where $\varphi_4 = \varphi_5 = 0$ or $\varphi_2 = 0$ is a very small subset. But in an analysis of a given data set it may hold that, say, φ_2 is not significantly different from zero, and hence a test that $\varphi_2 = 0$ will reveal that the identification rests on an assumption that is not sustained by the data. A general formulation of this is that if a submodel, given by further restrictions, is accepted by the data, and if this submodel is not identified, then the true parameter corresponds to one of the exceptional points where the rank condition fails. Such a general problem is difficult to formulate and solve, and we shall instead give another formulation that allows a simple answer, but still solves the basic problem, see Boswijk (1995).

In order to formulate this solution consider the situation where we assume that $\mathrm{rank}(R_1'\beta) < r - 1$, such that a linear combination of $\beta_2, \ldots, \beta_r$ satisfies the restrictions given by R_1 and hence is contained in the space spanned by H_1. This situation can be formulated as the hypothesis

$$\beta = (H_1\varphi_1, \varphi_2) \tag{5.7}$$

where φ_1 is $s_1 \times 2$ and φ_2 is $p \times (r - 2)$. If this hypothesis is rejected then clearly it will also be rejected if further identifying restrictions are enforced upon $\beta_3, \ldots, \beta_r$, and hence the relation defined by $R_1'\beta_1 = 0$ is identified. This hypothesis, however, is of the form (5.5), and will be analysed in Chapter 6.

If it is accepted one can achieve two cointegrating relations which satisfy $R_1'\beta_1 = 0$ and $R_1'\beta_2 = 0$. This shows that R_1 does not identify a relation if the remaining cointegrating vectors vary freely. This type of restrictions is treated in detail in Johansen and Juselius (1990), (1992), and (1994).

5.4 Hypotheses on the Adjustment Coefficients α

The natural question to ask about the adjustment vectors is whether the coefficients in α are zero for a certain subset of equations. This hypothesis means that the subset of variables is weakly exogenous for the long-run parameters and the remaining adjustment parameters, see Chapter 8. Thus if for instance $r = 1$ one can ask if the equations for income and interest rates contain any information on the cointegrating vector. If not the analysis can proceed conditional on current values of y_t, i_t^b, and i_t^d. The hypothesis can be formulated as a linear restriction on the columns of α as follows

$$\alpha = A\psi, \qquad (5.8)$$

where A is $(p \times m)$ and known and ψ is the $(m \times r)$ parameter to be estimated.

If $r = 1$, we formulate the weak exogeneity of y_t, i_t^b, and i_t^d as

$$A = \begin{bmatrix} 1 \\ 0 \\ 0 \\ 0 \end{bmatrix}.$$

The geometric formulation is

$$sp\,(\alpha) \subset sp\,(A).$$

Note that zeros in a row of α means that disturbances from this equation cumulate to a common trend since $\alpha_\perp$ contains the corresponding unit vector. In view of the interpretation of $\alpha_\perp$ as the coefficients of the common trends it seems natural to impose also linear restrictions on the common trends. Such a hypothesis can be formulated as

$$\alpha_\perp = K\psi, \qquad (5.9)$$

or geometrically

$$sp\,(\alpha_\perp) \subset sp\,(K).$$

This statement, however, is equivalent to

$$sp\,(K_\perp) \subset sp\,(\alpha).$$

Thus we are back in the formulation of the type (5.4), namely that certain vectors of α are assumed known. Hypotheses on α and in particular the coefficients of $\alpha_\perp$ have been studied by Warne (1993), with the purpose of identifying structural shocks. Such hypotheses as well as hypotheses on weak exogeneity are in general not invariant to an extension of the information set and should thus be interpreted within a given information set.

5.5   The Structural Error Correction Model

Even though the purpose of an econometric analysis is to find a good structural model we discuss this rather briefly and refer to the book by

Banerjee *et al.* (1993) for a more comprehensive treatment.

Multiplying equation (5.2) by a matrix Γ_0^* gives the structural error correction model

$$\Gamma_0^* \Delta X_t = \alpha^* \beta' X_{t-1} + \sum_{i=1}^{k-1} \Gamma_i^* \Delta X_{t-i} + \Phi^* D_t + \epsilon_t^*, \qquad (5.10)$$

where $\epsilon_t^* = \Gamma_0^* \epsilon_t$ is Gaussian $N_p\left(0, \Omega^*\right)$, $\Omega^* = \Gamma_0^* \Omega \Gamma_0^{*\prime}$.

Note that the parameter β is the same as in (5.2) but that all the other coefficients have changed. In order that the parameters

$$\left(\alpha^*, \beta, \Gamma_0^*, \ldots, \Gamma_{k-1}^*, \Phi^*, \Omega^*\right)$$

be identified one can impose restrictions on the coefficients

$$\vartheta = \left(\alpha^*, \Gamma_0^*, \ldots, \Gamma_{k-1}^*, \Phi^*\right). \qquad (5.11)$$

Such restrictions are of course well known from econometric textbooks, see Fisher (1966), and the usual rank condition again applies, as well as the formulations in connection with the identification of β.

Note that if $\Pi^* = \alpha^* \beta'$ then the hypothesis of cointegration is a cross-equation restriction on the coefficients of Π^* and a linear hypothesis on β is in general a non-linear restriction on Π^*.

The conclusion of this is that the presence of non-stationary variables allows two distinct identification problems to be formulated. First the long-run relations must be identified uniquely in order that one can estimate and interpret them and then the short-run parameters ϑ must be identified uniquely in the usual way. See Johansen and Juselius (1992) for an empirical investigation involving both identification problems, and Hendry (1995) for a discussion of many aspects of the identification problem.

The cointegration analysis allows us to formulate long-run *relations between variables*, but the structural error correction model formulates *equations for the variables* in the system. Thus if $r = 1$ in the example with money, income, and interest rates we can think of the cointegrating relation as a *money relation* if we solve it for money, but the equation for Δm_t in the structural model is a *money equation* and models the dynamic adjustment of money to the past and the other simultaneous variables in the system.

5.6   General Hypotheses

It is easy to formulate simultaneous linear restrictions on α and β of the type considered above. This allows for instance an estimation of β under linear restrictions when weak exogeneity is imposed. This has been formulated in Johansen (1991b).

As an example of a complicated model, where something still can be said, consider the hypothesis of neutrality as formulated by Mosconi and Giannini (1992). The hypothesis can be defined by splitting X_t into X_{1t} and X_{2t} of dimensions p_1 and p_2 respectively. The hypothesis of neutrality then says that $\Pi_{21} = 0$. In the presence of cointegration this can be formulated as

$$\Pi = \alpha\beta' \text{ and } \alpha_2\beta_1' = 0.$$

This can be satisfied if either $\alpha_2 = 0$, or $\beta_1 = 0$ or if the rows of α_2 are orthogonal to those of β_1. A direct parametrization is given by

$$\alpha = \begin{pmatrix} \alpha_{11} & \alpha_{12} & \alpha_{13} \\ 0 & 0 & \alpha_{23} \end{pmatrix}, \quad \beta = \begin{pmatrix} \beta_{11} & 0 & 0 \\ \beta_{21} & \beta_{22} & \beta_{23} \end{pmatrix}$$

or

$$\Pi = \begin{bmatrix} \alpha_{11}\beta_{11}' & \alpha_{11}\beta_{21}' \\ 0 & 0 \end{bmatrix} + \begin{bmatrix} 0 & \alpha_{12}\beta_{22}' \\ 0 & 0 \end{bmatrix} + \begin{bmatrix} 0 & \alpha_{13}\beta_{23}' \\ 0 & \alpha_{23}\beta_{23}' \end{bmatrix}.$$

Another example is given in Johansen and Swensen (1994) where some simple rational expectation models are treated. Let the expectation equation be formulated as

$$d'X_t + c'E_t\Delta X_{t+1} = 0,$$

for some fixed and known matrices d and c, and let the process be governed by the equations

$$\Delta X_t = \alpha\beta'X_{t-1} + \Gamma_1\Delta X_{t-1} + \epsilon_t.$$

For the expectation equation to be consistent with the model for the data the parameters have to be restricted as

$$d' + c'\alpha\beta' = 0, \quad c'\Gamma_1 = 0.$$

This submodel allows an explicit solution, see exercise 6.3.

5.7   Models for Deterministic Terms

In this section we consider various choices of the deterministic terms D_t, and discuss the interpretation of restrictions on the coefficients.

It follows from Granger's theorem (Theorem 4.2) that the solution X_t to (5.1) under condition (4.5), has the representation

$$X_t = C\sum_{i=1}^{t}(\epsilon_i + \Phi D_i) + C(L)(\epsilon_t + \Phi D_t) + P_{\beta_\perp}X_0, \tag{5.12}$$

where $C = \beta_\perp(\alpha_\perp'\Gamma\beta_\perp)^{-1}\alpha_\perp'$. This shows that the process X_t in general has a deterministic trend of the form $C\Phi\sum_{i=1}^{t}D_i + C(L)\Phi D_t$. We use

TABLE 5.1 The relation between the $I(1)$ models defined by restrictions on the constant and the linear drift terms

$$
\begin{array}{ccccc}
H\left(0\right) & \subset \cdots \subset & H\left(r\right) & \subset \cdots \subset & H\left(p\right) \\
\cup & & \cup & & \cup \\
H^{*}\left(0\right) & \subset \cdots \subset & H^{*}\left(r\right) & \subset \cdots \subset & H^{*}\left(p\right) \\
\| & & \cup & & \cup \\
H_{1}\left(0\right) & \subset \cdots \subset & H_{1}\left(r\right) & \subset \cdots \subset & H_{1}\left(p\right) \\
\cup & & \cup & . & \cup \\
H_{1}^{*}\left(0\right) & \subset \cdots \subset & H_{1}^{*}\left(r\right) & \subset \cdots \subset & H_{1}^{*}\left(p\right) \\
\| & & \cup & & \cup \\
H_{2}\left(0\right) & \subset \cdots \subset & H_{2}\left(r\right) & \subset \cdots \subset & H_{2}\left(p\right)
\end{array}
$$

the following notation: the deterministic term D_t is called a drift term whereas the deterministic term in the expression for X_t is called a trend. Thus a constant drift term in the equation will generate a linear trend term in the process, and a linear drift term in the equation will generate a quadratic trend term in the process via Granger's representation theorem, see Johansen (1994).

We consider for illustrative purpose in detail the situation where $\Phi D_t = \mu_0 + \mu_1 t$. It follows from the representation (5.12) that the quadratic trend has a coefficient $\frac{1}{2}C\mu_1$, that is, μ_1 enters into X_t only through $C\mu_1$, that is, through the combination $\alpha'_\perp \mu_1$. If $\mu_1 = 0$ then μ_0 enters the linear trend only through $C\mu_0$. Thus the behaviour of the deterministic trend of the process X_t depends on the relation between C and μ_i, or whether $\alpha'_\perp \mu_i$ is zero or not. In order to discuss this we decompose the parameters μ_i in the directions of α and $\alpha_\perp$ as follows:

$$
\mu_i = \alpha \rho_i + \alpha_\perp \gamma_i, \ i = 0, 1,
$$

and let $\mu_t = \mu_0 + \mu_1 t$ denote the deterministic part of the model. Thus $\rho_i = (\alpha'\alpha)^{-1} \alpha' \mu_i$ and $\gamma_i = (\alpha'_\perp \alpha_\perp)^{-1} \alpha'_\perp \mu_i$. We then define a number of nested sub-models of the general model derived from (5.1) under the assumption of cointegration, and with successive restrictions on the deterministic part of the process:

$$H(r) : \mu_t = \alpha \rho_0 + \alpha_\perp \gamma_0 + (\alpha \rho_1 + \alpha_\perp \gamma_1) t, \tag{5.13}$$

$$H^*(r) : \mu_t = \alpha \rho_0 + \alpha_\perp \gamma_0 + \alpha \rho_1 t, \tag{5.14}$$

$$H_1(r) : \mu_t = \alpha \rho_0 + \alpha_\perp \gamma_0, \tag{5.15}$$

$$H_1^*(r) : \mu_t = \alpha \rho_0, \tag{5.16}$$

$$H_2(r) : \mu_t = 0. \tag{5.17}$$

Model $H(r)$: the model is given by $\mu_t = \mu_0 + \mu_1 t$, and X_t has the representation

$$X_t = C \sum_{i=1}^{t} \epsilon_i + \frac{1}{2}\tau_2 t^2 + \tau_1 t + \tau_0 + Y_t + P_{\beta_\perp} X_0, \qquad (5.18)$$

where $Y_t = C(L) \epsilon_t$, and $C = \beta_\perp (\alpha'_\perp \Gamma \beta_\perp)^{-1} \alpha'_\perp$. Thus the process allows for a quadratic trend determined by

$$\tau_2 = C\mu_1 = \beta_\perp (\alpha'_\perp \Gamma \beta_\perp)^{-1} \alpha'_\perp \mu_1 = \beta_\perp (\alpha'_\perp \Gamma \beta_\perp)^{-1} \alpha'_\perp \alpha_\perp \gamma_1. \qquad (5.19)$$

Note, however, that the linear combinations $\beta' X_t$ have no quadratic trend, since $\beta' C = 0$. Thus the quadratic trend can be eliminated by the linear combinations β, but $\beta' X_t$ still has a linear trend.

Model $H^*(r)$: this model is given by $\mu_t = \mu_0 + \alpha \rho_1 t$, and is characterized by the absence of the quadratic trend since $\alpha'_\perp \mu_1 = 0$ or $\gamma_1 = 0$ and hence $\tau_2 = 0$. It still allows the possibility of a linear trend in all components of the process, a trend which cannot be eliminated by the cointegrating relations β. Thus a linear trend is allowed even in the cointegrating relations, each of which therefore represents a stationary process plus a linear trend or a trend stationary process. In particular if a unit vector is cointegrating then the corresponding component of X_t is trend stationary. The expression for the linear trend τ_1 when $\mu_1 = \alpha \rho_1$ can be found to be

$$\tau_1 = \bar{\beta}_\perp \Gamma^{-1}_{\alpha_\perp \beta_\perp} \gamma_0 + \bar{\beta}_\perp \Gamma^{-1}_{\alpha_\perp \beta_\perp} \Gamma_{\alpha_\perp \beta} \rho_1 - \bar{\beta} \rho_1, \qquad (5.20)$$

see exercise 6.1.

Here $\bar{\beta} = \beta (\beta' \beta)^{-1}$, and $\Gamma_{\alpha_\perp \beta_\perp} = \bar{\alpha}'_\perp \Gamma \bar{\beta}_\perp$, and X_t has in this case the representation

$$X_t = C \sum_{i=1}^{t} \epsilon_i + \tau_1 t + \tau_0 + Y_t + P_{\beta_\perp} X_0. \qquad (5.21)$$

For the present purpose we define a trend stationary process as a process that can be decomposed into a stationary process plus a linear deterministic trend. A problem that often faces the econometrician is to make a choice between describing a given time series as a trend stationary process or an $I(1)$ process plus a linear trend. Since the sample paths of two such processes observed over a short interval can easily be mistaken, one will expect that the real decision to choose between the two descriptions should be based on economic insight. In some cases, however, it is of interest to conduct a statistical test to see if one can make the distinction on the basis of the data.

Model $H^*(r)$ allows for r trend stationary variables, and $p - r$ variables that are composed of $I(1)$ variables and a linear trend. Thus if one wants to test that X_{1t} is trend stationary, one has to check that the unit vector

$(1, 0, \ldots, 0)$ is contained in the β space, see (5.4). If the hypothesis is rejected, a better description of the variable is as an $I(1)$ variable plus a trend. For a different formulation of $H^*(r)$, see exercise 5.2.

Model $H_1(r)$: in this model $\mu_t = \mu_0$, such that the process X_t has the form (5.21), that is, it still has a linear trend given by the coefficients $\tau_1 = C\mu_0$, but this can be eliminated by the cointegrating relations β, and the process contains no trend stationary components. Thus the model allows for a linear trend in each variable but not in the cointegrating relations.

Model $H_1^*(r)$: in model $H_1^*(r)$ there are no trends whatsoever, since $\alpha'_\perp \mu_0 = 0$, such that $\mu_t = \alpha\rho_0$, but a constant term is allowed in the cointegrating relations, and

$$X_t = C\sum_{i=1}^{t} \epsilon_i + \tau_0 + Y_t + P_{\beta_\perp} X_0.$$

Another way of formulating model $H_1^*(r)$ is as

$$X_t = \kappa + Y_t$$

$$\Delta Y_t = \alpha\beta' Y_{t-1} + \sum_{i=1}^{k-1} \Gamma_i \Delta Y_{t-i} + \epsilon_t. \tag{5.22}$$

It follows that the equation for X_t is given by

$$\Delta X_t = \alpha\beta'(X_{t-1} - \kappa) + \sum_{i=1}^{k-1} \Gamma_i \Delta X_{t-i} + \epsilon_t,$$

that is, (5.1) with $\mu_1 = 0$ and $\mu_0 = -\alpha\beta'\kappa$ which satisfies the condition $\alpha'_\perp \mu_0 = 0$. Such a formulation gives an easy interpretation of κ as the level of X_t, but note that the parameter κ is not identified, since only $\beta'\kappa$ enters the model. This is reasonable since for the non-stationary component, $\beta'_\perp X_t$, say, the role of the level of the process is taken over by the initial value $\beta'_\perp X_0$.

Model $H_2(r)$: this model does not allow for a constant term which means that all stationary linear combinations will have mean zero.

In summary we have seen that the role of the deterministic part depends on the relation between α and the coefficients μ_0 and μ_1. By restricting the deterministic terms suitably we can use equation (5.1) to generate processes with different trending behaviour. Not only can we get variables that are integrated of order 0 and 1, but we can also get deterministic trends of order 0, 1, and 2. The formulation of the different hypotheses as restrictions will allow us to derive likelihood ratio tests in the next section.

5.8   Intervention and Seasonal Dummies

Often the deterministic component D_t in (5.1) contains dummies, either seasonal dummies or intervention dummies. By applying Granger's representation theorem we can see that the drift term D_t will imply a trend term of the form

$$C\Phi \sum_{i=1}^{t} D_i + \sum_{i=0}^{\infty} C_i \Phi D_{t-i}. \tag{5.23}$$

Consider as an example an intervention dummy of the form

$$D_t = \begin{cases} 0 & t \le t_0, \\ 1 & t > t_0. \end{cases}$$

In this case $\sum_{i=1}^{t} D_i$ is a broken trend

$$\sum_{i=1}^{t} D_i = \begin{cases} 0 & t \le t_0, \\ t - t_0 & t > t_0, \end{cases}$$

and

$$\sum_{i=0}^{\infty} C_i \Phi D_{t-i} = \begin{cases} 0 & t \le t_0, \\ \sum_{i=0}^{t-t_0} C_i \Phi & t > t_0. \end{cases}$$

That is, the trend in the process has a broken linear component, as well as a smoothed version of the intervention dummy. If D_t is a seasonal dummy, then the cumulated seasonal dummy will grow linearly with a slope $\frac{1}{4}$, whereas the term $C(L)\Phi D_t$ will give rise to a seasonally varying mean.

Thus the inclusion of seasonal dummies is a simple way of allowing for a seasonally varying mean, but one should note the implications for the linear trend in the process. In practice it is more convenient to orthogonalize the seasonal dummies on the constant term such that the seasonal dummies sum to zero over a year. In this way the linear term from the dummies disappears and is taken over completely by the constant term, and only the seasonally varying means remain.

The expression (5.23) for the deterministic trend can be subtracted from the process X_t and would correspond, in the present framework, to seasonal correction if D_t are seasonal dummies and detrending if D_t contain a constant.

A systematic theory of dummies is attempted in Johansen and Nielsen (1994), since the presence of dummies influences the asymptotic theory as explained in more detail in the following chapters. Mosconi (1993) has investigated hypotheses about the trend coefficients in $C\Phi$ in order to check the presence of a deterministic trend in the individual series.

5.9   Exercises

5.1

A statistical model for a p-dimensional autoregressive process with an intercept can be formulated as the solution of the equations:

$$\Delta \left(X_t - m\right) = \alpha\beta' \left(X_{t-1} - m\right) + \epsilon_t,$$

where α and β are $(p \times r)$ and m is $(p \times 1)$.
  1. Show that this model is a submodel of

$$\Delta X_t = \alpha\beta' X_{t-1} + \mu + \epsilon_t,$$

where α and β are $(p \times r)$ and μ is $(p \times 1)$, with the constraint $\alpha'_\perp \mu = 0$, and find μ as a function of m.
  2. Show that m is not identified unless α and β are of rank p.

5.2

A model for a p-dimensional autoregressive process with an intercept and trend can be formulated as the solution of the equations

$$\Delta \left(X_t - m_0 - m_1 t\right) = \alpha\beta' \left(X_{t-1} - m_0 - m_1 \left(t - 1\right)\right) + \epsilon_t,$$

where α and β are $(p \times r)$ and m_0 and m_1 are $(p \times 1)$.
  1. Show that this model is a submodel of

$$\Delta X_t = \alpha\beta' X_{t-1} + \mu_0 + \mu_1 t + \epsilon_t,$$

where α and β are $(p \times r)$ and μ_0 and μ_1 are $(p \times 1)$ with the constraint $\alpha'_\perp \mu_1 = 0$, and express μ_0 and μ_1 as functions of m_0 and m_1.
  2. Show that m_0 is not identified unless α and β are of rank p, but that m_1 is always identified.

5.3

Consider the four variables m_t, y_t, i_{1t}, and i_{2t}, that is, money, income, and two interests rates. We think of the money equation

$$m_t = y_t + c\left(i_{1t} - i_{2t}\right) + \mu_1,$$

and the interest equation

$$i_{1t} = i_{2t} + \mu_2,$$

as describing stable economic relations.

This hypothesis is formulated in a vector autoregressive model as the statement that the vectors

$$\beta_1 = (1, -1, -c, c)',$$
$$\beta_2 = (0, 0, 1, -1)',$$

are cointegrating vectors.

Let us assume that the cointegrating rank is $r = 2$, and that we, in order to check the restrictions implicit in the above relations, first formulate the hypothesis

$$\beta_1 = (a_1, a_2, a_3, a_4)',$$
$$\beta_2 = (0, 0, a_5, a_6)'.$$

1. Formulate this hypothesis in the form

$$\beta = (H_1\varphi_1, H_2\varphi_2),$$

and check whether this hypothesis is a restriction on the cointegrating space. Are the equations identified?

2. Consider the same questions for

$$\beta_1 = (a_1, -a_1, a_3, a_4)',$$
$$\beta_2 = (0, 0, a_5, a_6)'.$$

3. Consider the same questions for

$$\beta_1 = (a_1, -a_1, a_3, -a_3)',$$
$$\beta_2 = (0, 0, a_5, a_6)'.$$

4. Consider the same questions for

$$\beta_1 = (a_1, -a_1, a_3, -a_3)',$$
$$\beta_2 = (0, 0, a_5, -a_5)'.$$

5.4

Consider the model

$$\Delta X_t = \alpha\beta' X_{t-1} + \Gamma_1 \Delta X_{t-1} + \epsilon_t,$$

and assume that all parameters vary freely except for $\alpha = A\psi$. Show that $A'_\perp X_t$ is weakly exogenous for (ψ, β).

The combinations $\alpha'_\perp \sum_{i=1}^{t} \epsilon_i$ are the common trends. The hypothesis that the shocks from a given equation, a price equation say, cumulate to a common trend can be formulated as $\alpha_\perp = (a_0, \psi)$, for a suitable unit vector a_0. Show that in this case $a'_0 X_t$ is weakly exogenous for (ψ, β), see Chapter 8.

5.5

In the cointegration model

$$\Delta X_t = \alpha\beta' X_{t-1} + \epsilon_t,$$

where $\epsilon_1, \ldots, \epsilon_T$ are independent Gaussian $N_p(0, \Omega)$, we split X_t in X_{1t} and X_{2t} of dimensions p_1 and p_2 respectively corresponding to two subsystems. We want to test if the cointegration in the full system can be expressed by requiring that the subsystems cointegrate. This is called separate cointegration. The precise definition is that there exist matrices β_1 $(p_1 \times r_1)$ and β_2 $(p_2 \times r_2)$ with $r_1 + r_2 = r$, such that the cointegrating relations $\beta' X_t$ are linear combinations of $\beta_1' X_{1t}$ and $\beta_2' X_{2t}$, that is, that there exist matrices A_1 $(r \times r_1)$ and A_2 $(r \times r_2)$, such that $\beta' X_t = A_1\beta_1' X_{1t} + A_2\beta_2' X_{2t}$.

1. Show that this hypotheses can be formulated as one of the hypotheses which is treated in Chapter 5 and discuss an algorithm for calculating the maximum likelihood estimator.

We call the system *strongly separated* if it is separated and it holds that the equations for ΔX_{1t} contain only $\beta_1' X_{1t-1}$ and the equations for ΔX_{2t} contain only $\beta_2' X_{2t-1}$.

2. Formulate this hypothesis as a hypothesis about α and show that even if the system is strongly separated it does not hold that X_{2t} is weakly exogenous for β_1 (Granger and Konishi 1993).

5.6

Consider the cointegration model

$$\Delta X_{1t} = \alpha_1\beta' X_{t-1} + \epsilon_{1t},$$
$$\Delta X_{2t} = \alpha_2\beta' X_{t-1} + \epsilon_{2t},$$

where $\epsilon_1, \ldots, \epsilon_T$ are independent Gaussian $N_p(0, \Omega)$.

1. Show how the hypothesis that X_2 is weakly exogenous for β can be formulated as a hypothesis on α.

We define the stochastic trends

$$\alpha_\perp' \sum_{i=1}^t \epsilon_i.$$

2. Show that the hypothesis that the first component of $\sum_{i=1}^t \epsilon_{1i}$ is a common stochastic trend can be formulated in the form

$$\alpha_\perp = (a_0, \psi)$$

and find a_0.

Assume that $X_t = (p^{au}, p^{us}, exch, i^{au}, i^{us})_t$, that is, prices and interest rates in Australia and United States together with the exchange rate. We assume that the cointegrating rank is three, that is, that there are two common trends. We want to investigate if there is a stochastic trend that comes from the price variables and the exchange rate (the goods sector) and another from the interest variables (the financial sector).

3. Formulate this hypothesis as a hypothesis on $\alpha_\perp$.

6

The Statistical Analysis of $I(1)$ Models

THIS chapter contains an analysis of the likelihood function of the $I(1)$ models discussed in Chapter 5. The main result in section 6.1 is the derivation of the method of reduced rank regression which solves the estimation problem for the unrestricted cointegration vectors, and which solves the problem of deriving a test statistic for the hypothesis of cointegrating rank. The asymptotic distribution of this test statistic is discussed in Chapter 12, and the way it should be applied is discussed in Chapter 13.

It turns out that the method of reduced rank regression solves a number of different models defined by various restrictions on the parameters. We give here the estimator of the unrestricted cointegrating vectors, and show in section 6.2 how it should be modified if restrictions are imposed on the deterministic terms. In Chapter 7 we discuss the modification needed for the estimation of cointegrating relations, when they are restricted by linear restrictions, and in Chapter 8 how it should be modified when α is restricted.

6.1 Likelihood Analysis of $H(r)$

We define the reduced form error correction model as given by

$$\Delta X_t = \alpha \beta' X_{t-1} + \sum_{i=1}^{k-1} \Gamma_i \Delta X_{t-i} + \Phi D_t + \epsilon_t, \, t = 1, \ldots, T, \qquad (6.1)$$

where ϵ_t are independent $N_p(0, \Omega)$ and $(\alpha, \beta, \Gamma_1, \ldots, \Gamma_{k-1}, \Phi, \Omega)$ are freely varying parameters.

The advantage of this parametrization is in the interpretation of the coefficients, where the effect of the levels is isolated in the matrix $\alpha \beta'$ and where $\Gamma_1, \ldots, \Gamma_{k-1}$ describe the short-term dynamics of the process. Sometimes the form

$$\Delta X_t = \sum_{i=1}^{k-1} \tilde{\Gamma}_i \Delta X_{t-i} + \alpha \beta' X_{t-k} + \Phi D_t + \epsilon_t,$$

is given, where $\tilde{\Gamma}_i = \Pi_1 + \cdots + \Pi_i - I$. This reparametrization leads to the same statistical analysis.

In (6.1) we introduce the notation $Z_{0t} = \Delta X_t$, $Z_{1t} = X_{t-1}$ and let Z_{2t} be the stacked variables $\Delta X_{t-1}, \ldots, \Delta X_{t-k+1}$, and D_t. We let Ψ be the matrix of parameters corresponding to Z_{2t}, that is, the matrix consisting of $\Gamma_1, \ldots, \Gamma_{k-1}$, and Φ. Thus Z_{2t} is a vector of dimension $p(k-1) + m$ and Ψ is a matrix of dimension $p \times (p(k-1) + m)$.

The model expressed in these variables becomes

$$Z_{0t} = \alpha\beta' Z_{1t} + \Psi Z_{2t} + \epsilon_t, \ t = 1, \ldots, T. \tag{6.2}$$

This is clearly a non-linear regression model where the parameters Ψ are unrestricted and the coefficient matrix to the levels Z_{1t} is of reduced rank. The analysis of the likelihood function leads to the technique developed by Anderson (1951) of reduced rank regression. We give the details here since the notation is needed for the asymptotic analysis. The log likelihood function is given apart from a constant by

$$\log L(\Psi, \alpha, \beta, \Omega)$$
$$= -\frac{1}{2}T\log|\Omega| - \frac{1}{2}\sum_{t=1}^{T}(Z_{0t} - \alpha\beta' Z_{1t} - \Psi Z_{2t})'\Omega^{-1}(Z_{0t} - \alpha\beta' Z_{1t} - \Psi Z_{2t}).$$

The first order conditions for estimating Ψ are given by

$$\sum_{t=1}^{T}(Z_{0t} - \alpha\beta' Z_{1t} - \hat{\Psi} Z_{2t})Z_{2t}' = 0. \tag{6.3}$$

We introduce the notation for the product moment matrices

$$M_{ij} = T^{-1}\sum_{t=1}^{T} Z_{it} Z_{jt}', \quad i, j = 0, 1, 2, \tag{6.4}$$

and note that

$$M_{ij} = M_{ji}', \ i, j = 0, 1, 2.$$

We write (6.3) as

$$M_{02} = \alpha\beta' M_{12} + \hat{\Psi} M_{22},$$

such that

$$\hat{\Psi}(\alpha, \beta) = M_{02} M_{22}^{-1} - \alpha\beta' M_{12} M_{22}^{-1}. \tag{6.5}$$

This leads to the definition of the residuals

$$R_{0t} = Z_{0t} - M_{02} M_{22}^{-1} Z_{2t}, \tag{6.6}$$

$$R_{1t} = Z_{1t} - M_{12} M_{22}^{-1} Z_{2t}, \tag{6.7}$$

i.e. the residuals we would obtain by regressing ΔX_t and X_{t-1} on the lagged differences $\Delta X_{t-1}, \ldots, \Delta X_{t-k+1}$, and D_t or Z_{0t} and Z_{1t} on Z_{2t}. The concentrated likelihood function is

$$\log L(\alpha, \beta, \Omega) = -\frac{1}{2}T\log|\Omega| - \frac{1}{2}\sum_{t=1}^{T}(R_{0t} - \alpha\beta' R_{1t})'\Omega^{-1}(R_{0t} - \alpha\beta' R_{1t}),$$

(6.8)

see also (A.29). Another way of writing this is as a regression equation in the residuals

$$R_{0t} = \alpha\beta' R_{1t} + \hat{\epsilon}_t,$$

(6.9)

which would give the same likelihood as (6.8). Thus the parameters Ψ can be eliminated by regression and what remains in (6.9) is a reduced rank regression as investigated by Anderson (1951).

As a final piece of notation consider

$$S_{ij} = T^{-1}\sum_{t=1}^{T} R_{it}R_{jt}' = M_{ij} - M_{i2}M_{22}^{-1}M_{2j}, \; ; \; i, j = 0, 1.$$

(6.10)

For fixed β it is easy to estimate α and Ω by regressing R_{0t} on $\beta' R_{1t}$ and obtain

$$\hat{\alpha}(\beta) = S_{01}\beta(\beta' S_{11}\beta)^{-1},$$

(6.11)

$$\hat{\Omega}(\beta) = S_{00} - S_{01}\beta(\beta' S_{11}\beta)^{-1}\beta' S_{10} = S_{00} - \hat{\alpha}(\beta)(\beta' S_{11}\beta)\hat{\alpha}(\beta)', \quad (6.12)$$

and apart from the constant $(2\pi e)^p$, which disappears when forming ratios, we find

$$L_{\max}^{-2/T}(\hat{\alpha}(\beta), \beta, \hat{\Omega}(\beta)) = L_{\max}^{-2/T}(\beta) = |\hat{\Omega}(\beta)| = |S_{00} - S_{01}\beta(\beta' S_{11}\beta)^{-1}\beta' S_{10}|.$$

We next rewrite this expression, using the identity

$$\begin{vmatrix} \Sigma_{11} & \Sigma_{12} \\ \Sigma_{21} & \Sigma_{22} \end{vmatrix} = |\Sigma_{11}||\Sigma_{22} - \Sigma_{21}\Sigma_{11}^{-1}\Sigma_{12}| = |\Sigma_{22}||\Sigma_{11} - \Sigma_{12}\Sigma_{22}^{-1}\Sigma_{21}|,$$

which is discussed in (A.26). Applying the identity to the matrix

$$\begin{vmatrix} S_{00} & S_{01}\beta \\ \beta' S_{10} & \beta' S_{11}\beta \end{vmatrix} = |S_{00}||\beta'(S_{11} - S_{10}S_{00}^{-1}S_{01})\beta|$$

$$= |\beta' S_{11}\beta||S_{00} - S_{01}\beta(\beta' S_{11}\beta)^{-1}\beta' S_{10}|,$$

we find that

$$|S_{00} - S_{01}\beta(\beta'S_{11}\beta)^{-1}\beta'S_{10}|$$

$$= |S_{00}||\beta'S_{11}\beta - \beta'S_{10}S_{00}^{-1}S_{01}\beta|/|\beta'S_{11}\beta| \qquad (6.13)$$

$$= |S_{00}||\beta'(S_{11} - S_{10}S_{00}^{-1}S_{01})\beta|/|\beta'S_{11}\beta|.$$

Thus the maximization of the likelihood function is equivalent to the minimization of the last factor of (6.13). This factor is minimized among all $p \times r$ matrices β, by applying Lemma A.8, that is, by solving the eigenvalue problem

$$|\rho S_{11} - (S_{11} - S_{10}S_{00}^{-1}S_{01})| = 0,$$

or, for $\lambda = 1 - \rho$, the eigenvalue problem

$$|\lambda S_{11} - S_{10}S_{00}^{-1}S_{01}| = 0,$$

for eigenvalues λ_i and eigenvectors v_i, such that

$$\lambda_i S_{11} v_i = S_{10}S_{00}^{-1}S_{01} v_i,$$

and $v_j'S_{11}v_i = 1$ if $i = j$ and 0 otherwise, see Lemma A.8. Note that the eigenvectors diagonalize the matrix $S_{10}S_{00}^{-1}S_{01}$ since $v_j'S_{10}S_{00}^{-1}S_{01}v_i = \lambda_i$ if $i = j$ and zero otherwise. Thus by simultaneously diagonalizing the matrices S_{11} and $S_{10}S_{00}^{-1}S_{01}$ we can estimate the r-dimensional cointegrating space as the space spanned by the eigenvectors corresponding to the r largest eigenvalues. With this choice of $\hat{\beta}$ we find from Lemma A.8, that

$$L_{\max}^{-2/T} = |S_{00}|\frac{|\hat{\beta}'(S_{11} - S_{10}S_{00}^{-1}S_{01})\hat{\beta}|}{|\hat{\beta}'S_{11}\hat{\beta}|} = |S_{00}|\prod_{i=1}^{r}(1 - \hat{\lambda}_i), \qquad (6.14)$$

since by the choice of $\hat{\beta}$ we have $\hat{\beta}'S_{11}\hat{\beta} = I$, as well as $\hat{\beta}'S_{10}S_{00}^{-1}S_{01}\hat{\beta} = \text{diag}(\hat{\lambda}_1, \ldots, \hat{\lambda}_r)$.

For $r = 0$ we choose $sp(\hat{\beta}) = \{0\}$, and find $\Pi = \hat{\Pi} = 0$, and for $r = p$ we can take $sp(\hat{\beta}) = R^p$, and the estimate of Π is $\hat{\Pi} = S_{01}S_{11}^{-1}$. Note that we have solved all the models $H(r)$, $r = 0, \ldots, p$ by the same eigenvalue calculation. The maximized likelihood is given for each r by (6.14) and by dividing the maximized likelihood function for r with the corresponding expression for $r = p$ we get the likelihood ratio test

$$Q(H(r)|H(p))^{-\frac{2}{T}} = \frac{|S_{00}|\prod_{i=1}^{r}(1 - \hat{\lambda}_i)}{|S_{00}|\prod_{i=1}^{p}(1 - \hat{\lambda}_i)}.$$

The factor $|S_{00}|$ cancels and we find the so-called trace statistic

$$-2\log Q(H(r)|H(p)) = -T\sum_{i=r+1}^{p}\log(1 - \hat{\lambda}_i).$$

Under hypothesis $H(r)$ the estimates of β and α are related to the canonical variates between R_{0t} and R_{1t}, and the eigenvalues are the squared canonical correlations, see Appendix A or Anderson (1984). The estimate of β is given as the eigenvectors of (6.15), see below, corresponding to the r largest eigenvalues, that is, the choice of $\hat{\beta}$ is the choice of the r linear combinations of X_{t-1} which have the largest squared partial correlations with the stationary process ΔX_t after correcting for lags and deterministic terms. We call such an analysis a reduced rank regression of ΔX_t on X_{t-1} corrected for $(\Delta X_{t-1}, \ldots, \Delta X_{t-k+1}, D_t)$. The results are formulated in Theorem 6.1, where we also give the asymptotic distributions of the test statistics even though they will be derived in Chapter 12. Note that the estimate of β given here is the unrestricted estimator, which is relevant if we do not want to impose any restrictions.

THEOREM 6.1 *Under hypothesis*

$$H(r) : \Pi = \alpha\beta',$$

the maximum likelihood estimator of β is found by the following procedure: first solve the equation

$$|\lambda S_{11} - S_{10}S_{00}^{-1}S_{01}| = 0, \tag{6.15}$$

for the eigenvalues $1 > \hat{\lambda}_1 > \cdots > \hat{\lambda}_p > 0$ and eigenvectors $\hat{V} = (\hat{v}_1, \ldots, \hat{v}_p)$ which we normalize by $\hat{V}'S_{11}\hat{V} = I$.
The cointegrating relations are estimated by

$$\hat{\beta} = (\hat{v}_1, \ldots, \hat{v}_r), \tag{6.16}$$

and the maximized likelihood function is found from

$$L_{\max}^{-2/T}(H(r)) = |S_{00}| \prod_{i=1}^{r}(1 - \hat{\lambda}_i). \tag{6.17}$$

The estimates of the other parameters are found by inserting $\hat{\beta}$ into the above equations, i.e. by ordinary least squares for $\beta = \hat{\beta}$.
The likelihood ratio test statistic $Q(H(r)|H(p))$ for $H(r)$ in $H(p)$, is found by comparing two expressions like (6.17). This gives the result

$$-2\log Q(H(r)|H(p)) = -T \sum_{i=r+1}^{p} \log(1 - \hat{\lambda}_i). \tag{6.18}$$

The likelihood ratio test statistic for testing $H(r)$ in $H(r+1)$ is given by

$$-2\log Q(H(r)|H(r+1)) = -T\log(1 - \hat{\lambda}_{r+1}). \tag{6.19}$$

*The asymptotic distribution of (6.18) depends on the deterministic terms
present in the model, and is derived in Chapter 11. We assume here that
rank$(\Pi) = r$.*
   If $\mu_t = 0$ we find

$$-2\log Q(H(r)|H(p)) \overset{w}{\to} tr\left\{\int_0^1 (dB)F'\left[\int_0^1 FF'du\right]^{-1}\int_0^1 F(dB)'\right\},$$
(6.20)

*where $F = B$ is a $p - r$ dimensional Brownian motion. The distribution is
tabulated in Chapter 15, Table 15.1.*
   *If $\mu_t = \mu_0$ and $\alpha'_\perp \mu_0 \neq 0$, the asymptotic distribution is given by (6.20)
with F defined by*

$$F_i(u) = B_i(u) - \int_0^1 B_i(u)du, \quad i = 1, \ldots, p - r - 1,$$
$$F_{p-r}(u) = u - \tfrac{1}{2}.$$
(6.21)

The distribution is tabulated in Chapter 15, Table 15.3.
   If $\mu_t = \mu_0 + \mu_1 t$, and $\alpha'_\perp \mu_1 \neq 0$ then F is given by

$$F_i(u) = B_i(u) - a_i - b_i t, \quad i = 1, \ldots, p - r - 1,$$
$$F_{p-r}(u) = u^2 - a - bu,$$
(6.22)

*where the random coefficients a, b, a_i, and b_i are found by regressing u, re-
spectively B_i, on a constant and a linear term. The distribution is tabulated
in Chapter 15, Table 15.5.*

Another way of formulating this basic estimation result is that we have
performed a singular value decomposition of the unrestricted regression
estimator $\hat{\Pi} = S_{01}S_{11}^{-1}$ with respect to its 'covariance matrix' $S_{00.1} \otimes S_{11}^{-1}$,
that is, of the matrix $\tilde{\Pi} = S_{00.1}^{-\frac{1}{2}}\hat{\Pi}S_{11}^{\frac{1}{2}}$ since

$$|\rho I - \tilde{\Pi}\tilde{\Pi}'| = |\rho I - S_{00.1}^{-\frac{1}{2}}S_{01}S_{11}^{-1}S_{10}S_{00.1}^{-\frac{1}{2}}|,$$

which is zero if

$$|\rho S_{00.1} - S_{01}S_{11}^{-1}S_{10}| = |\rho S_{00} - (1+\rho)S_{01}S_{11}^{-1}S_{10}| = 0,$$

which gives $\lambda = \rho/(1 + \rho)$, where we have used the notation

$$S_{00.1} = S_{00} - S_{01}S_{11}^{-1}S_{10}.$$

The normalization $\hat{\beta}'S_{11}\hat{\beta} = I$ is convenient from a mathematical point of
view but may not be economically meaningful. It has the advantage that
such normalizations can be made without assuming anything about which
variables cointegrate, that is, without normalizing β.

Note that since $\hat{\alpha} = S_{01}\hat{\beta}$ we have

$$\hat{\alpha}'S_{00}^{-1}\hat{\alpha} = \hat{\beta}'S_{10}S_{00}^{-1}S_{01}\hat{\beta} = \mathrm{diag}(\hat{\lambda}_1, \ldots, \hat{\lambda}_r).$$

Thus the eigenvalues measure the size of the coefficients to the cointegrating relations, and the test statistics can be interpreted as measuring the 'length' of the coefficients measured by S_{00}^{-1} of the supposedly nonstationary components of X_t.

The calculation of the eigenvalues of equation (6.15) is performed as follows: first the matrix S_{11} is diagonalized by solving the eigenvalue problem

$$|\rho I - S_{11}| = 0,$$

for eigenvalues $\rho_1, \ldots, \rho_p$ and eigenvectors $W = (w_1, \ldots, w_p)$, that is, we have the decomposition

$$S_{11} = W\mathrm{diag}(\rho_1, \ldots, \rho_p)W'$$

Then we define $S_{11}^{-\frac{1}{2}} = W\mathrm{diag}(\rho_1^{-\frac{1}{2}}, \ldots, \rho_p^{-\frac{1}{2}})W'$ and solve the eigenvalue problem

$$|\lambda I - S_{11}^{-\frac{1}{2}}S_{10}S_{00}^{-1}S_{01}S_{11}^{-\frac{1}{2}}| = 0,$$

for eigenvalues $\hat{\lambda}_1, \ldots, \hat{\lambda}_p$ and eigenvectors $U = (u_1, \ldots, u_p)$. Finally we define the eigenvectors $V = S_{11}^{-\frac{1}{2}}U$. Thus we diagonalize the matrices S_{11} and $S_{10}S_{00}^{-1}S_{01}$ simultaneously by the transformation V. The matrix S_{11} is reduced to the identity and $S_{10}S_{00}^{-1}S_{01}$ is reduced to $\mathrm{diag}(\hat{\lambda}_1, \ldots, \hat{\lambda}_p)$. One could also just say that we find the eigenvalues of $S_{11}^{-1}S_{10}S_{00}^{-1}S_{01}$, but this matrix is not symmetric, hence a different numerical algorithm should be used.

It is sometimes necessary to estimate the orthogonal complements of α and β. This can easily be done by the above results since

$$\hat{\beta}_\perp = S_{11}(v_{r+1}, \ldots, v_p),$$

$$\hat{\alpha}_\perp = S_{00}^{-1}S_{01}(v_{r+1}, \ldots, v_p).$$

satisfy the relation $\hat{\alpha}'\hat{\alpha}_\perp = \hat{\beta}'\hat{\beta}_\perp = 0$. These relations follow from the fact that the eigenvectors $v_1, \ldots, v_p$ diagonalize both S_{11} and $S_{10}S_{00}^{-1}S_{01}$.

Note that the asymptotic distribution of the test statistic $\lambda_{\max}$ in (6.19) is not given here but left as an exercise 11.5 in Chapter 11. The properties of the test are posed as a problem in Chapter 12.

6.2   Models for the Deterministic Terms

In this section we analyse the hypotheses given by (5.13), ..., (5.17). The analysis of (5.13), (5.15), and (5.17) is given in section 6.1 where the analysis is for a general form of the deterministic term D_t. If we take $\Phi D_t = \mu_0 + \mu_1 t$ we get the analysis of $H(r)$, for $\Phi D_t = \mu_0$ we get the analysis of $H_1(r)$ and finally $H_2(r)$ is analysed with $\Phi D_t = 0$. What remains is to discuss the models with a restriction on the deterministic terms: $H^*(r)$ where $\alpha'_\perp \mu_1 = 0$ and $H_1^*(r)$ where $\mu_1 = 0$ and $\alpha'_\perp \mu_0 = 0$. The analysis is very similar to the one given in section 6.1 and the new models will not be treated in so much detail.

Consider first $H^*(r)$ given by (5.14), that is, $\Pi = \alpha\beta'$, $\Phi D_t = \mu_0 + \mu_1 t$, and $\alpha'_\perp \mu_1 = 0$. We note the following relation

$$\alpha\beta' X_{t-1} + \mu_1 t = \alpha\beta' X_{t-1} + \alpha\rho_1 t = \alpha(\beta', \rho_1)(X'_{t-1}, t)' = \alpha\beta^{*\prime} Z_{1t}^*, \quad (6.23)$$

where we define $\beta^* = (\beta', \rho_1)'$ and $Z_{0t}^* = Z_{0t} = \Delta X_t$ and let Z_{2t}^* be the stacked variables $\Delta X_{t-1}, \ldots, \Delta X_{t-k+1}, 1$ whereas $Z_{1t}^* = X_{t-1}^* = (X'_{t-1}, t)'$. Further we define Ψ^* as the matrix $\{\Gamma_1, \ldots, \Gamma_{k-1}, \mu_0\}$. The regression model then becomes

$$Z_{0t}^* = \alpha\beta^{*\prime} Z_{1t}^* + \Psi^* Z_{2t}^* + \epsilon_t. \quad (6.24)$$

It is seen that by this reformulation we can estimate model $H^*(r)$ by reduced rank regression of Z_{0t}^* on Z_{1t}^* corrected for Z_{2t}^*. This defines residuals R_{0t}^*, R_{1t}^*, and product moment matrices S_{ij}^*. Note in particular that S_{11}^* is $p1 \times p1$, whereas S_{10}^* is $p1 \times p$ and S_{00}^* is $p \times p$ as before, with $p1 = p + 1$.

Thus we solve the eigenvalue problem

$$|\lambda^* S_{11}^* - S_{10}^* S_{00}^{*-1} S_{01}^*| = 0,$$

for eigenvalues $\lambda_1^*, \ldots, \lambda_{p1}^*$. Note that $\lambda_{p1}^* = 0$ since the matrix $S_{10}^* S_{00}^{*-1} S_{01}^*$ is of dimension $p1 \times p1$, but has rank p, such that $|S_{10}^* S_{00}^{*-1} S_{01}^*| = 0$. The likelihood ratio test of $H^*(r)$ in $H(r)$ is calculated from

$$Q(H^*(r)|H(r))^{-\frac{2}{T}} = \frac{|S_{00}^*| \prod_{i=1}^r (1 - \lambda_i^*)}{|S_{00}| \prod_{i=1}^r (1 - \hat{\lambda}_i)}.$$

The hypotheses $H^*(p)$ and $H(p)$ are so close that the likelihood function attains the same maximal value, see p.161.

Hence we find for $r = p$ that

$$|S_{00}^*| \prod_{i=1}^p (1 - \lambda_i^*) = |S_{00}| \prod_{i=1}^p (1 - \hat{\lambda}_i),$$

which shows that

$$-2\log Q(H^*(r)|H(r)) = T \log \frac{\prod_{i=r+1}^p (1 - \hat{\lambda}_i)}{\prod_{i=r+1}^p (1 - \lambda_i^*)}.$$

The results are formulated in

THEOREM 6.2 *Under the restrictions* $\Pi = \alpha\beta'$, $\Phi D_t = \mu_0 + \mu_1 t$, *and* $\alpha'_\perp \mu_1 = 0$ *the cointegrating vectors are estimated by reduced rank regression of* ΔX_t *on* (X_{t-1}, t) *corrected for lagged differences and the constant. The likelihood ratio test for the rank of* Π, *is given by*

$$-2\log Q(H^*(r)|H^*(p)) = -T \sum_{i=r+1}^{p} \log(1 - \lambda_i^*), \qquad (6.25)$$

where λ_i^* *solves the eigenvalue problem*

$$|\lambda^* S_{11}^* - S_{10}^* S_{00}^{*-1} S_{01}^*| = 0, \qquad (6.26)$$

for eigenvalues $1 > \lambda_1^* > \cdots > \lambda_p^* > \lambda_{p1}^* = 0$, *and eigenvectors* $v_1^*, \ldots, v_{p1}^*$. *The estimator for* β^* *is given by* $\hat\beta^* = (v_1^*, \ldots, v_r^*)$. *The likelihood ratio test of the restriction* $\alpha'_\perp \mu_1 = 0$ *when there are* r *cointegrating vectors, that is, of* $H^*(r)$ *in* $H(r)$, *is given by*

$$-2\log Q(H^*(r)|H(r)) = T \sum_{i=r+1}^{p} \log\{(1 - \hat\lambda_i)/(1 - \lambda_i^*)\}, \qquad (6.27)$$

where $\hat\lambda_i$ *solves (6.15).*

The asymptotic distribution of the likelihood ratio test statistic (6.25) is derived in Theorem 11.1, and is given by (6.20) with F defined by

$$F_i(u) = B_i(u) - \int_0^1 B_i(u)du, \ i = 1, \ldots, p - r,$$
$$F_{p-r+1}(u) = u - \tfrac{1}{2}. \qquad (6.28)$$

The distribution is tabulated by simulation in Chapter 15, Table 15.4. The asymptotic distribution of the likelihood ratio test statistic (6.27) is shown in Corollary 11.2 to be $\chi^2(p - r)$.

In a completely analogous way we can estimate in the model $H_1^*(r)$ where $\Phi D_t = \mu_0$ and $\alpha'_\perp \mu_0 = 0$. In this case we note that

$$\alpha\beta' X_{t-1} + \alpha\rho_0 = \alpha(\beta', \rho_0)'(X'_{t-1}, 1)' = \alpha\beta^{*'} Z_{1t}^*. \qquad (6.29)$$

For $Z_{2t}^* = (\Delta X'_{t-1}, \ldots, \Delta X'_{t-k+1})'$ we find the reduced rank regression (6.24) again giving rise to new residuals and product moment matrices S_{ij}^*. We formulate the results in

THEOREM 6.3 *Under the restrictions* $\Pi = \alpha\beta'$ *and* $\Phi D_t = \mu_0$ *and* $\alpha'_\perp \mu_0 = 0$ *the cointegration vectors are estimated by reduced rank regression of* ΔX_t *on* $(X_{t-1}, 1)$ *corrected for lagged differences. The likelihood ratio test for the rank of* Π, *when* $\alpha'_\perp \mu_0 = 0$ *is given by*

$$-2\log Q(H_1^*(r)|H_1^*(p)) = -T \sum_{i=r+1}^{p} \log(1 - \lambda_i^*), \qquad (6.30)$$

where λ_i^* solves the eigenvalue problem (6.26). The likelihood ratio test of the restriction $\alpha_{\perp}'\mu_0 = 0$ when there are r cointegration vectors, that is, of $H_1(r)^*$ in $H_1(r)$ is given by

$$-2\log Q(H_1^*(r)|H_1(r)) = -T \sum_{i=r+1}^{p} \log\{1 - \lambda_i^*)/(1 - \hat{\lambda}_i)\}, \qquad (6.31)$$

where $\hat{\lambda}_i$ solves (6.15).

The asymptotic distribution of the likelihood ratio test (6.30) is derived from Theorem 11.1 and is given by (6.20) with F defined by

$$F_i(u) = B_i(u), \quad i = 1, \ldots, p - r,$$
$$\qquad (6.32)$$
$$F_{p-r+1}(u) = 1.$$

The distribution is tabulated by simulation in Chapter 15, Table 15.2.

The asymptotic distribution of the likelihood ratio test statistic (6.31) is shown in Corollary 11.2 to be $\chi^2(p - r)$.

6.3   Determination of Cointegrating Rank

The problem of determining the cointegrating rank will be discussed in detail in Chapter 12, but we give here some rules for the application of the results in Theorem 6.1, 6.2, and 6.3.

Consider for simplicity first the situation where $\Phi D_t = 0$, that is, there are no deterministic terms in the model. In this case the test statistic is given by (6.18) where the preliminary regression does not involve correction for any deterministic terms, since they are not present in the model. The limit distribution of the likelihood ratio test statistic is given by (6.20) with $F = B$, and is tabulated in Chapter 15, Table 15.1. The tables are then used as follows.

If r represents a priori knowledge we simply calculate the test statistic $Q_r = -2\log Q(H(r)|H(p))$ and compare it with the relevant quantile in Table 15.1. Note that the tables give the asymptotic distribution only, and that the actual distribution depends not only on the finite value of T but also on all the short-term parameters as well as on α and β. If one wants to be absolutely sure that the quantiles reported are at all reasonable, one would have to supplement the comparison with the asymptotic tables with a simulation investigation. This will not be attempted here.

A small sample correction has been suggested by Reinsel and Ahn (1992). It consists of using the factor $(T - kp)$ instead of the sample size T

in the calculation of the test statistic for cointegrating rank. This idea has been investigated by Reimers (1992) and it seems that the approximation to the limit distribution is better with the corrected sample size. The theoretical justification for this result presents a very difficult mathematical problem, which it would be extremely useful to solve.

A common situation is that one has no or very little prior information about r, and in this case it seems more reasonable to estimate r from the data. This is done as follows. First compare Q_0 with its quantile c_0, say, from Table 15.1. If $Q_0 < c_0$, then we let $\hat{r} = 0$, if $Q_0 \geq c_0$ we calculate Q_1 and compare it with c_1. If now $Q_1 < c_1$ we define $\hat{r} = 1$, and if not we compare Q_2 with its quantile c_2, etc. This defines an estimator $\hat{r}$ which takes on the values $0, 1, \ldots, p$ and which converges in probability to the true value in a sense discussed in Chapter 12.

Next consider the case $\Phi D_t = \mu_0$, where μ_0 is allowed to vary freely. We see from Theorem 6.1 that the limit distribution depends on the assumption that $\alpha'_\perp \mu_0 \neq 0$.

Sometimes inspection of the graphs shows that the trend is present and we proceed as above and calculate $Q_0, \ldots, Q_{p-1}$, and compare them with the relevant quantiles from Table 15.3, since now the limit distribution is given by (6.21). We start comparing Q_0 with its quantile and proceed to Q_1, etc. This gives the possibility of estimating the value of r.

If it is clear that there is no deterministic trend it seems more reasonable to analyse the model $H_1^*(r)$, and calculate the relevant test statistic $-2 \log Q(H_1^*(r)|H_1^*(p))$. That is, we take the consequence of the assumption that $\alpha'_\perp \mu_0 = 0$ and analyse the model thus specified instead of applying another limit distribution to the previous statistic. That is, we change the test statistic to reflect the hypothesis we are interested in, rather than changing the limit distribution of the previous statistic.

If we are in the situation that we do not know whether there is a trend or not, we have to determine the presence of the trend as well as the cointegrating rank at the same time, since the tests are not similar, not even asymptotically, that is, the distribution and the limit distribution depends on which parameter point is considered under the null hypothesis. We then have a non-nested set of hypotheses, see Table 5.1

$$H_1(0) \subset \cdots \subset H_1(r) \subset \cdots \subset H_1(p)$$
$$\cup \qquad\qquad \cup \qquad\qquad \cup$$
$$H_1^*(0) \subset \cdots \subset H_1^*(r) \subset \cdots \subset H_1^*(p)$$

It holds that $H_1(p)$ is almost the same hypothesis as $H_1^*(p)$, in the sense that $-2\log Q(H_1^*(r)|H_1(p)) = -2\log Q(H_1^*(r)|H_1^*(p))$.

Thus we test all hypotheses against $H_1(p)$. The simultaneous determination of trend and cointegrating rank is now performed as follows:

We calculate $Q_0, \ldots, Q_{p-1}, Q_0^*, \ldots, Q_{p-1}^*$. We accept rank r and the presence of a trend if $H_1(0), \ldots, H_1(r-1)$ are rejected and if also the models $H_1^*(0), \ldots, H_1^*(r-1)$ as well as $H_1^*(r)$ are rejected but $H_1(r)$ is accepted.

We accept cointegrating rank r and the absence of a trend if $H_1^*(r)$ is accepted and $H_1(0), \ldots, H_1(r-1)$ as well as $H_1^*(0), \ldots, H_1^*(r-1)$ are rejected. This solution represents a choice and reflects a priority in the ordering of the hypotheses.

If instead we assume no quadratic trend in the process but allow a linear trend in all directions, we can analyse model $H^*(r)$. These models are nested and the rank is determined as above by calculating the $-2\log Q(H(r)^*|H(p)^*)$ for $r = 0, \ldots, p-1$, and compare them with their quantiles from Table 15.4, starting with $r = 0$.

6.4   Exercises

6.1

Consider the model

$$\Delta X_t = \alpha\beta' X_{t-1} + \mu_0 + \mu_1 t + \epsilon_t.$$

We define the parameters

$$\mu_0 = \alpha\rho_0 + \alpha_\perp \gamma_0,$$

$$\mu_1 = \alpha\rho_1 + \alpha_\perp \gamma_1.$$

1. Show by Granger's representation theorem that X_t in general has a quadratic trend and show how this model can be estimated by reduced rank regression.

2. Show that if $\alpha'_\perp \mu_1 = 0$ then the quadratic trend disappears, but the process still has a linear trend given by

$$\tau_1 = \beta_\perp \left(\alpha'_\perp \beta_\perp\right)^{-1} \alpha'_\perp \alpha_\perp \left(\gamma_0 + \left(\alpha'_\perp \alpha_\perp\right)^{-1} \alpha'_\perp \beta(\beta'\beta)^{-1}\rho_1\right) - \beta\left(\beta'\beta\right)^{-1}\rho_1,$$

see Chapter 5, formula (5.20).

3. Show how one can estimate the parameters of the model by reduced rank regression under the constraint $\alpha'_\perp \mu_1 = 0$.

4. What happens under the constraint $\alpha'_\perp \mu_0 = 0$, and μ_1 unrestricted?

5. Under the restriction $\alpha'_\perp \mu_1 = 0$, the hypothesis of trend stationarity of X_{1t}, say, can be formulated as the hypothesis that the unit vector $(1, 0, \ldots, 0)$ is one of the cointegrating vectors. Discuss how the parameters can be estimated by reduced rank regression in this case.

6.2

A normalization or identification of the cointegrating vectors. Consider the model

$$\Delta X_t = \alpha \beta' X_{t-1} + \epsilon_t.$$

The equation

$$|\lambda \Sigma_{\beta\beta} - \Sigma_{\beta 0}\Sigma_{00}^{-1}\Sigma_{0\beta}| = 0$$

has solutions $\lambda_1 > \cdots > \lambda_r$ and $V = (v_1, \ldots, v_r)$ such that $V'\Sigma_{\beta\beta}V = I$. Now define $\tilde{\beta} = \beta V$, that is, $\tilde{\beta}_i = \beta v_i$, and define $\tilde{\alpha} = \alpha V'^{-1}$, such that $\tilde{\alpha}\tilde{\beta}' = \alpha\beta'$.

1. Show that

$$\text{Var}(\tilde{\beta}' X_{t-1}) = I,$$

$$\tilde{\alpha} = \Sigma_{0\tilde{\beta}} = \text{Cov}(\Delta X_t, \tilde{\beta}' X_{t-1}),$$

$$\tilde{\alpha}'\Sigma_{00}^{-1}\tilde{\alpha} = \text{diag}(\lambda_1, \ldots, \lambda_r).$$

2. Show that similar relations hold for the estimated values of α and β.

6.3

An example of a model based on rational expectations can be formulated as

$$E_t(c_0' X_t + c_1' X_{t+1}) + c = 0, \tag{6.33}$$

for a process X_t which we assume is generated by the equation

$$\Delta X_t = \Pi X_{t-1} + \mu + \epsilon_t, \ t = 1, \ldots, T. \tag{6.34}$$

Here X_t is p-dimensional and the matrix c is $(q \times 1)$ and c_0 and c_1 are $(p \times q)$ known matrices. As an example of this situation consider the variables $(i_t^{au}, i_t^{us}, exch_t, p_t^{us}, p_t^{au})$. The hypothesis of uncovered interest parity is formulated as

$$i_t^{us} - i_t^{au} = E_t \Delta exch_{t+1}, \tag{6.35}$$

and the hypothesis of equal expected real interest rates is formulated as

$$i_t^{us} - E_t \Delta p_{t+1}^{us} = i_t^{au} - E_t \Delta p_{t+1}^{au}. \tag{6.36}$$

1. Show that (6.35) and (6.36) taken together are a special case of (6.33) and find the matrices c, c_0, and c_1.

2. Show that in order for (6.33) to be consistent with (6.34) it must hold that

$$c_1' \Pi = -(c_0 + c_1)', \text{ and } c_1' \mu + c = 0. \tag{6.37}$$

In the presence of cointegration these restrictions give more restrictions on the matrix Π and it is these restrictions that we want to test in the following. We define

$$a = c_1, \quad b = -(c_0 + c_1).$$

and assume that the matrix b has full rank.

3. Show that under the assumption that Π has reduced rank r ($0 < r < p$) and the restrictions (6.37) hold, we have that a has full rank and that

$$(a, a_\perp)' \Pi(b, b_\perp) = \begin{bmatrix} b'b & 0 \\ \Theta & \xi\eta' \end{bmatrix},$$

for matrices ξ and η of dimension $(p - q) \times (r - q)$ and rank $(r - q)$ and a matrix Θ of dimension $(p - q) \times q$. Find Π as a function of Θ, ξ, and η and show that this expression implies that Π has reduced rank and satisfies the restrictions (6.37).

4. Find the dimension of the parameter space spanned by Π and μ under the restrictions (6.37), and find an expression for the cointegrating vectors β expressed in terms of η, and an expression for α.

5. Show by multiplying the equations for X_t by a and $a_\perp$ respectively that the estimators for η, ξ, Θ, and μ can be determined by reduced rank regression.

6. Find an expression for the likelihood ratio test for the hypothesis (6.37). The asymptotic distribution is χ^2. Find the degrees of freedom.

6.4

Discuss the estimation problem for the statistical models discussed in the exercises given in Chapter 5.

6.5

Consider the model

$$\Delta X_t = \alpha\beta' X_{t-1} + \Gamma_1 \Delta X_{t-1} + \epsilon_t. \tag{6.38}$$

Let H be a $p \times s$ matrix.

1. Show that the hypothesis

$$\Gamma_1 H_\perp = 0$$

can be formulated as $\Gamma_1 = \xi H'$ for some ξ ($p \times s$) and derive the likelihood ratio test for this hypothesis. The asymptotic distribution of the test statistic is χ^2. Determine the degrees of freedom.

2. Show that if $\beta = H\varphi$ and $\Gamma_1 = \xi H'$ then $Y_t = H' X_t$ is an autoregressive process. Find the parameters and give the condition for the process Y_t to be an $I(1)$ process.

3. Consider now the following special case

$$\Delta Y_t = \gamma \Delta Z_{t-1} + \epsilon_{1t}, \qquad (6.39)$$

$$\Delta Z_t = \alpha_2 \left(Y_{t-1} + \beta_2 Z_{t-1} \right) + \epsilon_{2t}. \qquad (6.40)$$

Find the characteristic polynomial and its roots and show that if

$$\beta_2 + \gamma \ \neq 0$$
$$-1 \quad < \gamma \alpha_2$$
$$\gamma \alpha_2 + \beta_2 \alpha_2 < 0$$
$$\alpha_2 \left(\gamma - \beta_2 \right) < 2$$

then the process $X_t = (Y_t, \ Z_t)'$ is an $I(1)$ process and $Y_t + \beta_2 Z_t$ is stationary.

4. For $H = (1, \ 0)'$ the hypothesis $\beta = H\varphi$ reduces to $\beta_2 = 0$. Find the autoregressive representation of Y_t given by (6.39) and (6.40) under the assumption that $\beta = H\varphi$ and $\Gamma_1 = \xi H'$ and determine the properties of the process depending on the parameters.

The problem is inspired by the following situation. In an investigation of money m_t, income y_t, price p_t and interest rates i_{1t} and i_{2t}, both money and income are in nominal values. The variables m_t, y_t, and p_t are in logarithms. An analysis of the data shows that a model with $r = 3$ and $k = 2$ describes the data. We now want to investigate if we could have analysed the variables in real terms, that is, the variables $(m_t - p_t, \ y_t - p_t, \ i_{1t}, \ i_{2t})$.

5. Determine in this case the matrix H and determine explicitly the condition that Γ_1 has to satisfy in order that the real variables are described by an AR(2) model.

7

Hypothesis Testing for the Long-Run Coefficients β

THIS chapter contains a derivation of the estimator and test statistics under hypotheses expressed as linear restrictions of the long-run coefficients β. We saw in Chapter 6 how a number of hypotheses can be analysed by various versions of the reduced rank regression algorithm. In this chapter we show that a number of the models defined by restrictions on β in Chapter 5 can be solved by reduced rank regression or slight modifications of it. For each of the hypotheses we give an algorithm for estimation of the parameters and the maximized likelihood function, and hence the likelihood ratio statistics. All the asymptotic distributions for hypotheses on either β or α turn out to be χ^2 distributions by the results in Chapter 13. We give here the calculation of the degrees of freedom for the various hypotheses. The last section 7.3 shows how some of the results are applied to an analysis of the Purchasing Power Parity between Australia and United States as well as an analysis of demand for money in Denmark.

7.1   Degrees of Freedom

The tests on β all turn out to be asymptotically distributed as χ^2. The reason for this is that the asymptotic distribution of β, suitably normalized, will be mixed Gaussian, see Chapter 13, with a dimension determined by the dimension of the tangent space of the statistical model.

In order to understand the determination of the degrees of freedom the following should be kept in mind. In the usual linear regression model $y_t = \theta' x_t + \epsilon_t$ or $Y = X\theta + \epsilon$ with fixed regressors and Gaussian errors, the space spanned by the columns of the design matrix X, gives the dimension of the model or the number of free parameters. If linear restrictions are imposed on the parameters: $\theta = H\varphi$, a submodel is defined, and the space spanned by XH forms a subspace, the dimension of which determines the number of free parameters of the hypothesis. The decrease in number of parameters gives the degrees of freedom for the test of the restrictions on the parameter. For non-linear models $y_t = \theta(\eta)' x_t + \epsilon_t$ one applies a Taylor expansion to find that locally we have linearity:

$$\theta(\hat{\eta}) = \theta(\eta) + D\theta(\hat{\eta} - \eta) + O(|\hat{\eta} - \eta|^2).$$

Using the consistency of $\hat{\eta}$ we can in the asymptotic analysis replace the non-linear model by the linear model with regressors $(D\theta)'x_t$, such that the number of parameters is given by the dimension of the space spanned by $XD\theta$. Thus the tangent space of the non-linear function takes the role of the linear space in usual linear regressions and the dimension of the tangent space gives the number of free parameters. Similarly the information matrix is proportional to the matrix $(D\theta)'X'XD\theta$ and the inverse if it exists is proportional to the asymptotic variance.

A non-linear restriction then gives a subspace with a new tangent space, which is a subspace of the old tangent space and the difference in dimension is the degrees of freedom for the test of the non-linear restrictions. In a cointegration model, which is a non-linear restriction on Π expressed as $\Pi = \alpha\beta'$, we will first determine the dimension of the tangent space at a point where α and β are of full rank, and then use this result to determine the degrees of freedom for some of the tests for restrictions on β discussed in Chapter 5.

LEMMA 7.1 *The function $f(x, y) = xy'$, where x is $p \times r$ $(r \le p)$ and y is $m \times r$ $(r \le m)$, is differentiable at all points, with a differential given by*

$$Df(x, y, h, k) = xk' + hy', \ h\,(p \times r) \ and \ k\,(m \times r).$$

If x and y have full rank then the tangent space has dimension

$$pm - (p - r)(m - r) = (p + m - r)r.$$

PROOF From the expansion

$$f(x + h, y + k) = f(x, y) + xk' + hy' + hk'$$

the first result follows, and the tangent space consists of the matrices

$$\mathcal{T} = \{xk' + hy'|h\,(p \times r), \ k\,(m \times r)\}.$$

It is easier to determine the dimension of the normal space, that is, the space orthogonal to the tangent space at the point (x, y). This space must satisfy the conditions

$$\mathcal{N} = \{M\,(m \times p)\,|tr\,(M\,(xk' + hy')) = 0, \ \text{for all } h\,(p \times r) \ \text{and } k\,(m \times r)\}$$

$$= \{M|Mx = 0 \ \text{and} \ y'M = 0\}.$$

We next want to determine the number of free parameters in a matrix with these restrictions.

We assume without loss of generality, since x and y have full rank, that x, y, and M have the form

$$x = \begin{bmatrix} I \\ 0 \end{bmatrix}, \; y = \begin{bmatrix} I \\ 0 \end{bmatrix}, \; M = \begin{bmatrix} M_{11} & M_{12} \\ M_{21} & M_{22} \end{bmatrix}.$$

The condition $Mx = 0$ implies that $M_{11} = M_{21} = 0$ and $y'M = 0$ implies that $M_{11} = M_{12} = 0$, such that the only parameters remaining in M are the parameters of M_{22}, that is, a total of $(p - r)(m - r)$. Thus $\mathcal{N}$ has dimension $(p - r)(m - r)$ and hence the tangent space has dimension $pm - (p - r)(m - r)$. $\square$

Another way of determining the dimension of the space of matrices defined by xy' of full rank is the following. Since x and y have full rank there is no loss of generality in assuming that $y' = (y_1', y_2')$, where y_1 $(r \times r)$ has full rank, such that

$$f(x, y) = xy' = xy_1' \left(I, \, y_1^{-1'}y_2' \right) = \bar{x}\bar{y}',$$

say. Now $\bar{x}$ and $\bar{y}$ can be recovered from the value of $f(x, y)$ by the identifying restrictions imposed and the dimension of the space of matrices of the form xy' must be equal to the number of parameters in the arguments $\bar{x}$ and $\bar{y}$, that is, $pr + r(m - r)$ which is equal to $pm - (p - r)(m - r)$.

7.2   Linear Restrictions on β

We analyse some of the models discussed in Chapter 5 defined by linear restrictions on β and show that some can be estimated by reduced rank regression, whereas others need an iteration which can be performed conveniently by a switching algorithm. For each such hypothesis the degrees of freedom are calculated by the above result.

7.2.1   The same restriction on all β

The basic $I(1)$ model is given by the equations

$$\Delta X_t = \alpha\beta' X_{t-1} + \sum_{i=1}^{k-1} \Gamma_i \Delta X_{t-i} + \Phi D_t + \epsilon_t,$$

where the parameters $(\alpha, \beta, \Gamma_1, \ldots, \Gamma_{k-1}, \Phi, \Omega)$ vary freely. Consider first the restriction $H_0 : \beta = H\varphi$ for some known matrix H of dimension $p \times s$ which corresponds to imposing the same restriction on all cointegrating vectors.

THEOREM 7.2 *Under hypothesis $H_0 : \beta = H\varphi$, we find the maximum likelihood estimator of β by reduced rank regression of ΔX_t on $H'X_{t-1}$ corrected for lagged differences and dummies, that is, first we solve*

$$|\lambda^* H' S_{11} H - H' S_{10} S_{00}^{-1} S_{01} H| = 0, \qquad (7.1)$$

for $1 > \lambda_1^* > \cdots > \lambda_s^* > 0$ and $V = (v_1, \ldots, v_s)$ which we normalize by $V'H'S_{11}HV = I$. Then choose

$$\hat{\varphi} = (v_1, \ldots, v_r) \text{ and } \hat{\beta} = H\hat{\varphi},$$

and find the estimates of the remaining parameters by ordinary least squares for $\beta = \hat{\beta}$. The maximized likelihood becomes

$$L_{\max}^{-2/T}(H_0) = |S_{00}| \prod_{i=1}^{r} (1 - \lambda_i^*),$$

and the likelihood ratio test $Q(H_0|H(r))$ of the hypothesis H_0 in $H(r)$ is

$$-2\log Q(H_0|H(r)) = T \sum_{i=1}^{r} \log\{(1 - \lambda_i^*)/(1 - \hat{\lambda}_i)\}, \qquad (7.2)$$

which is asymptotically distributed as χ^2 with $r(p - s)$ degrees of freedom.

PROOF For fixed β we get the concentrated likelihood function as before and the regression equation

$$R_{0t} = \alpha\varphi'H'R_{1t} + \hat{\epsilon}_t,$$

see (6.8) and (6.9), which shows that α and φ can be found by reduced rank regression of R_{0t} on $H'R_{1t}$, that is, φ now has to be chosen to minimize

$$\frac{|\beta'(S_{11} - S_{10}S_{00}^{-1}S_{01})\beta|}{|\beta'S_{11}\beta|} = \frac{|\varphi'(H'S_{11}H - H'S_{10}S_{00}^{-1}S_{01}H)\varphi|}{|\varphi'H'S_{11}H\varphi|}, \qquad (7.3)$$

over the set of all $s \times r$ matrices. This shows most of the results of Theorem 7.2, it only remains to discuss the degrees of freedom for the test.

From Lemma 7.1 it follows that the number of parameters in the matrix $\Pi = \alpha\beta'$ with unrestricted α and β is $p^2 - (p - r)^2 = pr + r(p - r)$. If $\beta = H\varphi$, then $\Pi = \alpha\varphi'H'$ which according to Lemma 7.1 has $pr + r(s - r)$ parameters since H is $p \times s$. The difference is $r(p - r) - r(s - r) = r(p - s)$, which determines the degrees of freedom for the test of the hypothesis $\beta = H\varphi$. □

7.2.2 Some β assumed known

Next consider the hypothesis (5.4) $H_0 : \beta = (b, \varphi)$ where b is $p \times s$ and φ is $p \times (r - s)$. Thus of the r cointegrating relations the first b are assumed known, and the remaining $r - s$ are to be estimated unrestrictedly. Before formulating the result we introduce some notation. We decompose the adjustment parameter $\alpha = (\alpha_1, \alpha_2)$ correspondingly into α_1 $(p \times s)$ and α_2 $(p \times (r - s))$ and find that under H_0 it holds that

$$\Pi = \alpha\beta' = \alpha_1 b' + \alpha_2 \varphi',$$

and equation (6.9) becomes

$$R_{0t} = \alpha_1 b' R_{1t} + \alpha_2 \varphi' R_{1t} + \hat{\epsilon}_t. \tag{7.4}$$

The analysis of these equations can be performed by first concentrating out α_1, that is, regressing R_{0t} and R_{1t} on $b' R_{1t}$. This gives new residuals

$$R_{0.bt} = R_{0t} - S_{01}b(b'S_{11}b)^{-1}b'R_{1t},$$

$$R_{1.bt} = R_{1t} - S_{11}b(b'S_{11}b)^{-1}b'R_{1t},$$

and new product moment matrices

$$S_{ij.b} = S_{ij} - S_{i1}b\left(b'S_{11}b\right)^{-1}b'S_{1j}.$$

The concentrated likelihood function now has the form

$$L_{\max}^{-2/T} = |S_{00.b} - S_{01.b}\varphi\left(\varphi'S_{11.b}\varphi\right)^{-1}\varphi'S_{10.b}|$$

$$= |S_{00.b}||\varphi'\left(S_{11.b} - S_{10.b}S_{00.b}^{-1}S_{01.b}\right)\varphi|/|\varphi'S_{11.b}\varphi|.$$

Note that if φ is chosen to lie in $sp(b)$ then both the numerator and denominator are zero. This problem is treated in Lemma A.10, where it is shown that we need only consider vectors which are orthogonal to b. We therefore restrict attention to vectors in the space $sp(b_\perp)$, and solve the eigenvalue problem

$$|\tilde{\lambda}b'_\perp S_{11.b}b_\perp - b'_\perp S_{10.b}S_{00.b}^{-1}S_{01.b}b_\perp| = 0,$$

for eigenvalues $1 > \tilde{\lambda}_1 > \cdots > \tilde{\lambda}_{p-s} > 0$.

It is convenient also to solve the eigenvalue problem

$$|\tilde{\rho}S_{00} - S_{01}b\left(b'S_{11}b\right)^{-1}b'S_{10}| = 0,$$

for eigenvalues $\tilde{\rho}_1 > \cdots > \tilde{\rho}_s > \tilde{\rho}_{s+1} = \cdots = \tilde{\rho}_p = 0$. We then get the representation

$$|S_{00.b}|/|S_{00}| = |S_{00} - S_{01}b\,(b'S_{11}b)^{-1}\,b'S_{10}|/|S_{00}| = \prod_{i=1}^{s}(1 - \tilde{\rho}_i)\,.$$

From this we find the maximized likelihood function

$$L_{\max}^{-2/T} = |S_{00}| \prod_{i=1}^{s}(1 - \tilde{\rho}_i) \prod_{i=1}^{r-s}(1 - \tilde{\lambda}_i).$$

The degrees of freedom for this model can also be determined by Lemma 7.1. Since φ can be chosen in $sp(b_\perp)$, that is, $\varphi = b_\perp \psi$, equation (7.4) can be written as

$$R_{0t} = \alpha_1 b' R_{1t} + \alpha_2 \psi' b'_\perp R_{1t} + \hat{\epsilon}_t.$$

It is seen from Lemma 7.1 that the number of parameters is

$$ps + p\,(p - s) - (p - (r - s))\,(p - s - (r - s)) = p^2 - (p - r)^2 - s\,(p - r)$$

since α_1 is $(p \times s)$, α_2 is $(p \times (r - s))$, and ψ is $(p - s) \times (r - s)$. The number of parameters in the model with unrestricted α and β of dimension $p \times r$ is $p^2 - (p - r)^2$. The difference gives $s\,(p - r)$ degrees of freedom for the test. The results are formulated in

THEOREM 7.3 *Under hypothesis $H_0 : \beta = (b,\ \varphi)$ the estimate of φ is found by solving the eigenvalue problem*

$$|\tilde{\lambda}b'_\perp S_{11.b}b_\perp - b'_\perp S_{10.b}S_{00.b}^{-1}S_{01.b}b_\perp| = 0,$$

for eigenvalues $\tilde{\lambda}_1 > \cdots > \tilde{\lambda}_{p-s} > 0$ and eigenvectors w, and the eigenvalue problem

$$|\tilde{\rho}S_{00} - S_{01}b\,(b'S_{11}b)^{-1}\,b'S_{10}| = 0, \tag{7.5}$$

for eigenvalues $\tilde{\rho}_1 > \cdots > \tilde{\rho}_s > \tilde{\rho}_{s+1} = \cdots = \tilde{\rho}_p = 0$. The maximum likelihood estimator for β is

$$\tilde{\beta} = (b,\ b_\perp(w_1,\ \ldots,\ w_{r-s})),$$

and the maximized likelihood function is

$$L_{\max}^{-2/T} = |S_{00}| \prod_{i=1}^{s}(1 - \tilde{\rho}_i) \prod_{i=1}^{r-s}(1 - \tilde{\lambda}_i). \tag{7.6}$$

Hence the likelihood ratio test of the hypothesis H_0 in $H\,(r)$ is given by

$$-2\log Q\,(H_0|H\,(r))$$

$$= T\left\{ \textstyle\sum_{i=1}^{s}\log(1 - \tilde{\rho}_i) + \sum_{i=1}^{r-s}\log(1 - \tilde{\lambda}_i) - \sum_{i=1}^{r}\log(1 - \hat{\lambda}_i) \right\} \tag{7.7}$$

which is asymptotically distributed as χ^2 with $s\,(p - r)$ degrees of freedom.

We can compare the eigenvalue problem (7.3) corresponding to restrictions on β and (7.5) corresponding to assuming some known cointegrating relations.

The problem of estimating β subject to the restrictions $\beta = H\varphi$ leads to a transformation of the levels of the process by H' and the problem of estimating β when some of the vectors are known leads to conditioning on the levels transformed by b.

Thus if we imposed both sets of restrictions we should solve the eigenvalue problem where we have conditioned on $b'R_{1t}$ and transformed by $H'R_{1t}$. That is, we should solve the eigenvalue problem

$$|\lambda H'S_{11.b}H - H'S_{10.b}S_{00.b}^{-1}S_{01.b}H| = 0. \tag{7.8}$$

7.2.3   Individual restrictions on β

We first consider the model defined by the restrictions

$$\beta = (H_1\varphi_1, H_2\varphi_2),$$

where H_i is $p \times s_i$, and φ_i is $s_i \times r_i$, see (5.5). Note that the relations are not necessarily identified in the above model, since in particular we allow the matrices H_i to be the same, in which case we are in the situation considered in Theorem 7.2.

We decompose the α matrix similarly, that is, $\alpha = (\alpha_1, \alpha_2)$ where α_i is $p \times r_i$, and the basic equation (6.9) becomes

$$R_{0t} = \alpha_1\varphi_1'H_1'R_{1t} + \alpha_2\varphi_2'H_2'R_{1t} + \hat{\epsilon}_t. \tag{7.9}$$

This is evidently a reduced rank problem but with two reduced rank conditions. The solution is not given by an eigenvalue problem, but the following algorithm is easy to implement and is found to converge. Moreover it has the property that the likelihood function is increasing in each step. The algorithm is based on the observation that for known φ_1, the analysis of (7.9) is just a reduced rank regression of R_{0t} on $H_2'R_{1t}$ corrected for $\beta_1'R_{1t} = \varphi_1'H_1'R_{1t}$, that is, the solution given in Theorem 7.3.

As starting values it is not a good idea to use the unrestricted estimates of the vectors in β since the ordering of the vectors need not correspond to the ordering given in the model. Instead one can find among the r vectors in the unrestricted estimator $\hat{\beta}$ a total of r_1 linear combinations that are as close to $sp(H_1)$ as possible. This is done by solving the eigenvalue problem

$$\left|\lambda\hat{\beta}'\hat{\beta} - \hat{\beta}'H_1(H_1'H_1)^{-1}H_1'\hat{\beta}\right| = 0,$$

for eigenvalues and eigenvectors $(v_1, \ldots, v_r)$ and choose as initial value for the iteration the vectors $\hat{\beta}_1 = \hat{\beta}(v_1, \ldots, v_{r_1})$.

Thus the algorithm consists of the following steps:

1. Estimate β_1 and β_2 unrestricted as described in Theorem 6.1 and construct an initial estimate $\hat{\beta}_1$ as described above.

2. For fixed value of $\beta_1 = \hat{\beta}_1$ estimate α_2 and φ_2 by reduced rank regression of R_{0t} on $H_2' R_{1t}$ corrected for $\beta_1' R_{1t}$. This defines $\hat{\beta}_2 = H_2 \hat{\varphi}_2$.

3. For fixed value of $\beta_2 = \hat{\beta}_2$ estimate α_1 and φ_1 by reduced rank regression of R_{0t} on $H_1' R_{1t}$ corrected for $\beta_2' R_{1t}$. This defines $\hat{\beta}_1 = H_1 \hat{\varphi}_1$.

4. Continue with 2. and 3. until convergence.

We do not know that a unique maximum exists, and hence cannot prove that the algorithm always converges to the correct value but the algorithm has the property that the likelihood function is maximized in each step. The maximum value of the likelihood function is given by expressions like (7.6). We summarize the results in

THEOREM 7.4 *The model* $H_0 : \beta = (H_1 \varphi_1, H_2 \varphi_2)$ *is estimated by the switching algorithm described above. The maximized value of the likelihood function is given by*

$$L_{\max}^{-2/T} = |S_{00}| \prod_{i=1}^{r_1} (1 - \hat{\rho}_i) \prod_{i=1}^{r_2} \left(1 - \hat{\lambda}_i\right).$$

where $1 > \hat{\lambda}_1 > \cdots > \hat{\lambda}_{s_2}$ *are defined as the solutions to the eigenvalue problem for* $\beta_1 = \hat{\beta}_1$:

$$|\hat{\lambda} H_2' S_{11.\beta_1} H_2 - H_2' S_{10.\beta_1} S_{00.\beta_1}^{-1} S_{01.\beta_1} H_2| = 0,$$

and $1 > \hat{\rho}_1 > \cdots > \hat{\rho}_{s_1}$ *are defined by the eigenvalue problem for* $\beta_2 = \hat{\beta}_2$:

$$|\hat{\rho} H_1' S_{11.\beta_2} H_1 - H_1' S_{10.\beta_2} S_{00.\beta_2}^{-1} S_{01.\beta_2} H_1| = 0.$$

Theorem 7.4 can immediately be applied to calculate likelihood ratio tests for further restrictions on the variation of the cointegrating relations. Thus in particular this is the test of over-identifying restrictions and also the test for the identification as given by (5.7). There is no general simple formula for calculating the degrees of freedom for models of this type, since it depends on how the matrices H_1 and H_2 are related and on their dimensions. We give without proof a result for identified models with individual restrictions on the cointegrating relations.

THEOREM 7.5 *The model $H_0 : \beta = (H_1\varphi_1, \ldots, H_r\varphi_r)$ where H_i is $p \times s_i$ and φ_i is $s_i \times 1$ is estimated by the above switching algorithm, and the asymptotic distribution of the likelihood ratio test statistic for this model, in the general model of β unrestricted, is χ^2 with degrees of freedom given by $\sum_{i=1}^{r}(p - r - s_i + 1)$, provided that β is identified.*

The degrees of freedom can be calculated from Lemma 7.1 and are simply the sum of the number of restrictions in each equation, that is $p - s_i + 1$ less the number of restrictions r needed to just identify the parameters.

7.2.4 Structural error correction model

The structural error correction model is given by (5.10). Instead of estimating the restricted short-run and long-run parameters simultaneously it seems reasonable, in view of the super-consistency of the estimated long-run parameters, see Chapter 13, to estimate first the restricted long-run parameters from the reduced form error correction model with no restrictions on the short-run parameters. Next for fixed values of the long-run parameters apply the usual maximum likelihood procedure (FIML) to estimate the restricted structural error correction model since all regressors entering the error correction model are now stationary. An algorithm for performing the FIML estimation can be constructed as the algorithm for estimating the identified long-run parameters, see Johansen (1995b), but of course a general optimizing algorithm can be used if more complicated hypotheses are considered, see Doornik and Hendry (1994) and Boswijk (1995). In Johansen and Juselius (1994) an analysis of the IS-LM model is given from this point of view using Australian money data.

7.3 Illustrative Examples

7.3.1 The Danish data

In this section we analyse the Danish data using model $H_1^*(r)$, since inspection of the plots indicates that the data have no deterministic trend, which means that the constant term should be restricted by $\alpha_\perp' \mu = 0$. A formal test of this can be performed using the result of Corollary 11.2.

In this model, the value 1 is appended to the data vector and a set of coefficients to the β matrix, see (6.29), and then a reduced rank regression is performed. Hence $p = 4$ and $p1 = p + 1 = 5$. The result of the analysis is given in Table 7.1.

From Table 7.1 we find that there is no clear evidence for cointegration. The hypothesis $r = 0$ gives a test statistic of 49.14, which corresponds roughly to the 90 per cent quantile from Table 15.2. We choose to maintain the hypothesis that $r = 1$, that is, that there is one cointegrating relation.

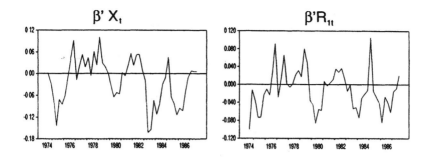

FIG. 7.1. The unrestricted cointegrating relation for the Danish data

Table 7.2 contains the estimated long-run coefficients and Table 7.3 the adjustment coefficients.

From these tables we see the cointegrating relation as the first column. In this case it seems natural to normalize on $m2$.

$$\hat{\beta}^{*\prime} = (1.00, \ -1.03, \ 5.21, \ -4.22, \ -6.06).$$

This makes it straightforward to interpret the cointegrating vector in terms of an error correction mechanism measuring the excess demand for money, where the equilibrium relation is given by

$$m2 = 1.03y - 5.21i^b + 4.22i^d + 6.06.$$

The corresponding α is

TABLE 7.1 The eigenvalues, trace statistic, and 95% quantiles for the Danish data

r	λ_{r+1}	Trace	95%
0	0.433	49.14	53.42
1	0.178	19.06	34.80
2	0.113	8.89	19.99
3	0.043	2.35	9.13

TABLE 7.2 The estimates of the long-run parameters β for the Danish data

	$\hat{\beta}_1^*$	$\hat{\beta}_2^*$	$\hat{\beta}_3^*$	$\hat{\beta}_4^*$	$\hat{\beta}_5^*$
$m2$	−21.97	14.66	7.95	1.02	11.36
y	22.70	−20.05	−25.64	−1.93	−7.20
i^b	−114.42	3.56	4.28	25.00	19.20
i^d	92.64	100.26	−44.88	−14.65	−21.53
1	133.16	−62.59	62.75	−2.32	−91.28

TABLE 7.3 The estimates of the adjustment parameters α ($\times 10^3$) for the Danish data

	$\hat{\alpha}_1$	$\hat{\alpha}_2$	$\hat{\alpha}_3$	$\hat{\alpha}_4$
$\Delta m2$	9.69	−0.33	4.41	1.98
Δy	−5.23	1.35	6.28	1.08
Δi^b	−1.05	−0.72	0.44	−1.53
Δi^d	−1.34	−2.06	−0.35	−0.05

$$\hat{\alpha}^{*\prime} = (-0.213,\ 0.115,\ 0.023,\ 0.029).$$

The normalized coefficients of α can now be interpreted as adjustment coefficients with which excess demand for money enters the four equations of our system. A low coefficient indicates slow adjustment and a high coefficient indicates rapid adjustment. It is seen that in the first equation which measures the changes in money balances, the adjustment coefficient is approximately 0.213, whereas in the last two equations the adjustment coefficients are lower. Note, however, that the interpretation of the coefficient α is the effect of a change in the disequilibrium error corrected for the lagged differences, and hence involves all parameters in the model. The cointegrating linear combination $\beta' X_t$ is plotted in Fig. 7.1, together with $\beta' R_{1t}$. It is seen that the processes appear considerably more stationary than the original variables, and that there is little difference in the behaviour of the two processes in this case.

The hypothesis of weak exogeneity is tested below, but first we test the hypothesis that money and income have equal coefficients with opposite sign.

With the notation $\beta^{*\prime} = (\beta_1, \beta_2, \beta_3, \beta_4, \beta_5)$ the hypothesis becomes:

$$H_0 : \beta_1 = -\beta_2.$$

In matrix formulation this hypothesis is expressed as

$$\beta^* = \begin{bmatrix} 1 & 0 & 0 & 0 \\ -1 & 0 & 0 & 0 \\ 0 & 1 & 0 & 0 \\ 0 & 0 & 1 & 0 \\ 0 & 0 & 0 & 1 \end{bmatrix} \varphi, \quad \varphi \ (4 \times 1)$$

The test of $\beta_1 + \beta_2 = 0$ is determined by the first eigenvalue with and without the restriction, see (7.2), and we find under this hypothesis the eigenvalues

$$\lambda = (0.4327,\ 0.1721,\ 0.0436,\ 0.0056,\ 0).$$

The eigenvector is

$$\hat{\beta}^{*\prime} = (-21.55,\ 21.55,\ -114.22,\ 92.45,\ 134.99),$$

with the adjustment coefficients

$$\hat{\alpha}^{*\prime} = (-9.83, \ 4.99, \ 1.05, \ -1.38).$$

The test statistic becomes

$$-2\mathrm{log}Q(\beta_1 + \beta_2 = 0 | H_1^*(2)) = 53\mathrm{log}\{(1 - 0.4327)/(1 - 0.4332)\} = 0.043.$$

The asymptotic distribution of this quantity is given by the χ^2 distribution with degrees of freedom $r(p1 - s) = 1(5 - 4) = 1$. Note that β is $(p+1) \times s$ since the constant is adjoined to the process X_t when we analyse the model with the constant term restricted such that no trend can appear. It is clearly not significant, and we thus accept the hypothesis that for the Danish data the coefficients to $m2$ and y are equal with opposite sign.

The second hypothesis is that the coefficients for bond rate and deposit rate are equal with opposite sign. This hypothesis implies that the cost of holding money can be measured as the difference between the bond yield and the yield from holding money in bank deposits. Since $\beta_1 + \beta_2 = 0$ was strongly supported by the data, we will test $\beta_3 + \beta_4 = 0$ within the hypothesis that $\beta_1 + \beta_2 = 0$. We then impose the restrictions on β given by the matrix

$$\beta^* = \begin{bmatrix} 1 & 0 & 0 \\ -1 & 0 & 0 \\ 0 & 1 & 0 \\ 0 & -1 & 0 \\ 0 & 0 & 1 \end{bmatrix} \varphi,$$

where φ is a 3×1 vector. Solving the eigenvalue problem we get the largest eigenvalue 0.4231. The test for the hypothesis is given by

$$-2\mathrm{log}(Q) = 53\mathrm{log}\{(1 - 0.4231)/(1 - 0.4327)\} = 0.89,$$

which should be compared with the χ^2 quantiles with $r(s_1 - s_2) = 1(4-3) = 1$ degree of freedom. Again this is not significant and we conclude the analysis of the cointegration vectors for the Danish demand for money by the restricted estimate

$$\hat{\beta}^{*\prime} = (1.00, \ -1.00, \ 5.88, \ -5.88, \ -6.21).$$

The corresponding estimate of α is

$$\hat{\alpha}^{*\prime} = (-0.177, \ 0.095, \ 0.023, \ 0.032).$$

If we want to test that we can restrict further the coefficients $\alpha_3 = \alpha_4 = 0$, that is, test the weak exogeneity of the two interest rates, we can calculate the likelihood ratio test and find that the largest eigenvalue is $\lambda_1 = 0.356$, such that the test statistic is given by

$$-2\log Q(\alpha_3 = \alpha_4 = 0 | \beta_1 + \beta_2 = \beta_3 + \beta_4 = 0)$$
$$= 53\log\{(1 - 0.356)/(1 - 0.423)\} = 5.81,$$

which compared with the quantiles in the $\chi^2(2)$ distribution gives a p-value of 5 per cent.

7.3.2   The Australian data

We first determine the cointegrating rank, and then test some hypotheses as discussed above. The eigenvalues and the related test statistics and quantiles are given in Table 7.4. The asymptotic distributions of the test statistics given in Theorem 6.1 are derived in Chapter 11, and the relevant tables are given in Chapter 15. Here we shall just use the results without comments on how they are obtained. The asymptotic distribution of

$$-2\log Q\left(H\left(r\right)|H\left(p\right)\right) = -T \sum_{i=r+1}^{p} \log(1 - \hat{\lambda}_i)$$

depends on the fact that the linear trend is present, hence Table 15.3 is chosen and the quantiles also depend on the number of common trends $p - r$ in the model being tested.

It appears that $r = 0$ is rejected, $r = 1$ is rejected, and that $r = 2$ can be accepted by the data. See Chapter 12 for a discussion of the rank determination. This is of course a rather formal test, since we only have the asymptotic distribution and not the actual distribution of the test statistic. Furthermore if we choose a 90 per cent quantile we can reject $r = 2$ but accept $r = 3$. Thus there is no clear-cut decision to make about whether $r = 2$ or 3. We started out looking for two cointegrating relations: the real exchange rate and the interest differential. These combinations are probably not stationary themselves, but we seem to have found two other combinations that are stationary.

TABLE 7.4 The eigenvalues, trace statistic and 95% quantile from Table 15.3 for the Australian data

r	λ_{r+1}	Trace	95%
0	0.484	101.38	68.91
1	0.268	51.78	47.18
2	0.215	28.43	29.51
3	0.074	10.24	15.20
4	0.058	4.45	3.96

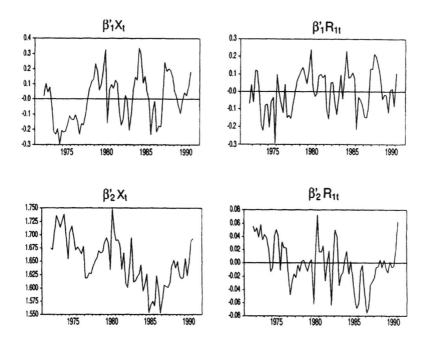

FIG. 7.2. The unrestricted cointegrating relations for the Australian data

We continue with the model $H\,(2)$ which assumes $r = 2$, and now illustrate some of the test procedures for hypotheses on β and α. Note that the calculated eigenvectors are normalized by $\hat{\beta}'S_{11}\hat{\beta} =$ diagonal matrix. The chosen normalization from Theorem 6.1 is supplemented by choosing the coefficient to p^{au} to 1.00, and the adjustment coefficients are normalized similarly. If $r = 1$ the maximum likelihood estimator is the first column of the long-run coefficients β, and the first column of the adjustment coefficients then gives the estimator of the corresponding adjustment coefficients in model $H\,(1)$. If $r = 2$, then the maximum likelihood estimator for the two cointegrating relations is given as the space spanned by the first two β-vectors etc. Thus the estimation problem for all the models is solved simultaneously. It must be emphasized that the estimates in Table 7.5 are the unrestricted estimates, because we have analysed the general cointegration model. If we have prior assumptions on the cointegrating vectors we must incorporate this in the estimation method as discussed in this chapter.

The two cointegrating linear combinations $\beta_1'X_t$ and $\beta_2'X_t$ together with $\beta_1'R_{1t}$ and $\beta_2'R_{2t}$ are plotted in Fig. 7.2. Note that the latter which are corrected for short-term dynamics and seasonals appear more stationary.

Since we can only estimate the cointegrating space and not the individual vectors (without further restrictions) we should be prepared to take linear combinations of the vectors into account before we interpret them,

TABLE 7.5 Estimates of the long-run parameters β for the Australian data

	$\hat{\beta}_1$	$\hat{\beta}_2$	$\hat{\beta}_3$	$\hat{\beta}_4$	$\hat{\beta}_5$
p^{au}	1.00	1.00	1.00	1.00	1.00
p^{us}	-0.95	-1.98	-1.12	-1.65	-1.01
$exch$	0.38	0.76	-0.81	0.14	-0.35
i^{au}	-11.75	2.77	4.16	0.42	-0.98
i^{us}	9.34	3.88	2.03	3.28	-1.39

TABLE 7.6 Estimates of the adjustment parameters α for the Australian data

	$\hat{\alpha}_1$	$\hat{\alpha}_2$	$\hat{\alpha}_3$	$\hat{\alpha}_4$	$\hat{\alpha}_5$
Δp^{au}	-0.030	-0.013	-0.007	0.012	-0.018
Δp^{us}	0.004	-0.034	-0.001	0.028	0.008
$\Delta exch$	-0.035	-0.124	0.159	0.043	-0.064
Δi^{au}	0.028	-0.043	0.005	-0.007	-0.009
Δi^{us}	-0.008	-0.052	-0.000	-0.027	0.018

or rather formulate the questions in terms of the cointegrating space. Note that it does not look possible to take linear combinations of the first two vectors and obtain the vector $(1, -1, -1, 0, 0)$, but that it seems that the two prices enter with equal coefficient with opposite sign. If they do so in the chosen representation they will do so for any linear combination, hence such a question is a question that involves the whole cointegrating space. Thus we would expect that the hypothesis that the coefficients to the prices sum to zero is accepted, but it looks as if the hypothesis that the real exchange rate is stationary is not satisfied.

Similarly with the interest differential which seems to enter the first relation but not the second. Note that we can always find a linear combination of the first two vectors that have exactly the coefficient 1 and -1 to the interest rates, hence this hypothesis is not testable. The hypothesis that the interest differential enters both relations, however, is testable. Next note that the third vector seems to contain the real exchange rate together with a linear combination of the interest rates. The proper formulation of this observation is that a vector of the form $(1, -1, -1, \varphi, \psi)$ seems to lie in the space spanned by the first three cointegration vectors. Thus rather than becoming a question about the third vector, which is identified in a peculiar way, we formulate it as a question about the cointegrating space, which is identified.

First note that the interest rate in US has some very strange behaviour around 1980 which has resulted in an ARCH(2) which is far too big. Somehow the US interest rate is not well modelled by the chosen set of data, and it is tempting to check if some of the variables can be assumed weakly

TABLE 7.7 The estimates of α and β for the Australian data when $r = 2$ and i^{us} and p^{us} are weakly exogenous

	$\hat{\beta}_1$	$\hat{\beta}_2$	$\hat{\alpha}_1$	$\hat{\alpha}_2$
p^{au}	1.000	1.000	−0.027	−0.005
p^{us}	−0.776	−1.055	0.000	−0.000
$exch$	0.399	−0.968	−0.036	0.153
i^{au}	−14.444	4.296	0.022	−0.004
i^{us}	10.541	1.878	0.000	0.000

exogenous, in particular the US interest, as it is not modelled so well by the chosen information set, and p^{us} which also needs a different information set to get a relevant model. We formulate this as a hypothesis on α, namely the hypothesis of weak exogeneity of i^{us} and p^{us} or in matrix formulation that rows 2 and 5 of α are zero, see (5.8). The likelihood ratio test for this hypothesis is 7.34, and should be evaluated in a $\chi^2(4)$ corresponding to a p-value of 12 per cent. Thus it is not against the data to assume that i^{us} and p^{us} are weakly exogenous, and we continue the analysis under this assumption. The interpretation of the weak exogeneity is that some rows of α are zero, but that means that the corresponding unit vectors are contained in $\alpha_\perp$, which again means that the cumulated ϵ from these equations are common trends. Thus we find that the cumulated unexplained variation from the interest and price equation for US are two of the common trends. This question will be treated in detail in Chapter 8.

Table 7.7 gives the restricted estimates for $r = 2$ and under the assumption that i^{us} and p^{us} are weakly exogenous.

Note how the new estimates contain the real exchange rates in the second vector, or more precisely the cointegrating space now seems to contain a vector with coefficients corresponding to the real exchange rate together with a combination of the interest rates. The first relation is quite close to the interest differential, which means that we can now formulate a hypothesis about restrictions on both the cointegrating vectors in the form (5.5).

Strictly speaking the previous cointegration analysis where r was determined and the test for weak exogeneity rested on the assumption that the model actually fitted the data, that is, that even the US interest rate could be described by the model. We shall continue the analysis in the conditional model given current values of p^{us} and i^{us}, that is, under the assumption that the corresponding rows of α are zero.

We can then test various hypotheses about the cointegrating vectors. First consider the hypothesis that the interest rate differential is stationary. We formulate this as the hypothesis that $(0, 0, 0, 1, -1)$ is a cointegrating vector. The likelihood ratio test, assuming the restriction on α, is calculated to be 11.61 which is significant in a $\chi^2(3)$ distribution. Theorem 7.3

contains the limit result and the degrees of freedom $s(p-r) = 1(5-2) = 3$.

Note that the degrees of freedom can also be found as follows. We can easily find a cointegrating relation with coefficients to the interest rates summing to zero, just by taking a suitable linear combination. This is no restriction, but the moment we require the first three coefficients to be zero as well we get genuine restrictions, that is, we get three degrees of freedom.

Another hypothesis that can be tested is that one equation contains the interest rate differential and the other the real exchange rate. This is formulated as a hypothesis on the individual cointegrating vectors see (5.5). One vector is restricted by the requirement that the coefficients to the interest rates sum to zero, and the other is restricted by requiring that the real exchange rate enters. The first restriction is given by the matrix $R_1' = (0, 0, 0, 1, 1)$ and R_2' has two rows $(1, 1, 0, 0, 0)$ and $(1, 0, 1, 0, 0)$. Thus $\beta = (H_1\varphi_1, H_2\varphi_2)$ where

$$H_1 = \begin{bmatrix} 1 & 0 & 0 & 0 \\ 0 & 1 & 0 & 0 \\ 0 & 0 & 1 & 0 \\ 0 & 0 & 0 & 1 \\ 0 & 0 & 0 & -1 \end{bmatrix}, \quad H_2 = \begin{bmatrix} 1 & 0 & 0 \\ -1 & 0 & 0 \\ -1 & 0 & 0 \\ 0 & 1 & 0 \\ 0 & 0 & 1 \end{bmatrix}.$$

In other words

$$\beta_1' = (\varphi_{11}, \varphi_{21}, \varphi_{31}, \varphi_{41}, -\varphi_{41}),$$

$$\beta_2' = (\varphi_{12}, -\varphi_{12}, -\varphi_{12}, \varphi_{22}, \varphi_{32}).$$

The likelihood ratio test is 0.1 which is not significant in a $\chi^2 (1)$ distribution.

7.4   Exercises

7.1

Consider the model

$$\Delta X_{1t} = \tfrac{1}{2} (X_{1t-1} - \beta_1 X_{2t-1}) + \epsilon_{1t},$$

$$\Delta X_{2t} = \tfrac{1}{2} (X_{1t-1} - \beta_2 X_{2t-1}) + \epsilon_{2t},$$

where ϵ_t, $t = 1, \ldots, T$ are i.i.d. $N_2 (0, \Omega)$. Find the maximum likelihood estimator of β_1 and β_2 and derive the likelihood ratio test of the hypothesis $\beta_1 = \beta_2$. Discuss the properties of the process X_t when $\beta_1 = \beta_2$, and when $\beta_1 \neq \beta_2$.

8

Partial Systems and Hypotheses on α

THIS chapter contains a brief discussion of partial systems, that is, systems which are formulated as conditional models of some variables, the endogenous, given others, the exogenous. We discuss such models in the framework of the full VAR model and focus on the notion of weak exogeneity in section 8.1, and use that in section 8.2 as an example of hypothesis testing on α. There is an interesting similarity, or duality, between the interpretation as well as the estimation procedure for β and that of $\alpha_\perp$. This is explained in section 8.3.

8.1   Partial Systems

When choosing the information set or the variables for an econometric investigation there are often some variables of primary interest, the endogenous that we want to describe by means of others, the exogenous variables. Sometimes it is easier to model satisfactorily the conditional model of the endogenous variables given the exogenous variables, and the marginal distribution of the exogenous variables show an irregular behaviour which is difficult to model using a VAR. It is tempting in such a situation to make inference from the conditional or partial model (8.3) and leave the exogenous variables unspecified or at least modelled less carefully. Thus one would like to make inference on the cointegrating rank in the partial system, to estimate β in the partial system and finally to test hypotheses on β.

It turns out that such an analysis can only be valid if the assumption of weak exogeneity is satisfied, see Engle *et al.* (1983). The reason for this is that the asymptotic distribution theory for the estimate of β becomes very difficult, not to say impossible, without the assumption of weak exogeneity. This problem is discussed in some detail in Johansen (1992c), Boswijk (1992), and Urbain (1992). The assumption of weak exogeneity, however, is an assumption about the full system.

The problem of rank determination in partial systems is discussed in Harboe *et al.* (1995) where it is shown that even if weak exogeneity is assumed the deterministic term makes it difficult to determine the rank without modelling the full system. Thus in the following we work in the full system, and assume weak exogeneity and that the value of the cointegrating rank is known.

Let the process be decomposed as $X_t = (X'_{1t}, X'_{2t})'$ and the matrices decomposed similarly, that is,

$$\alpha = \begin{bmatrix} \alpha_1 \\ \alpha_2 \end{bmatrix}, \Gamma_j = \begin{bmatrix} \Gamma_{1j} \\ \Gamma_{2j} \end{bmatrix}, \Phi = \begin{bmatrix} \Phi_1 \\ \Phi_2 \end{bmatrix}.$$

The basic model equations can be rewritten as

$$\Delta X_{1t} = \alpha_1 \beta' X_{t-1} + \sum_{i=1}^{k-1} \Gamma_{1i} \Delta X_{t-i} + \Phi_1 D_t + \epsilon_{1t}, \quad (8.1)$$

$$\Delta X_{2t} = \alpha_2 \beta' X_{t-1} + \sum_{i=1}^{k-1} \Gamma_{2i} \Delta X_{t-i} + \Phi_2 D_t + \epsilon_{2t}. \quad (8.2)$$

Here the ϵ are i.i.d. Gaussian with mean zero and variance matrix

$$\Omega = \begin{bmatrix} \Omega_{11} & \Omega_{12} \\ \Omega_{21} & \Omega_{22} \end{bmatrix}.$$

The conditional model for ΔX_{1t} given the past and ΔX_{2t} is found from these equations:

$$\Delta X_{1t} = \omega \Delta X_{2t} + (\alpha_1 - \omega \alpha_2) \beta' X_{t-1} + \sum_{i=1}^{k-1} \tilde{\Gamma}_{1i} \Delta X_{t-i} + \tilde{\Phi}_1 D_t + \tilde{\epsilon}_{1t}, \quad (8.3)$$

where $\omega = \Omega_{12} \Omega_{22}^{-1}$, $\tilde{\Gamma}_{1i} = \Gamma_{1i} - \omega \Gamma_{2i}$, $\tilde{\Phi}_1 = \Phi_1 - \omega \Phi_2$, and $\tilde{\epsilon}_{1t} = \epsilon_{1t} - \omega \epsilon_{2t}$ with variance $\Omega_{11.2} = \Omega_{11} - \Omega_{12} \Omega_{22}^{-1} \Omega_{21}$. It is seen that β enters both equations (8.2) and (8.3) and there can be a considerable problem, as well as a loss of information, in the analysis of the conditional equation (8.3) without taking into account the second equation (8.2).

We formulate a simple result about a condition for when the analysis of the conditional model is efficient.

THEOREM 8.1 *If $\alpha_2 = 0$, then X_{2t} is weakly exogenous for the parameter (β, α_1), and the maximum likelihood estimator of β and α_1 can be calculated from the conditional model.*

PROOF Under the assumption that $\alpha_2 = 0$, equations (8.2) and (8.3) become

$$\Delta X_{2t} = \sum_{i=1}^{k-1} \Gamma_{2i} \Delta X_{t-i} + \Phi_2 D_t + \epsilon_{2t}, \quad (8.4)$$

$$\Delta X_{1t} = \omega \Delta X_{2t} + \alpha_1 \beta' X_{t-1} + \sum_{i=1}^{k-1} \tilde{\Gamma}_{1i} \Delta X_{t-i} + \tilde{\Phi}_1 D_t + \tilde{\epsilon}_{1t}. \quad (8.5)$$

It is seen that the parameters in the marginal model (8.4) are

$$\theta_m = (\Gamma_{21}, \ldots, \Gamma_{2k-1}, \Phi_2, \Omega_{22}),$$

and the parameters in the conditional model (8.5) are

$$\theta_c = (\alpha_1, \beta, \tilde{\Gamma}_{11}, \ldots, \tilde{\Gamma}_{1k-1}, \tilde{\Phi}_1, \omega, \Omega_{11.2}).$$

It is clear that the parameter space with parameters

$$\theta = (\alpha_1, \beta, \Gamma_1, \ldots, \Gamma_{k-1}, \Phi, \Omega),$$

is decomposed into a product space of the parameters in the marginal model θ_m and the parameters in the conditional model θ_c. This is seen by selecting arbitrary values for θ_m and θ_c (satisfying that Ω_{22} and $\Omega_{11.2}$ are positive definite) and then constructing θ which satisfies that Ω is positive definite. We have here used the fact that for the multivariate Gaussian distribution the parameter Ω_{22} is variation independent of the parameters $(\omega, \Omega_{11.2})$, see Barndorff-Nielsen (1978). Since finally the parameters of interest, (α_1, β), are functions of the parameters of the conditional model we have proved that X_{2t} is weakly exogenous.

This shows that the likelihood function factors as

$$L(\theta) = \prod_{t=1}^{T} f(\Delta X_{2t} | \Delta X_{t-1}, \ldots, \Delta X_{t-k+1}, \theta_m)$$

$$\times \prod_{t=1}^{T} f(\Delta X_{1t} | \Delta X_{2t}, X_{t-1}, \Delta X_{t-1}, \ldots, \Delta X_{t-k+1}, \theta_c),$$

which shows that the maximum likelihood estimator $\hat{\theta}_c$, and hence $(\hat{\alpha}_1, \hat{\beta})$, can be calculated from the second factor, the partial likelihood. $\square$

Another interpretation of the hypothesis of weak exogeneity is the following: if $\alpha_2 = 0$ then $sp((0, I)')$ is contained in $sp(\alpha_\perp)$ which means that $\sum_{i=1}^{t} \epsilon_{2i}$ is a common trend in the sense that the errors in the equations for X_{2t} cumulate in the system and give rise to the non-stationarity. This does not mean that the process X_{2t} cannot cointegrate, in fact it can be stationary, see exercise 4.3.

If in particular X_{1t} is univariate then (8.5) consists of a single equation which is an error correction model for the changes in X_{1t} as explained by simultaneous values of ΔX_{2t}, the lags of ΔX_t and the error correction term $\beta' X_{t-1}$ as well as the dummies. What the theorem states is a condition which guarantees that for inference concerning β and α_1 we only need to do a single equation analysis, which is easier since usual regression analysis will provide estimates for the parameters. It therefore becomes important to have a test for the adequacy of single equation analysis, and this is treated in the next section. See also Corollary 8.3.

8.2   Test of Restrictions on α

This section discusses estimation of β when α is restricted by hypotheses like (5.8) and (5.9).

8.2.1   The same restriction on all α

Consider the hypothesis (5.8) where α is restricted by $H_0 : \alpha = A\psi$ in model $H(r)$. Here A is a $(p \times m)$ matrix with $m \geq r$. As a special case we get the situation considered above where $A = (I, 0)'$, that is, weak exogeneity of X_{2t} for the parameters of interest (α_1, β). The hypothesis H_0 can be expressed in indirect form as $A'_\perp \alpha = 0$.

The concentrated likelihood function will be expressed in the form of two regression equations derived from (6.9). Recall the notation $\bar{A} = A(A'A)^{-1}$, with the property that $A'\bar{A} = I$. We then get from

$$R_{0t} = \alpha\beta'R_{1t} + \hat{\epsilon}_t = A\psi\beta'R_{1t} + \hat{\epsilon}_t,$$

the equations

$$\bar{A}'R_{0t} = \psi\beta'R_{1t} + \bar{A}'\hat{\epsilon}_t, \tag{8.6}$$

$$A'_\perp R_{0t} = A'_\perp \hat{\epsilon}_t. \tag{8.7}$$

In the following we apply the same trick as above of analysing first equation (8.7) and then equation (8.6) given (8.7). That is, we first factor out that part of the likelihood function which depends on $A'_\perp R_{0t}$, since it does not contain the parameters ψ and β. To save notation we define $\Omega_{11} = \bar{A}'\Omega\bar{A}$, $\Omega_{12} = \bar{A}'\Omega A_\perp$, $\Omega_{22} = A'_\perp \Omega A_\perp$, $\Omega_{11.2} = \Omega_{12}\Omega_{22}^{-1}\Omega_{21}$, $\omega = \Omega_{12}\Omega_{22}^{-1}$ and finally

$$S_{ij.A_\perp} = S_{ij} - S_{i0}A_\perp(A'_\perp S_{00}A_\perp)^{-1}A'_\perp S_{0j}, \; i,j = 0,1.$$

We then get the two equations

$$\bar{A}'R_{0t} = \psi\beta'R_{1t} + \omega A'_\perp R_{0t} + \bar{A}'\hat{\epsilon}_t - \omega A'_\perp \hat{\epsilon}_t, \tag{8.8}$$

$$A'_\perp R_{0t} = A'_\perp \hat{\epsilon}_t, \tag{8.9}$$

which have independent error terms. Note that the properties of the multivariate Gaussian distribution imply that $(\psi, \beta, \omega, \Omega_{11.2})$, the parameters of (8.8), are variation independent of the parameters from (8.9) given by Ω_{22}. Thus the two equations can be analysed separately. Strictly speaking these calculations should be performed in equation (6.2) before correcting for the variable Z_{2t}. That is, first one should derive the conditional and marginal models and then eliminate the regression parameters Ψ. The result is the same, however. We next find the two factors corresponding to the marginal and the conditional distribution.

The factor of the likelihood function corresponding to the marginal distribution of $A'_\perp R_{0t}$ in (8.9) is given by

$$|A'_\perp A_\perp|^{\frac{1}{2}T}|\Omega_{22}|^{-\frac{1}{2}T}\exp\{-\frac{1}{2}\sum_{t=1}^{T}(A'_\perp R_{0t})'\Omega_{22}^{-1}(A'_\perp R_{0t})\}, \qquad (8.10)$$

which gives the estimate

$$\hat{\Omega}_{22} = A'_\perp S_{00} A_\perp, \qquad (8.11)$$

and the maximized likelihood function from the marginal distribution

$$L_{\max}^{-2/T} = |A'_\perp S_{00} A_\perp|/|A'_\perp A_\perp|. \qquad (8.12)$$

The other factor of the likelihood function corresponds to the conditional distribution of $\bar{A}' R_{0t}$ conditional on $A'_\perp R_{0t}$ and R_{1t}, and is given by

$$|\bar{A}'\bar{A}|^{\frac{1}{2}T}|\Omega_{11.2}|^{-\frac{1}{2}T}\exp\{-\frac{1}{2}\sum_{t=1}^{T}\left(\bar{A}' R_{0t} - \psi\beta' R_{1t} - \omega A'_\perp R_{0t}\right)'$$
$$\times\Omega_{11.2}^{-1}\left(\bar{A}' R_{0t} - \psi\beta' R_{1t} - \omega A'_\perp R_{0t}\right)\}. \qquad (8.13)$$

The analysis of (8.13) or (8.8) is seen to be performed by reduced rank regression of $\bar{A}' R_{0t}$ on R_{1t} corrected for $A'_\perp R_{0t}$. Hence the estimator of $\omega = \Omega_{12}\Omega_{22}^{-1}$ is found by regression for fixed ψ and β giving

$$\hat{\omega}(\psi, \beta) = \left(\bar{A}' S_{00} - \psi\beta' S_{10}\right) A_\perp (A'_\perp S_{00} A_\perp)^{-1}, \qquad (8.14)$$

and new residuals defined by

$$\tilde{R}_{0t} = R_{0t} - S_{00} A_\perp (A'_\perp S_{00} A_\perp)^{-1} A'_\perp R_{0t},$$

$$\tilde{R}_{1t} = R_{1t} - S_{10} A_\perp (A'_\perp S_{00} A_\perp)^{-1} A'_\perp R_{0t}.$$

In terms of $\tilde{R}_{0t}$ and $\tilde{R}_{1t}$ the concentrated likelihood function has the form (6.8) which means that estimation of β follows as before by reduced rank regression. It is convenient to calculate the relevant product moment matrices as

$$S_{ij.A_\perp} = T^{-1}\sum_{t=1}^{T}\tilde{R}_{it}\tilde{R}'_{jt}, \quad i, j = 0, 1.$$

The results are formulated in Theorem 8.2, where we also state the asymptotic distribution of the test statistic.

THEOREM 8.2 *Under hypothesis* $H_0 : \alpha = A\psi$, *the maximum likelihood estimator of* β *is found as follows: first solve the equation*

$$|\tilde{\lambda} S_{11.A_\perp} - S_{10.A_\perp} \bar{A} (\bar{A}' S_{00.A_\perp} \bar{A})^{-1} \bar{A}' S_{01.A_\perp}| = 0, \qquad (8.15)$$

for $1 > \tilde{\lambda}_1 > \cdots > \tilde{\lambda}_m > \tilde{\lambda}_{m+1} = \cdots = \tilde{\lambda}_p = 0$ *and* $\tilde{V} = (\tilde{v}_1, \ldots, \tilde{v}_p)$ *normalized by* $\tilde{V}' S_{11.A_\perp} \tilde{V} = I$.

The estimator of the cointegrating relations is

$$\tilde{\beta} = (\tilde{v}_1, \ldots, \tilde{v}_r). \qquad (8.16)$$

The estimators of the other parameters can be found by regression from (8.8) and (8.9) for $\beta = \tilde{\beta}$. *The maximized likelihood function is*

$$L_{\max}^{-2/T} (H_0) = |A'_\perp A_\perp|^{-1} |\bar{A}' \bar{A}|^{-1} |A'_\perp S_{00} A_\perp| |\bar{A}' S_{00.A_\perp} \bar{A}| \prod_{i=1}^r (1 - \tilde{\lambda}_i)$$

$$= |S_{00}| \prod_{i=1}^r (1 - \tilde{\lambda}_i). \qquad (8.17)$$

The likelihood ratio test statistic of H_0 *in* $H(r)$ *is*

$$-2\log(Q(H_0|H(r)) = T \sum_{i=1}^r \log\{(1 - \tilde{\lambda}_i)/(1 - \hat{\lambda}_i)\},$$

which is asymptotically distributed as χ^2 *with* $r(p - m)$ *degrees of freedom.*

Notice that equation (8.9) does not contain cointegrating terms, such that inference on β can be conducted from equation (8.8) given (8.9), as explained in Chapter 7. If further $m = r$ then the restriction $\alpha = A\psi$ corresponds to choosing $sp(\alpha) = sp(A)$, that is, the space of the adjustment coefficients is known. The degrees of freedom are found from Lemma 7.1, since evidently $\Pi = A\psi\beta'$ or rather $\psi\beta'$ contains $mp - (m - r)(p - r)$ parameters, which compared to $p^2 - (p - r)^2$ gives $r(p - m)$ degrees of freedom.

COROLLARY 8.3 *If* $m = r$, *that is, the adjustment coefficients are known up to normalization, then the maximum likelihood estimate of* β *is found as the coefficients of* X_{t-1} *in the regression of* $\bar{A}' \Delta X_t$ *on* X_{t-1}, $A'_\perp \Delta X_t$, $\Delta X_{t-1}, \ldots, \Delta X_{t-k+1}$ *and* D_t.

PROOF The estimator for β is found from (8.8). If $m = r$ we absorb the $r \times r$ matrix ψ into β and it is seen that the coefficients β can be found by regressing $\bar{A}' R_{0t}$ on R_{1t} corrected for $A'_\perp R_{0t}$. Thus in particular if α is proportional to $(1, 0, \ldots, 0)$ and $r = 1$ then ordinary least squares analysis of the first equation will give the maximum likelihood estimator of the cointegrating vector.   □

8.2.2 Some adjustment coefficients assumed known

Next we consider the situation where the restrictions on α are given by $\alpha = (a, \tau)$, where $a\,(p \times s)$ is known $s \leq r$ and the remaining vectors τ are to be estimated. It is not so easy to give an interpretation of this model as it stands but $sp(a) \subset sp(\alpha)$ is equivalent to $sp(a_\perp) \supset sp(\alpha_\perp)$, that is, $\alpha_\perp = a_\perp \xi$ for some matrix ξ. Thus these hypotheses are concerned with testing the same restriction on all common trends. Again we only need to consider vectors τ in $sp\,(a_\perp)$, and define $\tau = a_\perp \psi$.

We concentrate the likelihood function, see (6.8), and obtain the equation

$$R_{0t} = a\beta_1' R_{1t} + a_\perp \psi \beta_2' R_{1t} + \hat{\epsilon}_t,$$

where $\beta = (\beta_1, \beta_2)$. Now multiply by $\bar{a}'$ and $\bar{a}'_\perp$ to obtain

$$\bar{a}' R_{0t} = \beta_1' R_{1t} + \bar{a}' \hat{\epsilon}_t, \tag{8.18}$$

$$\bar{a}'_\perp R_{0t} = \psi \beta_2' R_{1t} + \bar{a}'_\perp \hat{\epsilon}_t. \tag{8.19}$$

The conditional equation for $\bar{a}' R_{0t}$ given $\bar{a}'_\perp R_{0t}$ and the past is given by

$$\bar{a}' R_{0t} = \left(\beta_1' - \omega\psi\beta_2'\right) R_{1t} + \omega \bar{a}'_\perp R_{0t} + \bar{a}' \hat{\epsilon}_t - \omega \bar{a}'_\perp \hat{\epsilon}_t. \tag{8.20}$$

where $\omega = \Omega_{aa}\Omega_{aa_\perp}^{-1}$, such that the errors are independent in (8.19) and (8.20). Moreover the parameters $(\beta_1 - \beta_2\psi'\omega', \omega, \Omega_{aa.a_\perp})$ from (8.20) are variation independent of the parameters $(\psi, \beta_2, \Omega_{a_\perp a_\perp})$ from (8.19). Hence the marginal distribution (8.19) gives rise to estimation of the parameters ψ and β_2 by a reduced rank regression. We find the regression estimate for ψ, see (8.19),

$$\hat{\psi}\,(\beta_2) = \bar{a}'_\perp S_{01}\beta_2 \left(\beta_2' S_{11}\beta_2\right)^{-1},$$

and then $\hat{\beta}_2\,(p \times (r-s))$ solves the eigenvalue problem

$$|\lambda S_{11} - S_{10}\bar{a}_\perp \left(\bar{a}'_\perp S_{00}\bar{a}_\perp\right)^{-1} \bar{a}'_\perp S_{01}| = 0.$$

Finally (8.20) gives a solution for β_1 by regressing $\bar{a}' R_{0t}$ on R_{1t} and $\bar{a}'_\perp R_{0t}$. We formulate the results in a theorem.

THEOREM 8.4 *Under hypothesis* $H_0 : \alpha = (a, a_\perp\psi)$ *the estimate of* β *is found as the eigenvectors corresponding to the largest* $r - s$ *solutions of the equations*

$$|\tilde{\lambda} S_{11} - S_{10}\bar{a}_\perp \left(\bar{a}'_\perp S_{00}\bar{a}_\perp\right)^{-1} \bar{a}'_\perp S_{01}| = 0.$$

The remaining parameters are found by regression from equation (8.19) and (8.20). The asymptotic distribution of the likelihood ratio test is χ^2 *with* $s(p-r)$ *degrees of freedom.*

8.3 The Duality between $\hat{\beta}$ and $\hat{\alpha}_\perp$

The two hypotheses considered above are both solved by an eigenvalue problem. The restriction $sp(\alpha) \subset sp(A)$ gives rise to conditioning on $A'_\perp R_{0t}$, whereas the assumption that $sp(\alpha)$ contains $sp(a)$ implies that one should transform by $\bar{a}'_\perp R_{0t}$. This is the opposite of the corresponding result for β, see section 7.2, and we add some remarks to explain this, thereby gaining some insight into the estimation procedure considered in (8.19) and (8.20).

The duality in the estimation of $\alpha_\perp$ and β is really a consequence of Lemma A.9 but we formulate it as a theorem:

THEOREM 8.5 *The estimator of the unrestricted β is found as the eigenvectors corresponding to the largest r eigenvalues of the problem*

$$|\lambda S_{11} - S_{10}S_{00}^{-1}S_{01}| = 0,$$

and the estimator of the unrestricted $\alpha_\perp$ is found as the eigenvectors corresponding to the $p - r$ smallest eigenvalues of the problem

$$|\lambda S_{00} - S_{01}S_{11}^{-1}S_{10}| = 0.$$

PROOF The statement about β is contained in Theorem 6.2. The dual problem, see Lemma A.9, is

$$|\lambda S_{00} - S_{01}S_{11}^{-1}S_{10}| = 0,$$

which has the same eigenvalues but eigenvectors $\hat{W}$ which can be chosen as $\hat{w}_i = \hat{\lambda}_i^{-\frac{1}{2}} S_{00}^{-1}S_{01}\hat{v}_i$, $i = 1, \ldots, p$. But for $i = 1, \ldots, r$, $\hat{\alpha}_i = S_{01}\hat{\beta}_i = S_{01}v_i$, such that $\hat{w}_i = \hat{\lambda}_i^{-\frac{1}{2}} S_{00}^{-1}\hat{\alpha}_i$, and

$$\hat{\alpha} = S_{00}\left(\hat{w}_1\hat{\lambda}_1^{\frac{1}{2}}, \ldots, \hat{w}_r\hat{\lambda}_r^{\frac{1}{2}}\right).$$

Note that the vectors $(\hat{w}_{r+1}, \ldots, \hat{w}_p)$ are orthogonal to $\hat{\alpha}$, since

$$\hat{w}'_j\hat{\alpha}_i = \hat{w}'_j S_{00}\hat{w}_i\hat{\lambda}_i^{\frac{1}{2}} = 0, \, i = 1, \ldots, r \text{ and } j = r+1, \ldots, p,$$

by the normalization of $\hat{W}$. Thus $\hat{\alpha}_\perp$ is directly estimated by $(\hat{w}_{r+1}, \ldots, \hat{w}_p)$. With this formulation one can see that the analysis of the hypothesis

$$sp(b) \subset sp(\beta) \subset sp(H),$$

which consists in conditioning on $b'R_{1t}$ and transforming by $H'R_{1t}$, is mathematically the same as the analysis of the hypothesis

$$sp\,(a) \subset sp\,(\alpha) \subset sp\,(A)\,,$$

since this can be formulated as

$$sp\,(A_\perp) \subset sp\,(\alpha_\perp) \subset sp\,(a_\perp)\,.$$

Now $\hat{\alpha}_\perp$ is found as the solution to an eigenvalue problem just as $\hat{\beta}$, hence in this dual problem one conditions on $A'_\perp R_{0t}$ and transforms by $\bar{a}'_\perp R_{0t}$ and hence solve

$$|\lambda \bar{a}'_\perp (S_{00.A_\perp} - S_{01.A_\perp} S_{11.A_\perp}^{-1} S_{10.A_\perp}) \bar{a}'_\perp| = 0,$$

which again shows that $\hat{\beta}$ should be found as eigenvectors of the dual problem

$$|\lambda S_{11.A_\perp} - S_{10.A_\perp} \bar{a}_\perp (\bar{a}'_\perp S_{00.A_\perp} \bar{a}_\perp)^{-1} \bar{a}'_\perp S_{01.A_\perp}| = 0.$$

$\square$

One can interpret β as determining the variables that are cointegrating whereas $\alpha_\perp$ determine the coefficients of the common trends. Thus the two concepts of cointegration and common trends that have been created as economic concepts, and defined precisely in the VAR model, are estimated in this dual manner, see also Gonzalo and Granger (1995).

It is now clear how in principle one should analyse the rather complicated model where both restrictions on α and β are imposed. One conditions the levels on the known cointegrating relations $(b' R_{1t})$ and conditions on the equations which are known to contain no cointegrating relations, i.e. $A'_\perp R_{0t}$. Similarly one transforms the levels to the linear combinations which are postulated as the only possible cointegrating relations $(H' R_{1t})$ and restricts attention to the equations that contain the cointegrating relation, i.e. transforms to $\bar{a}'_\perp R_{0t}$.

Finally one can get a different formulation by calculating the likelihood function concentrated to be a function of α alone. We go back to (6.9) and derive the two equations

$$\bar{\alpha}' R_{0t} = \beta' R_{1t} + \alpha' \hat{\epsilon}_t, \qquad (8.21)$$
$$\alpha'_\perp R_{0t} = \alpha'_\perp \hat{\epsilon}_t, \qquad (8.22)$$

and then condition (8.21) on (8.22) and get

$$\bar{\alpha}' R_{0t} = \beta' R_{1t} + \omega \alpha'_\perp R_{0t} + \bar{\alpha}' \hat{\epsilon}_t - \omega \alpha'_\perp \hat{\epsilon}_t, \qquad (8.23)$$

for $\omega = \Omega_{\alpha \alpha_\perp} \Omega_{\alpha_\perp \alpha_\perp}^{-1}$.

For fixed α the analysis of (8.22) and (8.23) is performed by regression leading to two contributions to the likelihood function. Equation (8.22) gives the contribution

$$L_{\max}^{-2/T}(\alpha) = |\alpha'_\perp S_{00}\alpha_\perp|/|\alpha'_\perp \alpha_\perp|$$

and equation (8.23) leads to a regression of $\bar{\alpha}' R_{0t}$ on R_{1t} and $\alpha'_\perp R_{0t}$ which gives the contribution

$$L_{\max}^{-2/T}(\alpha) = |\bar{\alpha}' S_{00.\alpha_\perp}\bar{\alpha} - \bar{\alpha}' S_{01.\alpha_\perp} S_{11.\alpha_\perp}^{-1} S_{10.\alpha_\perp}\bar{\alpha}|/|\bar{\alpha}'\bar{\alpha}|,$$

and β is, for fixed α, given by the regression estimate

$$\hat{\beta}(\alpha) = S_{11.\alpha_\perp}^{-1} S_{10.\alpha_\perp}\bar{\alpha}.$$

The maximized likelihood function is found from

$$L_{\max}^{-2/T}(\alpha) = |S_{\alpha_\perp\alpha_\perp}||S_{\alpha\alpha.1,\alpha_\perp}|/|\bar{\alpha}'\bar{\alpha}||\alpha'_\perp\alpha_\perp|.$$

From the identity

$$\begin{bmatrix} (\bar{\alpha},\alpha_\perp)' & 0 \\ 0 & I \end{bmatrix} \begin{bmatrix} S_{00} & S_{01} \\ S_{10} & S_{11} \end{bmatrix} \begin{bmatrix} (\bar{\alpha},\alpha_\perp) & 0 \\ 0 & I \end{bmatrix} = \begin{bmatrix} S_{\alpha\alpha} & S_{\alpha\alpha_\perp} & S_{\alpha1} \\ S_{\alpha_\perp\alpha} & S_{\alpha_\perp\alpha_\perp} & S_{\alpha_\perp1} \\ S_{1\alpha} & S_{1\alpha_\perp} & S_{11} \end{bmatrix}$$

it follows that

$$|\bar{\alpha}'\bar{\alpha}||\alpha'_\perp\alpha_\perp| \begin{vmatrix} S_{00} & S_{01} \\ S_{10} & S_{11} \end{vmatrix} = |S_{11}||S_{\alpha_\perp\alpha_\perp.1}||S_{\alpha\alpha.1,\alpha_\perp}|.$$

Hence

$$L_{\max}^{-2/T}(\alpha) = |S_{00.1}||\alpha'_\perp S_{00}\alpha_\perp|/|\alpha'_\perp \left(S_{00} - S_{01}S_{11}^{-1}S_{10}\right)\alpha_\perp|.$$

Thus L is maximized by maximizing

$$|\alpha'_\perp \left(S_{00} - S_{01}S_{11}^{-1}S_{10}\right)\alpha_\perp|/|\alpha'_\perp S_{00}\alpha_\perp|,$$

i.e. by choosing $\alpha_\perp$ to be the eigenvectors corresponding to the $p-r$ smallest eigenvalues of

$$|\lambda S_{00} - S_{01}S_{11}^{-1}S_{10}| = 0.$$

This explains explicitly why $\hat{\alpha}_\perp$ is found as the solution to an eigenvalue problem.

8.4 Exercises

8.1

Consider the model

$$\Delta X_{1t} = \alpha_1 \left(X_{1t-1} - X_{2t-1} \right) + \epsilon_{1t},$$

$$\Delta X_{2t} = \alpha_2 \left(X_{1t-1} - X_{2t-1} \right) + \epsilon_{2t},$$

where ϵ_t, $t = 1, \ldots, T$ are i.i.d. $N_2 \left(0, \Omega \right)$. Find the maximum likelihood estimator of α_1 and α_2 and derive the likelihood ratio test of the hypothesis $\alpha_1 = \alpha_2$. Discuss the properties of the process X_t when $\alpha_1 = \alpha_2$, and when $\alpha_1 \neq \alpha_2$.

9

The $I(2)$ Model and a Test for $I(2)$

WE consider again equation (4.1) with deterministic term D_t

$$\Delta X_t = \Pi X_{t-1} + \sum_{i=1}^{k-1} \Gamma_i \Delta X_{t-i} + \Phi D_t + \epsilon_t. \tag{9.1}$$

The $I(2)$ model is defined by two reduced rank conditions, see (4.4) and (4.5), and it is therefore convenient to reparametrize the model such that the matrices involved in the reduced rank conditions are displayed directly. We rewrite (9.1) as

$$\Delta^2 X_t = \Pi X_{t-1} - \Gamma \Delta X_{t-1} + \sum_{i=1}^{k-2} \Psi_i \Delta^2 X_{t-i} + \Phi D_t + \epsilon_t, \tag{9.2}$$

where $\Gamma = I - \sum_{i=1}^{k-1} \Gamma_i$, as before and $\Psi_i = -\sum_{j=i+1}^{k-1} \Gamma_i, i = 1, \ldots, k-2$.

In this chapter we define in section 9.1 the $I(2)$ model as a submodel of the general VAR and discuss various modifications of the model by restricting the deterministic terms. In section 9.2 we derive a misspecification test for the presence of $I(2)$ components, in order to check the validity of the $I(1)$ model and in section 9.3 we analyse the Australian data in order to see if the data indicates the presence of an $I(2)$ component.

The statistical theory of the $I(2)$ model is much less developed than the theory for the $I(1)$ model, and we do not attempt to give a genuine statistical analysis of the $I(2)$ model here. The discussion given is only sufficient for an introduction to the problems. We refer to Johansen (1992c, d) for illustrative examples and to Juselius (1992), (1995) for applications of the $I(2)$ analysis.

9.1   A Statistical Model for $I(2)$

The $I(2)$ model $H_{r,s}$ is defined as the submodel of the VAR (9.2). We shall not analyse the model in detail, since the theory is quite involved. Instead we shall give a simple two step procedure for estimating the model and deriving test statistics for the presence of $I(2)$ components in the data.

DEFINITION 9.1 *For* $s = 0, 1, \ldots, p-r$, $r = 0, 1, \ldots, p-1$ *the* $I(2)$ *models* H_{rs} *are defined as submodels of the* VAR *by the two reduced rank conditions*

$$\Pi = \alpha\beta, \qquad (9.3)$$

where α *and* β *are* $p \times r$ *matrices of full rank with* $r < p$, *and*

$$\alpha'_\perp \Gamma \beta_\perp = \xi\eta', \qquad (9.4)$$

where ξ *and* η *are* $(p - r) \times s$ *matrices, with* $s \leq p - r$.

Thus the model is defined by two reduced rank conditions but the remaining parameters vary freely, that is, the parameter space is described by the parameters

$$(\alpha, \beta, \Psi_1, \ldots, \Psi_{k-2}, \Phi, \Omega),$$

where the only restriction is (9.4). It is convenient to have a notation for the submodels H_r^0 of $H(r)$ defined by α and β having full rank r. Similarly we define $H_{r,s}^0$ as the submodel of $H_{r,s}$, where also ξ and η have full rank. In Table 9.1 it is shown how the $I(1)$ and $I(2)$ models are nested.

Many other models can be defined by specializing the variable D_t. In particular if $\Phi D_t = \mu$, it is seen from (4.28) that μ gives rise to a quadratic trend with a coefficient $\frac{1}{2}C_2\mu$. Thus a submodel of $H_{r,s}$ can be defined by the restriction $\alpha'_2\mu = 0$, which corresponds to assuming that there is no quadratic trend in the process. Similarly a further submodel is obtained by assuming that $\alpha'_1\mu = 0$ too. We shall use the notation $H_{r,s}^*$ for the submodel of $H_{r,s}$ with $\Phi D_t = \mu$ and $\alpha'_2\mu = 0$, such that no quadratic trend is present. The likelihood analysis of these models is given in Johansen (1995a, 1996) and Paruolo (1995b, 1996). The likelihood analysis is not easy in the sense that there are no simple algorithms for the calculation of the maximum likelihood estimator, and we do not have any information about uniqueness and existence, see, however, Johansen (1996) for an algorithm. The asymptotic distributions are derived in the above references and they are more complicated than those that are valid for the $I(1)$ analysis.

The next section contains a simple analysis of the likelihood function that leads to manageable calculations consisting of repeated applications of reduced rank regression and a test for the presence of $I(2)$ components, that can be analysed using the tables given in Chapter 15.

TABLE 9.1 The relation between the $I(2)$ models and the $I(1)$ models for $p = 3$

r	The $I(2)$ models					The $I(1)$ models		
0	$H_{0,0}$	$\subset$ $H_{0,1}$	$\subset$ $H_{0,2}$	$\subset$ $H_{0,3}$	$=$	H_0^0	$\subset$	$H(0)$
1		$H_{1,0}$	$\subset$ $H_{1,1}$	$\subset$ $H_{1,2}$	$=$	H_1^0	$\subset$	$H(1)$
2			$H_{2,0}$	$\subset$ $H_{2,1}$	$=$	H_2	$\subset$	$H(2)$

9.2   A Misspecification Test for the Presence of $I(2)$

In (9.2) only Π and Γ enter the reduced rank conditions and the remaining parameters $\Psi = (\Psi_1, \ldots, \Psi_{k-2}, \Phi)$ are unrestricted. It is therefore convenient to introduce the short-hand notation

$$Z_t' = (\Delta^2 X_{t-1}', \ldots, \Delta^2 X_{t-k+2}', D_t'),$$

such that the equations are written as

$$\Delta^2 X_t = \Pi X_{t-1} - \Gamma \Delta X_{t-1} + \Psi Z_t + \epsilon_t. \tag{9.5}$$

Let us now assume that we have performed an $I(1)$ analysis which in view of (9.5) is a reduced rank analysis of $\Delta^2 X_t$ on X_{t-1} corrected for lagged differences and second differences and the dummies as collected in Z_t. We want to guard ourselves against the presence of $I(2)$ components which will invalidate the conclusions from the $I(1)$ analysis.

Before performing the $I(1)$ analysis we have calculated the roots of the characteristic polynomial, and noted that some of them are close to $z = 1$. We can also calculate the roots using the coefficients estimated under the $I(1)$ model, that is, after having imposed $p - r$ unit roots. It may turn out that there are still roots close to $z = 1$. This can now have two explanations, the first is that we have not imposed enough unit roots and have determined the rank incorrectly. The rank determination tests should have taken care of this possibility. The other possibility is that there are $I(2)$ components in the system, since we know, see Corollary 4.5, that for an $I(1)$ process the number of unit roots plus the cointegrating rank should be the dimension.

Since it is difficult to assess the uncertainty of the roots of the characteristic polynomial we propose here a test derived from the likelihood function.

The test is based upon an analysis of the $I(2)$ model as defined in section 9.1, in particular the reduced rank condition (9.4) under the assumption that (α, β, r) are known.

If (α, β, r) are known we can reformulate model (9.5) by multiplying by $(\bar{\alpha}, \alpha_\perp)'$ and we find the equations

$$\alpha_\perp' \Delta^2 X_t = -\alpha_\perp' \Gamma \Delta X_{t-1} + \alpha_\perp' \Psi Z_t + \alpha_\perp' \epsilon_t, \tag{9.6}$$

$$\bar{\alpha}' \Delta^2 X_t = \beta' X_{t-1} - \bar{\alpha}' \Gamma \Delta X_{t-1} + \bar{\alpha}' \Psi Z_t + \bar{\alpha}' \epsilon_t. \tag{9.7}$$

Next define $\Omega_{\alpha\alpha} = \bar{\alpha}' \Omega \bar{\alpha}$, $\Omega_{\alpha\alpha_\perp} = \bar{\alpha}' \Omega \alpha_\perp$, $\Omega_{\alpha_\perp \alpha_\perp} = \alpha_\perp' \Omega \alpha_\perp$, $\Omega_{\alpha\alpha.\alpha_\perp} = \Omega_{\alpha\alpha} - \Omega_{\alpha\alpha_\perp} \Omega_{\alpha_\perp \alpha_\perp}^{-1} \Omega_{\alpha_\perp \alpha}$, and $\omega = \Omega_{\alpha\alpha_\perp} \Omega_{\alpha_\perp \alpha_\perp}^{-1}$ and subtract ω times (9.6) from (9.7) to obtain

$$\bar{\alpha}' \Delta^2 X_t = \omega \alpha_\perp' \Delta^2 X_t + \beta' X_{t-1} - (\bar{\alpha}' - \omega \alpha_\perp') \Gamma \Delta X_{t-1}$$

$$+ (\bar{\alpha}' - \omega \alpha_\perp') \Psi Z_t + (\bar{\alpha}' - \omega \alpha_\perp') \epsilon_t.$$

The equations (9.6) and (9.2) have independent error terms and parameters $(\alpha'_\perp \Gamma, \alpha'_\perp \Psi, \Omega_{\alpha_\perp \alpha_\perp})$ and $(\omega, (\bar{\alpha}' - \omega \alpha'_\perp)\Gamma, (\bar{\alpha}' - \omega \alpha'_\perp)\Psi, \Omega_{\alpha \alpha . \alpha_\perp})$ respectively, and it is seen that the two sets of parameters are variation free, in the sense that for any value of the respective sets of parameters one can reconstruct the original parameters $(\Gamma, \Psi_1, \ldots, \Psi_{k-2}, \Phi, \Omega)$ still for known values of α, β, and r. Thus the equations can be analysed independently as long as no cross-equation restrictions are imposed. It is furthermore seen that the reduced rank condition (9.4) is a restriction of the parameters for (9.6) only, and that the maximum likelihood estimator of equation (9.2) is found by a regression analysis of $\bar{\alpha}' \Delta^2 X_t - \beta' X_{t-1}$ on $\alpha'_\perp \Delta^2 X_t$, ΔX_{t-1}, and Z_t.

In order to analyse (9.6) we introduce the new variables $\beta' \Delta X_{t-1}$ and $\bar{\beta}'_\perp \Delta X_{t-1}$ through the usual trick of writing $I = \bar{\beta}\beta' + \beta_\perp \bar{\beta}'_\perp$, such that

$$\alpha'_\perp \Delta^2 X_t = -\alpha'_\perp \Gamma \bar{\beta}\beta' \Delta X_{t-1} - \alpha'_\perp \Gamma \beta_\perp \bar{\beta}'_\perp \Delta X_{t-1} + \alpha'_\perp \Psi Z_t + \alpha'_\perp \epsilon_t.$$

From (9.4) it follows that

$$\alpha'_\perp \Delta^2 X_t = -\alpha'_\perp \Gamma \bar{\beta}\beta' \Delta X_{t-1} - \xi \eta' \bar{\beta}'_\perp \Delta X_{t-1} + \alpha'_\perp \Psi Z_t + \alpha'_\perp \epsilon_t. \quad (9.8)$$

Equation (9.8) is an equation for the differences of the process which explicitly contains the parameters ξ and η. This shows that the likelihood analysis of (9.6) or (9.8) can be performed by reduced rank regression of $\alpha'_\perp \Delta^2 X_t$ on $\bar{\beta}'_\perp \Delta X_{t-1}$ corrected for $\beta' \Delta X_{t-1}$ and lagged second differences and dummies as collected in Z_t.

What is achieved here by the analysis of (9.8) and (9.7) is to derive an equation in differences (9.8) using the information in the levels matrix $\Pi = \alpha\beta'$. Thus model $H_{r,s}$ is analysed by reduced rank regression if (α, β, r) were known.

The likelihood ratio test $Q_{r,s} = -2 \log Q(H_{r,s}|H_r^0)$ of $H_{r,s}$ in H_r^0 (or $H(r)$) is found by analysing (9.8) for the value s as well as for the value $s = p - r$ and comparing the achieved values of the maximum. Note that the contribution from equation (9.2) is the same for the analysis of $H_{r,s}$ as for the analysis of $H_{r,p-r} = H_r^0$, since the parameters in the two equations are variation free. Hence the contribution from (9.2) to the maximized likelihood function cancels when calculating the likelihood ratio statistic.

This shows that the likelihood ratio test has the form (6.18) where the coefficients λ_i are calculated from an eigenvalue problem like (6.15) where S_{11} equals the product moments of $\bar{\beta}'_\perp \Delta X_{t-1}$, S_{00} equals the product moments of $\alpha'_\perp \Delta^2 X_t$, and S_{01} the mixed moments all corrected for $\beta' \Delta X_{t-1}$ and lagged second differences and dummies.

Notice that this analysis can easily be modified if we want to restrict the constant term in the analysis of the differences, thereby ruling out the possibility of a quadratic trend. The modification is described in Chapter 6, section 6.2.

Thus for instance if $\Phi D_t = \mu$, the analysis of (9.8) will involve correcting for the constant term. If we want to restrict this we assume that $\xi'_\perp \alpha'_\perp \mu = 0$ and perform a reduced rank regression of $\alpha'_\perp \Delta^2 X_t$ on the stacked variable $(\Delta X'_{t-1} \bar{\beta}_\perp, 1)$ corrected for lagged second differences, see (6.29).

We now give a misspecification test for the presence of $I(2)$ variables in the system. We give it in the case where we are willing to assume that there is a trend in the system but no quadratic trend. Thus the analysis, which is illustrated in the next section, runs as follows: first we perform an $I(1)$ analysis as described in Chapter 7 and determine $(\hat{\alpha}, \hat{\beta}, \hat{r})$ using the test statistics $Q_r = -2\log Q(H(r)|H(p))$. Next we analyse equation (9.8) using $(\alpha, \beta, r) = (\hat{\alpha}, \hat{\beta}, \hat{r})$ but this time with a restricted constant in order to avoid the presence of a quadratic trend. This gives the test statistics $Q^*_{r,s} = -2\log Q(H^*_{r,s}|H^0_r)$, $s = 0, \ldots, p - r - 1$.

THEOREM 9.2 *Consider model (9.2) with $\Phi D_t = \mu$. Let Q_r denote the likelihood ratio test (6.18) of $H(r)$ in $H(p)$, and let $c_{p-r}(\delta)$ denote the $1 - \delta$ quantiles as derived from (6.20) with F given by (6.21).*

Let $Q^*_{r,s}$ denote the likelihood ratio test statistic of $H^*_{r,s}$ in H^0_r of the form (6.18) calculated with the estimated values of (α, β, r) from the $I(1)$ analysis, and let $c^*_{p-r-s}(\delta)$ denote the quantiles as derived from (6.20) with F given by (6.32).

We choose to accept r cointegrating relations and no $I(2)$ components on the set A_r defined by

$$Q_i \geq c_{p-i}(\delta), \, i = 0, \ldots, r-1, \quad Q_r < c_{p-r}(\delta),$$

$$Q^*_{r,i} \geq c^*_{p-r-i}(\delta), \, i = 0, \ldots, p-r-1.$$

This procedure has the properties

$$\lim_{T\to\infty} P(A_r) = 1 - \delta \text{ if } H^0_{r,p-r} \text{ holds} \qquad (9.9)$$

and

$$\lim_{T\to\infty} P(A_r) = 0 \text{ if } H(p) \backslash H(r) \text{ holds} \qquad (9.10)$$

and

$$\lim_{T\to\infty} P(A_r) \leq \delta \text{ if } H^*_{r,s} \text{ holds for } s = 0, \ldots, p-r-1. \qquad (9.11)$$

Thus if the rank of Π is r and there are no $I(2)$ components the procedure picks out the true value of r with a high probability $(1 - \delta)$ in the limit. It picks out a too low value with limiting probability zero. Finally if there are $I(2)$ components the procedure will under $H^*_{r,s}$ accept no $I(2)$ components with a small probability. A discussion of the proof of this result will be given in Chapter 12.

9.3 A Test for $I(2)$ in the Australian Data

The $I(1)$ analysis from Chapter 7 gives the estimated values of (α, β, r). The transformed equations leading to (9.8) can then be solved and we do this for each value of $r = 0, 1, \ldots, 5$. The likelihood ratio test statistics are calculated as in (6.30).

Note that we choose in the initial $I(1)$ analysis to have the constant unrestricted, but prefer to restrict it in the second analysis in order to avoid the possibility of a quadratic trend. The test statistics are given in Table 9.2.

Based upon the $I(1)$ analysis from Chapter 7 we have chosen $r = 2$ and we then proceed by comparing $Q_{2,s}^*$, $s = 0, 1, 2$ with the quantiles $c_{p-r-s}^*(5\%)$ from Table 15.2. It is seen that there seems to be evidence of $I(2)$ in the data, since $s = 0$ is rejected, as is $s = 1$, but the hypothesis that $s = 2$ gives a test statistic of $-2\log Q(H_{2,2}^*|H_2^0) = 4.21$ which should be compared with the (asymptotic) 95 per cent quantile of 9.09.

The evidence for $I(2)$ that we find is the following: the test statistics seem to indicate that $s = 2$, and the plot of Δp_t^{us} in Fig 2.4 suggests that the inflation rate is non-stationary and drifts like a random walk. There is of course the possibility that the shift in inflation rate after 1980 is better described as a deterministic shift. But for now we shall continue with the idea that the shift is random and indicates a persistent shift corresponding to the $I(1)$ nature of the inflation rate.

It is noteworthy that the graph of $\hat{\beta}'X_t$ looks more non-stationary than the graph of $\hat{\beta}'R_{1t}$ see Fig. 7.2. This is also evidence of $I(2)$ since the result of Theorem 4.6 shows that $\beta'X_t$ corrected for ΔX_t is stationary even if X_t is $I(2)$, whereas $\beta'X_t$ is not in general stationary by itself.

The final piece of evidence is that when calculating the roots of the characteristic polynomial for the estimated values we see from Table 9.3 that apart from the three imposed unit roots there is a root close to one with the value 0.83. If this corresponds to a unit root we seem to have a case where the number of unit roots cannot be calculated from the Π matrix alone.

TABLE 9.2 The likelihood ratio statistics $Q_{r,s}^*$ and Q_r together with the critical values $c_{p-r}(5\%)$ and $c_{p-r-s}^*(5\%)$.

r	$Q_{r,s}^*$					Q_r	c_{p-r}
$p-r-s$	5	4	3	2	1		
0	261.50	157.44	95.96	45.86	10.91	101.38	68.91
1		178.48	84.48	32.61	9.18	51.78	47.18
2			82.26	28.10	4.21	28.43	29.51
3				28.82	10.04	10.24	15.20
4					8.84	4.45	3.96
c_{p-r-s}^*	75.33	53.35	35.07	20.17	9.09		

TABLE 9.3 The eigenvalues of the companion matrix for the Australian data. The cointegrating rank is $r = 2$ and β is unrestricted and α restricted as in Table 7.7.

Root	Real	Complex	Modulus
ρ_1	1.00	0.00	1.00
ρ_2	1.00	0.00	1.00
ρ_3	1.00	0.00	1.00
ρ_4	0.83	0.00	0.83
ρ_5	0.72	0.06	0.72
ρ_6	0.72	−0.06	0.72
ρ_7	0.11	0.00	0.11
ρ_8	−0.02	−0.21	0.21
ρ_9	−0.02	0.21	0.21
ρ_{10}	−0.29	0.00	0.29

Taken by themselves these pieces of evidence are perhaps not very convincing, but taken together they seem to point towards the conclusion that there is $I(2)$ in the data.

The question then arises to what extent this invalidates the $I(1)$ analysis and the conclusions reached.

It is somewhat surprising that hypothesis tests on α and β remain valid in the sense that inference is still asymptotically χ^2. What is no longer valid is the interpretation of these hypotheses, since $\beta' X_t$ is no longer stationary, and $\alpha_2 = 0$ is no longer a hypothesis about weak exogeneity.

Thus there is a need for the analysis of the data from the point of view of $I(2)$.

Part II

The Probability Analysis of Cointegration

10

Probability Properties of $I(1)$ Processes

IN this chapter we discuss basic properties of $I(1)$ processes given by the autoregressive model (4.1) allowing for a constant term, that is, $\Phi D_t = \mu$. The process is by (4.6) given as a mixture of a trend, a random walk, and a stationary process:

$$X_t = C \sum_{i=1}^{t} \epsilon_i + C\mu t + C_1(L)(\epsilon_t + \mu) + P_{\beta_\perp} X_0, \qquad (10.1)$$

where $C = \beta_\perp(\alpha'_\perp \Gamma \beta_\perp)^{-1}\alpha'_\perp$. We discuss the behaviour of the process in different directions, and apply these results to find asymptotic properties of various product moment matrices needed to derive properties of likelihood ratio tests and estimators in Chapters 11 and 13.

All estimators and test statistics are derived under the assumption of Gaussian errors, but we prove limit results for the process under the slightly more general assumption that the errors are independent with the same distribution with mean zero and variance Ω, such that ΔX_t becomes a linear process.

First, however, we discuss some useful identities between variances and covariances of the various stationary processes. The results are taken from Johansen (1991b).

10.1 Finite Sample Results

There are very few exact results in the theory of autoregressive processes. The main ones that we use here are relations between the second order moments conditional on the past values of the process. Under the assumptions of $I(1)$ and cointegration we have that $\beta'X_t$ is stationary and that ΔX_t is stationary, see Theorem 4.2. We define

$$\text{Var}\left[\begin{array}{c} \Delta X_t \\ \beta'X_{t-1} \end{array} \mid \Delta X_{t-1}, \ldots, \Delta X_{t-k+1}\right] = \left[\begin{array}{cc} \Sigma_{00} & \Sigma_{0\beta} \\ \Sigma_{\beta 0} & \Sigma_{\beta\beta} \end{array}\right],$$

and the first result concerns relations between these variance-covariance matrices and the parameters α and β in model $H_1(r)$.

LEMMA 10.1 *Under the $I(1)$ assumptions and the assumption of i.i.d. errors the following relations hold*

$$\Sigma_{00} = \alpha\Sigma_{\beta 0} + \Omega, \qquad (10.2)$$

$$\Sigma_{0\beta} = \alpha\Sigma_{\beta\beta}, \qquad (10.3)$$

and hence

$$\Sigma_{00} = \alpha\Sigma_{\beta\beta}\alpha' + \Omega \qquad (10.4)$$

These relations imply that

$$(\alpha'\Sigma_{00}^{-1}\alpha)^{-1}\alpha'\Sigma_{00}^{-1} = (\alpha'\Omega^{-1}\alpha)^{-1}\alpha'\Omega^{-1}, \qquad (10.5)$$

$$\Sigma_{00}^{-1} - \Sigma_{00}^{-1}\alpha\left(\alpha'\Sigma_{00}^{-1}\alpha\right)^{-1}\alpha'\Sigma_{00}^{-1} = \alpha_\perp\left(\alpha'_\perp\Sigma_{00}\alpha_\perp\right)^{-1}\alpha'_\perp$$

$$= \Omega^{-1} - \Omega^{-1}\alpha\left(\alpha'\Omega^{-1}\alpha\right)^{-1}\alpha'\Omega^{-1} = \alpha_\perp\left(\alpha'_\perp\Omega\alpha_\perp\right)^{-1}\alpha'_\perp \qquad (10.6)$$

$$\Sigma_{\beta\beta}\left(\Sigma_{\beta 0}\Sigma_{00}^{-1}\Sigma_{0\beta}\right)^{-1}\Sigma_{\beta\beta} - \Sigma_{\beta\beta} = \left(\alpha'\Omega^{-1}\alpha\right)^{-1} \qquad (10.7)$$

$$\alpha'\Sigma_{00}^{-1}\alpha = (\Sigma_{\beta\beta} + \left(\alpha'\Omega^{-1}\alpha\right)^{-1})^{-1} \qquad (10.8)$$

$$\Sigma_{\beta\beta}^{-1} - \left(\Sigma_{\beta\beta} - \Sigma_{\beta 0}\Sigma_{00}^{-1}\Sigma_{0\beta}\right)^{-1} = -\alpha'\Omega^{-1}\alpha. \qquad (10.9)$$

PROOF From the model equation

$$\Delta X_t = \alpha\beta'X_{t-1} + \sum_{i=1}^{k-1}\Gamma_i\Delta X_{t-i} + \mu + \epsilon_t,$$

one finds immediately the results (10.2), (10.3), and (10.4) by calculating the conditional variances given lagged differences $\Delta X_{t-1}, \ldots, \Delta X_{t-k+1}$. To prove (10.5) multiply first by α from the right, and both sides become the identity, then multiply by $\Sigma_{00}\alpha_\perp = \Omega\alpha_\perp$, see (10.4), and both sides reduce to zero. Since the $p \times p$ matrix $(\alpha, \Omega\alpha_\perp)$ has full rank the relation (10.5) has been proved.

The relation (10.6) is proved by applying the identity $\alpha'_\perp\Sigma_{00} = \alpha'_\perp\Omega$, see (10.4), and by multiplying by the matrix $(\alpha, \Sigma_{00}\alpha_\perp) = (\alpha, \Omega\alpha_\perp)$.

The relation (10.7) is proved by inserting $\alpha = \Sigma_{0\beta}\Sigma_{\beta\beta}^{-1}$ such that (10.7) becomes

$$\left(\alpha'\Sigma_{00}^{-1}\alpha\right)^{-1} - \Sigma_{\beta\beta} = \left(\alpha'\Omega^{-1}\alpha\right)^{-1}.$$

This relation can be proved by multiplying (10.5) by

$$\Sigma_{00}\alpha\left(\alpha'\alpha\right)^{-1} = \left(\alpha\Sigma_{\beta\beta}\alpha' + \Omega\right)\alpha\left(\alpha'\alpha\right)^{-1}.$$

The proof of (10.8) follows by noting that the $p \times p$ matrix $K = \left(\Omega^{-1}\alpha, \alpha_\perp\right)$ has full rank, such that we can write, see (10.4),

$$\alpha' \Sigma_{00}^{-1} \alpha = \alpha' \left(\Omega + \alpha \Sigma_{\beta\beta} \alpha' \right)^{-1} \alpha = \alpha' K (K'(\Omega + \alpha \Sigma_{\beta\beta} \alpha')K)^{-1} K' \alpha$$

$$= \begin{bmatrix} \alpha' \Omega^{-1} \alpha \\ 0 \end{bmatrix}' \begin{bmatrix} \alpha' \Omega^{-1} \alpha + \alpha' \Omega^{-1} \alpha \Sigma_{\beta\beta} \alpha' \Omega^{-1} \alpha & 0 \\ 0 & \alpha'_{\perp} \Omega \alpha_{\perp} \end{bmatrix}^{-1} \begin{bmatrix} \alpha' \Omega^{-1} \alpha \\ 0 \end{bmatrix}$$

$$= (\Sigma_{\beta\beta} + (\alpha' \Omega^{-1} \alpha)^{-1})^{-1}.$$

Finally (10.9) is proved as follows: first note that

$$\Sigma_{\beta\beta} - \Sigma_{\beta\beta} (\Sigma_{\beta\beta} + (\alpha' \Omega^{-1} \alpha)^{-1})^{-1} \Sigma_{\beta\beta}$$

$$= \Sigma_{\beta\beta} (\Sigma_{\beta\beta} + (\alpha' \Omega^{-1} \alpha)^{-1})^{-1} (\Sigma_{\beta\beta} + (\alpha' \Omega^{-1} \alpha)^{-1} - \Sigma_{\beta\beta})$$

$$= \Sigma_{\beta\beta} (\Sigma_{\beta\beta} + (\alpha' \Omega^{-1} \alpha)^{-1})^{-1} (\alpha' \Omega^{-1} \alpha)^{-1}.$$

Then we find

$$\Sigma_{\beta\beta}^{-1} - (\Sigma_{\beta\beta} - \Sigma_{\beta\beta} (\Sigma_{\beta\beta} + (\alpha' \Omega^{-1} \alpha)^{-1})^{-1} \Sigma_{\beta\beta})^{-1}$$

$$= \Sigma_{\beta\beta}^{-1} - (\alpha' \Omega^{-1} \alpha) (\Sigma_{\beta\beta} + (\alpha' \Omega^{-1} \alpha)^{-1}) \Sigma_{\beta\beta}^{-1} = - (\alpha' \Omega^{-1} \alpha).$$

This completes the proof of Lemma 9.1. □

10.2 Asymptotic Results

The process generated by the autoregressive equations has the property that ΔX_t is a linear process, see Chapter 2. We have given in Theorem B.13 some basic limit results for such processes, and here we apply them to the process X_t. The asymptotic properties of the non-stationary process X_t are described by a Brownian motion W in p dimensions on the unit interval. This Brownian motion is the weak limit of the random walk $\sum_{i=1}^{t} \epsilon_i$, which appears in the representation (10.1) and can be found by rescaling the time axis and the variables as follows:

$$S_T(u) = T^{-\frac{1}{2}} \sum_{i=1}^{[Tu]} \epsilon_i \xrightarrow{w} W(u), u \in [0, 1].$$

We apply the results in Theorem B.13 in order to find the asymptotic properties of the test statistics and estimators derived from the cointegration model. We have only given the results in Appendix B for $C[0, 1]$ but here we apply the results for $D[0, 1]$, since the normalization above leaves $S_T(u)$ a piecewise constant function rather than a continuous function.

From the representation (10.1) it follows that X_t is composed of a random walk $(C \sum_{i=1}^{t} \epsilon_i)$, a linear trend $(\tau t = C \mu t)$, a stationary process which is a linear process with exponentially decreasing coefficients and the initial values $P_{\beta_\perp} X_t$. The asymptotic properties of the process therefore depend on which linear combination of the process we consider. If we consider $\tau' X_t$ it is clear that the process is dominated by the linear trend, whereas if we take vectors γ which are orthogonal to τ and linearly independent of β then the dominating term is the random walk $\gamma' C \Sigma_{i=1}^t \epsilon_i$ since $\gamma' \tau t = 0$. Finally if we take the linear combinations $\beta' X_t$ then both the trend and the random walk are multiplied by $\beta' C = 0$, and $\beta' X_t$ is stationary since the initial values cancel. Thus let $\gamma \, (p \times (p - r - 1))$ be chosen orthogonal to τ and β, such that (β, γ, τ) span all of R^p. We give some examples which illustrate the choice of τ and γ.

EXAMPLE 10.1 We consider the two-dimensional process given by the equations

$$\Delta X_{1t} = \mu_1 + \epsilon_{1t},$$

$$\Delta X_{2t} = \mu_2 + \epsilon_{2t}.$$

The equations are solved to give

$$X_{1t} = \sum_{i=1}^t \epsilon_{1i} + t\mu_1 + X_{10},$$

$$X_{2t} = \sum_{i=1}^t \epsilon_{2i} + t\mu_2 + X_{20}.$$

Thus both processes are random walks with a trend, and the processes do not cointegrate. It is, however, easily seen that the linear combination

$$\mu_2 X_{1t} - \mu_1 X_{2t} = \mu_2 \sum_{i=1}^t \epsilon_{1i} - \mu_1 \sum_{i=1}^t \epsilon_{2i} + \mu_2 X_{10} - \mu_1 X_{10},$$

is a random walk with no trend. Thus the trend can be eliminated by multiplying by $\tau_\perp = (\mu_2, -\mu_1)'$. In this case there is no cointegration and we can take $\beta = 0$ and $\gamma = \tau_\perp$.

EXAMPLE 10.2 We next consider the three-dimensional process given by the equations

$$\Delta X_{1t} = \alpha_1 \left(X_{1t-1} - X_{2t-1} \right) + \mu_1 + \epsilon_{1t},$$

$$\Delta X_{2t} = \mu_2 + \epsilon_{2t},$$

$$\Delta X_{3t} = \mu_3 + \epsilon_{3t},$$

where $-2 < \alpha_1 < 0$. These equations are solved to give

$$X_{1t} = \sum_{i=1}^t \epsilon_{2i} + \mu_2 t + X_{20} + \sum_{i=0}^\infty (1 + \alpha_1)^i \left(\epsilon_{1t-i} - \epsilon_{2t-i} \right) - \alpha_1^{-1} \left(\mu_1 - \mu_2 \right).$$

It is seen that X_{1t}, X_{2t}, and X_{3t} have a linear trend, which in this case is eliminated by the cointegrating vector $\beta = (1, -1, 0)'$. This is an instance of a general result that $\beta'C = 0$, which annihilates both the stochastic and the deterministic trends. We find that $\tau = (\mu_2, \mu_2, \mu_3)'$ and $\gamma = (\mu_3, \mu_3, -2\mu_2)'$ which together with β span the whole space.

We next give the asymptotic behaviour of the process in the directions τ and γ. Recall the definition $\bar{\gamma} = \gamma(\gamma'\gamma)^{-1}$.

LEMMA 10.2 *Let the process X_t be given by (10.1), let $\tau = C\mu$ and choose γ orthogonal to β and τ such that (β, τ, γ) has full rank p. Then as $T \to \infty$ and $u \in [0, 1]$*

$$T^{-\frac{1}{2}}\bar{\gamma}'X_{[Tu]} \xrightarrow{w} \bar{\gamma}'CW(u), \qquad (10.10)$$

$$T^{-1}\bar{\tau}'X_{[Tu]} \xrightarrow{w} u. \qquad (10.11)$$

We define the normalization matrix $B_T = (\bar{\gamma}, T^{-\frac{1}{2}}\bar{\tau})$ and combine the results into

$$T^{-\frac{1}{2}}B_T'X_{[Tu]} \xrightarrow{w} G_0(u) = \begin{bmatrix} \bar{\gamma}'CW(u) \\ u \end{bmatrix}.$$

It then follows for $\bar{X}_T = T^{-1}\sum_{t=1}^{T} X_{t-1}$ that

$$T^{-\frac{1}{2}}B_T'\left(X_{[Tu]} - \bar{X}_T\right) \xrightarrow{w} G_0(u) - \bar{G}_0 = G(u) = \begin{bmatrix} \bar{\gamma}'C(W(u) - \bar{W}) \\ u - \frac{1}{2} \end{bmatrix}, \qquad (10.12)$$

where $\bar{G}_0 = \int_0^1 G_0(u)du$.

PROOF We apply Theorem B.13. From the representation (10.1) we see that X_t is decomposed into a random walk, a linear trend, and a stationary process. Weak convergence of $T^{-\frac{1}{2}}\bar{\gamma}'X_{[Tu]}$ now follows from (10.1). The random walk term gives $\bar{\gamma}'CW(u)$ in the limit, the trend term vanishes since $\gamma'\tau = 0$, and the stationary term disappears by (B.17).

Weak convergence of $T^{-1}\bar{\tau}'X_{[Tu]}$ follows from (10.1). The random walk part tends to zero by the factor T^{-1}, the linear term converges to u, and the stationary part vanishes by (B.17).

Finally weak convergence of the average

$$T^{-\frac{1}{2}}B_T'\bar{X}_T = T^{-1}\sum_{t=1}^{T} T^{-\frac{1}{2}}B_T'X_{t-1}$$

follows from the continuous mapping theorem, Theorem B.5, since the mapping $x \to \int_0^1 x(u)\,du$ is continuous. $\qquad \square$

Note that the limiting behaviour of the non-stationary part of the process is completely described by the matrix C, see (10.1), the direction $\tau = C\mu$, and the variance matrix of the errors Ω.

Using these results one can describe asymptotic properties of the product moment matrices and S_{ij} defined in Chapter 6, which are basic for the properties of the estimators and tests. Recall that the residuals R_{0t} and R_{1t} are defined by regressing ΔX_t and X_{t-1} respectively on lagged differences and a constant, and that

$$S_{ij} = T^{-1} \sum_{t=1}^{T} R_{it} R'_{jt}, \ i, j = 0, 1.$$

LEMMA 10.3 *Under the assumptions of Lemma 10.2*

$$S_{00} \xrightarrow{P} \Sigma_{00}, \tag{10.13}$$

$$\beta' S_{11} \beta \xrightarrow{P} \Sigma_{\beta\beta}, \tag{10.14}$$

$$\beta' S_{10} \xrightarrow{P} \Sigma_{\beta 0}, \tag{10.15}$$

$$T^{-1} B'_T S_{11} B_T \xrightarrow{w} \int_0^1 GG' du, \tag{10.16}$$

$$B'_T S_{1\epsilon} = B'_T (S_{10} - S_{11}\beta\alpha') \xrightarrow{w} \int_0^1 G (dW)', \tag{10.17}$$

$$B'_T S_{11}\beta \in O_P (1). \tag{10.18}$$

PROOF We apply repeatedly the results of Theorem B.13 about the proper normalization of product moments. In the following we use [ ] to indicate that a product moment has been normalized such that it converges in distribution. The basic rules are that if Y_{jt} is a process that is $I(j)$, $j = 0, 1$, then

$$T^{-1} \sum_{t=1}^{T} Y_{0t}^2, \ T^{-2} \sum_{t=1}^{T} Y_{1t}^2, \ T^{-1} \sum_{t=1}^{T} Y_{0t} Y_{1t},$$

$$T^{-3/2} \sum_{t=1}^{T} t Y_{0t}, \ T^{-5/2} \sum_{t=1}^{T} t Y_{1t}$$

are all normalized to converge weakly.

We apply the notation $Z_{2t} = (\Delta X'_{t-1}, \ldots, \Delta X'_{t-k+1})'$ from Chapter 6, and let $\bar{\Delta} X = T^{-1} \sum_{t=1}^{T} \Delta X_t$. Since the process ΔX_t is a stationary and ergodic process it follows from the law of large numbers that the different product moments in the expression

$$S_{00} = S_{\Delta\Delta} - S_{\Delta z} S_{zz}^{-1} S_{z\Delta},$$

where

$$S_{\Delta\Delta} = T^{-1} \sum_{t=1}^{T} (\Delta X_t - \bar{\Delta} X) (\Delta X_t - \bar{\Delta} X)',$$

$$S_{\Delta z} = -T^{-1} \sum_{t=1}^{T} (\Delta X_t - \bar{\Delta} X) (Z_{2t} - \bar{Z}_2)',$$

and

$$S_{zz} = T^{-1} \sum_{t=1}^{T} \left(Z_{2t} - \bar{Z}_2\right) \left(Z_{2t} - \bar{Z}_2\right)',$$

converge in probability to the corresponding population values. Thus

$$S_{00} \xrightarrow{P} \mathrm{Var}\left(\Delta X_t\right) - \mathrm{Cov}\left(\Delta X_t, Z_{2t}\right) \mathrm{Var}\left(Z_{2t}\right)^{-1} \mathrm{Cov}\left(Z_{2t}, \Delta X_t\right)$$

$$= \mathrm{Var}\left(\Delta X_t | Z_{2t}\right) = \Sigma_{00}.$$

EXERCISE 10.1 This proves (10.13). In order to prove (10.14) we use the notation

$$S_{xx} = T^{-1} \sum_{t=1}^{T} \left(X_{t-1} - \bar{X}_T\right) \left(X_{t-1} - \bar{X}_T\right)',$$

and write with an obvious notation

$$\beta' S_{11} \beta = [\beta' S_{xx} \beta] - [\beta' S_{xz} S_{zz}^{-1} S_{zx} \beta].$$

Since the process $\beta' X_t$ is stationary and ergodic it follows again from the law of large numbers that $\beta' S_{11} \beta$ converges in probability towards its population value

$$\beta' S_{11} \beta \xrightarrow{P} \mathrm{Var}\left(\beta' X_t | Z_{2t}\right) = \Sigma_{\beta\beta}.$$

The proof of (10.15) is similar.

For the proof of (10.16) we investigate the matrix S_{11} in the directions given by $\bar{\gamma} = \gamma(\gamma'\gamma)^{-1}$ and $\bar{\tau} = \tau(\tau'\tau)^{-1}$. We find

$$T^{-1}\bar{\gamma}' S_{11} \bar{\gamma} = [T^{-1}\bar{\gamma}' S_{xx} \bar{\gamma}] - T^{-1}[\bar{\gamma}' S_{xz} S_{zz}^{-1} S_{zx} \bar{\gamma}]. \qquad (10.19)$$

The convergence of the first term follows from (10.12) together with the continuous mapping theorem applied to the mapping $x \to \int_0^1 x(u) x'(u) \, du$. We find

$$T^{-1}\bar{\gamma}' S_{xx} \bar{\gamma} = \left[T^{-1} \sum_{t=1}^{T} T^{-\frac{1}{2}}\bar{\gamma}' \left(X_{t-1} - \bar{X}_T\right) \left(X_{t-1} - \bar{X}_T\right) \bar{\gamma}' T^{-\frac{1}{2}} \right]$$

$$\xrightarrow{w} \bar{\gamma}' C \int_0^1 \left(W(u) - \bar{W}\right) \left(W(u) - \bar{W}\right)' \, du C' \bar{\gamma}.$$

It next follows from Theorem B.13 that $\bar{\gamma}' S_{xz} S_{zz}^{-1} S_{zx} \bar{\gamma}$ is of the order of 1, since Z_{2t} is $I(0)$ and $\bar{\gamma}' X_t$ is $I(1)$. Thus the extra factor of T^{-1} ensures that the first term in (10.19) is dominating and gives the required limit. In the direction $\bar{\tau}$ we find

$$T^{-2}\bar{\tau}' S_{11} \bar{\tau} = [T^{-2}\bar{\tau}' S_{xx} \bar{\tau}] - T^{-1}[T^{-\frac{1}{2}}\bar{\tau}' S_{xz} S_{zz}^{-1} S_{zx} \bar{\tau} T^{-\frac{1}{2}}].$$

The terms in brackets have been normalized to converge in distribution, see Theorem B.13, and the extra factor of T^{-1} makes sure that the first term is dominating, giving the limit

$$\int_0^1 (u - 1/2)^2 \, du = 1/12.$$

The term $T^{-3/2}\bar{\tau}'S_{11}\bar{\gamma}$ is treated in the same way and the results are collected to prove (10.16).

The result (10.18) follows from Theorem B.13 in a similar way.

The proof of (10.17) follows from

$$\bar{\gamma}'(S_{10} - S_{11}\beta\alpha') = \bar{\gamma}'S_{1\epsilon} = [\bar{\gamma}'S_{x\epsilon}] - T^{-\frac{1}{2}}[\bar{\gamma}'S_{xz}S_{zz}^{-1}S_{z\epsilon}T^{\frac{1}{2}}].$$

The extra factor $T^{-\frac{1}{2}}$ in the second term makes sure that in the limit the first term is dominating and we find from (10.12)

$$\bar{\gamma}'(S_{10} - S_{11}\beta\alpha') \overset{w}{\to} \bar{\gamma}'C \int_0^1 (W - \bar{W}) \, (dW)'.$$

In the direction $\bar{\tau}$ we find

$$T^{-\frac{1}{2}}\bar{\tau}'(S_{10} - S_{11}\beta\alpha') = T^{-\frac{1}{2}}\bar{\tau}'S_{1\epsilon}$$

$$= \left[T^{-\frac{1}{2}}\bar{\tau}'S_{x\epsilon}\right] - T^{-\frac{1}{2}}\left[T^{-\frac{1}{2}}\bar{\tau}'S_{xz}S_{zz}^{-1}S_{z\epsilon}T^{\frac{1}{2}}\right].$$

As before the first term is dominating and we find the limit

$$\int_0^1 (u - 1/2) \, (dW)'.$$

Combining these results we have finally proved Lemma 10.3.   □

EXAMPLE 10.3 As an application of the above results consider the test for no cointegration $\Pi = 0$ in the model

$$\Delta X_t = \Pi X_{t-1} + \epsilon_t, \, t = 1, \ldots, T.$$

Under the null hypothesis X_t is a random walk $X_t = X_0 + \sum_{i=1}^t \epsilon_i$. In this case there is no trend and no cointegration under the null hypothesis, hence we can take $\beta = \bar{\tau} = 0$ and $\bar{\gamma} = I$ in the above results. Thus we find from (10.10) that in this very special case we have

$$T^{-\frac{1}{2}}X_{[Tu]} = T^{-\frac{1}{2}}\sum_{i=1}^{[Tu]} \epsilon_i \overset{w}{\to} W(u).$$

From (B.13) we find

$$T^{-2} \sum_{t=1}^{T} X_{t-1} X'_{t-1} \xrightarrow{w} \int_0^1 W(u) W(u)' \, du = \int_0^1 WW' du,$$

and finally from (B.14) we get

$$T^{-1} \sum_{t=1}^{T} X_{t-1} \epsilon'_t \xrightarrow{w} \int_0^1 W(dW)'.$$

These are the three basic results needed for the asymptotic behaviour of the test statistic for the hypothesis that $\Pi = 0$. The general problem will be taken up in Chapter 11.

10.3 Exercises

10.1

Consider the model

$$\Delta X_t = \Pi X_{t-1} + \Gamma_1 \Delta X_{t-1} + \epsilon_t, \ t = 1, \ldots, T.$$

In Chapter 2 it is mentioned that the likelihood ratio test for $\Gamma_1 = 0$ in the unrestricted VAR model is asymptotically distributed as χ^2 with p^2 degrees of freedom.

With the notation

$$Z_{0t} = \Delta X_t, \ Z_{1t} = X_{t-1}, \ Z_{2t} = \Delta X_{t-1}$$

we define

$$M_{ij} = T^{-1} \sum_{t=1}^{T} Z_{it} Z'_{jt}, \ i, j = 0, 1, 2.$$

1. Show that the estimator of Ω in the unrestricted VAR is given by

$$\hat{\Omega} = M_{00.12} = M_{00} - \begin{bmatrix} M_{10} \\ M_{20} \end{bmatrix}' \begin{bmatrix} M_{11} & M_{12} \\ M_{21} & M_{22} \end{bmatrix}^{-1} \begin{bmatrix} M_{10} \\ M_{20} \end{bmatrix},$$

whereas the estimator under the null hypothesis that $\Gamma_1 = 0$ is given by

$$\hat{\Omega}_0 = M_{00.1} = M_{00} - M_{01} M_{11}^{-1} M_{10}.$$

2. Find an expression for the likelihood ratio test statistic for the null that $\Gamma_1 = 0$ expressed in terms of $\hat{\Omega}$ and $\hat{\Omega}_0$.

3. Show that if also $\Pi = 0$ such that the process X_t is a random walk, then $T(\hat{\Omega}_0 - \hat{\Omega})$ has the same limit distribution as $TM_{02}M_{22}^{-1}M_{20}$, which implies that $-2\log Q(\Gamma_1 = 0) \overset{w}{\to} \chi^2(p^2)$. Hence the asymptotic distribution does not depend on the presence of $I(1)$ variables in this case.

10.2

Let the $I(2)$ process X_t be given as a cumulated random walk:

$$X_t = \sum_{i=1}^{t}\sum_{j=1}^{i}\epsilon_j,$$

where as usual the ϵ are i.i.d. with mean zero and finite variance. Consider the mapping from $C[0,1]$ to $C[0,1]$ given by associating to every continuous function f its integral $F(\cdot) = \int_0^{\cdot} f(u)du$.

1. Prove by the continuous mapping theorem applied to this functional that

$$T^{-\frac{3}{2}}X_{[Tu]} \overset{w}{\to} \int_0^u W(s)ds.$$

2. Use the result in 1. to show that

$$T^{-4}\sum_{t=1}^{T}X_tX_t' \overset{w}{\to} \int_0^1 \left(\int_0^u W(s)ds\right)\left(\int_0^u W(s)'ds\right)du.$$

10.3

Consider the regression

$$Y_t = \beta'X_t + \epsilon_t,$$

where $\{\epsilon_t\}$ is as before, and X_t a random walk with finite variance, which is independent of the ϵ. 1. Find the limit distribution of the regression estimator for β

$$\hat{\beta}_{\text{ols}} = (\sum_{t=1}^{T}X_tX_t')^{-1}(\sum_{t=1}^{T}X_tY_t').$$

2. Solve the same problem if X_t is an $I(2)$ process given as a cumulated random walk, but still independent of the ϵ.

11

The Asymptotic Distribution of the Test for Cointegrating Rank

IN this chapter we give various forms for the limit distribution of the likelihood ratio test for cointegrating rank. The limit distribution depends on the model for the deterministic terms, and we give the different formulae that can be obtained for a constant and a linear term in the equation even when there are restrictions as discussed in Chapter 6. The proofs and concepts are rather technical, and we therefore first give some special cases which introduce the basic notation and illustrate the type of analysis that is necessary for understanding the limit theory of test statistics in the presence of unit roots and cointegration.

11.1 Testing $\Pi = 0$ in the Basic Model

We assume here that ϵ_t are independent identically distributed with mean zero and variance Ω in p dimensions.

Consider first the situation from Example 10.3, where

$$\Delta X_t = \Pi X_{t-1} + \epsilon_t,$$

and we want to test that $\Pi = 0$, that is, we are testing model $H_2(0)$ in model $H_2(p)$, see (5.15), where the hypothesis without deterministic terms is defined. The test statistic is given by

$$-2\log Q\left(H_2(0) \mid H_2(p)\right) = -T\sum_{i=1}^{p}\log(1-\hat{\lambda}_i), \qquad (11.1)$$

see (6.18), where $\hat{\lambda}_1, \ldots, \hat{\lambda}_p$ solve the equation

$$|\lambda S_{11} - S_{10}S_{00}^{-1}S_{01}| = 0. \qquad (11.2)$$

These product moments were investigated in Example 10.3, where it was found that

$$T^{-1}S_{11} \xrightarrow{w} \int_0^1 WW'du, \qquad (11.3)$$

$$S_{10} \overset{w}{\to} \int_0^1 W\,(dW)', \tag{11.4}$$

$$S_{00} \overset{P}{\to} \Omega. \tag{11.5}$$

With these results we can now discuss the limit behaviour of the test statistic (11.1). We first note that S_{11} is $O_P(T)$ whereas S_{01} and S_{00} are $O_p(1)$ such that the roots $\hat{\lambda}_i$ of equation (11.2) converge to zero like T^{-1}. This on the other hand implies that

$$-T\sum_{i=1}^{p} \log(1 - \hat{\lambda}_i) = T\sum_{i=1}^{p} \hat{\lambda}_i + o_P(1).$$

The sum of the eigenvalues can be found as follows:

$$|\lambda S_{11} - S_{10}S_{00}^{-1}S_{01}| = 0 \text{ if and only if } |\lambda I - S_{11}^{-1}S_{10}S_{00}^{-1}S_{01}| = 0,$$

which shows that

$$T\sum_{i=1}^{p} \hat{\lambda}_i = T tr\{S_{11}^{-1}S_{10}S_{00}^{-1}S_{01}\}.$$

From (11.3), (11.4), and (11.5), we find that the limit of the likelihood ratio test statistic is given by

$$-2\log Q\,(H_2(0)\,|H_2(p))$$

$$\overset{w}{\to} tr\left\{\left[\int_0^1 WW'du\right]^{-1} \int_0^1 W\,(dW)'\,\Omega^{-1}\int_0^1 (dW)\,W'\right\}.$$

If we define the standard Brownian motion $B = \Omega^{-\frac{1}{2}}W$, we get the result

$$-2\log Q\,(H_2(0)\,|H_2(p)) \overset{w}{\to} tr\left\{\int_0^1 (dB)\,B'\left[\int_0^1 BB'du\right]^{-1} \int_0^1 B(dB)'\right\}.$$
$$\tag{11.6}$$

If the null hypothesis is not valid, and we have cointegration, then one of the eigenvalues will be positive in the limit. In this case

$$-2\log Q(H_2(0)|H_2(p)) \geq -T\log(1 - \hat{\lambda}_1) \overset{P}{\to} \infty,$$

which shows that the asymptotic power of the test is 1.

Note that the limit distribution does not depend on the parameter Ω, but only on the dimension p or the number of random walks.

If $p = 1$ the limit distribution is the squared Dickey–Fuller distribution see Fuller (1976) and we shall call the distribution (11.6) the Dickey–Fuller distribution with p degrees of freedom, DF_p. The reason that we get the squared DF distribution is that we test the hypothesis $\Pi = 0$ against $\Pi \neq 0$, whereas the univariate problem is usually formulated as $\Pi = 0$ against $\Pi < 0$, which is a one-sided test. One should be aware that a significantly large value of the test statistic (11.6) which rejects $\Pi = 0$, could mean that the process is stationary, but of course also that the process has explosive roots.

It turns out in the following that we get various versions of this fundamental distribution, and we illustrate this in the next case that we consider, namely the modification of the basic model with a constant term added in the equation. In this case the process is a random walk with a trend under the null hypothesis $\Pi = 0$:

$$X_t = \mu t + \sum_{i=1}^{t} \epsilon_i + X_0.$$

The test statistic is calculated in the usual way with the product moments corrected for a constant term. In order to find the limit distribution we assume first that $\mu \neq 0$, such that there is actually a linear trend in the process. The component X_{it} of the process X_t grows linearly if $\mu_i \neq 0$. If, however, we consider X_t in the $p-1$ directions $\mu_\perp$ then the process has no trend since

$$\mu'_\perp X_t = \sum_{i=1}^{t} \mu'_\perp \epsilon_i + \mu'_\perp X_0.$$

Thus the directions applied in Chapter 10 become $\beta = 0$, $\gamma = \mu_\perp$, and $\tau = \mu$. In the direction μ we have

$$\mu' X_t = \mu' \mu t + \sum_{i=1}^{t} \mu' \epsilon_i + \mu' X_0.$$

The asymptotic behaviour of the process is given by

$$T^{-\frac{1}{2}} \mu'_\perp X_{[Tu]} = T^{-\frac{1}{2}} \sum_{i=1}^{[Tu]} \mu'_\perp \epsilon_i + T^{-\frac{1}{2}} \mu'_\perp X_0 \qquad \xrightarrow{w} \mu'_\perp W(u)$$

$$T^{-1} \mu' X_{[Tu]} = T^{-1}[Tu] + T^{-1} \sum_{i=1}^{[Tu]} \mu' \epsilon_i + T^{-1} \mu' X_0 \xrightarrow{w} u,$$

since the trend dominates the random walk. Lemma 10.2 implies that

$$T^{-1} \mu' \left(X_{[Tu]} - \bar{X}_T \right) \xrightarrow{w} (u - 1/2),$$

and that

$$T^{-\frac{1}{2}}\bar{\mu}'_{\perp}\left(X_{[Tu]} - \bar{X}_T\right) \xrightarrow{w} \bar{\mu}'_{\perp}\left(W\left(u\right) - \bar{W}\right).$$

Applying these results to the product moment matrices we find from Lemma 10.3 that the asymptotic behaviour is different in different directions. Thus

$$T^{-2}\bar{\mu}'S_{11}\bar{\mu} \xrightarrow{P} \int_0^1 \left(u - 1/2\right)^2 du,$$

$$T^{-3/2}\bar{\mu}'S_{11}\bar{\mu}_{\perp} \xrightarrow{w} \int_0^1 \left(u - 1/2\right)\left(W\left(u\right) - \bar{W}\right)' du\bar{\mu}_{\perp},$$

and finally

$$T^{-1}\bar{\mu}'_{\perp}S_{11}\bar{\mu}_{\perp} \xrightarrow{w} \bar{\mu}'_{\perp}\int_0^1 \left(W\left(u\right) - \bar{W}\right)\left(W\left(u\right) - \bar{W}\right)' du\bar{\mu}_{\perp}.$$

Using the same arguments we find

$$\bar{\mu}'_{\perp}S_{10} = T^{-1}\sum_{t=1}^T \bar{\mu}'_{\perp}\left(X_{t-1} - \bar{X}_T\right)\epsilon'_t \xrightarrow{w} \bar{\mu}'_{\perp}\int_0^1 \left(W\left(u\right) - \bar{W}\right)\left(dW\right)',$$

and

$$T^{-\frac{1}{2}}\bar{\mu}'S_{10} = T^{-1}\sum_{t=1}^T \bar{\mu}'\left(X_{t-1} - \bar{X}_T\right)\epsilon'_t T^{-\frac{1}{2}} \xrightarrow{w} \int_0^1 \left(u - 1/2\right)\left(dW\right)',$$

and finally $S_{00} \xrightarrow{P} \Omega$.

We combine these results by introducing the matrix $B_T = (\bar{\mu}_{\perp}, T^{-\frac{1}{2}}\bar{\mu})$ and the process $G = (G'_1, G'_2)'$ with components

$$G_1\left(u\right) = \bar{\mu}'_{\perp}\left(W\left(u\right) - \bar{W}\right),$$

$$G_2\left(u\right) = u - 1/2.$$

We then get the results from Lemma 10.3

$$T^{-1}B'_T S_{11}B_T \xrightarrow{w} \int_0^1 GG' du,$$

$$B'_T S_{10} \xrightarrow{w} \int_0^1 G\left(dW\right)'.$$

It is seen that again S_{11} tends to infinity which implies that the eigenvalues $\hat{\lambda}_i$ of equation (11.2) tend to zero, and that the test statistic has the same limit distribution as

$$T tr\{S_{11}^{-1}S_{10}S_{00}^{-1}S_{01}\} = tr\{[T^{-1}B'_T S_{11}B_T]^{-1} B'_T S_{10}S_{00}^{-1}S_{01}B_T\}$$

$$\xrightarrow{w} tr\left\{\left[\int_0^1 GG' du\right]^{-1}\int_0^1 G\left(dW\right)'\Omega^{-1}\int_0^1 \left(dW\right)G'\right\}.$$

This quantity is invariant under linear transformations of G and W. We therefore define the standard Brownian motion $B = (B_1', B_2')'$ as follows

$$B_1(u) = (\bar{\mu}_\perp' \Omega \bar{\mu}_\perp)^{-\frac{1}{2}} \bar{\mu}_\perp' W(u),$$

$$B_2(u) = (\bar{\mu}' \Omega^{-1} \bar{\mu})^{-\frac{1}{2}} \bar{\mu}' \Omega^{-1} W(u),$$

such that B is a linear transformation of W and has variance I. Similarly we define the process $F = (F_1', F_2')'$ by

$$F_1(u) = B_1 - \bar{B} = (\bar{\mu}_\perp' \Omega \bar{\mu}_\perp)^{-\frac{1}{2}} G_1(u),$$

$$F_2(u) = u - \tfrac{1}{2} \quad = G_2(u).$$

Note that F is a linear transformation of G. Applying these transformations and using the invariance of the test statistic under linear transformations we find that the limit distribution of the trace test statistic where we correct for the intercept has the form

$$tr\left\{ \int_0^1 (dB) F' \left[\int_0^1 FF' du \right]^{-1} \int_0^1 F(dB)' \right\}. \tag{11.7}$$

This limit distribution is the most general form we get in the context of testing for cointegration and it depends on the degrees of freedom but also on the choice of F. The distribution is non-standard and has to be tabulated by simulation, see **Chapter 15**.

The process F reflects the properties of the process X_t, in the sense that in one direction it behaves like a trend and orthogonal to this it behaves like a random walk. The process is corrected for its mean as is X_t in the statistical calculation. Thus the presence of the linear term in the model changes the statistical calculations by correcting the processes X_t and ΔX_t for their mean and it changes the limit process F by making it linear in one component.

In the univariate case only the linear part of the process F is present and we find an expression which is just a $\chi^2(1)$.

$$tr\left\{ \int_0^1 (dB) F' \left[\int_0^1 FF' du \right]^{-1} \int_0^1 F(dB)' \right\}$$
$$= \left[\int_0^1 (u - \tfrac{1}{2})(dB) \right]^2 / \int_0^1 (u - \tfrac{1}{2})^2 du.$$

Note that if we investigate the limit distribution of the test statistic (11.1) with the parameter value $\mu = 0$, then the process X_t has no linear trend and the above argument has to be modified. The limit distribution is given by (11.7) but now with $F = B - \bar{B}$, since X_t is corrected for an intercept. This limit distribution has broader tails than (11.7), which is unfortunate since it means that under the hypothesis $\Pi = 0$, there are two different limit distributions, which means that not even in the limit the test is similar. This leads to complications in the procedure for testing for cointegrating rank which will be dealt with in Chapter 12.

Next we turn to the formulation of the general result for the test for cointegration.

11.2   The Limit Distribution of the Test for Cointegrating Rank

In this section we consider the full model

$$\Delta X_t = \Pi X_{t-1} + \sum_{i=1}^{k-1} \Gamma_i \Delta X_{t-i} + \mu_0 + \mu_1 t + \epsilon_t, \qquad (11.8)$$

and the hypothesis $\Pi = \alpha \beta'$ for α and β of dimension $p \times r$ as well as the submodels discussed in Chapter 5 defined by restrictions on μ_0 and μ_1. We find the limit distribution under various assumptions on the process X_t, the main one being that there are no $I(2)$ processes present, see Theorem 4.2, that is, that $\alpha'_\perp \Gamma \beta_\perp$ is of full rank. The limit distribution is independent of the choice of $\Gamma_1, \ldots, \Gamma_{k-1}$ as long as the assumptions of Theorem 4.2 are satisfied, but depends on the rank of α and β and to some extent on the value of μ_0 and μ_1. We apply the notation from Chapter 6 for the various models defined by restrictions on the deterministic terms. In order not to overburden the notation we assume throughout that α and β have full rank r and that the process X_t is $I(1)$. We can then prove

THEOREM 11.1 *The limit distribution of the likelihood ratio test statistic for the hypothesis $\Pi = \alpha \beta'$ where α and β are $p \times r$ is in general given by the DF distribution with $p - r$ degrees of freedom*

$$tr \left\{ \int_0^1 (dB) F' \left[\int_0^1 FF' du \right]^{-1} \int_0^1 F (dB)' \right\}, \qquad (11.9)$$

where B is a $p - r$ dimensional Brownian motion on the unit interval and F depends on B and on the model in which the hypothesis is being tested. If the deterministic term is $\mu_t = \mu_0 + \mu_1 t$, and if $\alpha'_\perp \mu_1 \neq 0$ then

$$F_i (u) = B_i (u) - a_i - b_i u, \ i = 1, \ldots, p - r - 1,$$

$$F_{p-r} (u) = u^2 - a - bu, \qquad (11.10)$$

where the random coefficients $(a, b, a_i, b_i, i = 1, \ldots, p - r - 1)$ are found by correcting u^2 and $B_i (u)$ for a linear trend and a constant. The distribu-

tion is tabulated by simulation in Chapter 15, Table 15.5. If $\alpha'_\perp \mu_1 = 0$, there is no quadratic trend and we define $F_i = B_i - a_i - b_i u$, $i = 1, \ldots, p - r$. If the deterministic term is $\mu_t = \mu_0 + \alpha \rho_1 t$ then

$$F_i(u) = B_i(u) - a_i, \quad i = 1, \ldots, p - r,$$
$$F_{p-r+1}(u) = u - a, \tag{11.11}$$

where the random coefficients $(a, a_i, i = 1, \ldots, p - r)$ are found by correcting u and $B_i(u)$ for a constant. The distribution is tabulated by simulation in Chapter 15, Table 15.4.

If the deterministic term is $\mu_t = \mu_0$, and $\alpha'_\perp \mu_0 \neq 0$,

$$F_i(u) = B_i(u) - a_i, \quad i = 1, \ldots, p - r - 1,$$
$$F_{p-r}(u) = u - a, \tag{11.12}$$

where the random coefficients $(a, a_i, i = 1, \ldots, p - r - 1)$ are found by correcting u respectively $B_i(u)$ for a constant. The distribution is tabulated by simulation in Chapter 15, Table 15.3. If $\alpha'_\perp \mu_0 = 0$ there is no trend in the process and we can take $F_i = B_i - a_i$, $i = 1, \ldots, p - r$.

If the deterministic term is $\mu_t = \alpha \rho_0$ then

$$F_i(u) = B_i(u), \quad i = 1, \ldots, p - r,$$
$$F_{p-r+1}(u) = 1. \tag{11.13}$$

The distribution is tabulated by simulation in Chapter 15, Table 15.2.
If the deterministic term is $\mu_t = 0$, then

$$F_i(u) = B_i(u), \quad i = 1, \ldots, p - r. \tag{11.14}$$

The distribution is tabulated by simulation in Chapter 15, Table 15.1.
Finally all tests are consistent, in the sense that if the parameter is a point in the alternative then the power tends to 1.

The proof will be given below, but some comments will be given here. Note that the limit distribution has the same form (11.9) in all cases. Note that the statistical model $H(r)$, say, has freely varying parameters but that the limit distribution of the test statistic depends not only on the number of common trends but also on whether $\alpha'_\perp \mu_1 = 0$ or not. We have chosen to simulate the asymptotic distribution only in the generic case of full rank of α and β and such that $\alpha'_\perp \mu_1 \neq 0$, and $\alpha'_\perp \mu_0 \neq 0$. Take for instance the test for $H(r)$ in $H(p)$. The test statistic is calculated by first correcting for a constant and a linear term, and it is defined as the sum of the smallest $p - r$ eigenvalues of a suitable eigenvalue problem. If in fact α or β has rank

$s < r$, then the limit distribution is not given by (11.9) but rather as the sum of the smallest $p - r$ eigenvalues of an eigenvalue problem

$$\left| \rho \int_0^1 FF'du - \int_0^1 F\,(dB)' \int_0^1 (dB)\,F' \right| = 0,$$

where F consists of a $p - s$ dimensional Brownian motion and where the last component is u^2, all corrected for a constant and a linear term, see exercise 11.3 for an example. Similarly if in fact $\alpha_{\perp}'\mu_1 = 0$, such that no quadratic trend appears, the limit distribution again has to be modified, since the quadratic trend does not appear. These exceptional cases form a small subset of the parameter set defined by the model, and we discuss in Chapter 12 how they influence the determination of the cointegrating rank. Basically we assert that if there is any doubt in practice if, say, $\alpha_{\perp}'\mu_1 = 0$ or not this should be tested and included in the determination of the cointegrating rank.

PROOF We next turn to the proof of Theorem 11.1, that is, we want to focus on the proof of (11.9) in the case where F is given by (11.12) since the other cases are entirely similar. The likelihood ratio test statistic of $H_1(r)$ in $H_1(p)$ is given in the form

$$-2\log Q(H_1(r)|H_1(p)) = -T \sum_{i=r+1}^{p} \log(1 - \hat{\lambda}_i), \qquad (11.15)$$

where the eigenvalues $\hat{\lambda}_{r+1}, \ldots, \hat{\lambda}_p$ are the smallest solutions to the equation

$$|\lambda S_{11} - S_{10}S_{00}^{-1}S_{01}| = 0,$$

see (6.15). Let $S(\lambda) = \lambda S_{11} - S_{10}S_{00}^{-1}S_{01}$. We apply Lemma 10.3 to investigate the asymptotic properties of $S(\lambda)$ and use the fact that the ordered solutions of (11.2) are continuous functions of the coefficient matrices.

We then find from Lemma 10.3, that for $B_T = (\bar{\gamma}, T^{-\frac{1}{2}}\bar{\tau})$ and $A_T = (\beta, T^{-\frac{1}{2}}B_T)$ we get

$$|A_T'\,(S\,(\lambda))\,A_T| \overset{w}{\to} \left| \begin{bmatrix} \lambda\Sigma_{\beta\beta} & 0 \\ 0 & \lambda \int_0^1 GG'du \end{bmatrix} - \begin{bmatrix} \Sigma_{\beta0}\Sigma_{00}^{-1}\Sigma_{0\beta} & 0 \\ 0 & 0 \end{bmatrix} \right| \qquad (11.16)$$

$$= \quad |\lambda\Sigma_{\beta\beta} - \Sigma_{\beta0}\Sigma_{00}^{-1}\Sigma_{0\beta}| \left| \lambda \int_0^1 GG'du \right|.$$

This equation has $p - r$ zero roots and r positive roots given by the solutions of

$$|\lambda\Sigma_{\beta\beta} - \Sigma_{\beta0}\Sigma_{00}^{-1}\Sigma_{0\beta}| = 0. \qquad (11.17)$$

This shows that the r largest solutions of (11.2) converge to the roots of (11.17) and that the rest converge to zero.

Next consider the decomposition

$$|(\beta, B_T)' S(\lambda)(\beta, B_T)| = \left| \begin{bmatrix} \beta' S(\lambda)\beta & \beta' S(\lambda) B_T \\ B_T' S(\lambda)\beta & B_T' S(\lambda) B_T \end{bmatrix} \right|$$

$$= |\beta' S(\lambda)\beta| \left| B_T' \{ S(\lambda) - S(\lambda)\beta [\beta' S(\lambda)\beta]^{-1} \beta' S(\lambda) \} B_T \right|, \qquad (11.18)$$

and let $T \to \infty$ and $\lambda \to 0$, such that $\rho = T\lambda$ is fixed. From Lemma 10.3 it follows that

$$\beta' S(\lambda)\beta = \rho T^{-1} \beta' S_{11}\beta - \beta' S_{10} S_{00}^{-1} S_{01}\beta = -\Sigma_{\beta 0}\Sigma_{00}^{-1}\Sigma_{0\beta} + o_P(1), \qquad (11.19)$$

since the first term tends to zero, which shows that in the limit the first factor in (11.18) has no roots. In order to investigate the next factor we note the following consequence of Lemma 10.3:

$$B_T' S(\lambda)\beta = \rho T^{-1} B_T' S_{11}\beta - B_T' S_{10} S_{00}^{-1} S_{01}\beta$$

$$= -B_T' S_{10}\Sigma_{00}^{-1}\Sigma_{0\beta} + o_P(1). \qquad (11.20)$$

Inserting (11.19) and (11.20) into the second factor in (11.18) we find

$$B_T' \{ S(\lambda) - S(\lambda)\beta [\beta' S(\lambda)\beta]^{-1} \beta' S(\lambda) \} B_T$$

$$= \rho T^{-1} B_T' S_{11} B_T - B_T' S_{10} N S_{01} B_T + o_P(1),$$

where N is a notation for the matrix

$$N = \Sigma_{00}^{-1} - \Sigma_{00}^{-1}\Sigma_{0\beta} \left[\Sigma_{\beta 0}\Sigma_{00}^{-1}\Sigma_{0\beta} \right]^{-1} \Sigma_{\beta 0}\Sigma_{00}^{-1}.$$

By Lemma 10.1 this matrix equals

$$\alpha_\perp (\alpha_\perp' \Omega \alpha_\perp)^{-1} \alpha_\perp' = \alpha_\perp (\text{Var}(\alpha_\perp' W))^{-1} \alpha_\perp',$$

which shows that the limit distribution of $B_T' S_{10}\alpha_\perp = B_T'(S_{10} - S_{11}\beta\alpha')\alpha_\perp$ can be found from Lemma 10.3, that is,

$$B_T' S_{10}\alpha_\perp \overset{w}{\to} \int_0^1 G(dW)'\alpha_\perp.$$

Finally Lemma 10.3 implies that

$$T^{-1} B_T' S_{11} B_T \overset{w}{\to} \int_0^1 GG' du.$$

The above results imply that the $p - r$ smallest solutions of (11.2) normalized by T converge to those of the equation

$$\left| \rho \int_0^1 GG' du - \int_0^1 G(dW)' \alpha_\perp (\text{Var}(\alpha'_\perp W))^{-1} \alpha'_\perp \int_0^1 (dW) G' \right| = 0.$$
(11.20)

In order to simplify this expression note that the roots are invariant to linear transformations of G and of $\alpha'_\perp W$. Define therefore the standard Brownian motions

$$B_1 = (\bar{\gamma}' C \Omega C' \bar{\gamma})^{-\frac{1}{2}} \bar{\gamma}' CW ,$$

$$B_2 = (\mu' \alpha_\perp (\alpha'_\perp \Omega \alpha_\perp)^{-1} \alpha'_\perp \mu)^{-\frac{1}{2}} \mu' \alpha_\perp (\alpha'_\perp \Omega \alpha_\perp)^{-1} \alpha'_\perp W.$$

It is seen that $B = (B'_1, B'_2)'$ is a standard Brownian motion since the covariance between B_1 and B_2 contains the factor

$$\mu' \alpha_\perp (\alpha'_\perp \Omega \alpha_\perp)^{-1} \alpha'_\perp \Omega C' \gamma = \mu' C' \gamma = \tau' \gamma = 0,$$

where the last equality follows by the choice of γ. The process $B = (B'_1, B_2)'$ is a linear function of $\alpha'_\perp W$, and can be inserted instead of this process into (11.20). We also see that with the definition $F_1 = B_1 - \bar{B}_1$ and $F_2 = G_2$, we can express the equation (11.20) as

$$\left| \rho \int_0^1 FF' du - \int_0^1 F(dB)' \int_0^1 (dB) F' \right| = 0,$$
(11.21)

where F is given by (11.12). This equation has $p - r$ roots. Thus we have seen that the $p - r$ smallest roots of (11.2) decrease to zero at the rate T^{-1} and that $T\hat{\lambda}$ converges to the roots of (11.21). From the expression for the likelihood ratio test statistic (11.15) we find that

$$-2 \log Q(H_1(r) | H_1(p)) = T \sum_{i=r+1}^p \hat{\lambda}_i + o_P(1) \xrightarrow{w} \sum_{i=r+1}^p \rho_i$$

$$= tr \left\{ \int_0^1 (dB) F' \left[\int_0^1 FF' du \right]^{-1} \int_0^1 F(dB)' \right\},$$

which is the desired result.

Next note that if $\alpha'_\perp \mu = 0$ there is no trend in the process and we need not take it into account in the discussion of the derivation of the limit result. Thus we can take $\gamma = \beta_\perp$ in the proof above and find the same result but with $F = B - \bar{B}$. The proof of the results for $H(r)$ where F is given by (11.10) is similar. The same holds for the proof of the result about $H_2(r)$ where the constant term is absent. As a final remark note that if the parameter is a point in the alternative then we have more than r cointegrating relations, and $\hat{\lambda}_{r+1}$ is positive in the limit. Hence

$$-2 \log Q(H_1(r) | H_1(p)) \geq -T \log(1 - \hat{\lambda}_{r+1}) \xrightarrow{P} \infty.$$

This shows that any test based upon $\{-2 \log Q(H_1(r)\,|H_1(p)) \geq c\}$ will have asymptotic power 1. $\qquad\qquad\qquad\qquad\qquad\qquad\qquad\qquad\qquad$ □

COROLLARY 11.2 *The likelihood ratio test in $H(r)$ that the quadratic trend is absent: $\alpha'_\perp \mu_1 = 0$ satisfies*

$$-2 \log Q(H^*(r)\,|H(r)) \overset{w}{\to} \chi^2(p-r).$$

The likelihood ratio test in $H_1(r)$ that the linear trend is absent: $\alpha'_\perp \mu_0 = 0$ satisfies

$$-2 \log Q(H_1^*(r)\,|H_1(r)) \overset{w}{\to} \chi^2(p-r).$$

PROOF We prove the result for $H_1(r)$. We first note that the parameter space of $H_1^*(p)$ is dense in that of $H_1(p)$. In order to see that, take any parameter value μ_0 and Π in $H_1(p)$. If Π has full rank then $\alpha_\perp = 0$ such that the condition $\alpha'_\perp \mu_0 = 0$ is satisfied. Hence (μ_0, Π) is a point in $H_1^*(p)$. If Π has reduced rank, we can find a full rank matrix $\tilde{\Pi}$ as close to Π as we wish, but then $(\mu_0, \tilde{\Pi})$ is a parameter point in $H_1^*(p)$ which is close to (μ_0, Π). Thus maximizing over $H_1(p)$ will lead to the same maximum, since the parameter points which are in $H_1(p)$ but not in $H_1^*(p)$ comprise a very small set.

This proves that

$$|S_{00}| \prod_{i=1}^{p}(1 - \hat{\lambda}_i) = L_{\max}^{-\frac{2}{T}}(H_1(p)) = L_{\max}^{-\frac{2}{T}}(H_1^*(p)) = |S_{00}^*| \prod_{i=1}^{p}(1 - \lambda_i^*).$$

Next consider

$$Q^{-2/T}(H_1^*(r)\,|H_1(r)) = L_{\max}^{-2/T}(H_1^*(r))\,/L_{\max}^{-2/T}(H_1(r))$$

$$= Q^{-2/T}(H_1^*(r)\,|H_1^*(p))\,/Q^{-2/T}(H_1(r)\,|H_1(p))$$

$$= \prod_{i=r+1}^{p}(1 - \hat{\lambda}_i)\,/\prod_{i=r+1}^{p}(1 - \lambda_i^*).$$

This shows that

$$-2 \log Q(H_1^*(r)\,|H_1(r))$$

$$= 2 \log Q(H_1(r)\,|H_1(p)) - 2 \log Q(H_1^*(r)\,|H_1^*(p))$$

$$= T \sum_{i=r+1}^{p} \log((1 - \hat{\lambda}_i)/(1 - \lambda_i^*)).$$

By the results in the proof of Theorem 11.1 we find that the limit distribution can be expressed by the $p - r$ dimensional Brownian motion B as

$$-\int_0^1 (dB)(B-\bar{B})'\left[\int_0^1 (B-\bar{B})(B-\bar{B})'\right]^{-1}\int_0^1 (B-\bar{B})(dB)'$$

$$+\int_0^1 (dB)(B',1)\left[\int_0^1 (B',1)'(B',1)du\right]^{-1}\int_0^1 (B',1)'(dB)' \tag{11.22}$$

$$=\int_0^1 (dB)\left[\int_0^1 1du\right]^{-1}\int_0^1 (dB)'.$$

We have here used the identity

$$\begin{bmatrix} X_1 \\ X_2 \end{bmatrix}'\begin{bmatrix} A & B \\ B' & D \end{bmatrix}^{-1}\begin{bmatrix} Y_1 \\ Y_2 \end{bmatrix}$$

$$= X_1 A^{-1}Y_1 + \left(X_2 - B'A^{-1}X_1\right)'\left(D - B'A^{-1}B\right)^{-1}\left(Y_2 - B'A^{-1}Y_1\right).$$

Taking the trace of (11.22) the right hand side is $\chi^2(p-r)$. The proof for $H(r)$ is similar. $\qquad\square$

THEOREM 11.3 *The likelihood ratio test of $H_1(r)$ in $H^*(r)$, that is $\alpha'\mu_1 = 0$, or that the trend stationary linear combinations are in fact stationary, satisfies*

$$-2\log Q(H_1(r)|H^*(r)) \xrightarrow{w} \chi^2(r).$$

The likelihood ratio test of $H_2(r)$ in $H_1^*(r)$, that is $\alpha'\mu_0 = 0$, or that all stationary linear combinations have mean zero, satisfies

$$-2\log Q(H_2(r)|H_1^*(r)) \xrightarrow{w} \chi^2(r).$$

PROOF   The model $H^*(r)$ is given by the equations

$$\Delta X_t = \alpha\beta'X_{t-1} + \mu_0 + \alpha\rho_1 t + \sum_{i=1}^{k-1}\Gamma_i\Delta X_{t-i} + \epsilon_t$$

$$= \alpha\beta^{*\prime}X_{t-1}^* + \mu_0 + \sum_{i=1}^{k-1}\Gamma_i\Delta X_{t-i} + \epsilon_t,$$

where $\beta^{*\prime} = (\beta', \rho_1)$ and $X_{t-1}^{*\prime} = (X_{t-1}', t)$. Thus the test of $H_1(r)$ is the test that $\rho_1 = 0$ and is really a test β^* of the form $\beta^* = H\varphi$. Thus the test statistic is given by

$$-2\log Q(H_1(r)|H^*(r)) = T\sum_{i=1}^{r}\log(1-\hat{\lambda}_i)/(1-\lambda_i^*),$$

where $\hat{\lambda}_i$ solves (6.15) and λ_i^* the corresponding eigenvalue problem based upon X_t^*. The asymptotic distribution is then found by the same methods as explained in Chapter 13 in the proof of Theorem 13.9. $\qquad\square$

The difficulty in understanding and applying these results is in keeping the distinction between the statistical model as defined by its parameter space and the data-generating process as specified by the parameter value.

In constructing a statistical test we apply the maximum of the likelihood function over the parameter space with and without parameter constraints, but when calculating the distribution of the test we need to specify the actual parameter value. Unfortunately it turns out that the *same statistic* can have not only different distributions under the null hypothesis, but also different limit distributions. Thus the statistic derived allowing for a linear trend has a different limit distribution if the trend is actually absent. This should not be confused with the fact that if the statistical model specifies the absence of the trend then clearly a *different statistic* is derived.

11.3   Asymptotic Properties of the Test for $I(2)$

We want to give an indication of the properties of the test for $I(2)$ as derived in Chapter 9, by discussing the proof of Theorem 9.2. Let us first consider the situation where (α, β, r) are known, just as in the derivation of the test statistic. In this case $Q^*_{r,s}$ will have the limit distribution given by (11.13) since the analysis of (9.3) is an $I(1)$ analysis with restricted constant term. It turns out that this result holds even if (α, β) are estimated by an $I(1)$ analysis disregarding the possibility of $I(2)$. We shall not give the proof of this result which requires that we go into the asymptotics of $I(2)$ processes, but refer to Johansen (1995a) and Paruolo (1995b) for a more complete discussion.

In the proof of Theorem 9.2 given now we thus assume that $Q^*_{r,s}$ has the limit distribution as given by (11.13) if model $H^{*0}_{r,s}$ holds. The set A_r on which we choose r cointegrating relations and no $I(2)$ components is given by

$$Q_i \geq c_{p-i}(\delta), \ i = 0, \ldots, r-1, \ Q_r < c_{p-r}(\delta),$$

$$Q^*_{r,i} \geq c^*_{p-r-i}(\delta), \ i = 0, \ldots, p-r-1.$$

PROOF   of Theorem 9.2. Under $H^0_{r,p-r}$ we have $\operatorname{rank}(\alpha) = \operatorname{rank}(\beta) = r$ and that $\alpha'_\perp \Gamma \beta_\perp$ has full rank such that no $I(2)$ components are present. It then follows from Lemma 12.1 that

$$Q_i \xrightarrow{P} \infty, \ i = 0, \ldots, r-1, \ Q^*_{r,i} \xrightarrow{P} \infty, \ i = 0, \ldots, p-r-1.$$

Hence

$$\lim_{T \to \infty} P(A_r) = \lim_{T \to \infty} P(Q_r < c_{p-r}(\delta)) = 1 - \delta,$$

by the choice of the quantile.

If $H(p)\backslash H(r)$ holds then the cointegrating rank is larger than r and in this case $Q_r \xrightarrow{P} \infty$ which shows that

$$\lim_{T \to \infty} P(A_r) \leq \lim_{T \to \infty} P(Q_r < c_{p-r}(\delta)) = 0.$$

Finally assume that H_r^0 and that there is no quadratic trend. Then $H_{r,s}^*$ holds for some $s = 0, \ldots, p - r - 1$, and

$$\lim_{T \to \infty} P(A_r) \leq \lim_{T \to \infty} P(Q_{r,s}^* \geq c_{p-r-s}^*(\delta)) = \delta.$$

This completes the proof of Theorem 9.2.   □

11.4   Exercises

11.1

Consider the model

$$\Delta X_t = \alpha \beta' X_{t-1} + \mu + \epsilon_t,$$

and the test statistic of the hypothesis $H_1(r)$ in $H_1(p)$, see Chapter 5. In Chapters 10 and 11 the asymptotic properties of X_t, S_{ij}, and the test statistic $-2\log Q(H_1(r)|H_1(p))$ were discussed under the assumption that $\text{rank}(\alpha) = \text{rank}(\beta) = r$ and that $\alpha'_\perp \mu \neq 0$. In the following assume that $\alpha'_\perp \mu = 0$.

1. Show that

$$T^{-\frac{1}{2}} \beta'_\perp X_{[Tu]} \xrightarrow{w} \beta'_\perp C W(u).$$

2. Show that

$$T^{-1} \beta'_\perp S_{11} \beta_\perp \xrightarrow{w} \beta'_\perp C \int_0^1 (W(u) - \bar{W}) (W(u) - \bar{W})' du C' \beta_\perp,$$

$$\beta'_\perp S_{10} \alpha_\perp \xrightarrow{w} \beta'_\perp C \int_0^1 (W - \bar{W}) (dW)' \alpha_\perp.$$

3. Finally show that

$$-2\log Q(H_1(r)|H_1(p)) \xrightarrow{w} tr \left\{ \int_0^1 (dB) F' \left[\int_0^1 FF' du \right]^{-1} \int_0^1 F(dB)' \right\},$$

where $F = B - \bar{B}$.

11.2

Consider instead the model

$$\Delta X_t = \alpha \beta' X_{t-1} + \alpha \rho_0 + \epsilon_t,$$

and the test statistic of the hypothesis $H_1^*(r)$ in $H_1^*(p)$, see Chapter 5. Assume again that $\text{rank}(\alpha) = \text{rank}(\beta) = r$.

1. Show that

$$T^{-\frac{1}{2}}\beta'_\perp X_{[Tu]} \xrightarrow{w} \beta'_\perp CW(u).$$

2. Show that if $\bar{X} = T^{-1}\sum_{t=1}^T X_{t-1}$ and $\bar{\Delta}X = T^{-1}\sum_{t=1}^T \Delta X_t$, then

$$S^*_{11} = \begin{bmatrix} S_{xx} & \bar{X} \\ \bar{X}' & 1 \end{bmatrix} \text{ and } S^*_{10} = \begin{bmatrix} S_{x0} \\ \bar{\Delta}X' \end{bmatrix}.$$

Hence

$$T^{-1}\begin{bmatrix} \beta_\perp & 0 \\ 0 & T^{\frac{1}{2}} \end{bmatrix}' S^*_{11} \begin{bmatrix} \beta_\perp & 0 \\ 0 & T^{\frac{1}{2}} \end{bmatrix}$$

$$\xrightarrow{w} \begin{bmatrix} \beta'_\perp C \int_0^1 WW' du C'\beta_\perp & \beta'_\perp C \int_0^1 W(u)du \\ \int_0^1 W(u)' du C'\beta_\perp & 1 \end{bmatrix},$$

$$\begin{bmatrix} \beta_\perp & 0 \\ 0 & T^{\frac{1}{2}} \end{bmatrix}' S^*_{10}\alpha_\perp \xrightarrow{w} \begin{bmatrix} \beta'_\perp C \int_0^1 W(dW)' \alpha_\perp \\ \int_0^1 (dW)' \alpha_\perp \end{bmatrix}.$$

3. Finally show that

$$-2\log Q\left(H^*_1(r)|H^*_1(p)\right) \xrightarrow{w} tr\left\{\int_0^1 (dB)F'\left[\int_0^1 FF'du\right]^{-1}\int_0^1 F(dB)'\right\},$$

where $F' = (B', 1)$.

11.3

Consider the model

$$\Delta X_t = \alpha\beta' X_{t-1} + \epsilon_t,$$

and the test statistic of the hypothesis $H_2(r)$ in $H_2(p)$, see Chapter 5.

In Chapters 10 and 11 the asymptotic properties of the test statistic $-2\log Q(H_1(r)|H_1(p))$, X_t, and S_{ij} were discussed under the assumption that $\text{rank}(\alpha) = \text{rank}(\beta) = r$. In the following assume that $\text{rank}(\alpha) = \text{rank}(\beta) = 0$.

1. Show that

$$T^{-\frac{1}{2}}X_{[Tu]} \xrightarrow{w} W(u).$$

2. Show that

$$T^{-1}S_{11} \xrightarrow{w} \int_0^1 W(u)W(u)'\, du,$$

$$S_{10} \xrightarrow{w} \int_0^1 W(dW)'.$$

3. Finally show that

$$-2\log Q\left(H_2(r)|H_2(p)\right) \xrightarrow{w} tr_{p-r}\left\{\int_0^1 (dB)B'\left[\int_0^1 BB'du\right]^{-1}\int_0^1 B(dB)'\right\},$$

that is, the sum of the $p - r$ smallest solutions of the equation

$$\left| \lambda \int_0^1 BB'du - \int_0^1 B\,(dB)' \int_0^1 (dB)\,B' \right| = 0,$$

where B is p-dimensional Brownian motion.

11.4

Consider next the model

$$\Delta X_t = \alpha\beta' X_{t-1} + \mu + \Phi D_t + \epsilon_t,$$

where D_t are three quarterly dummies, which have been orthogonalized to the constant term, that is, they sum to zero over a year. Consider again the test statistic of the hypothesis $H_1(r)$ in $H_1(p)$, see Chapter 5, and assume that α and β have full rank r, and that $\alpha'_\perp \mu \neq 0$. Granger's theorem shows that

$$X_t = C \sum_{i=1}^t (\epsilon_i + \mu + \Phi D_i) + C_0(L)(\epsilon_t + \mu + \Phi D_t) + P_{\beta_\perp} X_0,$$

for $C = \beta_\perp (\alpha'_\perp \beta_\perp)^{-1} \alpha'_\perp$. Let $\tau = C\mu \neq 0$ and define the coordinate system (β, γ, τ) which spans R^p. The purpose of this exercise is to show that the seasonal dummies do not matter for the asymptotics, once they have been ortogonalized to the constant.
  1. Show that (10.10) and (10.11) hold.
  2. Use this to show that Lemma 10.3 holds.
  3. Finally show that

$$-2\log Q\left(H_1(r)\,|\,H_1(p)\right) \overset{w}{\to} tr\left\{ \int_0^1 (dB)F' \left[\int_0^1 FF'du \right]^{-1} \int_0^1 F\,(dB)' \right\},$$

where F is given by (11.12), such that the conclusions of Theorem 11.1 hold.

11.5

Consider model $H_2(r)$, where $\Phi D_t = 0$. Show that the asymptotic distribution of the test statistic $\lambda_{\max}$, see (6.19), is given as the smallest eigenvalue of the matrix

$$\int_0^1 (dB)B' \left[\int_0^1 BB'du \right]^{-1} \int_0^1 B(dB)',$$

where B is a $p - r$ dimensional standard Brownian motion.

12

Determination of Cointegrating Rank

THIS chapter contains a procedure for determining the cointegrating rank in the vector autoregressive model. In some cases there may be strong a priori beliefs about the value of the rank. In this case it is of course important to test this assumption against the data. Another situation is when little is known a priori, and the rank has to be determined mainly by the data. This situation can also be formulated as an estimation problem, see Theorems 12.3, 12.7, and 12.9.

In the presence of deterministic terms we meet the problem that the limit distribution under the null of cointegrating rank r depends on nuisance parameters, namely the presence or absence of the trend and the value of the actual cointegrating rank, see Theorem 11.1. In this case we suggest a procedure, based on an idea of Pantula (1989), which, briefly explained, says that if the distribution of the test statistic for a given hypothesis depends on the parameter under the null hypothesis, then subhypotheses should be identified where the distribution is constant and has broader tails, and each of these should be tested. The hypothesis should then only be rejected if all the subhypotheses are also rejected. This idea is known from statistical literature, see Berger and Sinclair (1984). The results are taken from Johansen (1994b).

Another problem that we meet is that the hypothesis $H(r)$ is formulated as rank $(\Pi) \leq r$, which makes the hypotheses nested, but having found that $H(r)$ is consistent with the data we still want to know what the rank is. We therefore test successively the hypotheses $H(0)$, $H(1)$, ..., and this gives a consistent way of determining the rank.

In section 12.1 we treat the simplest case where there is no linear term in the model, since then the hypotheses are nested linearly. In section 12.2 we then give the general case of a constant term in the equation, and in section 12.3 we deal briefly with the case of a linear term in the equation.

The inference conducted here is asymptotic and simulations show that one can easily find situations in practice where the number of observations is not sufficient to apply the asymptotic results. One should also note that in testing for cointegrating rank r, one is testing for the number of common trends $p - r$ as well. Thus the final acceptance of the number r should allow an interpretation of the number of cointegrating relations, but also be consistent with an interpretation of the number of common trends.

12.1   Model Without Constant Term

The model

$$\Delta X_t = \alpha\beta' X_{t-1} + \sum_{i=1}^{k-1} \Gamma_i \Delta X_{t-i} + \epsilon_t, \tag{12.1}$$

allows one to test $H_2(r)$ in $H_2(p)$ as described in Chapter 5. In Chapter 11 the asymptotic properties of the test statistic are derived under the assumption that the rank of α and β is r. If in fact α and β have lower rank $s < r$, then one can show, see exercise 11.3, that the limit distribution is different, that is, one can show the general result that

$$Q_r = -2\mathrm{log}Q\left(H_2(r) \,|\, H_2(p)\right)$$

$$\xrightarrow{w} tr_{p-r}\left\{\int_0^1 (dB)\, B'\left[\int_0^1 BB'du\right]^{-1}\int_0^1 B\,(dB)'\right\},$$

where tr_{p-r} is the sum of the $p-r$ smallest solutions of the equation

$$\left|\rho\int_0^1 BB'du - \int_0^1 B\,(dB)'\int_0^1 (dB)\, B'\right| = 0, \tag{12.2}$$

and B is $p-s$ dimensional Brownian motion, since under the assumption that α and β have rank s there are $p-s$ common trends.

The hypothesis $H_2(r)$ assumes that the rank is less than or equal to r. Thus when calculating the p−value

$$\max_{\theta \in H_2(r)} P_\theta\{Q_r \geq c\},$$

we also have to take into account the case where the rank is less than r. Simulations show that the distributions we find for rank of α and β less than r are shifted towards smaller values, and are hence not relevant for for calculating the p−value, and we therefore only give the tables for the situation of full rank of α and β.

Still if the test Q_r is not rejected we only know that the cointegrating rank is $\leq r$. Therefore we suggest here a procedure which consists of first testing if the hypotheses $H_2(0), \ldots, H_2(r-1)$ give reasonable descriptions of the data. We define the critical value $c_{p-r} = c_{p-r}(\delta)$ from Table 15.1 by

$$P_\vartheta\{Q_r \geq c_{p-r}\} \to \delta,$$

when $\vartheta \,\epsilon\, H_2(r)$ and α and β have rank r. Thus c_{p-r} is the $1-\delta$ quantile in the limit distribution given in Theorem 11.1, see (11.14).

All the calculations in the following depend on the result in

LEMMA 12.1 *If the cointegrating rank is r then $Q_s \xrightarrow{P} \infty$ if $s < r$.*

PROOF For $s < r$ we have

$$Q_s = -T \sum_{i=s+1}^{p} \log(1 - \hat{\lambda}_i) = -T \sum_{i=s+1}^{r} \log(1 - \hat{\lambda}_i) - T \sum_{i=r+1}^{p} \log(1 - \hat{\lambda}_i),$$

(12.3)

which shows that $Q_s \xrightarrow{P} \infty$ since $\hat{\lambda}_{s+1}, \ldots, \hat{\lambda}_r$ have positive limits, see (11.17). □

THEOREM 12.2 *The test that rejects $H_2(r)$ on the set*

$$\{Q_0 > c_p, \ldots, Q_r > c_{p-r}\},$$

has asymptotic size δ :

$$\lim_{T\to\infty} P_\vartheta\{Q_0 > c_p, \ldots, Q_r > c_{p-r}\} \le \delta, \quad \vartheta \in H_2(r),$$

where equality holds if rank $(\Pi) = r$. The asymptotic power is 1:

$$\lim_{T\to\infty} P_\vartheta\{Q_0 > c_p, \ldots, Q_r > c_{p-r}\} = 1, \quad \vartheta \notin H_2(r).$$

PROOF If $\vartheta \in H_2(r)$ then the corresponding Π-matrix has rank $s \le r$. It then holds that

$$P_\vartheta\{Q_0 > c_p, \ldots, Q_r > c_{p-r}\} \le P_\vartheta\{Q_s > c_{p-s}\},$$

which converges towards δ by the constructions of c_{p-s}. If rank $(\Pi) = r$, it follows from Lemma 12.1, that $Q_0, \ldots, Q_{r-1} \xrightarrow{P} \infty$. Thus

$$\lim_{T\to\infty} P_\vartheta\{Q_0 > c_p, \ldots, Q_r > c_{p-r}\} = \lim_{T\to\infty} P_\vartheta\{Q_r > c_{p-r}\} = \delta.$$

This shows that the size is δ. Finally if $\vartheta \notin H_2(r)$ then rank$(\Pi) > r$ and, by Lemma 12.1, $Q_0, \ldots, Q_r \xrightarrow{P} \infty$, which shows that

$$\lim_{T\to\infty} P_\vartheta\{Q_0 > c_p, \ldots, Q_r > c_{p-r}\} = 1,$$

which shows that the asymptotic power for a fixed alternative is 1. □

Another way of stating these results is that one can construct an estimator for the cointegrating rank as follows:

THEOREM 12.3 *The estimator $\hat{r}$ of the cointegrating rank defined by*

$$\{\hat{r} = r\} = \{Q_0 > c_p, \ldots, Q_{r-1} > c_{p-r+1}, Q_r \le c_{p-r}\}$$

has the property that for $\vartheta \in H_2(r) \backslash H_2(r-1)$, that is, rank$(\Pi) = r$,

$$P_\vartheta\{\hat{r} = i\} \to \begin{cases} 0 & i = 0, \ldots, r-1, \\ 1-\delta & i = r, \\ \leq \delta & i = r+1, \ldots, p. \end{cases}$$

PROOF If rank $(\Pi) = r$ it follows from Lemma 12.1 that $Q_0, \ldots, Q_{r-1} \xrightarrow{P} \infty$, such that for $i = 0, \ldots, r-1$,

$$P_\vartheta\{\hat{r} = i\} \leq P_\vartheta\{Q_i \leq c_{p-i}\} \to 0,$$

whereas

$$P_\vartheta\{\hat{r} = r\} = P_\vartheta\{Q_0 > c_p, \ldots, Q_{r-1} > c_{p-r+1}, Q_r \leq c_{p-r}\}$$

must have the same limit as $P_\vartheta\{Q_r \leq c_{p-r}\}$ which converges towards $1-\delta$ by the choice of c_{p-r}. Finally for $i = r+1, \ldots, p$ we find

$$P_\vartheta\{\hat{r} = i\} \leq P_\vartheta\{Q_0 > c_p, \ldots, Q_{i-1} > c_{p-i+1}\} \leq P_\vartheta\{Q_r > c_{p-r}\},$$

which converges to δ. This completes the proof of Theorem 12.3.   □

Thus in order to avoid the problem that the hypotheses of a given cointegrating rank are not nested, we suggest to formulate the hypotheses of interest as rank$(\Pi) \leq r$, and to test $H_2(r)$ by first checking if $H_2(0), \ldots, H_2(r-1)$ are acceptable as descriptions of the data. Only if none of these can be used do we accept or reject $H_2(r)$ on the basis of the test statistic Q_r.

12.2   Model With a Constant Term

If we consider the model with unrestricted constant term

$$\Delta X_t = \alpha\beta' X_{t-1} + \sum_{i=1}^{k-1} \Gamma_i \Delta X_{t-i} + \mu + \epsilon_t, \tag{12.4}$$

we need to discuss the test for cointegrating rank and the hypothesis about the absence of the trend $(\alpha'_\perp \mu = 0)$ at the same time, since the limit distribution of the test of cointegrating rank in (12.4), see (11.12), depends on the actual cointegrating rank and on the presence or absence of the trend, that is, on the condition $\alpha'_\perp \mu \neq 0$. Hence we have to discuss the hypotheses $H_1(r)$ and $H_1^*(r)$ simultaneously. These hypotheses are no longer linearly ordered in a natural way, see Table 5.1, where we have

$$\begin{array}{ccccc} H_1(0) & \subset \cdots \subset & H_1(r) & \subset \cdots \subset & H_1(p) \\ \cup & & \cup & & \cup \\ H_1^*(0) & \subset \cdots \subset & H_1^*(r) & \subset \cdots \subset & H_1^*(p). \end{array}$$

Another situation occurs if we consider the model with restricted constant term $H_1^*(r)$ $(\mu_0 = \alpha\rho_0)$, that is, if we are willing to assume that there is no linear trend in the data. In this case the distributions of the test statistics do not depend on ρ_0, and the hypotheses are nested as in the discussion in Section 12.1.

We first consider the case of the unrestricted constant and define the test statistics

$$Q_r = -2\mathrm{log}Q\left(H_1\left(r\right)|H_1\left(p\right)\right),$$

$$Q_r^* = -2\mathrm{log}Q\left(H_1^*\left(r\right)|H_1^*\left(p\right)\right).$$

We let $c_{p-r} = c_{p-r}(\delta)$ denote the $1-\delta$ quantile in the limit distribution of Q_r under the assumption that the rank of Π is r and that the trend is present. That is, c_{p-r} is taken from Table 15.3.

Similarly we let $c_{p-r}^* = c_{p-r}^*(\delta)$ denote the $1-\delta$ quantile in the limit distribution of Q_r^* when the rank of Π is r and the trend is absent, that is, taken from Table 15.2.

As stated in Theorem 11.1 the limit distribution of Q_r depends on the presence or absence of the trend. Simulations show that the distribution of Q_r, if the trend is absent, has heavier right tails than the distribution given in Theorem 11.1 when the trend is present. In order to test the hypothesis $H_1(r)$ we need to bound the size of the test, that is, we want

$$\mathrm{max}_{\vartheta \in H_1(r)}\, P_\vartheta\{Q_r \geq c\}, \tag{12.5}$$

to be 5 per cent, say. This way we make sure that for any parameter value in the null hypothesis $H_1(r)$, the probability of rejecting the null is at most 5 per cent. Since the parameter values corresponding to $\alpha'_\perp \mu = 0$ give the largest probability we thus have to calculate the probability distribution of $-2\mathrm{log}Q\left(H_1\left(r\right)|H_1\left(p\right)\right)$ when in fact $\alpha'_\perp \mu = 0$, that is, the trend is absent. This is clearly unreasonable since it leads to too high critical values and hence very low power against the alternative of more than r cointegrating relations.

In the following we denote by P_r the probability measure under the assumption that the cointegrating rank is r and that $\alpha'_\perp \mu \neq 0$, such that the process has a trend. If $\alpha'_\perp \mu = 0$, however, we denote the measure by P_r^*.

LEMMA 12.4 *With respect to P_r it holds that*

$$Q_0^*,\, \ldots,\, Q_{r-1}^*,\, Q_0,\, \ldots,\, Q_{r-1},\, Q_r^* \xrightarrow{P} \infty,$$

and with respect to P_r^* it holds that

$$Q_0^*,\, \ldots,\, Q_{r-1}^*,\, Q_0,\, \ldots,\, Q_{r-1} \xrightarrow{P} \infty.$$

PROOF   In the first case where the trend is present, (12.3) shows that $Q_0, \ldots, Q_{r-1}$ contain a contribution from a root that is positive in the limit and hence that they all tend to ∞ in probability. Since $Q_i^* \geq Q_i$ the same holds for Q_i^*, $i = 0, \ldots, r-1$.

From the relation

$$Q_r^* = Q_r - 2\log Q(H_1^*(r)|H_1(r)),$$

we find the result that $Q_r^* \xrightarrow{P} \infty$ since the last term is the test statistic for the hypothesis of the absence of the trend. This shows the first statement.

In the second case, that is, under P_r^* we find from (11.16) that even though $\tau = 0$, it still holds that the r largest roots of (11.16) converge to those of

$$\left|\lambda\Sigma_{\beta\beta} - \Sigma_{\beta 0}\Sigma_{00}^{-1}\Sigma_{0\beta}\right| = 0,$$

such that $Q_0, \ldots, Q_{r-1}$ tend to ∞ in probability. Since $Q_i^* \geq Q_i$ the same holds for Q_i^*, $i = 0, \ldots, r-1$.   □

We propose only to reject $H_1(r)$ if it and all hypotheses contained in it are rejected, that is, $H_1(r)$ is rejected if the observation belongs to the set

$$R_r = \{Q_0^* > c_p^*, \ldots, Q_r^* > c_{p-r}^*, Q_0 > c_p, \ldots, Q_r > c_{p-r}\},$$

and only accept $H_1(r)$ if the observation belongs to

$$A_r = \{Q_0^* > c_p^*, \ldots, Q_r^* > c_{p-r}^*, Q_0 > c_p, \ldots, Q_{r-1} > c_{p-r+1}, Q_r \leq c_{p-r}\}.$$

THEOREM 12.5   *The test that rejects $H_1(r)$ on R_r and accepts $H_1(r)$ on A_r has asymptotic size δ and asymptotic power 1.*

PROOF   First consider the size of the test for $\vartheta \in H_1(r)$. Then $\vartheta \in H_1^*(s)$ for some $s \leq r$ with $\alpha'_\perp\mu = 0$ or $\vartheta \in H_1(s)$ with $\alpha'_\perp\mu \neq 0$. In the first case, $\vartheta \in H_1^*(s)$, we find

$$P_s^*(R_r) \leq P_s^*(Q_s^* > c_{p-s}^*),$$

which converges to δ by the choice of c_{p-s}^*. In the second case, $\vartheta \in H_1(s)$ and $\alpha'_\perp\mu \neq 0$, we find

$$P_s(R_r) \leq P_s(Q_s > c_{p-s}),$$

which converges to δ by the choice of c_{p-s}.

Finally if $\vartheta \in H_1(r)\backslash H_1(r-1)$, $\alpha'_\perp\mu \neq 0$ then by Lemma 12.4

$$Q_0^*, \ldots, Q_{r-1}^*, Q_0, \ldots, Q_{r-1}, Q_r^* \xrightarrow{P} \infty$$

such that

$$\lim_{T\to\infty} P_r(R_r) = \lim_{T\to\infty} P_r(Q_r > c_{p-r}) = \delta.$$

Thus the size of the test is δ.

Next consider the power for $\vartheta \notin H_1(r)$. In this case we must have the cointegrating rank $s > r$ but then from Lemma 12.4 $Q_0^*, \ldots, Q_r^*$, as well as $Q_0, \ldots, Q_r$ converge to infinity in probability for both P_s and P_s^*, which shows that

$$\lim_{T \to \infty} P_s(R_r) = \lim_{T \to \infty} P_s^*(R_r) = 1.$$

$\square$

We next define the acceptance region for $H_1^*(r)$

$$A_r^* = \{Q_0^* > c_p^*, \ldots, Q_{r-1}^* > c_{p-r+1}^*,$$

$$Q_r^* \leq c_{p-r}^*, Q_0 > c_p, \ldots, Q_{r-1} > c_{p-r+1}\}.$$

The rejection region then becomes

$$R_r^* = \{Q_0^* > c_p^*, \ldots, Q_r^* > c_{p-r}^*, Q_0 > c_p, \ldots, Q_{r-1} > c_{p-r+1}\}.$$

THEOREM 12.6 *The test that rejects $H_1^*(r)$ on R_r^* and accepts $H_1^*(r)$ on A_r^* has asymptotic size δ and asymptotic power 1.*

PROOF   First consider the size of the test for $\vartheta \in H_1^*(r)$ which means that $\vartheta \in H_1^*(s)$ for some $s \leq r$.

If $s < r$,

$$\lim_{T \to \infty} P_s^*\{R_r^*\} \leq \lim_{T \to \infty} P_s^*\{Q_s^* > c_{p-s}^*\} = \delta.$$

If $s = r$ we get $Q_0, \ldots, Q_{r-1}, Q_0^*, \ldots, Q_{r-1}^* \xrightarrow{P} \infty$, with respect to P_r^* such that

$$\lim_{T \to \infty} P_r^*\{R_r^*\} = \lim_{T \to \infty} P_r^*\{Q_r^* > c_{p-r}^*\} = \delta,$$

which show that the test has the asymptotic size δ.

Next consider the power. If $\vartheta \notin H_1^*(r)$ then either $\vartheta \in H_1^*(s)$ for some $s > r$, or $\vartheta \in H_1(s)$ for some $s \geq r$, where $\alpha_\perp' \mu \neq 0$, that is, $\vartheta \in H_1(s)\backslash H_1^*(s)$ for some $s \geq r$.

If $s > r$ then it follows from Lemma 12.4 that with respect to P_s^* as well as P_s it holds that in particular

$$Q_0, \ldots, Q_{r-1}, Q_0^*, \ldots, Q_{r-1}^* \xrightarrow{P} \infty,$$

such that

$$\lim_{T \to \infty} P_s^*(R_r^*) = \lim_{T \to \infty} P_s(R_r^*) = 1.$$

If $s = r$ and $\alpha_\perp' \mu \neq 0$ then from Lemma 12.4 we see that not only do we have that $Q_0, \ldots, Q_{r-1}, Q_0^*, \ldots, Q_{r-1}^* \xrightarrow{P} \infty$, but also $Q_r^* \xrightarrow{P} \infty$, such that

$$\lim_{T \to \infty} P_r(R_r^*) = 1.$$

This completes the proof of Theorem 12.6.

$\square$

The results can also be formulated as an estimation problem. We define the parameter κ as 1 or zero depending on the presence or absence of the trend.

THEOREM 12.7 *The estimator defined by*

$$\{\hat{r} = r, \, \hat{\kappa} = 1\} = A_r,$$

and

$$\{\hat{r} = r, \, \hat{\kappa} = 0\} = A_r^*,$$

is consistent in the sense that if r is the cointegrating rank then

$$\lim_{T \to \infty} P_r\{\hat{r} = i\} = \lim_{T \to \infty} P_r^*\{\hat{r} = i\} = 0, \, i = 0, 1, \ldots, r - 1. \qquad (12.6)$$

If $\kappa = 1$, that is, $\alpha'_\perp \mu \neq 0$, then

$$\lim_{T \to \infty} P_r\{\hat{r} = r, \, \hat{\kappa} = 1\} = 1 - \delta,$$

$$\lim_{T \to \infty} P_r\{\hat{r} = r, \, \hat{\kappa} = 0\} = 0.$$

If $\kappa = 0$, that is, $\alpha'_\perp \mu = 0$, then

$$\lim_{T \to \infty} P_r^*\{\hat{r} = r, \, \hat{\kappa} = 0\} = 1 - \delta,$$

$$\lim_{T \to \infty} P_r^*\{\hat{r} = r, \, \hat{\kappa} = 1\} \le \delta.$$

PROOF Let the cointegrating rank be r. If $i = 0, 1, \ldots, r-1$ then $Q_i \overset{P}{\to} \infty$ with respect to both P_r and P_r^*, and

$$P_r\{\hat{r} = i, \, \hat{\kappa} = 1\} = P_r(A_i) \le P_r\{Q_i \le c_{p-i}\} \to 0,$$

$$P_r\{\hat{r} = i, \, \hat{\kappa} = 0\} = P_r(A_i^*) \le P_r\{Q_i^* \le c_{p-i}^*\} \to 0.$$

Similarly with respect to P_r^* we have $Q_i^* \overset{P}{\to} \infty$ and $Q_i \overset{P}{\to} \infty, \, i = 0, \ldots, r - 1$, such that

$$P_r^*\{\hat{r} = i, \, \hat{\kappa} = 1\} = P_r^*(A_i) \le P_r^*\{Q_i \le c_{p-i}\} \to 0,$$

$$P_r^*\{\hat{r} = i, \, \hat{\kappa} = 0\} = P_r^*(A_i^*) \le P_r^*\{Q_i^* \le c_{p-i}^*\} \to 0,$$

which proves (12.6). If we take $i = r$, and $\kappa = 1$, then from Lemma 12.4

$$\lim_{T \to \infty} P_r\{\hat{r} = r, \, \hat{\kappa} = 1\} = \lim_{T \to \infty} P_r\{Q_r \le c_{p-r}\} = 1 - \delta,$$

and

$$\lim_{T \to \infty} P_r\{\hat{r} = r,\ \hat{\kappa} = 0\} = \lim_{T \to \infty} P_r\{Q_r^* \leq c_{p-r}^*\} = 0,$$

since $Q_r^* \xrightarrow{P} \infty$. Finally we let $\kappa = 0$ and investigate the measure P_r^*, where we find

$$\lim_{T \to \infty} P_r^*\{\hat{r} = r,\ \hat{\kappa} = 0\} = \lim_{T \to \infty} P_r^*\{Q_r^* \leq c_{p-r}^*\} = 1 - \delta,$$

and

$$\lim_{T \to \infty} P_r^*\{\hat{r} = r,\ \hat{\kappa} = 1\} = \lim_{T \to \infty} P_r^*\{Q_r^* > c_{p-r}^*,\ Q_r \leq c_{p-r}\}$$

$$\leq \lim_{T \to \infty} P_r^*\{Q_r^* > c_{p-r}^*\} = \delta.$$

□

Next consider the situation where the constant is assumed to be restricted. In this case the hypotheses $H_1^*(r)$ are nested and the distribution is invariant to the value of ρ_0. Thus the results of Theorem 12.3 hold for the statistic Q_r^* and the quantiles c_{p-r}^*.

As a final comment, note that the above procedures are of course rather formal, and that in practice it is sometimes quite clear that the trend is present, such that we need not worry about $H_1^*(r)$, or that the trend cannot be present such that we can disregard $H_1(r)$.

12.3   Models with a Linear Term

Models with linear term can be treated along the same lines, see Johansen (1994b). Thus if the possibility of a quadratic trend is allowed one should consider simultaneously the models $H(r)$ and $H^*(r)$ and determine the presence or absence of the quadratic trend at the same time as the cointegrating rank, since the limit distribution in this case depends on the presence of the quadratic trend.

If, however, one is willing to assume that the quadratic trend is absent, as one would normally do, one can see that the distribution of the test statistic does not depend on ρ_1 and we can apply results like Theorem 12.2 and Theorem 12.3. Thus if

$$Q_r^* = -2 \log Q(H^*(r)|H^*(p))$$

the limit distribution is given by (11.11), which only depends on the number of common trends $p - r$. In particular it does not depend on the values of μ_0 and ρ_1. If $c_{p-r}^* = c_{p-r}^*(\delta)$ denotes the $1 - \delta$ quantile as tabulated in Table 15.4 we find

THEOREM 12.8 *The test that rejects $H^*(r)$ on*

$$\{Q_0^* > c_p^*, \ldots, Q_r^* > c_{p-r}^*\}$$

has asymptotic size δ and asymptotic power 1.

THEOREM 12.9 *The estimator $\hat{r}$ of the cointegrating rank defined by*

$$\{\hat{r} = i\} = \{Q_0^* > c_p^*, \ldots, Q_{r-1}^* > c_{p-r+1}^*, Q_r^* \leq c_{p-r}^*\}$$

has the property

$$P_\theta\{\hat{r} = i\} \rightarrow \begin{cases} 0 & i = 0, 1, \ldots, r-1 \\ 1 - \delta & i = r \\ \leq \delta & i = r+1, \ldots, p \end{cases}$$

Thus by allowing for a linear trend in the process even in the stationary directions one can avoid the joint determination of the cointegrating rank and the presence of the trend as in section 12.2. Having determined the rank one can then proceed to test for the absence of the trend in the stationary linear combinations by testing model $H(r)$ in $H^*(r)$ as described in Theorem 11.3. See also Perron and Campbell (1993) for a different discussion of the problem of determining the rank.

Finally it should be emphasized again that all the results are asymptotic and that the amount of data in macro economic series are not always enough to apply the results without a detailed simulation study of small sample properties. I do not know how to improve the approximation, and see this as the most important problem for further work in this area.

12.4   Exercises

12.1

In (6.19) the test of $H(r)$ in $H(r+1)$ is given. This test statistic is sometimes called the $\lambda_{\max}$ statistic. Discuss its properties with respect to size and power as a procedure for selecting the cointegrating rank using $\lambda_{\max}$.

12.2

1. Show that the distribution of the likelihood ratio test statistic

$$Q_r^* = -2logQ(H_1^*(r)|H_1^*(p))$$

does not depend on the parameter ρ_0, see (5.15).

2. Show that the distribution of the likelihood ratio test statistic

$$Q_r^* = -2logQ(H^*(r)|H^*(p))$$

does not depend on the parameters μ_0 and ρ_1, see (5.13).

13

Asymptotic Properties of the Estimators

WE treat in detail the model $H_1(r)$ where the deterministic term is given by $\Phi D_t = \mu_t = \mu$. We assume throughout that the trend is present, that is, $\alpha'_\perp \mu \neq 0$. We also assume that the process is $I(1)$, that is, that the conditions of Theorem 4.2 are satisfied.

One of the problems in the estimation of α and β is that they are not identified, as discussed in Chapter 5. We derive in section 13.4 the asymptotic properties of the estimators for α and β under the assumption that they have been estimated unrestricted, and that they are normalized or uniquely identified by a $p \times r$ matrix c, that is, we find properties of the estimators $\hat{\beta}_c = \hat{\beta}(c'\hat{\beta})^{-1}$, which is normalized by $c'\hat{\beta}_c = I$, and $\hat{\alpha}_c = \hat{\alpha}\hat{\beta}'c$. We also state the asymptotic distribution of $\hat{\beta}$ when it is estimated under identifying restrictions. We then find in section 13.5 the asymptotic distribution of the remaining parameter estimators as well as some relevant parametric functions. In section 13.6 we discuss the asymptotic distribution of the likelihood ratio test statistic for hypotheses on β and derive the limit distribution in some cases. Since the asymptotic distribution of $\hat{\beta}$ is mixed Gaussian we start in section 13.1 with a brief discussion of this distribution.

13.1   The Mixed Gaussian Distribution

The Gaussian distribution plays two important roles in statistics, namely as error distribution and as limit distribution. In the first role it provides an error distribution for which, in some simple cases, the maximum likelihood estimator equals ordinary least squares. We apply the Gaussian distribution in this role in this presentation, since we use the Gaussian distribution to formulate a likelihood function and it is the analysis of the likelihood function that tells us how to modify the estimators and test statistics when new information is incorporated in the model in the form of restrictions on the parameters.

Most of the models we work with here are so complicated that no exact inference can be conducted, and we have to do with asymptotic inference. Hence the emphasis in the following is on asymptotic distributions and asymptotic Gaussian distributions which by transformation implies that some test statistics are asymptotically χ^2 distributed. The mixed Gaussian distribution appears in the present work as a limit distribution. By a mixed Gaussian distribution we understand the following: let there be given two stochastic variables: X which is p-dimensional and Y which is a positive semi-definite matrix of dimension $p \times p$. We assume that the distribution of X given Y is Gaussian $N_p(\xi, Y)$, and call the marginal distribution of X a mixed Gaussian distribution with centre ξ and mixing parameter Y. Note that if Y is degenerate then X is actually Gaussian such that the Gaussian distribution is a special case of the mixed Gaussian distribution. Typically the mixed Gaussian distribution has thicker tails than the Gaussian distribution. Thus the Student distribution and the Cauchy distribution are mixed Gaussian distributions.

It is a property of the mixed Gaussian distribution that the statistic constructed by $(X - \xi)' Y^{-1} (X - \xi)$ is χ^2 with p^2 degrees of freedom, since for fixed Y the distribution clearly has this property, and since this conditional distribution does not depend on Y it also holds marginally. This argument will be used many times in the derivation of the limit distribution of test statistics in the following.

If one observed only X one would have to make inference in the marginal distribution of X, and take into account the fat tails. Thus for instance for a univariate variable X one could construct a confidence set for ξ of the form $(X - c, X + c)$ where c was determined by $P_\xi(|X - \xi| > c) = 0.05$. This would require a tabulation of the mixed Gaussian distribution of X. If, however, one has measurements of both X and Y then inference is a lot easier, since we can construct a confidence set of the form $(X - cY^{\frac{1}{2}}, X + cY^{\frac{1}{2}})$, and determine c such that

$$P_\xi(|X - \xi| > cY^{\frac{1}{2}}) = P_\xi(|X - \xi| > cY^{\frac{1}{2}}|Y) = 0.05.$$

This last calculation only requires the Gaussian distribution or the χ^2 distribution. Thus despite the heavy tails in the distribution of X we can make inference using the usual Gaussian distribution by conditioning on Y. It is not difficult to see that if the parameters in the distribution of Y are free of ξ, then the information about ξ in the sample as measured by minus the second derivative of the likelihood function is given by Y^{-1}, such that if the data X and the information Y are measured then inference can most easily be conducted conditional on the observed information or equivalently the observed common trends. The conditioning argument is discussed in more detail in Johansen (1995c).

We shall meet $p \times r$ matrices X with a mixed Gaussian distribution, and they all have the form that given Y $(p \times p)$ the distribution of X is Gaussian with mean zero and variance $Y \otimes \Omega$, meaning that $\nu' X \mu$ given Y is univariate Gaussian with mean zero and variance $\nu' Y \nu \mu' \Omega \mu$, for any $\nu \in R^p$ and $\mu \in R^r$.

13.2 A Convenient Normalization of β

The estimator $\hat{\beta}$ derived in Chapter 6 is found as the eigenvectors of equation (6.15) and are normalized in the natural way for eigenvectors: $\hat{\beta}'S_{11}\hat{\beta} = I$. This normalization is convenient for the calculations and clearly determines the estimates uniquely but is often not the most natural way of interpreting the results.

We here discuss a different normalization which is convenient for the mathematical analysis and which is also not natural for interpretation since it depends on the unknown parameters. We choose the coordinate system (β, γ, τ), see Lemma 10.2, and expand

$$\hat{\beta} = \beta\bar{\beta}'\hat{\beta} + \bar{\gamma}\gamma'\hat{\beta} + \bar{\tau}\tau'\hat{\beta},$$

where $\bar{\beta} = \beta(\beta'\beta)^{-1}$ etc. and define the estimator

$$\tilde{\beta} = \hat{\beta}(\bar{\beta}'\hat{\beta})^{-1} = \beta + \bar{\gamma}\gamma'\tilde{\beta} + \bar{\tau}\tau'\tilde{\beta}$$

$$= \beta + \bar{\gamma}U_{1T} + T^{-\frac{1}{2}}\bar{\tau}U_{2T} = \beta + B_TU_T, \tag{13.1}$$

where

$$B_T = (\bar{\gamma}, T^{-\frac{1}{2}}\bar{\tau}), \text{ and } U_T = (U'_{1T}, U'_{2T})' = (\gamma, T^{\frac{1}{2}}\tau)'\tilde{\beta}. \tag{13.2}$$

This way of normalizing is convenient for the analysis, since it has the property that $\tilde{\beta} - \beta$ is contained in the space spanned by γ and τ, and hence orthogonal to β. Note that since $\tilde{\beta}$ is just a linear transformation of the columns of $\hat{\beta}$ it also maximizes the likelihood function and hence $\tilde{\beta}$ satisfies the likelihood equations. The normalization depends on β, so for practice it is not so useful, but it is convenient in the analysis. We define $\tilde{\alpha} = \hat{\alpha}\hat{\beta}'\bar{\beta}$ so that $\tilde{\alpha}\tilde{\beta}' = \hat{\alpha}\hat{\beta}'$.

The normalization by c denoted by $\beta_c = \beta(c'\beta)^{-1}$, has the advantage that it can be used in practice and that a measure can be given of the (asymptotic) variation of the individual estimated coefficients which can be used for Wald tests for hypotheses on the coefficients. If in particular we take $c' = (I, 0)$ and decompose $X = (X'_1, X'_2)'$ and $\beta = (\beta'_1, \beta'_2)'$ then $\beta_c = (I, \beta'^{-1}_1\beta'_2)'$. Whether this normalization is useful for applications is of course an empirical question. In general structural equations look different and are not just solved for some of the variables. The estimation of coefficients identified by restrictions within each equation will be treated in section 13.4.

We first derive the properties of $\tilde{\beta}$ and then derive those of $\hat{\beta}_c$ by the expansion

$$\hat{\beta}_c = \hat{\beta}(c'\hat{\beta})^{-1} = \tilde{\beta}(c'\tilde{\beta})^{-1}$$

$$= \beta(c'\beta)^{-1} + \left[I - \beta(c'\beta)^{-1}c'\right](\tilde{\beta} - \beta)(c'\beta)^{-1} + O_P(|\tilde{\beta} - \beta|^2).$$

Hence if β and $\hat{\beta}$ are normalized by $c'\beta = c'\hat{\beta} = I$, we have

$$\hat{\beta} - \beta = (I - \beta c')(\tilde{\beta} - \beta) + O_P(|\tilde{\beta} - \beta|^2). \tag{13.3}$$

Note that $I - \beta c' = c_\perp(\beta'_\perp c_\perp)^{-1}\beta'_\perp$.

13.3   Consistency of the Estimators

We prove here that the estimators of α, β, and Ω in model $H_1(r)$ are consistent and find some auxiliary results on the order of magnitude of various product moments.

LEMMA 13.1   *The estimators* $\tilde{\beta} = \hat{\beta}(\bar{\beta}'\hat{\beta})^{-1}$, $\tilde{\alpha} = \hat{\alpha}\hat{\beta}'\tilde{\beta}$, *and* $\hat{\Omega}$ *are consistent. Moreover* $\tilde{\beta} - \beta \in o_P(T^{-\frac{1}{2}})$ *such that*

$$\tilde{\beta}'S_{11}\tilde{\beta} = \beta'S_{11}\beta + o_P(1) \xrightarrow{P} \Sigma_{\beta\beta}, \tag{13.4}$$

$$\tilde{\beta}'S_{10} = \beta'S_{10} + o_P(T^{-\frac{1}{2}}) \xrightarrow{P} \Sigma_{\beta 0}. \tag{13.5}$$

PROOF   The estimator $\hat{\beta}$ is determined by the eigenvectors corresponding to the r largest eigenvalues of (6.15). We multiply the equation by the matrix $A_T = (\beta, T^{-\frac{1}{2}}\bar{\gamma}, T^{-1}\bar{\tau})$ and A'_T, see (11.17), and find

$$|\lambda A'_T S_{11} A_T - A'_T S_{10} S_{00}^{-1} S_{01} A_T| = 0. \tag{13.6}$$

This equation has the same eigenvalues as (6.15) and eigenvectors $A_T^{-1}V$, where V are the eigenvectors of (6.15). For $T \to \infty$ the ordered eigenvalues of (13.6) converge to those of the equation,

$$|\lambda\Sigma_{\beta\beta} - \Sigma_{\beta 0}\Sigma_{00}^{-1}\Sigma_{0\beta}||\lambda \int_0^1 GG'du| = 0,$$

see (11.17), and the space spanned by the r first eigenvectors of (13.6) converges to the space spanned by the first r unit vectors or equivalently the space spanned by vectors with zeros in the last $p - r$ coordinates. The space spanned by the first r eigenvectors of (13.6) is $sp(A_T^{-1}\hat{\beta}) = sp(A_T^{-1}\tilde{\beta})$, where

$$A_T^{-1}\tilde{\beta} = (\bar{\beta}, T^{\frac{1}{2}}\gamma, T\tau)'\tilde{\beta} = (I, T^{\frac{1}{2}}U'_T)', \tag{13.7}$$

see (13.2). Thus we find that $T^{\frac{1}{2}}U_T \xrightarrow{P} 0$. This shows consistency of $\tilde{\beta}$ and moreover that

$$(\tilde{\beta} - \beta) \in o_P(T^{-\frac{1}{2}}).$$

Next consider the expression

$$\tilde{\beta}' S_{11} \tilde{\beta} = (\beta + B_T U_T)' S_{11} (\beta + B_T U_T).$$

From Lemma 10.3 it follows that $B_T' S_{11} B_T$ is $O_P(T)$ and that $B_T' S_{11} \beta$ is $O_P(1)$, and since $U_T \in o_P(T^{-\frac{1}{2}})$, see (13.7), we find (13.4). The proof of (13.5) is similar. Finally (13.4) and (13.5) imply the consistency of $\tilde{\alpha} = S_{01} \tilde{\beta} (\tilde{\beta}' S_{11} \tilde{\beta})^{-1}$ which converges towards $\Sigma_{0\beta} \Sigma_{\beta\beta}^{-1} = \alpha$, see (10.3). The estimator of Ω is

$$\hat{\Omega} = S_{00} - S_{01} \tilde{\beta} (\tilde{\beta}' S_{11} \tilde{\beta})^{-1} \tilde{\beta}' S_{10},$$

which by (13.4) and (13.5) converges towards

$$\Sigma_{00} - \Sigma_{0\beta} \Sigma_{\beta\beta}^{-1} \Sigma_{\beta 0} = \Sigma_{00} - \alpha \Sigma_{\beta\beta} \alpha' = \Omega,$$

see (10.4).   □

If instead of an unrestricted β we estimate β under restrictions, the proof of consistency is not so simple, see Saikkonen(1995) and Johansen (1996). We shall not go into this problem, but whenever needed we assume that the estimator of β is superconsistent in the sense above, that is, $\hat{\beta} - \beta \in o_P(T^{-\frac{1}{2}})$.

13.4   Asymptotic Distribution of $\hat{\beta}$ and $\hat{\alpha}$

We next give the asymptotic distribution of the estimator $\hat{\beta}_c$ and the corresponding $\hat{\alpha}_c$. We give the details for the proof of the normalized unrestricted estimator and quote the result for β when estimated under identifying linear restrictions. But first we give a result for the normalized estimators $\tilde{\beta}$ and $\tilde{\alpha}$.

LEMMA 13.2   *The asymptotic distribution of $\tilde{\beta}$ is mixed Gaussian and given by*

$$TU_T = \left(T\gamma, T^{3/2}\tau\right)' \left(\tilde{\beta} - \beta\right) \xrightarrow{w} \left[\int_0^1 GG' du\right]^{-1} \int_0^1 G\left(dV_\alpha'\right),$$

hence $\tilde{\beta} - \beta \in O_P\left(T^{-1}\right)$. The conditional variance of the limit distribution is given by

$$\left[\int_0^1 GG' du\right]^{-1} \otimes \left(\alpha' \Omega^{-1} \alpha\right)^{-1}.$$

The asymptotic distribution of $\tilde{\alpha}$ is given by

$$T^{\frac{1}{2}} (\tilde{\alpha} - \alpha) \xrightarrow{w} N_{p \times r} \left(0, \Omega \otimes \Sigma_{\beta\beta}^{-1}\right).$$

Here

$$G(u) = \begin{bmatrix} \bar{\gamma}' C(W(u) - \bar{W}) \\ u - \frac{1}{2} \end{bmatrix},$$

and $V_\alpha(u) = \left(\alpha'\Omega^{-1}\alpha\right)^{-1} \alpha'\Omega^{-1} W(u)$, *see Lemma 10.2, are independent.*

Note that the speed of convergence is different in the directions τ and γ corresponding to different behaviour of the process X_t in these directions as given in Lemma 10.2.

PROOF   The estimators $\tilde{\alpha}$ and $\tilde{\beta}$ satisfy the likelihood equations, and we therefore derive expressions for the derivative of $\log L(\alpha, \beta, \Omega)$, the concentrated likelihood function, see (6.8), with respect to β and α in the directions b and a respectively:

$$D_\beta \log L(\alpha, \beta, \Omega)(b) = tr\{\Omega^{-1}(\textstyle\sum_{t=1}^{T} \hat{\epsilon}_t R'_{1t} b\alpha')\}$$

$$= T tr\{\alpha'\Omega^{-1}(S_{01} - \alpha\beta' S_{11}) b\},$$

$$D_\alpha \log L(\alpha, \beta, \Omega)(a) = tr\{\Omega^{-1}(\textstyle\sum_{t=1}^{T} \hat{\epsilon}_t R'_{1t} \beta a')\}$$

$$= T tr\{\Omega^{-1}(S_{01} - \alpha\beta' S_{11}) \beta a'\}.$$

From these results we can derive the first order conditions that are satisfied at a maximum point. At the point $(\tilde{\alpha}, \tilde{\beta})$ the derivatives are zero in all directions hence the likelihood equations are

$$\tilde{\alpha}'\hat{\Omega}^{-1}(S_{01} - \tilde{\alpha}\tilde{\beta}' S_{11}) = 0, \tag{13.8}$$

$$(S_{01} - \tilde{\alpha}\tilde{\beta}' S_{11})\tilde{\beta} = 0. \tag{13.9}$$

Define

$$S_{\epsilon 1} = T^{-1} \sum_{t=1}^{T} \hat{\epsilon}_t R'_{1t} = S_{01} - \alpha\beta' S_{11}.$$

Consider first equation (13.8) and insert $S_{01} = \alpha\beta' S_{11} + S_{\epsilon 1}$ to get

$$0 = \tilde{\alpha}'\hat{\Omega}^{-1}(S_{01} - \tilde{\alpha}\tilde{\beta}' S_{11}) = \tilde{\alpha}'\hat{\Omega}^{-1}(S_{\epsilon 1} + \alpha\beta' S_{11} - \tilde{\alpha}\tilde{\beta}' S_{11})$$

$$= \tilde{\alpha}'\hat{\Omega}^{-1}(S_{\epsilon 1} - \tilde{\alpha}(\tilde{\beta} - \beta)' S_{11} - (\tilde{\alpha} - \alpha)\beta' S_{11}).$$

We next multiply by $B_T = (\bar{\gamma}, T^{-\frac{1}{2}}\bar{\tau})$ from the right and insert $\tilde{\beta} - \beta = B_T U_T$. We then get

$$0 = \tilde{\alpha}'\hat{\Omega}^{-1}(S_{\epsilon 1} B_T - \tilde{\alpha} T U_T' \left[T^{-1} B_T' S_{11} B_T\right] - (\tilde{\alpha} - \alpha)\beta' S_{11} B_T).$$

By Lemma 10.3 and the consistency of $\tilde{\alpha}$ the last term tends to zero and the consistency of $\hat{\Omega}$ then implies that

$$TU_T = \left[T^{-1}B'_T S_{11} B_T\right]^{-1} B'_T S'_{1\epsilon} \Omega^{-1}\alpha \left(\alpha'\Omega^{-1}\alpha\right)^{-1} + o_P(1),$$

which by (10.16) and (10.17) converges towards

$$\left[\int_0^1 GG' du\right]^{-1} \int_0^1 G\,(dW)'\,\Omega^{-1}\alpha \left(\alpha'\Omega^{-1}\alpha\right)^{-1},$$

as was to be shown. This result implies that $\tilde{\beta} - \beta \in O_P\left(T^{-1}\right)$. Next consider (13.9) and insert $S_{01} = \alpha\beta' S_{11} + S_{\epsilon 1}$. Then

$$0 = (S_{\epsilon 1} + \alpha\beta' S_{11} - \tilde{\alpha}\tilde{\beta}' S_{11})\tilde{\beta}$$

$$= S_{\epsilon 1}\tilde{\beta} - (\tilde{\alpha} - \alpha)\tilde{\beta}' S_{11}\tilde{\beta} - \alpha(\tilde{\beta} - \beta)' S_{11}\tilde{\beta}.$$

Multiplying by $T^{\frac{1}{2}}$ we find

$$\left[T^{\frac{1}{2}}(\tilde{\alpha} - \alpha)\right]\tilde{\beta}' S_{11}\tilde{\beta} = T^{\frac{1}{2}} S_{\epsilon 1}\tilde{\beta} - T^{\frac{1}{2}}\alpha(\tilde{\beta} - \beta)' S_{11}\tilde{\beta}$$

$$= T^{\frac{1}{2}} S_{\epsilon 1}\beta + T^{\frac{1}{2}} S_{\epsilon 1}(\tilde{\beta} - \beta) - T^{\frac{1}{2}}\alpha(\tilde{\beta} - \beta)' S_{11}\tilde{\beta}.$$

It was shown above that $\tilde{\beta} - \beta$ is $O_P\left(T^{-1}\right)$ such that it follows that the last two terms tend to zero, and the first converges weakly by the central limit theorem to $N_{p\times r}(0, \Omega \otimes \Sigma_{\beta\beta})$. Since also $\tilde{\beta}' S_{11}\tilde{\beta} \xrightarrow{P} \Sigma_{\beta\beta}$ the result about $\tilde{\alpha}$ follows.   □

We next give the result for $\hat{\beta}$ normalized by c.

THEOREM 13.3 *Let $\hat{\beta}$ and β be normalized by $c'\beta = c'\hat{\beta} = I$, then*

$$T(\hat{\beta} - \beta) \xrightarrow{w} (I - \beta c')\bar{\gamma}\left[\int_0^1 G_{1.2} G'_{1.2} du\right]^{-1} \int_0^1 G_{1.2}\,(dV'_\alpha), \qquad (13.10)$$

where

$$G_{1.2}(u) = G_1(u) - \int_0^1 G_1 G'_2 du \left[\int_0^1 G_2 G'_2 du\right]^{-1} G_2(u),$$

that is, $\bar{\gamma}' CW$ corrected for intercept and trend, and

$$V_\alpha = (\alpha'\Omega^{-1}\alpha)^{-1}\alpha'\Omega^{-1}W.$$

Hence the asymptotic distribution is mixed Gaussian with conditional variance

$$(I - \beta c')\,\bar{\gamma} \left[\int_0^1 G_{1.2}G'_{1.2}du \right]^{-1} \bar{\gamma}'\,(I - c\beta') \otimes (\alpha'\Omega^{-1}\alpha)^{-1}, \qquad (13.11)$$

which is consistently estimated by

$$T(I - \hat{\beta}c')S_{11}^{-1}(I - c\hat{\beta}') \otimes (\hat{\alpha}'\hat{\Omega}^{-1}\hat{\alpha})^{-1}. \qquad (13.12)$$

The asymptotic distribution of $\hat{\alpha}$ when $\hat{\beta}$ is normalized by c is given by

$$T^{\frac{1}{2}}(\hat{\alpha} - \alpha) \xrightarrow{w} N_{p\times r}(0, \Omega \otimes \Sigma_{\beta\beta}^{-1}).$$

Note that if we consider the linear combination $\tau'(\hat{\beta} - \beta)$ then the limit distribution is singular since $\tau'\gamma = 0$ and $\tau'\beta = 0$. Thus a different normalization is needed. The results can be derived from Lemma 13.2 but will not be given here.

PROOF   The expansion (13.3) implies that if $\hat{\beta}$ and β are normalized by c, then
$$T(\hat{\beta} - \beta) = (I - \beta c')\,T(\tilde{\beta} - \beta) + O_P(T|\tilde{\beta} - \beta|^2).$$
From (13.1) we then get that

$$T(\hat{\beta} - \beta) = (I - \beta c')\,(\bar{\gamma}TU_{1T} + T^{-\frac{1}{2}}\bar{\tau}TU_{2T}) + O_P(T|\tilde{\beta} - \beta|^2).$$

Since $|\tilde{\beta} - \beta|^2$ is $O_P(T^{-2})$ and TU_T is convergent it follows that $T(\hat{\beta} - \beta)$ has the same limit distribution as $(I - \beta c')\,\bar{\gamma}TU_{1T}$, that is, the marginal distribution of the first components as given by Lemma 13.2.
From the definition

$$\hat{\alpha}_c = \tilde{\alpha}\tilde{\beta}'c = \tilde{\alpha}((\tilde{\beta} - \beta)'c) + \tilde{\alpha},$$

it follows that

$$T^{\frac{1}{2}}(\hat{\alpha}_c - \alpha) = T^{\frac{1}{2}}(\tilde{\alpha} - \alpha) + T^{\frac{1}{2}}\tilde{\alpha}((\tilde{\beta} - \beta)'c),$$

which is seen to have the same limit distribution as $T^{\frac{1}{2}}(\tilde{\alpha} - \alpha)$, since $|\tilde{\beta} - \beta|$ is $O_P(T^{-1})$. The result then follows from Lemma 13.2.   □

The asymptotic results on the estimator should be interpreted carefully. The asymptotic distribution of $\hat{\beta}$ is mixed Gaussian, that is, for fixed value of the mixing process G, the distribution is Gaussian. This means that the distribution of the estimator has much broader tails than the Gaussian, with the result that once in a while an extreme value of the estimator appears. Note, however, that when testing hypotheses one does not normalize by the variance of $\hat{\beta}$, but by the asymptotic conditional variance, or the limit of the inverse information, which even in the limit is random. This means that one does not apply the distribution of $\hat{\beta}$ for testing, hence the values of $\hat{\beta}$ have to be interpreted with a 'variance' given by (13.12) not by its population variance. Another way of saying this is that whereas one normally applies the asymptotic distribution of the estimator for testing, in the case of β we need the joint limit distribution of $\hat{\beta}$ and the information in the sample.

A general result about a smooth parametrization $\beta(\vartheta)$, $\vartheta \in \Theta$ is proved in Johansen (1991b), Phillips (1991), and Reinsel and Ahn (1992). This result implies that for any linear or non-linear restriction on the coefficients of the cointegrating relations one can apply the usual result that $\hat{\vartheta}$ is asymptotically mixed Gaussian with an estimator of the asymptotic conditional variance as would be found from the second derivative of the likelihood function. What remains in such a general situation is to find conditions for the existence and uniqueness of the maximum likelihood estimator and to find an efficient algorithm for the calculation of the estimators.

We give here a result from Johansen (1995b) on the asymptotic distribution of $\hat{\beta}$ when it is estimated under identifying restrictions. Let $R_1, \ldots, R_r$ be the restrictions, such that $R_i'\beta_i = 0$, see Chapter 5.

We let $H_i = R_{i\perp}$ and use the formulation

$$\beta = (H_1\varphi_1, \ldots, H_r\varphi_r).$$

We also want to normalize the vectors, and a general version of this is given by

$$\beta_i = h_i + H^i\psi_i,$$

where $sp\left(h_i, H^i\right) = sp\left(H_i\right)$.

The limit distribution is most conveniently expressed in terms of the following notation. The block diagonal matrix with blocks A_i, $i = 1, \ldots, s$ is denoted by $\{A_i\}$, and the block matrix with blocks A_{ij} is denoted by $\{A_{ij}\}$.

THEOREM 13.4 *The maximum likelihood estimator of the identified β is consistent and the asymptotic distribution is mixed Gaussian. An estimator of the asymptotic conditional variance of $T(\hat{\beta} - \beta)$ is given by*

$$T\{H^i\}\{\hat{\rho}_{ij}H^{i\prime}S_{11}H^j\}^{-1}\{H^{j\prime}\}, \ \hat{\rho}_{ij} = \hat{\alpha}_i'\hat{\Omega}^{-1}\hat{\alpha}_j.$$

The difficulty in the proof is the discussion of consistency. Since the maximum likelihood estimator is not explicitly defined one will have to derive the consistency from the asymptotic behaviour of the likelihood function. This will not be attempted here, but exercise 13.8 is a guided tour through the easy part of the proof, which involves the asymptotic distribution under the assumption that the estimator is consistent. Here we illustrate the result by an example.

EXAMPLE 13.1 Consider the basic model

$$\Delta X_t = \alpha \beta' X_{t-1} + \epsilon_t, \, t = 1, \ldots, T,$$

with $p = 4$, $r = 2$, and β of the form

$$\beta = \begin{bmatrix} 1 & \chi \\ 0 & 1 \\ \varphi & 0 \\ \psi & \eta \end{bmatrix}, \, (\varphi, \psi, \chi, \eta) \in R^4.$$

It is seen that the rank condition is satisfied for β if $\varphi \neq 0$, in which case β is just identified. We define the matrices

$$h_1 = \begin{bmatrix} 1 \\ 0 \\ 0 \\ 0 \end{bmatrix}, \, H^1 = \begin{bmatrix} 0 & 0 \\ 0 & 0 \\ 1 & 0 \\ 0 & 1 \end{bmatrix}, \, h_2 = \begin{bmatrix} 0 \\ 1 \\ 0 \\ 0 \end{bmatrix}, \, H^2 = \begin{bmatrix} 1 & 0 \\ 0 & 0 \\ 0 & 0 \\ 0 & 1 \end{bmatrix}.$$

Then the identifying restrictions can be expressed as

$$\beta_1 = h_1 + H^1 \begin{bmatrix} \varphi \\ \psi \end{bmatrix}, \, \beta_2 = h_2 + H^2 \begin{bmatrix} \chi \\ \eta \end{bmatrix}.$$

The asymptotic distribution of the estimators of $(\varphi, \psi, \chi, \eta)$ is mixed Gaussian around the true values with an asymptotic quadratic variation process for $T((\hat{\varphi}, \hat{\psi}, \hat{\chi}, \hat{\eta}) - (\varphi, \psi, \chi, \eta))$ estimated by

$$T \begin{bmatrix} \hat{\rho}_{11} H^{1\prime} S_{11} H^1 & \hat{\rho}_{12} H^{1\prime} S_{11} H^2 \\ \hat{\rho}_{21} H^{2\prime} S_{11} H^1 & \hat{\rho}_{22} H^{2\prime} S_{11} H^2 \end{bmatrix}^{-1}, \, \hat{\rho}_{ij} = \hat{\alpha}_i \hat{\Omega}^{-1} \hat{\alpha}_j.$$

Thus asymptotic inference concerning the parameters can be conducted as if they are Gaussian with the above variance matrix, provided parameters are estimated by the maximum likelihood procedure.

Perhaps an even better way of writing the result is as follows:

$$\begin{bmatrix} T^{-1} \hat{\rho}_{11} H^{1\prime} S_{11} H^1 & T^{-1} \hat{\rho}_{12} H^{1\prime} S_{11} H^2 \\ T^{-1} \hat{\rho}_{21} H^{2\prime} S_{11} H^1 & T^{-1} \hat{\rho}_{22} H^{2\prime} S_{11} H^2 \end{bmatrix}^{-\frac{1}{2}} T \begin{bmatrix} \hat{\varphi} - \varphi \\ \hat{\psi} - \psi \\ \hat{\chi} - \chi \\ \hat{\eta} - \eta \end{bmatrix} \xrightarrow{w} N_4(0, I).$$

If we would rather specify the asymptotic distribution of the estimated cointegrating vectors themselves we see that

$$\hat{\beta}_1 - \beta_1 = H^1 \begin{bmatrix} \hat{\varphi} - \varphi \\ \hat{\psi} - \psi \end{bmatrix}, \, \hat{\beta}_2 - \beta_2 = H^2 \begin{bmatrix} \hat{\chi} - \chi \\ \hat{\eta} - \eta \end{bmatrix},$$

which accounts for the extra factors $\{H^i\}$ and $\{H^{i\prime}\}$, with

$$\{H^i\} = \begin{bmatrix} H^1 & 0 \\ 0 & H^2 \end{bmatrix},$$

in the result of Theorem 13.4.

13.5 More Asymptotic Distributions

The results obtained in section 13.4 can be applied to find the asymptotic distribution of the remaining parameter estimates. We first discuss the distribution of the estimator for the parameters $\vartheta = (\alpha, \Gamma_1, \ldots, \Gamma_{k-1})$ and then find the asymptotic distribution of $\hat{\mu}$. In deriving the asymptotic distribution of $\hat{\vartheta}$ we use the fact that they are all coefficients to stationary variables, since both $\beta'X_t$ and ΔX_t are stationary. We define

$$Z_t(\beta)' = ((\beta'X_{t-1})', \Delta X'_{t-1}, \ldots, \Delta X'_{t-k+1}),$$

and $\bar{Z}_T(\beta) = T^{-1}\sum_{t=1}^T Z_t(\beta)$. Note that $E(\Delta X_t) = C\mu$ and that the expectation of $\beta'X_t$ can be found from the model equation (4.1),

$$C\mu = E(\Delta X_t) = \alpha E(\beta'X_{t-1}) + \sum_{i=1}^{k-1}\Gamma_iC\mu + \mu.$$

Multiplying by $\bar{\alpha}'$, gives

$$E(\beta'X_t) = \bar{\alpha}'(C - I - \sum_{i=1}^{k-1}\Gamma_iC)\mu = \bar{\alpha}'(\Gamma C - I)\mu,$$

with $\Gamma = I - \Sigma_{i=1}^{k-1}\Gamma_i$, see Theorem 4.2. Thus

$$E(Z_t(\beta))' = \mu'\{(C'\Gamma' - I)\bar{\alpha}, C', \ldots, C'\} = \mu'\xi',$$

say. We denote $\Sigma = \mathrm{Var}(Z_t(\beta))$. Clearly this can be calculated in terms of $\alpha, \beta, \Gamma_1, \ldots, \Gamma_{k-1}$ and Ω, but this will not be needed here, since we shall estimate it consistently from $Z_t(\hat{\beta})$.

THEOREM 13.5 *If β is normalized by $c'\beta = I$ then the asymptotic distribution of the estimator $\hat{\vartheta} = (\hat{\alpha}, \hat{\Gamma}_1, \ldots, \hat{\Gamma}_{k-1})$ is given by*

$$T^{\frac{1}{2}}(\hat{\vartheta} - \vartheta) \xrightarrow{w} N_{p\times(r+(k-1)p)}(0, \Omega \otimes \Sigma^{-1}),$$

where Σ is consistently estimated by

$$T^{-1} \sum_{t=1}^{T} (Z_t(\hat{\beta}) - \bar{Z}_T(\hat{\beta}))(Z_t(\hat{\beta}) - \bar{Z}_T(\hat{\beta}))' \xrightarrow{P} \Sigma = \text{Var}\,(Z_t(\beta)).$$

PROOF The model can be written as

$$\Delta X_t = \vartheta Z_t(\beta) + \mu + \epsilon_t.$$

For fixed β this is just a regression equation which determines the maximum likelihood estimator $\hat{\vartheta}(\beta)$ by the equation

$$T^{\frac{1}{2}}(\hat{\vartheta}(\beta) - \vartheta) \left[T^{-1} \sum_{t=1}^{T} (Z_t(\beta) - \bar{Z}_t(\beta)) (Z_t(\beta) - \bar{Z}_t(\beta))' \right]$$

$$= T^{-\frac{1}{2}} \sum_{t=1}^{T} \epsilon_t (Z_t(\beta) - \bar{Z}_t(\beta))'.$$

By Theorem B.13 this is weakly convergent to a Gaussian distribution with mean zero and variance $\Omega \otimes \Sigma$, such that

$$T^{\frac{1}{2}}(\hat{\vartheta}(\beta) - \vartheta) \xrightarrow{w} N\left(0, \Omega \otimes \Sigma^{-1}\right).$$

Here Σ is the probability limit of

$$T^{-1} \sum_{t=1}^{T} (Z_t(\beta) - \bar{Z}_t(\beta)) (Z_t(\beta) - \bar{Z}_t(\beta))'.$$

It is not difficult to see that we can replace β by $\hat{\beta}$ due to the relations (13.4) and (13.5), which shows Theorem 13.5 for $\hat{\vartheta} = \hat{\vartheta}(\hat{\beta})$. $\quad\square$

THEOREM 13.6 *The asymptotic distribution of* $T^{\frac{1}{2}}(\hat{\mu} - \mu)$ *is found from*

$$T^{\frac{1}{2}}(\hat{\mu} - \mu) \xrightarrow{w} N_p\left(0, \Omega\mu'\xi'\Sigma^{-1}\xi\mu\right)$$

$$+ W(1) - \alpha \int_0^1 (dV_\alpha)\, G' \left[\int_0^1 GG'du \right]^{-1} \bar{G}_0, \tag{13.13}$$

where $\xi\mu = E\,(Z_t(\beta))$, $\Sigma = \text{Var}\,(Z_t(\beta))$,

$$T^{-\frac{1}{2}} B_T' X_{[Tu]} \xrightarrow{w} G_0(u) = \begin{bmatrix} \bar{\gamma}'CW(u) \\ u \end{bmatrix},$$

and $G(u) = G_0(u) - \bar{G}_0$, *see Lemma 10.2. The first term in (13.13) is independent of the last two terms.*

Thus

$$T^{\frac{1}{2}}\alpha'_{\perp}\left(\hat{\mu}-\mu\right) \xrightarrow{w} N_{p-r}\left(0,\alpha'_{\perp}\Omega\alpha_{\perp}\left(\mu'\xi'\Sigma^{-1}\xi\mu+1\right)\right),$$

that is, asymptotically Gaussian, whereas

$$T^{\frac{1}{2}}\alpha'\Omega^{-1}\left(\hat{\mu}-\mu\right) \xrightarrow{w} N_r\left(0,\alpha'\Omega^{-1}\alpha\mu'\xi'\Sigma^{-1}\xi\mu\right)$$
$$+\ \alpha'\Omega^{-1}W\left(1\right)-\alpha'\Omega^{-1}\alpha\int_0^1\left(dV_\alpha\right)G'\left[\int_0^1 GG'du\right]^{-1}\bar{G}_0,$$

is asymptotically mixed Gaussian with conditional variance given by

$$\alpha'\Omega^{-1}\alpha(\mu'\xi'\Sigma^{-1}\xi\mu+1+\bar{G}'_0\left[\int_0^1 GG'du\right]^{-1}\bar{G}_0).$$

PROOF   The likelihood equation for μ is

$$T^{-1}\sum_{t=1}^{T}\Delta X_t = \hat{\alpha}\hat{\beta}'\bar{X}_T+\sum_{i=1}^{k-1}\hat{\Gamma}_iT^{-1}\sum_{t=1}^{T}\Delta X_{t-i}+\hat{\mu},$$

and the model equation implies

$$T^{-1}\sum_{t=1}^{T}\Delta X_t = \alpha\beta'\bar{X}_T+\sum_{i=1}^{k-1}\Gamma_iT^{-1}\sum_{t=1}^{T}\Delta X_{t-i}+\mu+\bar{\epsilon}_T.$$

From this we find since $\alpha\beta'-\hat{\alpha}\hat{\beta}'=-\hat{\alpha}(\hat{\beta}-\beta)'-(\hat{\alpha}-\alpha)\beta'$

$$T^{\frac{1}{2}}\left(\hat{\mu}-\mu\right)$$

$$=T^{\frac{1}{2}}(\alpha\beta'-\hat{\alpha}\hat{\beta}')\bar{X}_T+\sum_{i=1}^{k-1}T^{\frac{1}{2}}(\Gamma_i-\hat{\Gamma}_i)T^{-1}\sum_{t=1}^{T}\Delta X_{t-i}+T^{-\frac{1}{2}}\sum_{t=1}^{T}\epsilon_t$$

$$=-T^{\frac{1}{2}}\hat{\alpha}(\hat{\beta}-\beta)'\bar{X}_T-T^{\frac{1}{2}}(\hat{\vartheta}-\vartheta)\bar{Z}_T\left(\beta\right)+T^{-\frac{1}{2}}\sum_{t=1}^{T}\epsilon_t,$$

which we write

$$T^{\frac{1}{2}}\left(\hat{\mu}-\mu\right)$$

$$=-\hat{\alpha}\left[TU'_T\right]\left[T^{-\frac{1}{2}}B'_T\bar{X}_T\right]-T^{\frac{1}{2}}\left(\hat{\vartheta}-\vartheta\right)\bar{Z}_T\left(\beta\right)+T^{-\frac{1}{2}}\sum_{t=1}^{T}\epsilon_t. \tag{13.14}$$

From this expression we derive the limit distribution of $T^{\frac{1}{2}}\left(\hat{\mu}-\mu\right)$. From Lemma 10.2 we find that $T^{-\frac{1}{2}}B'_T\bar{X}_T \xrightarrow{w} \bar{G}_0$. From Theorem 13.5 we see that $T^{\frac{1}{2}}(\hat{\vartheta}-\vartheta)\bar{Z}_T\left(\beta\right) \xrightarrow{w} N\left(0,\Omega\mu'\xi'\Sigma^{-1}\xi\mu\right)$. Finally Lemma 13.2 shows that

$$TU'_T \xrightarrow{w} \int_0^1 (dV_\alpha)\, G' \left[\int_0^1 GG'\, du \right]^{-1}.$$

Combining the results we find (13.13). It only remains to see that the contribution from the limit of $T^{\frac{1}{2}}(\hat{\vartheta} - \vartheta)$ is independent of the other terms. It is seen from the proof of Theorem 13.5 that the limit of $T^{\frac{1}{2}}(\hat{\vartheta} - \vartheta)$ is derived from

$$T^{-\frac{1}{2}} \sum_{t=1}^{[Tu]} \epsilon_t \left(Z_t(\beta) - \bar{Z}_T(\beta) \right)'.$$

This process converges towards a Brownian motion with covariance matrix $\Omega \otimes \Sigma$, but the covariance with the process $T^{-\frac{1}{2}} \sum_{t=1}^{[Tu]} \epsilon_t$ is zero, implying that the two limit processes are independent. Since the contributions from $(\hat{\beta} - \beta)' \bar{X}_T$ and $T^{-\frac{1}{2}} \sum_{t=1}^{[Tu]} \epsilon_t$ in (13.14) only depend on W the result is proved. Multiplication by $\alpha'_\perp$ and $\alpha' \Omega^{-1}$ gives the final formulation. $\square$

The reason for the final formulation with $\alpha_\perp$ and $\alpha' \Omega^{-1}$ is that the asymptotic distribution of $T^{\frac{1}{2}}(\hat{\mu} - \mu)$ is not mixed Gaussian in the sense that if in (13.13) we condition on G the expectation is not zero. If, however, we consider the components in the direction $\alpha'_\perp$ and $\alpha' \Omega^{-1}$, then we get mixed Gaussian distributions with conditional expectation zero. The result implies that inference in the form of Wald tests is not so simple, but the hypothesis about the absence of the trend $\alpha'_\perp \mu = 0$ is easily tested, see Corollary 11.2.

THEOREM 13.7 *The asymptotic distribution of the estimators of* $\Pi = \alpha\beta'$, $C = \beta_\perp \left(\alpha'_\perp \Gamma \beta_\perp \right)^{-1} \alpha'_\perp$, *and* $\tau = C\mu$ *are given by*

$$T^{\frac{1}{2}}(\hat{\Pi} - \Pi) \xrightarrow{w} N_{p \times p}(0, \Omega \otimes \beta \Sigma_{\beta\beta}^{-1} \beta'),$$

$$T^{\frac{1}{2}}(\hat{C} - C) \xrightarrow{w} N_{p \times p}(0, C\Omega C' \otimes \xi' \Sigma^{-1} \xi),$$

$$T^{\frac{1}{2}}(\hat{\tau} - \tau) \xrightarrow{w} CW(1),$$

with $\xi' = ((C'\Gamma' - I)\bar{\alpha}, C', \ldots, C')$. *An efficient estimator of* τ *is* $T^{-1} X_T$.

PROOF We let β be normalized by a matrix c and apply Theorem 13.3. We find

$$T^{\frac{1}{2}}(\hat{\Pi} - \Pi) = T^{\frac{1}{2}}(\hat{\alpha}\hat{\beta}' - \alpha\beta') = T^{\frac{1}{2}}(\hat{\alpha} - \alpha)\beta' + O_P(T^{-\frac{1}{2}}),$$

since the superconsistency of $\hat{\beta}$ implies that $\hat{\beta} - \beta \in O_P(T^{-1})$. Thus the result about $\hat{\Pi}$ follows from that of $\hat{\alpha}$ and the asymptotic variation of $\hat{\beta}$ plays no role in the asymptotic variance of $\hat{\Pi}$ due to the superconsistency of $\hat{\beta}$. Note that the asymptotic variance matrix is singular, and that hypotheses on β require investigation of this singularity as indicated by the asymptotic distribution of $\hat{\beta}$.

If we choose $\hat{\alpha}_\perp = \alpha_\perp - \alpha\,(\hat{\alpha}'\alpha)^{-1}\,\hat{\alpha}'\alpha_\perp$ then $\hat{\alpha}'\hat{\alpha}_\perp = 0$ and

$$\hat{\alpha}_\perp - \alpha_\perp = -\bar{\alpha}\,(\hat{\alpha} - \alpha)'\,\alpha_\perp + O_P(T^{-1}).$$

The superconsistency of $\hat{\beta}$ implies that we can replace $\hat{\beta}_\perp$ by $\beta_\perp$ in the expression for $\hat{C}$ with an error of $O_P(T^{-1})$ and we then get, apart from terms of $O_P(T^{-1})$,

$$\hat{C} = \hat{\beta}_\perp(\hat{\alpha}'_\perp\hat{\Gamma}\hat{\beta}_\perp)^{-1}\hat{\alpha}'_\perp = \beta_\perp(\hat{\alpha}'_\perp\hat{\Gamma}\beta_\perp)^{-1}\hat{\alpha}'_\perp$$

$$= \beta_\perp[\alpha'_\perp\Gamma\beta_\perp + (\hat{\alpha}_\perp - \alpha_\perp)'\Gamma\beta_\perp + \hat{\alpha}'_\perp(\hat{\Gamma} - \Gamma)\beta_\perp]^{-1}(\alpha_\perp + \hat{\alpha}_\perp - \alpha_\perp)'$$

$$= C - \beta_\perp(\alpha'_\perp\Gamma\beta_\perp)^{-1}(\hat{\alpha}_\perp - \alpha_\perp)'\Gamma\beta_\perp(\alpha'_\perp\Gamma\beta_\perp)^{-1}\alpha'_\perp$$

$$- \beta_\perp(\alpha'_\perp\Gamma\beta_\perp)^{-1}\alpha'_\perp(\hat{\Gamma} - \Gamma)\beta_\perp(\alpha'_\perp\Gamma\beta_\perp)^{-1}\alpha'_\perp$$

$$+ \beta_\perp(\alpha'_\perp\Gamma\beta_\perp)^{-1}(\hat{\alpha}_\perp - \alpha_\perp)'.$$

Now insert $\hat{\alpha}_\perp - \alpha_\perp = -\bar{\alpha}\,(\hat{\alpha} - \alpha)'\,\alpha_\perp + O_P(T^{-1})$ and use the definition of C, and we find

$$\hat{C} - C = C(\hat{\alpha} - \alpha)\bar{\alpha}'(\Gamma C - I) - C(\hat{\Gamma} - \Gamma)C + O_P(T^{-1}) = C(\hat{\vartheta} - \vartheta)\xi + O_P(T^{-1}),$$

with $\xi' = ((C'\Gamma' - I)\bar{\alpha},\ C',\ \ldots,\ C')$, since $\Gamma = I - \sum_{i=1}^{k-1}\Gamma_i$, and $\vartheta = (\alpha,\ \Gamma_1,\ \ldots,\ \Gamma_{k-1})$

Thus the asymptotic distribution can be found from Theorem 13.5. This result can also be found in Paruolo (1995a).

Next consider the estimation of τ. From the likelihood equation for $\hat{\mu}$ we find by multiplying by $\hat{C}$ that

$$\hat{\tau} = \hat{C}\hat{\mu} = \hat{C}T^{-1}\,(X_T - X_0) - \sum_{i=1}^{k-1}\hat{C}\hat{\Gamma}_i T^{-1}\,(X_{T-i} - X_{-i})$$

$$= \hat{C}\hat{\Gamma}_i T^{-1}X_T - \sum_{i=1}^{k-1}\hat{C}\hat{\Gamma}_i T^{-1}\,(X_{T-i} - X_T - X_{-i}) + O_P(T^{-1})$$

$$= \hat{C}\hat{\Gamma}T^{-1}X_T + O_P(T^{-1}),$$

since $\hat{C}\hat{\alpha}\hat{\beta}'\bar{X}_T = 0$. From Granger's representation theorem we find

$$T^{-1}X_T = CT^{-1}\sum_{i=1}^{T}\epsilon_i + C\mu + O_P\left(T^{-1}\right),$$

and hence that

$$T^{\frac{1}{2}}\left(\hat{\tau} - \tau\right) = T^{\frac{1}{2}}(\hat{C}\hat{\Gamma}T^{-1}X_T - C\mu) + O_P(T^{-\frac{1}{2}})$$

$$= \hat{C}\hat{\Gamma}C\left[T^{-\frac{1}{2}}\sum_{i=1}^{T}\epsilon_i\right] + T^{\frac{1}{2}}(\hat{C}\hat{\Gamma}C - C)\mu + o_P(1).$$

In the expression for $\hat{C}\hat{\Gamma}C$ we can insert $\hat{\beta}_\perp = \beta_\perp + O_P(T^{-1})$ and find apart from terms of the order $O_P(T^{-1})$

$$\hat{C}\hat{\Gamma}C = \beta_\perp(\hat{\alpha}'_\perp\hat{\Gamma}\beta_\perp)^{-1}\hat{\alpha}'_\perp\hat{\Gamma}\beta_\perp(\alpha'_\perp\Gamma\beta_\perp)^{-1}\alpha'_\perp = C$$

□

13.6 The Likelihood Ratio Test for Hypotheses on the Long-Run Coefficients β

In this section we will exploit the mixed Gaussian distribution as obtained in section 13.4 to show that the likelihood ratio test statistics of hypotheses on β are asymptotically χ^2 distributed. This follows since a Taylor expansion of the likelihood function around the maximum value gives a quadratic approximation, and by conditioning on the mixing parameter one obtains an asymptotic χ^2 distribution.

We first derive a second order approximation to the likelihood function and then apply this to give the asymptotic distribution of the test statistic for a simple hypothesis on β, as well as the test statistic for $\beta = H\varphi$ and for general identifying restrictions on β.

LEMMA 13.8 *The likelihood ratio test for a simple hypothesis on β has the representation*

$$- 2\log Q\left(\beta|H\left(r\right)\right) = T tr\left\{\left(\alpha'\Omega^{-1}\alpha\right)(\tilde{\beta} - \beta)'S_{11}(\tilde{\beta} - \beta)\right\} + O_P\left(T^{-1}\right),$$
(13.15)

which is asymptotically distributed as

$$tr\left\{\left(\alpha'\Omega^{-1}\alpha\right)\int_0^1(dV_\alpha)\,G'\left[\int_0^1 GG'du\right]^{-1}\int_0^1 G\,(dV_\alpha)\right\},$$
(13.16)

where G is given in Lemma 13.2. The distribution of (13.16) is χ^2 with $r\,(p-r)$ degrees of freedom.

PROOF The likelihood ratio test has the form

$$-2\log Q\left(\beta|H\left(r\right)\right) = -2\log(L_{\max}\left(\beta\right)/L_{\max}(\tilde{\beta})),$$

where

$$L_{\max}^{-2/T}(\beta) = |S_{00}||\beta'(S_{11} - S_{10}S_{00}^{-1}S_{01})\beta|/|\beta'S_{11}\beta|, \qquad (13.17)$$

see (6.14).

In the following it is useful to evaluate the order of magnitude of various terms. From (13.2) we have $\tilde{\beta} - \beta = B_T U_T$, and the result of Lemma 13.2 is that $T U_T$ converges in distribution. Hence

$$(\tilde{\beta} - \beta)'S_{11}\beta \qquad = U_T' B_T' S_{11}\beta \qquad \in O_P(T^{-1}),$$

$$(\tilde{\beta} - \beta)'S_{11}(\tilde{\beta} - \beta) = U_T' B_T' S_{11} B_T U_T \in O_P(T^{-1}),$$

$$(\tilde{\beta} - \beta)'S_{10} \qquad = U_T' B_T' S_{10} \qquad \in O_P(T^{-1}).$$

The remainder terms of the expansion (A.11) is given as $O(||h||^3)$, but in the expression for $-2\log L_{\max}(\beta)$ the remainder terms contains apart from the factor T a product of terms like $(\tilde{\beta} - \beta)'S_{11}(\tilde{\beta} - \beta)$ and $(\tilde{\beta} - \beta)'S_{11}\beta$ which shows that the remainder term is of the order of T^{-1} in probability.

We now expand the logarithm of the expression for $L_{\max}^{-2}(\beta)$ around the value $\beta = \tilde{\beta}$ using the expansion (A.11). We find that $-2\log Q(\beta|H(r))$ equals the difference between two terms: the first we get for $\hat{x} = \tilde{\beta}$, $h = (\tilde{\beta} - \beta)$ and $M = S_{11} - S_{10}S_{00}^{-1}S_{01}$ and the other with $N = S_{11}$. The second term is

$$T\mathrm{tr}\{(\tilde{\beta}'S_{11}\tilde{\beta})^{-1}(\tilde{\beta} - \beta)'(S_{11} - S_{11}\tilde{\beta}(\tilde{\beta}'S_{11}\tilde{\beta})^{-1}\tilde{\beta}'S_{11})(\tilde{\beta} - \beta)\}$$

$$= T\mathrm{tr}\{\Sigma_{\beta\beta}^{-1}(\tilde{\beta} - \beta)'S_{11}(\tilde{\beta} - \beta)\} + O_P(T^{-1}).$$

In a similar way we find the first term can be reduced since

$$\tilde{\beta}'(S_{11} - S_{10}S_{00}^{-1}S_{01})\tilde{\beta} \xrightarrow{P} \Sigma_{\beta\beta} - \Sigma_{\beta 0}\Sigma_{00}^{-1}\Sigma_{0\beta},$$

$$(\tilde{\beta} - \beta)'(S_{11} - S_{10}S_{00}^{-1}S_{01})(\tilde{\beta} - \beta) = (\tilde{\beta} - \beta)'S_{11}(\tilde{\beta} - \beta) + O_P(T^{-2}),$$

$$(\tilde{\beta} - \beta)'(S_{11} - S_{10}S_{00}^{-1}S_{01})\tilde{\beta} = O_P(T^{-1}).$$

Combining these results we find that $-2\log Q(\beta|H(r))$ equals

$$T\mathrm{tr}\left\{\left[\left(\Sigma_{\beta\beta} - \Sigma_{\beta 0}\Sigma_{00}^{-1}\Sigma_{0\beta}\right)^{-1} - \Sigma_{\beta\beta}^{-1}\right](\tilde{\beta} - \beta)'S_{11}(\tilde{\beta} - \beta)\right\} + O_P\left(T^{-1}\right).$$

From (10.8) the first factor equals $\alpha'\Omega^{-1}\alpha$, which shows (13.15). Since $\tilde{\beta} - \beta = B_T U_T$, see Lemma 13.2, we find

$$-2\log Q(\beta|H(r)) = \mathrm{tr}\left\{\alpha'\Omega^{-1}\alpha\left[TU_T'\right]\left[T^{-1}B_T'S_{11}B_T\right]\left[TU_T\right]\right\},$$

apart from terms of the order of T^{-1} in probability. By Lemma 13.2 this converges towards

$$tr\left\{\alpha'\Omega^{-1}\alpha\int_0^1(dV_\alpha)\,G'\left[\int_0^1 GG'du\right]^{-1}\int_0^1 G\,(dV_\alpha)'\right\},$$

which shows (13.16). Now notice that conditionally on G the $r\times(p-r)$ matrix $\int_0^1(dV_\alpha)\,G'$ is Gaussian with mean zero and conditional variance $(\alpha'\Omega^{-1}\alpha)^{-1}\otimes\int_0^1 GG'du$, such that conditionally on G the distribution of the statistic (13.16) is χ^2 with $r\,(p-r)$ degrees of freedom. Hence this result also holds marginally, as was to be proved. $\square$

Another way of expressing this result is as follows: conditioning on G, the integral $\int_0^1(dV_\alpha)G'$ is Gaussian

$$N_{p\times(p-r)}\left(0,(\alpha'\Omega^{-1}\alpha)^{-1}\otimes\int_0^1 GG'du\right),$$

such that the variable

$$Z=(\alpha'\Omega^{-1}\alpha)^{\frac12}\int_0^1(dV_\alpha)G'\left(\int_0^1 GG'du\right)^{-\frac12}\tag{13.18}$$

is $N_{r\times(p-r)}(0,I)$. Expressed in terms of this variable the limit is just $tr\{ZZ'\}$ which is χ^2 with $r\times(p-r)$ degrees of freedom.

The results of Lemma 13.8 is of course not enough for applications where one typically wants to test a composite hypothesis on β as for instance $\beta=H\varphi$, $\beta=(b,\psi)$, $\beta=(H_1\varphi_1,H_2\varphi_2)$ etc. For each of these hypotheses, however, the method is the same. One obtains an expansion of the log-likelihood function around the maximum point with and without restrictions, and by subtracting the expressions one finds an expression for the asymptotic distribution, which turns out to be a χ^2 distribution.

In order to illustrate the technique consider the simple situation where we want to test $\beta=H\varphi$.

THEOREM 13.9 *The asymptotic distribution of the likelihood ratio test for the hypothesis $\beta=H\varphi$, see (7.2), is $\chi^2(r(p-s))$.*

PROOF For fixed $\beta=H\varphi$ we found the maximized likelihood function in (13.17). The asymptotic properties of the sample moments now depend on the asymptotic properties of the process

$$H'X_t=H'C\sum_{i=1}^t\epsilon_i+H'C\mu t+H'Y_t+H'P_{\beta_\perp}X_0,$$

where Y_t is a stationary process, see (4.2).

Let $P_H=H(H'H)^{-1}H'$ denote the projection onto the space $sp(H)$, and define $\tau_H=P_H\tau=\bar H H'C\mu$. Then $\beta=H\varphi$ is orthogonal to τ_H since

$\beta'\tau_H = \beta'P_H\tau = \beta'\tau = 0$. Let γ_H $(p \times (s-r-1))$ be chosen orthogonal to β and τ_H such that $(\beta, \tau_H, \gamma_H)$ span $sp(H)$. Then γ_H is also orthogonal to τ, since $\gamma_H'\tau = \gamma_H'P_H\tau = \gamma_H'\tau_H = 0$, and this shows that $\gamma_H = \gamma\xi_H$ for some matrix ξ_H, where γ is $p \times (p+r-1)$ is orthogonal to (β, τ). Thus $P_H X_t$ will be stationary in the direction β, dominated by a linear trends in the direction τ_H, and finally behave like a random walk without trend in the direction γ_H. Thus in particular we find

$$T^{-\frac{1}{2}}\bar{\gamma}_H' X_{[Tu]} \xrightarrow{w} \bar{\gamma}_H' CW(u),$$

$$T^{-1}\bar{\tau}_H' X_{[Tu]} \xrightarrow{P} u.$$

From these results we can find the asymptotic behaviour of the product moment matrices and derive an asymptotic expression for the log likelihood function of the form (13.16) except that G is now replace by

$$G_H(u) = \begin{bmatrix} \bar{\gamma}_H' C(W(u) - \bar{W}) \\ u - \frac{1}{2} \end{bmatrix} = \begin{bmatrix} (\gamma_H'\gamma_H)^{-1}\xi_H'\gamma'\gamma & 0 \\ 0 & 1 \end{bmatrix} G(u).$$

The likelihood ratio test of $\beta = H\varphi$ is now the difference of the two expressions like (13.16) with G and G_H. We want to simplify this by conditioning on G (and hence G_H), and introduce the $r \times (p-r)$ Gaussian variable Z (13.18) and the $(s-r) \times p$ matrix

$$M' = \begin{bmatrix} (\gamma_H'\gamma_H)^{-1}\xi_H'\gamma'\gamma & 0 \\ 0 & 1 \end{bmatrix} \left(\int_0^1 GG' du \right)^{\frac{1}{2}}$$

We then get the representation

$$-2\log Q(\beta = H\varphi | H_1(r)) \xrightarrow{w} tr\{ZZ'\} - tr\{ZM(M'M)^{-1}M'Z'\}$$

$$= tr\{ZM_\perp(M_\perp'M_\perp)^{-1}M_\perp'Z'\},$$

which is distributed as χ^2 with $r(p-s)$ degrees of freedom.   □

Finally we give the result for the case where the individual cointegrating vectors are identified by linear restrictions.

THEOREM 13.10 *The asymptotic distribution of the likelihood ratio test for the identifying restrictions* $\beta = (H_1\varphi_1, \ldots, H_r\varphi_r)$ *normalized by* $\beta_i = h_i + H^i\psi_i$ *is* χ^2 *with degrees of freedom* $\Sigma_{i=1}^r (p-r-s_i+1)$, *where* H_i *is* $p \times s_i$, *provided* β *is identified.*

PROOF We can write the hypothesis as

$$\beta = (h_1, \ldots, h_r) + (H^1, \ldots, H^r)\{\psi_i\},$$

where we have used the notation of Theorem 13.4, that is, $\{\psi_i\}$ is block diagonal with ψ_i, in the diagonal. By the expansion of the log likelihood function around the maximum point $\hat\beta$ we find that the first order condition is

$$tr\{(\hat\beta'(S_{11} - S_{10}S_{00}^{-1}S_{01})\hat\beta)^{-1}\hat\beta'(S_{11} - S_{10}S_{00}^{-1}S_{01})k\}$$

$$= tr\{(\hat\beta'S_{11}\hat\beta)^{-1}\hat\beta'S_{11}k\},$$

for all k of the form $k = (H^1, \ldots, H^r)\{k_i\}$. Thus at the maximum point we have

$$(\hat\beta'(S_{11} - S_{10}S_{00}^{-1}S_{01})\hat\beta)^{-1}\hat\beta'(S_{11} - S_{10}S_{00}^{-1}S_{01})H^i = (\hat\beta'S_{11}\hat\beta)^{-1}\hat\beta'S_{11}H^i,$$

and the expansion to the second order around the maximum point has the same form as in the proof of Lemma 13.8 and we get an expansion of the test statistic. We find

$$-2\log Q = Ttr\{\alpha'\Omega^{-1}\alpha(\hat\beta - \beta)'S_{11}(\hat\beta - \beta)\} + O_P(T^{-1})$$

$$= Ttr\{\alpha'\Omega^{-1}\alpha\{\hat\psi_i - \psi_i\}'\{H^{i'}S_{11}H^j\}\{\hat\psi_j - \psi_j\}\} + O_P(T^{-1})$$

$$= Ttr\{\{\hat\psi_i - \psi_i\}'\{\rho_{ij}H^{i'}S_{11}H^j\}\{\hat\psi_j - \psi_j\}\} + O_P(T^{-1}),$$

where $\rho_{ij} = \alpha_i\Omega^{-1}\alpha_j$. As in Theorem 13.4 we use the notation $\{A_{ij}\}$ for a block matrix with blocks A_{ij}.

From Theorem 13.4 we now see that the asymptotic distribution of this quantity is χ^2, and the degrees of freedom is the number of parameters in a just identified system $r(p-r)$ minus the number of parameters in the identified model which is $\Sigma_{i=1}^r(s_i - 1)$ which gives the result.   □

13.7   Exercises

13.1

Consider the cointegration model

$$\Delta X_t = a\tau b'X_{t-1} + \epsilon_t,$$

where a and b are known $p \times r$ matrices, Ω is a known variance matrix, whereas τ is the unknown parameter which varies freely in the space of $r \times r$ matrices.

1. Find the maximum likelihood estimator of τ.
2. Find the likelihood ratio test for the hypothesis $\tau = 0$.

Under the null hypothesis X_t is a random walk and we define the Brownian motion W by

$$T^{-\frac{1}{2}}X_{[Tu]} = T^{-\frac{1}{2}}\sum_{t=1}^{[Tu]}\epsilon_t \xrightarrow{w} W_u.$$

3. Show that under the null hypothesis, $T\hat{\tau}$ will converge weakly towards a stochastic variable Z, and determine Z expressed in terms of W. Find the distribution of Z given $b'W$.

4. Find also the distribution of the likelihood ratio test for $\tau = 0$. Show that when $a'b = 0$, then the likelihood ratio test is asymptotically χ^2 distributed with r^2 degrees of freedom, and when $b = \Omega^{-1}a$, then the likelihood ratio test is asymptotically distributed as

$$tr\left\{\int_0^1 (dB)\, B'\left[\int_0^1 BB'du\right]^{-1}\int_0^1 B\,(dB)'\right\},$$

where B is an r-dimensional standard Brownian motion.

13.2

Let as before

$$\Delta X_t = \alpha\beta' X_{t-1} + \epsilon_t.$$

Let $X_t = (X'_{1t}, X'_{2t})'$ where the dimension of X_{1t} is m and that of X_{2t} is $p - m$. Let α and Ω be decomposed similarly.

1. Find the distribution $f_{\alpha,\beta,\Omega}(\Delta X_{1t}|\Delta X_{2t}, X_{t-1})$ and find the partial likelihood function

$$L_{\text{part}}(\alpha, \beta, \Omega) = \prod_{t=1}^{T} f_{\alpha,\beta,\Omega}(\Delta X_{1t}|\Delta X_{2t}, X_{t-1}). \tag{13.19}$$

2. Show that the partial maximum likelihood estimator of β based on (13.19) is given by reduced rank regression if $r \leq m$, and find those functions of α and Ω that can be estimated. Show that if $\alpha_2 = 0$ one can estimate α_1 and β and then the estimator of β is the maximum likelihood estimator.

3. In the model with rank$(\Pi) = $ rank$(\alpha\beta') \leq p$ find the likelihood ratio test for the hypothesis $\Pi = 0$ based upon the conditional likelihood function and sketch the proof that the asymptotic distribution of the likelihood ratio test is given by

$$tr\left\{\int_0^1 (dB_1)\, B'\left[\int_0^1 BB'du\right]^{-1}\int_0^1 B\,(dB_1')\right\},$$

where B is a p-dimensional Brownian motion decomposed as $B = (B'_1, B'_2)'$ of dimension m and $p - m$ respectively.

In the above situation inference about β is difficult, and the next questions are attempts to find conditions for inference to be easier.

4. Assume again that α and Ω are known. Show that β can be estimated by regression and find the expression for the estimator of β based upon the partial likelihood function.

5. Show that the asymptotic distribution for $T(\hat{\beta}-\beta)$ is mixed Gaussian, but that the Brownian motions entering the asymptotic expression for the limit distribution are not independent.

6. Show that they are independent if $\alpha_2 = 0$, that is, if X_{2t} is weakly exogenous for β, and that this gives a possibility for conducting inference on β.

13.3

Consider the usual model

$$\Delta X_t = \alpha\beta'X_{t-1} + \epsilon_t.$$

1. Find the estimator of α for fixed β and Ω, and find the asymptotic distribution of

$$T^{\frac{1}{2}}(\hat{\alpha}(\beta) - \alpha).$$

2. Find the estimator of β for fixed α and Ω, and find the asymptotic distribution of

$$T\beta'_\perp(\hat{\beta}(\alpha) - \beta).$$

13.4

In the univariate case the model is given by

$$\Delta X_t = \pi X_{t-1} + \epsilon_t.$$

1. Show that

$$T^{\frac{1}{2}}(\hat{\pi} - \pi)$$

is asymptotically Gaussian when $-2 < \pi < 0$.

2. Find the asymptotic distribution of

$$T(\hat{\pi} - \pi),$$

for $\pi = 0$.

3. Discuss the above problems for the model

$$\Delta X_t = \pi X_{t-1} + \mu + \epsilon_t.$$

13.5

1. Show that in the model

$$\Delta X_t = \alpha\beta' X_{t-1} + \mu + \epsilon_t,$$

the likelihood equations for the parameters α, β, and μ when Ω is known are given by

$$(\tilde{\alpha} - \alpha)\beta' S_{xx}\tilde{\beta} + \tilde{\alpha}(\tilde{\beta} - \beta)' S_{xx}\tilde{\beta} + (\hat{\mu} - \mu)\,\bar{X}_T'\tilde{\beta} = S_{\epsilon x}\tilde{\beta},$$

$$\tilde{\alpha}'\Omega^{-1}(\tilde{\alpha} - \alpha)\beta' S_{xx} + \tilde{\alpha}'\Omega^{-1}\tilde{\alpha}(\tilde{\beta} - \beta)' S_{xx} + \tilde{\alpha}'\Omega^{-1}(\hat{\mu} - \mu)\,\bar{X}' = \tilde{\alpha}'\Omega^{-1}S_{\epsilon x},$$

$$(\tilde{\alpha} - \alpha)\beta'\bar{X}_T + \tilde{\alpha}(\tilde{\beta} - \beta)'\bar{X}_T + (\hat{\mu} - \mu) = \bar{\epsilon}.$$

Here $S_{xx} = T^{-1}\sum_{t=1}^T X_{t-1}X_{t-1}'$ and $\bar{X}_T = T^{-1}\sum_{t=1}^T X_{t-1}$.

We next introduce the notation U_α, U_β, and U_μ for the limit distributions, that is

$$T^{\frac{1}{2}}(\tilde{\alpha} - \alpha) \overset{w}{\to} U_\alpha,$$

$$T^{\frac{1}{2}}(\hat{\mu} - \mu) \overset{w}{\to} U_\mu,$$

$$TU_T = (T\gamma'(\tilde{\beta} - \beta), T^{3/2}\tau'(\tilde{\beta} - \beta)) \overset{w}{\to} U_\beta.$$

2. Show that in the limit we then have the equations to determine the distributions U_α, U_β, and U_μ:

$$U_\alpha E\left(\beta' XX'\beta\right) + \alpha U_\beta' \bar{G}_0 E\left(X'\beta\right) + U_\mu E\left(X'\beta\right) = W_0\left(1\right) + W\left(1\right)E\left(X'\beta\right),$$

$$\alpha'\Omega^{-1}U_\alpha E\left(\beta' X\right)\bar{G}_0' + \alpha'\Omega^{-1}\alpha U_\beta' \int_0^1 G_0 G_0' du + \alpha'\Omega^{-1}U_\mu\bar{G}_0'$$
$$= \alpha'\Omega^{-1}\int_0^1 (dW)\,G_0',$$

$$U_\alpha E\left(\beta' X\right) + \alpha U_\beta'\bar{G}_0 + U_\mu = W\left(1\right).$$

Here $W\left(u\right)$ is the weak limit of $T^{-\frac{1}{2}}\sum_{t=1}^{[Tu]}\epsilon_t$ and $W_0\left(u\right)$ is the weak limit of the process $T^{-\frac{1}{2}}\sum_{t=1}^{[Tu]}\epsilon_t\left(X_{t-1}'\beta - E\left(X_{t-1}'\beta\right)\right)$ and

$$G_0(u) = \begin{bmatrix} \bar{\gamma}'CW(u) \\ u \end{bmatrix}.$$

3. Show by eliminating U_μ that U_α and U_β are given by the results from Lemma 13.2. Note that although the equations determining the limit distributions have to be solved simultaneously, the equations we get by eliminating U_μ are block diagonal, indicating that inference concerning α and β can be conducted as if the other were known.

13.6

1. Find in the model described by (4.1) the maximum likelihood estimator of

$$E\left(\beta'X_t\right) = \bar{\alpha}'\left(\Gamma C - I\right)\mu.$$

2. Find its asymptotic distribution.
3. Show that an efficient estimator is $\hat{\beta}'\bar{X}_T$.

13.7

Consider the model

$$\Delta X_t = \alpha\beta'X_{t-1} + \epsilon_t, \tag{13.20}$$

where β is identified by the restrictions

$$\beta = (H_1\varphi_1, \ldots, H_r\varphi_r).$$

This means that $\text{rank}(H'_{i\perp}\beta) = r - 1$, since $H'_{i\perp}\beta_i = 0$ and the remaining columns are linearly independent. We normalize β_i as $\beta_i = h_i + H^i\psi_i$.

1. Show that the identification condition implies that there is no vector $\eta \neq 0$, such that $H^i\eta \in sp(\beta)$.
2. Show that

$$T^{-1}H^{i\prime}S_{11}H^j \xrightarrow{w} H^{i\prime}\int_0^1 CWW'C'du\,H^j.$$

3. Show that the likelihood equation for ψ_i is given by

$$\hat{\alpha}'_i\hat{\Omega}^{-1}(S_{01} - \hat{\alpha}\hat{\beta}'S_{11})H^i = 0, \quad i = 1, \ldots, r.$$

4. Show by going through the proof of Lemma 13.2 that Theorem 13.4 holds.

Next consider model (13.20) with a constant term μ in the equation. From Granger's representation theorem we have

$$H^{i\prime}X_t = H^{i\prime}C\sum_{i=1}^t \epsilon_i + H^{i\prime}C\mu t + H^{i\prime}Y_t + H^{i\prime}P_{\beta_\perp}.$$

This gives rise to the directions $\tau_i = H^{i\prime}C\mu$ and $\gamma_i = \tau_{i\perp}$, such that in the directions τ_i the processes $H^{i\prime}X_t$ are dominated by the linear trends and in the directions γ_i the trends are eliminated, and the processes converge towards Brownian motions.

5. Find the proper normalization of the matrix $H^{i\prime}S_{11}H^i$ and determine the limit.
6. Show that the results of Theorem 13.4 hold in this case.

14

The Power Function of the Test for Cointegrating Rank under Local Alternatives

THIS chapter contains a discussion of the power of the test for cointegrating rank for local alternatives, see Johansen (1991 a). The results use the formulation of local alternatives and near integrated processes as formulated by Phillips (1988). In the next section we define a local alternative, and study in section 14.2 the properties of the process under the local alternative. It turns out that the limit process is an Ornstein–Uhlenbeck process, and this means that product moments involving the near integrated processes will have a limit different from the one under the null hypothesis. In section 14.3 we then discuss the limit distribution for the likelihood ratio test under suitable assumptions on the cointegrating ranks. Throughout we treat the model without short-terms dynamics and constant term. The model with the constant term is treated by Rahbek (1994). The limit results do not depend on the short-term dynamics, and this result is formulated as an exercise.

Finally the results are illustrated by a simulation in Chapter 15 of the local power.

14.1 Local Alternatives

We consider the model

$$\Delta X_t = \Pi X_{t-1} + \epsilon_t, \ t = 1, \ldots, T, \tag{14.1}$$

where Π is $p \times p$ and unrestricted and $\epsilon_1, \ldots, \epsilon_T$ are independent identically distributed with mean zero and variance Ω. We assume that the initial value is zero. We then consider the null hypothesis

$$H(r): \quad \Pi = \alpha\beta',$$

where α and β are $p \times r$ such that X_t is cointegrated with cointegrating rank $\leq r$. A parameter point in the alternative must then correspond to a process with more that r cointegrating relations, and thus has the representation

$$\Pi = \alpha\beta' + \alpha_1\beta_1'.$$

Here Π has rank $r + s$, $s > 0$. We define a local alternative by

$$H_T\,(r,s): \qquad \Pi_T = \alpha\beta' + T^{-1}\alpha_1\beta_1'. \qquad (14.2)$$

The interpretation of this is that under the local alternative the process has s extra cointegrating vectors, β_1, which enter in the process with very small adjustment coefficients, $T^{-1}\alpha_1$, and are hence difficult to find. These extra components are near integrated in the sense of Phillips (1988). We want to investigate the power of the test for cointegrating rank under the local alternative and hence we first find the properties of the process under the local alternative.

Since the parameter depends on T we use the notation $X_t^{(T)}$ for the process generated by equation (14.1) with $\Pi = \Pi_T$, and apply the notation X_t for the process generated by the equation

$$\Delta X_t = \alpha\beta' X_{t-1} + \epsilon_t, \qquad (14.3)$$

with initial value $X_0 = 0$.

14.2 Properties of the Process under Local Alternatives

In order to derive properties of test statistics under local alternatives we have to assume that the process is $I(1)$ under the null hypothesis, that is, that the eigenvalues of $I + \beta'\alpha$ are bounded in absolute value by a number less than 1. See exercise 4.12, and Theorem 4.2. Since we need this condition in the formulation we write it as

$$|\mathrm{eig}\,(I + \beta'\alpha)| < 1.$$

A number of evaluations needed in this chapter are derived using the binomial formula for matrices. These have been collected in the mathematical results in Appendix A, section 2.

THEOREM 14.1 *If* $|\mathrm{eig}\,(I + \beta'\alpha)| < 1$ *then under the local alternative it holds that* $R_{\beta t} = \beta' X_t^{(T)} - \beta' X_t$ *satisfies*

$$\max_{t \le T} \|\mathrm{Var}\,(R_{\beta t})\| \in O(T^{-1}). \qquad (14.4)$$

Furthermore $T^{-\frac{1}{2}}\alpha_\perp' X_{[Tu]}^{(T)} \xrightarrow{w} K(u)$, *where* $K(u)$ *is an Ornstein–Uhlenbeck process defined by*

$$K(t) = \alpha_\perp' \int_0^t \exp\left(\alpha_1\beta_1' C\,(t-u)\right) dW(u), \qquad (14.5)$$

and W is p-dimensional Brownian motion with variance matrix Ω and $C = \beta_\perp (\alpha'_\perp \beta_\perp)^{-1} \alpha_\perp$. The process $K(u)$ satisfies the stochastic integral equation

$$K(u) = \alpha'_\perp W(u) + \alpha'_\perp \alpha_1 \beta'_1 \beta_\perp (\alpha'_\perp \beta_\perp)^{-1} \int_0^u K(s)ds. \qquad (14.6)$$

If further $|eig(I + (\beta, \beta_1)'(\alpha, \alpha_1))| < 1$ then $\alpha'_\perp \alpha_1 \beta'_1 \beta_\perp$ has rank s.

PROOF The process $X_t^{(T)}$ is given as solution to equation (14.1) by

$$X_t^{(T)} = \sum_{i=0}^{t-1} \left(I + \alpha\beta' + T^{-1}\alpha_1\beta'_1\right)^i \epsilon_{t-i}. \qquad (14.7)$$

In the direction β we find

$$R_{\beta t} = \beta' X_t^{(T)} - \beta' X_t$$

$$= \sum_{i=0}^{t-1} \left[\beta'(I + \alpha\beta' + T^{-1}\alpha_1\beta'_1)^i - \beta'(I + \alpha\beta')^i\right] \epsilon_{t-i}$$

$$= \sum_{i=0}^{t-1} \beta'((A + B_T)^i - A^i)\epsilon_{t-i},$$

with $A = I + \alpha\beta'$ and $B_T = T^{-1}\alpha_1\beta'_1$. This has variance

$$\text{Var}(R_{\beta t}) = \sum_{i=0}^{t-1} \beta'((A + B_T)^i - A^i)\Omega\beta((A + B_T)^i - A^i)'.$$

In order to evaluate the norm we apply (A.22) which assumes that $T\|B_T\|$ is bounded, and that $|eig(I + \beta'\alpha)| < 1$, and find

$$\|\text{Var}(R_{\beta t})\| \le Tc^2\|B_T\|^2\|\Omega\| = c^2 T^{-1}\|\alpha_1\beta'_1\|^2\|\Omega\|,$$

which shows the result (14.4) about the process $X_t^{(T)} - X_t$ in the direction β.

We next investigate the process $\alpha'_\perp X_{[Tu]}^{(T)}$. We find from (14.7)

$$T^{-\frac{1}{2}}\alpha'_\perp X_{[Tu]}^{(T)} = T^{-\frac{1}{2}}\alpha'_\perp \sum_{i=0}^{[Tu]-1} \left(I + \alpha\beta' + T^{-1}\alpha_1\beta'_1\right)^i \epsilon_{[Tu]-i}$$

$$= T^{-\frac{1}{2}}\alpha'_\perp \sum_{i=1}^{[Tu]} \left(I + \alpha\beta' + T^{-1}\alpha_1\beta'_1\right)^{[Tu]-i} \epsilon_i,$$

which by (B.15) converges towards

$$\alpha'_\perp \int_0^u C \exp\left(\alpha_1\beta'_1 C(u - s)\right) dW(s)$$

$$= \alpha'_\perp \int_0^u \exp\left(\alpha_1\beta'_1 C(u - s)\right) dW(s) = K(u).$$

This follows from Theorem A.14 where it is shown that if $|\text{eig}\,(I + \beta'\alpha)| < 1$, then

$$\left(I + \alpha\beta' + T^{-1}\alpha_1\beta_1'\right)^{[T(u-s)]} \to C\exp\left(\alpha_1\beta_1'C\,(u-s)\right).$$

The limit process $K(u)$ satisfies the stochastic integral equation

$$K(u) = \alpha_\perp'W(u) + \alpha_\perp'\alpha_1\beta_1'\beta_\perp\,(\alpha_\perp'\beta_\perp)^{-1}\int_0^u K(s)ds,$$

or equivalently the stochastic differential equation

$$dK(u) = \alpha_\perp'dW(u) + \alpha_\perp'\alpha_1\beta_1'\beta_\perp\,(\alpha_\perp'\beta_\perp)^{-1}K(u)du.$$

If further $|\text{eig}\,(I + (\beta,\beta_1)'\,(\alpha,\alpha_1))| < 1$ then

$$(\beta,\ \beta_1)'\,(\alpha,\ \alpha_1) = \begin{bmatrix} \beta'\alpha & \beta'\alpha_1 \\ \beta_1'\alpha & \beta_1'\alpha_1 \end{bmatrix}$$

has full rank, and since also $\beta'\alpha$ has full rank it implies that

$$\beta_1'\alpha_1 - \beta_1'\alpha\,(\beta'\alpha)^{-1}\,\beta'\alpha_1 = \beta_1'\beta_\perp\,(\alpha_\perp'\beta_\perp)^{-1}\,\alpha_\perp'\alpha_1,$$

has full rank, which again implies that $\alpha_\perp'\alpha_1\beta_1'\beta_\perp$,has rank s.   □

From the asymptotic behaviour of the process X_t we can derive asymptotic properties of the product moment matrices needed in the treatment of the likelihood ratio statistic. Under the null hypothesis these results are given in Lemma 10.3. The only new result that is needed under the local alternative is formulated in the next lemma. We apply the notation

$$S_{yy} = T^{-1}\sum_{t=1}^{T}Y_tY_t',$$

for any stochastic process Y_t.

LEMMA 14.2 *If*

$$Y_t^{(T)} = Z_t^{(T)} + R_t^{(T)},\ S_{zz}^{(T)} \in O_P\,(1)\,,\ E(R_t^{(T)}) = 0,$$

and

$$\max_{t\le T}\|\text{Var}(R_t^{(T)})\| \to 0,$$

then

$$S_{yy}^{(T)} - S_{zz}^{(T)} \xrightarrow{P} 0.$$

PROOF From the identity

$$S_{yy}^{(T)} = S_{zz}^{(T)} + S_{zr}^{(T)} + S_{rz}^{(T)} + S_{rr}^{(T)},$$

and the inequality

$$(\xi' S_{zr}^{(T)} \mu)^2 \le \xi' S_{zz}^{(T)} \xi \mu' S_{rr}^{(T)} \mu,$$

it is seen that it is enough to prove that $S_{rr}^{(T)} \xrightarrow{P} 0$. Since the matrix $S_{rr}^{(T)}$ is positive semi-definite it is enough to show that $E(S_{rr}^{(T)}) \to 0$, but

$$E(S_{rr}^{(T)}) = T^{-1} \sum_{t=1}^{T} E(R_t^{(T)} R_t^{(T)'}) = T^{-1} \sum_{t=1}^{T} \text{Var}(R_t^{(T)}),$$

which is bounded in norm by $\max_{t \le T} \|\text{Var}(R_t^{(T)})\|$ which is assumed to tend to zero.   □

In the next result we use the usual notation

$$S_{ij} = T^{-1} \sum_{t=1}^{T} \Delta^{1-i} X_{t-i} (\Delta^{1-j} X_{t-j})', \quad i, j = 0, 1,$$

and let $S_{ij}^{(T)}$ be the corresponding quantities calculated from $X_t^{(T)}$.

LEMMA 14.3 *If* $|eig(I + \alpha' \beta)| < 1$ *then under the local alternative it holds that*

$$S_{00}^{(T)} \xrightarrow{P} \Sigma_{00}, \tag{14.8}$$

$$\beta' S_{11}^{(T)} \beta \xrightarrow{P} \Sigma_{\beta\beta}, \tag{14.9}$$

$$\beta' S_{10}^{(T)} \xrightarrow{P} \Sigma_{\beta 0}, \tag{14.10}$$

$$T^{-1} \alpha'_\perp S_{11}^{(T)} \alpha_\perp \xrightarrow{w} \int_0^1 KK' du, \tag{14.11}$$

$$(S_{01}^{(T)} - \Pi_T S_{11}^{(T)}) \alpha_\perp \xrightarrow{w} \int_0^1 (dW) K', \tag{14.12}$$

$$\alpha'_\perp S_{11}^{(T)} \beta \in O_P(1). \tag{14.13}$$

PROOF From equations (14.1), (14.2), and (14.3), we have the relations

$$\Delta X_t^{(T)} = (\alpha \beta' + T^{-1} \alpha_1 \beta_1') X_{t-1}^{(T)} + \epsilon_t,$$

and

$$\Delta X_t = \alpha \beta' X_{t-1} + \epsilon_t,$$

which show that for $R_{\beta t} = \beta'(X_t^{(T)} - X_t)$

$$\Delta X_t^{(T)} - \Delta X_t = \alpha R_{\beta t-1} + T^{-1}\alpha_1\beta_1' X_{t-1}^{(T)}.$$

To prove (14.8) we want to apply Lemma 14.2 with $Y^{(T)} = \Delta X^{(T)}$ and $Z^{(T)} = \Delta X$. Since $E(\Delta X_t^{(T)}) = E(\Delta X_t) = 0$, we have $S_{zz}^{(T)} \xrightarrow{P} \text{Var}(\Delta X_t)$. Hence it is enough to check that $\max_{t \leq T} \|\text{Var}(\Delta X_t^{(T)} - \Delta X_t)\| \to 0$, and hence enough to show that $\text{Var}(R_{\beta t})$ and $\text{Var}(T^{-1}\alpha_1\beta_1' X_t^{(T)})$ tend to zero uniformly in t.

By Theorem 14.1, $\max_{t \leq T} \|\text{Var}(R_{\beta t})\| \to 0$. To investigate the second condition we evaluate the variance of $X_t^{(T)}$ as follows

$$\text{Var}(X_t^{(T)}) = \sum_{i=0}^{t-1} (I + \Pi_T)^i \, \Omega (I + \Pi_T')^i,$$

which by (A.21) is bounded in norm by a constant times T. This shows that also $\text{Var}(T^{-1}\alpha_1\beta_1' X_{t-1}^{(T)})$ tends to zero uniformly in t, and hence the conditions of Lemma 14.2 are satisfied and (14.8) follows from (10.13) in Lemma 10.3 combined with Lemma 14.2.

To prove (14.9) we apply Lemma 14.2 with $Y_t^{(T)} = \beta' X_t^{(T)}$ and $Z_t^{(T)} = \beta' X_t$ and use the result (14.4) about the variance of $R_{\beta t}$. Finally (14.10) is proved in a similar way.

The result (14.11) follows from the result about the process $X_t^{(T)}$ in the direction $\alpha_\perp$ and the continuous mapping theorem applied to the functional $x \to \int_0^1 xx'du$. The result (14.12) follows from (14.1) with $\Pi = \Pi_T$ and $X = X^{(T)}$ since

$$(S_{01}^{(T)} - \Pi_T S_{11}^{(T)})\alpha_\perp = S_{\epsilon 1}^{(T)}\alpha_\perp,$$

which converges as stated in Theorem B.13.

Finally the result (14.13) follows by applying Lemma 14.2 together with the results in Theorem B.13.   □

14.3   The Local Power of the Trace Test

If we consider a fixed alternative $\Pi = \alpha\beta' + \alpha_1\beta_1'$ (rank$(\Pi) = r + s$) then it follows from the proof of the asymptotic properties of the eigenvalues of

$$|\lambda S_{11} - S_{10}S_{00}^{-1}S_{01}| = 0,$$

that the largest $r + s$ of these converge to positive limits. Hence the likelihood ratio statistic $-T\Sigma_{i=r+1}^p \log(1-\hat{\lambda}_i)$ which contains s of these will tend to ∞. This shows that for fixed alternative the power of the cointegrating test tends to 1.

THEOREM 14.4 *The asymptotic distribution of the likelihood ratio test statistic* $-2\log Q\left(H\left(r\right)|H\left(p\right)\right)$ *for the hypothesis* $H(r): \Pi = \alpha\beta'$ *is investigated under the local alternative* $H_T(r,s): \Pi = \alpha\beta' + T^{-1}\alpha_1\beta_1'$. *If* $|eig(I+\alpha'\beta| < 1$ *the asymptotic distribution is given by*

$$tr\left\{\int_0^1 (dK^*)K^{*\prime}\left[\int_0^1 K^*K^{*\prime}du\right]^{-1}\int_0^1 K^*(dK^*)'\right\}. \quad (14.14)$$

Here K^* *is the* $p-r$ *dimensional Ornstein–Uhlenbeck process given by*

$$-ab'\int_0^t K^*(u)du + K^*(t) = B(t), \quad t \in [0,1]$$

$B(u)$ *is standard Brownian motion in* $p-r$ *dimensions, and the coefficients* a *and* b *are defined by*

$$a = (\alpha_\perp'\Omega\alpha_\perp)^{-\frac{1}{2}}\alpha_\perp'\alpha_1, \quad b = (\alpha_\perp'\Omega\alpha_\perp)^{\frac{1}{2}}(\beta_\perp'\alpha_\perp)^{-1}\beta_\perp'\beta_1. \quad (14.15)$$

PROOF The proof here mimics the proof in Chapter 11 for the distribution when $\Pi = \alpha\beta'$ applying the results about the product moment matrices derived in Lemma 14.3. We define as in Chapter 11, $S(\lambda) = \lambda S_{11} - S_{10}S_{00}^{-1}S_{01}$, but choose $A_T = (\beta, T^{-\frac{1}{2}}\alpha_\perp)$, and find from Lemma 14.3 that

$$|A_T'S(\lambda)A_T| \overset{w}{\to} \left|\lambda\begin{bmatrix}\Sigma_{\beta\beta} & 0 \\ 0 & \int_0^1 KK'du\end{bmatrix} - \begin{bmatrix}\Sigma_{\beta0}\Sigma_{00}^{-1}\Sigma_{0\beta} & 0 \\ 0 & 0\end{bmatrix}\right|$$

$$= \left|\lambda\Sigma_{\beta\beta} - \Sigma_{\beta0}\Sigma_{00}^{-1}\Sigma_{0\beta}\right|\left|\lambda\int_0^1 KK'du\right|.$$

This polynomial has r positive roots and $p-r$ zero roots. Thus the r largest eigenvalues converge towards the positive roots, and the $p-r$ smallest converge to zero. We next consider the decomposition

$$|(\beta, \alpha_\perp)'S(\lambda)(\beta, \alpha_\perp)|$$

$$= |\beta'S(\lambda)\beta||\alpha_\perp'(S(\lambda) - S(\lambda)\beta\beta'S(\lambda)\beta)^{-1}\beta'S(\lambda))\alpha_\perp|,$$

and let $T \to \infty$, $\lambda \to 0$ such that $\rho = T\lambda$ is fixed. From Lemma 14.3 we find

$$\beta'S(\lambda)\beta \overset{P}{\to} -\Sigma_{\beta0}\Sigma_{00}^{-1}\Sigma_{0\beta},$$

such that the roots have to be in the second factor. We find

$$\alpha_\perp'S(\lambda)\beta = -\alpha_\perp'S_{10}\Sigma_{00}^{-1}\Sigma_{0\beta} + o_P(1),$$

and

$$\alpha'_\perp (S(\lambda) - S(\lambda)\beta(\beta'S(\lambda)\beta)^{-1}\beta'S(\lambda))\alpha_\perp$$

$$= \rho T^{-1}\alpha'_\perp S_{11}\alpha_\perp - \alpha'_\perp S_{10}NS_{01}\alpha_\perp + o_P(1),$$

where N is given in Chapter 11 as the matrix $\alpha_\perp(\alpha'_\perp\Omega\alpha_\perp)^{-1}\alpha'_\perp$. This shows that we need the limit distribution of

$$\alpha'_\perp S_{10}\alpha_\perp = T^{-1}\alpha'_\perp S_{11}\beta_1\alpha'_1\alpha_\perp + \alpha'_\perp S_{1\epsilon}\alpha_\perp$$

$$= T^{-1}\alpha'_\perp S_{11}\alpha_\perp(\beta'_\perp\alpha_\perp)^{-1}\beta'_\perp\beta_1\alpha'_1\alpha_\perp + \alpha'_\perp S_{1\epsilon}\alpha_\perp + o_P(1)$$

$$\overset{w}{\to} \int_0^1 KK'du\,(\beta'_\perp\alpha_\perp)^{-1}\beta'_\perp\beta_1\alpha'_1\alpha_\perp + \int_0^1 K(dW)'\alpha_\perp$$

$$= \int_0^1 K(dK)',$$

where the convergence follows from Lemma 14.3. Combining these results we find that in the limit the roots ρ have to satisfy the equation

$$\left| \rho \int_0^1 KK'du - \int_0^1 K(dK)'(\alpha'_\perp\Omega\alpha_\perp)^{-1}\int_0^1 (dK)K' \right| = 0.$$

As in Chapter 11 the asymptotic distribution of the test statistic is now given as the sum of the roots times T which shows the result:

$$-2\log Q(H(r)|H(p))$$

$$\overset{w}{\to} tr\left\{ \left[\int_0^1 KK'du\right]^{-1}\int_0^1 K(dK)'(\alpha'_\perp\Omega\alpha_\perp)^{-1}\int_0^1 (dK)K' \right\}.$$

If we define the process $K^* = (\alpha'_\perp\Omega\alpha_\perp)^{-\frac{1}{2}}K$, we find the result of the Theorem.   □

It is seen that the asymptotic power only depends on the parameters a and b, but due to the invariance of the Brownian motion and the test statistic under orthogonal transformations one can show that in fact it only depends on the matrices $a'a$, $b'b$, and $b'a$. In order to see this consider the orthogonal transformation $O = (O_1, O_2, O_3)$ defined by

$$O_1 = b(b'b)^{-\frac{1}{2}},$$

$$O_2 = (a - b(b'b)^{-1}b'a)(a'a - a'b(b'b)^{-1}b'a)^{-\frac{1}{2}},$$

and choose O_3 to be orthogonal to O_1 and O_2, and such that O is an orthogonal transformation. Further define $K_i^* = O_i'K^*$, and $B_i = O_i'B$, then the equations for K_i^* are given by

$$-(b'b)^{-\frac{1}{2}} b'a (b'b)^{\frac{1}{2}} \int_0^u K_1^*(s)ds + K_1^*(u) = B_1(u), \quad (14.16)$$

$$-(a'a - a'b (b'b)^{-1} b'a)^{\frac{1}{2}} (b'b)^{\frac{1}{2}} \int_0^u K_1^*(s)ds + K_2^*(u) = B_2(u), \quad (14.17)$$

$$K_3^*(u) = B_3(u). \quad (14.18)$$

It is seen that only the matrices $a'a$, $b'b$, and $a'b$ enter in the equations. If $s = 1$ this result simplifies further, and will be applied in the simulation study of the power function in Chapter 15.

COROLLARY 14.5 *Under the local alternative* $\Pi_T = \alpha\beta' + T^{-1}\alpha_1\beta_1$, *where* α_1 *and* β_1 *are* $p \times 1$ *vectors, the asymptotic power depends only on the parameters through the numbers*

$$f = b'a = \beta_1' C\alpha_1 < 0,$$

and

$$g^2 = a'ab'b - (a'b)^2$$

$$= (\alpha_1'\alpha_\perp (\alpha_\perp' \Omega\alpha_\perp)^{-1} \alpha_\perp' \alpha_1)(\beta_1' C\Omega C'\beta_1) - (\beta_1' C\alpha_1)^2,$$

where $C = \beta_\perp (\alpha_\perp'\beta_\perp)^{-1} \alpha_\perp'$.

PROOF This follows from (14.16) and (14.17) since $b'b$ cancels in (14.16) and (14.17) only depends on g^2. The expressions for f and g are found by inserting the expressions for a and b. □

14.4 Exercises

14.1

In the model

$$\Delta X_t = \left(\alpha\beta' + T^{-1}\alpha_1\beta_1'\right) X_{t-1} + \sum_{i=1}^{k-1} \Gamma_i \Delta X_{t-i} + \epsilon_t, \quad (14.19)$$

define $\tilde{X}_t' = (X_t', \ldots, X_{t-k}')$, and $\tilde{\epsilon}_t = (\epsilon_t, 0, \ldots, 0)$.
1. Show that $\tilde{X}_t$ satisfies the equation

$$\Delta \tilde{X}_t = \tilde{\Pi}_T \tilde{X}_{t-1} + \tilde{\epsilon}_t,$$

and find an expression for $\tilde{\Pi}_T$ in terms of the other parameters.

2. Show that $\tilde{\beta}'_\perp = \beta'_\perp (I, \ldots, I)$, and $\tilde{\alpha}'_\perp = \alpha'_\perp (I, -\Gamma_1, \ldots, -\Gamma_{k-1})$, and hence that

$$\tilde{C} = \tilde{\beta}_\perp \left(\tilde{\alpha}'_\perp \tilde{\beta}_\perp \right)^{-1} \tilde{\alpha}'_\perp = \beta_\perp (\alpha'_\perp \Gamma \beta_\perp)^{-1} \alpha'_\perp,$$

where $\Gamma = I - \sum_{i=1}^{k-1} \Gamma_i$. Find expressions for $\tilde{\alpha}$, $\tilde{\beta}$, $\tilde{\alpha}_1$, and $\tilde{\beta}_1$.

3. Next apply Theorem 14.1 to the process $\tilde{X}_t^{(T)}$, and express the results for the process $\tilde{\beta}' \tilde{X}_t^{(T)} - \tilde{\beta}' \tilde{X}_t$ and $\tilde{\alpha}'_\perp \tilde{X}_{[Tu]}^{(T)}$ in terms of the original parameters and processes. Find the equation for the process K_t, and show that the results of Theorem 14.4 still hold with the same definition of a provided b is defined as $b = (\alpha'_\perp \Omega \alpha_\perp)^{\frac{1}{2}} (\beta'_\perp \Gamma \alpha_\perp)^{-1} \beta'_\perp \beta_1$. Thus the limit result for the power function only depends on the short-term dynamics through the matrix Γ.

15

Simulations and Tables

THE stochastic integrals that appear in the expressions for the limiting distributions really only serve the purpose of showing that we have normalized the statistics correctly.

The functionals obtained are so complicated as functions of the Brownian motion that no explicit results seem to be available. It turns out that for the limiting distribution of the test statistics, the main dependence is on the dimension of the problem, more precisely the number of non-stationary components. The only point where the parameters appear is through conditions like $\alpha'_\perp \mu_0 = 0$, or $\alpha'_\perp \mu_1 = 0$, which were shown to influence the limiting distribution, see Theorem 6.1 and Theorem 6.2.

15.1 Simulation of the Limit Distributions

The conclusion of the limit results is that the asymptotic distributions of the test statistics of $H(r)$ in $H(p)$ are the same as those of $H(0)$ in $H(p-r)$ in a $p-r$ dimensional system, that is, a test of $\Pi = 0$ in the model

$$\Delta X_t = \Pi X_{t-1} + \epsilon_t,$$

where Π is $(p-r) \times (p-r)$. Thus when one wants to simulate the limit distribution under the null $\Pi = 0$ one simply simulates the $(p-r)$-dimensional system

$$\Delta X_t = \epsilon_t, \ t = 1, \ldots, T, \tag{15.1}$$

where ϵ_t are independent $N_{p-r}(0, I)$. Summing over t we find the solution $X_t = \Sigma_{i=1}^t \epsilon_i + X_0$. In the simulations we take $T = 400$, and $X_0 = 0$.

The limit distribution (6.20) given by

$$tr\left\{ \int_0^1 (dB) F' \left[\int_0^1 FF' du \right]^{-1} \int_0^1 F (dB)' \right\}, \tag{15.2}$$

is approximated by

$$tr\left\{ \sum_{t=1}^T \epsilon_t S'_t \left[\sum_{t=1}^T S_t S'_t \right]^{-1} \sum_{t=1}^T S_t \epsilon'_t \right\} \tag{15.3}$$

for suitable choices of S. If $D_t = 0$, then F is given by Brownian motion in $p - r$ dimensions and S_t is chosen as the random walk X_{t-1}.

In case $D_t = 1$, and $\alpha'_\perp \mu_0 \neq 0$ then F is given by (6.21) and we define $S_t = \left(X'_{t-1} - \bar{X}', \; t - \frac{1}{2}(T+1) \right)'$, where $\bar{X} = T^{-1}\Sigma^T_{t=1}X_{t-1}$ for a $p - r - 1$ dimensional random walk. Finally if $D_t = 1$ and $\alpha'_\perp \mu_0 = 0$, then F is given by (6.32) and we define $S_t = \left(X'_{t-1}, 1 \right)'$ for a $p - r$ dimensional random walk.

The modifications needed to obtain the limit distribution where F is given by any of the other formulae in Theorem 6.1 and Theorem 6.2 should now be obvious. This section contains five tables for the asymptotic distribution of the trace test for the cointegration rank, and one table for the power of the cointegration test in a simple situation. The tables for the asymptotic distributions have been calculated by Bent Nielsen using the program Disco, see Johansen and Nielsen (1993), based on 100,000 replications of (15.2) in which B is replaced by a random walk with 400 observations and F is described below. With the notation from Chapter 5, see (5.11) – (5.15), an overview of the tables is given as follows:

Model	F'		Table
$\mu_t = 0$	$(B_1, \ldots, B_{p-r})$		15.1
$\mu_t = \alpha\rho_0$	$(B_1, \ldots, B_{p-r}, 1)$		15.2
$\mu_t = \mu_0$	$(B_1, \ldots, B_{p-r-1}, u)$	corrected for a constant	15.3
$\mu_t = \mu_0 + \alpha\rho_1 t$	$(B_1, \ldots, B_{p-r}, u)$	corrected for a constant	15.4
$\mu_t = \mu_0 + \mu_1 t$	$(B_1, \ldots, B_{p-r-1}, u^2)$	corrected for $(1, u)$.	15.5

15.2   Simulations of the Power Function

In this section we shall simulate the asymptotic power function in the case when only one cointegrating relation is missing, that is for $s = 1$. In this special case the equations (14.18), (14.19), and (14.20) are of the form

$$-f \int_0^t K^*_{1u}du + K^*_{1t} = B_{1t}, \qquad (15.4)$$

$$-g \int_0^t K^*_{1u}du + K^*_{2t} = B_{2t}, \qquad (15.5)$$

$$K^*_{3t} = B_{3t}. \qquad (15.6)$$

The functional (14.14) gives the asymptotic power of the trace test. The distribution of this functional is too complicated to find analytically but it can be found by simulation.

In order to simulate the processes we apply the discrete version of these equations

$$K_{1t}^* = \left(1 + T^{-1}f\right)K_{1t-1}^* + \epsilon_{1t}, \qquad (15.7)$$

$$K_{2t}^* = K_{2t-1}^* + (T^{-1}g)K_{1t-1}^* + \epsilon_{2t}, \qquad (15.8)$$

$$K_{3t}^* = K_{3t-1}^* + \epsilon_{3t}, \qquad (15.9)$$

$t = 1, \ldots, T$, starting with $K_0^* = 0$.

Note that the actual expression for the limit distribution is not so important. What is being used here is only the fact that the parameters of the original model (14.2) with $\Pi_T = \alpha\beta' + T^{-1}\alpha_1\beta_1'$ only enter through the dimension $p - r$ and through the parameters f and g. Thus the system we simulate consists of the last $p - r$ equations of model (14.2) with $\alpha = \beta = (I,\ 0)'$ and

$$\alpha_1 = (0, \ldots, 0, f, g, 0, \ldots, 0)', \qquad \beta_1 = (0, \ldots, 0, 1, 0, 0, \ldots, 0)',$$

where both vectors start with r zeros. Thus in order to simulate the system we choose the simplest possible system compatible with the given f and g.

We then easily solve the equations (15.7), (15.8), and (15.9) recursively and form the $T \times (p - r)$ matrix M with elements $M_{ti} = K_{it}^*$. Then we calculate ΔM and M_{-1}, i.e. the differences and lagged variables respectively and find the test statistic

$$\text{Test} = tr\{\Delta M'M_{-1}\left(M_{-1}'M_{-1}\right)^{-1}M_{-1}'\Delta M\}.$$

The number of observations T has to be chosen so large that the approximation of the random walk to the Brownian motion is sufficiently good. We have chosen $T = 400$.

We find the results for stationary alternatives and $p - r = 1, 2$, and 3 in Table 15.6. It is seen that, not surprisingly, the power decreases as the dimension increases, i.e. if there are many dimensions to hide in. This means that it is difficult to find the cointegrating vector, if it has a small loading. It was found that the non-stationary alternatives (not shown) are readily picked up by the test with large power. The test appears unbiased when considering f and g close to zero.

The table gives the limit distribution of (14.14) for the process defined by (15.4)–(15.6). If we apply the results for the approximation defined by (15.7)–(15.9) one can for a large value of T interpret the coefficient $1 + T^{-1}f = 1 + T^{-1}\alpha_1'\beta_1$ as the autoregressive parameter, see (15.7), in the stationary (or near-integrated) relation we are trying to find. Hence we can apply Table 15.6 as follows: assume we have $T = 100$ observations and an autoregressive coefficient of 0.79 say. Then the relation $0.79 = 1 - 21/100 = 1 + T^{-1}f$ shows that we can use Table 15.6 with $f = -21$. Now the power of finding such a process depends on the relation between the adjustment coefficients and the cointegration vector. If α_1 and β_1 are proportional, so that $g = 0$, then, if the number of non-stationary components is $p - r = 1$, we have a probability of 0.998 of rejecting the hypothesis of non-stationarity, and hence of finding a stationary relation. If, however, the system has $p - r = 3$ non-stationary components, then the probability of rejecting the non-stationarity hypothesis is only 0.346. For a given angle, that is, for fixed f/g, it is seen from the table that the larger the vectors the easier it is to find them.

The asymptotic power of the likelihood ratio test at 5 per cent for r cointegration vectors among p variables under the local alternative of one extra cointegrating vector is given in Table 15.6. The quantities f and g are defined in Corollary 14.5. The number of simulations is 5,000 for $p - r = 1$ and 2,000 for $p - r = 2$, 3, and $T = 400$.

15.3   Tables

TABLE 15.1 Quantiles of the likelihood ratio test for cointegrating rank (6.20) with constant term zero and $F = B$

$p - r$	50.0%	75.0%	80.0%	85.0%	90.0%	95.0%	97.5%	99.0%
1	0.60	1.56	1.89	2.32	2.98	4.14	5.30	7.02
2	5.47	7.77	8.41	9.22	10.35	12.21	13.94	16.16
3	14.31	17.85	18.83	20.00	21.58	24.08	26.42	29.19
4	27.14	31.86	33.10	34.62	36.58	39.71	42.59	46.00
5	43.75	49.71	51.25	53.11	55.54	59.24	62.68	66.71
6	64.37	71.44	73.27	75.48	78.30	82.61	86.36	91.12
7	88.73	97.02	99.12	101.67	104.93	109.93	114.24	119.58
8	116.81	126.20	128.61	131.49	135.16	140.74	145.80	151.70
9	148.76	159.27	161.98	165.22	169.30	175.47	181.20	187.82
10	184.44	196.13	199.11	202.65	207.21	214.07	220.00	226.95
11	223.98	236.82	240.09	243.88	248.77	256.23	262.69	270.47
12	266.92	280.71	284.36	288.47	293.83	301.95	309.08	318.14

TABLE 15.2 Quantiles of the likelihood ratio test for cointegration (6.32) with restricted constant and $F = (B_1, \ldots, B_{p-r}, 1)'$

$p - r$	50.0%	75.0%	80.0%	85.0%	90.0%	95.0%	97.5%	99.0%
1	3.43	5.28	5.85	6.54	7.50	9.13	10.73	12.73
2	11.34	14.45	15.31	16.39	17.79	19.99	22.07	24.74
3	23.15	27.50	28.65	30.05	31.88	34.80	37.56	40.84
4	38.90	44.39	45.86	47.60	49.92	53.42	56.57	60.42
5	58.47	65.19	66.92	69.01	71.66	75.74	79.60	83.93
6	81.85	89.71	91.75	94.13	97.17	101.84	106.07	111.38
7	109.11	118.12	120.52	123.26	126.71	132.00	136.69	142.34
8	140.01	150.10	152.75	155.86	159.74	165.73	171.18	177.42
9	174.65	185.99	188.92	192.27	196.66	203.34	209.28	216.08
10	213.14	225.67	228.81	232.63	237.35	244.56	250.86	258.31
11	255.33	269.01	272.44	276.46	281.63	289.71	296.70	304.89
12	315.69	319.50	323.90	329.51	333.26	338.10	345.77	354.32

TABLE 15.3 Quantiles of the likelihood ratio test for unrestricted constant (6.21) and $F = (B_1 - \bar{B}_1, \ldots, B_{p-r-1} - \bar{B}_{p-r-1}, u - \frac{1}{2})'$

$p - r$	50.0%	75.0%	80.0%	85.0%	90.0%	95.0%	97.5%	99.0%
1	0.46	1.32	1.64	2.07	2.71	3.84	5.02	6.64
2	7.59	10.29	11.06	12.03	13.31	15.34	17.24	19.69
3	18.65	22.63	23.72	25.03	26.70	29.38	31.76	34.87
4	33.52	38.68	40.08	41.73	43.84	47.21	50.19	53.91
5	52.21	58.55	60.23	62.25	64.74	68.68	72.21	76.37
6	74.62	82.14	84.10	86.41	89.37	93.92	97.97	102.95
7	100.93	109.61	111.79	114.40	117.73	123.04	127.59	133.04
8	130.89	140.66	143.19	146.17	149.99	155.75	160.87	166.95
9	164.61	175.58	178.33	181.66	185.83	192.30	198.19	204.64
10	214.07	217.18	220.86	225.49	228.55	232.60	238.69	246.17
11	256.44	259.80	263.79	268.72	272.03	276.37	283.24	291.58
12	302.23	305.85	310.17	315.53	319.21	323.93	331.22	339.64

TABLE 15.4 Quantiles of the likelihood ratio test for cointegrating rank with the linear term restricted (6.28) and hence no quadratic trend in the process, and $F = (B_1 - \bar{B}_1, \ldots, B_{p-r} - \bar{B}_{p-r}, u - \frac{1}{2})'$

$p - r$	50.0%	75.0%	80.0%	85.0%	90.0%	95.0%	97.5%	99.0%
1	5.62	7.92	8.59	9.43	10.56	12.39	14.13	16.39
2	15.68	19.24	20.22	21.40	22.95	25.47	27.87	30.65
3	29.56	34.30	35.58	37.11	39.08	42.20	45.04	48.59
4	47.19	53.16	54.73	56.56	58.96	62.61	66.04	70.22
5	68.70	75.87	77.65	79.85	82.68	86.96	90.87	95.38
6	93.88	102.16	104.29	106.79	110.00	114.96	119.43	124.61
7	122.99	132.35	134.77	137.55	141.31	146.75	151.70	157.53
8	155.60	166.08	168.85	172.10	176.13	182.45	187.80	194.12
9	192.11	203.70	206.64	210.21	214.72	221.56	227.61	234.65
10	232.31	245.06	248.24	252.18	257.08	264.23	270.90	278.80
11	290.06	293.60	297.73	302.88	306.47	311.13	318.03	326.73
12	338.46	342.33	346.88	352.61	356.39	361.07	368.75	377.54

TABLE 15.5 Quantiles of the likelihood ratio test for cointegrating rank with the linear term unrestricted allowing for a quadratic trend and $F = (B_1 - a_1 - b_1 u, \ldots, B_{p-r-1} - a_{p-r-1} - b_{p-r-1} u, u^2 - a - bu)'$

$p - r$	50.0%	75.0%	80.0%	85.0%	90.0%	95.0%	97.5%	99.0%
1	0.46	1.32	1.64	2.07	2.71	3.84	5.02	6.64
2	9.65	12.69	13.53	14.56	15.94	18.15	20.26	22.78
3	22.75	27.10	28.28	29.69	31.57	34.56	37.21	40.61
4	39.57	45.14	46.61	48.36	50.67	54.11	57.41	61.28
5	60.19	66.96	68.76	70.90	73.62	77.79	81.57	86.11
6	84.56	92.41	94.43	96.83	99.97	104.76	109.04	114.23
7	112.66	121.65	123.95	126.81	130.39	135.66	140.49	146.05
8	144.47	154.66	157.25	160.32	164.24	170.15	175.38	181.62
9	179.93	191.21	194.07	197.53	201.83	208.53	214.51	221.47
10	219.25	231.72	234.82	238.55	243.29	250.53	256.96	264.52
11	275.58	279.01	282.96	288.17	291.51	296.02	302.86	311.41
12	323.14	326.82	331.22	336.81	340.54	345.27	352.98	361.69

TABLE 15.6 The power function

$p - r$	g	$f = 0$	-3	-6	-9	-12	-15	-18	-21
1		0.052	0.141	0.350	0.620	0.820	0.945	0.987	0.998
2	0	0.060	0.069	0.105	0.175	0.272	0.416	0.565	0.714
2	6	0.615	0.335	0.269	0.298	0.390	0.513	0.642	0.772
2	12	0.944	0.850	0.760	0.716	0.717	0.760	0.830	0.874
3	0	0.054	0.059	0.073	0.105	0.136	0.187	0.266	0.346
3	6	0.510	0.211	0.143	0.142	0.188	0.233	0.305	0.383
3	12	0.834	0.694	0.536	0.424	0.407	0.429	0.476	0.543

Part III

Appendices

Some Mathematical Results

THIS appendix contains some results from various branches of mathematics, that I consider useful for the analysis of the autoregressive models. Most are concerned with classical results about eigenvalues and eigenvectors, see Magnus and Neudecker (1988) but some are more specialized, like the results on the binomial and exponential functions in section A.2, which are used in the discussion of the local power of the cointegration test. Finally I have collected a few results about regression and multivariate statistics in section A.3, see Anderson (1984).

A.1   Eigenvalues and Eigenvectors

Let M be a $p \times p$ matrix. We let $|M|$ be the absolute value of the determinant of M, and let I be an identity matrix. The norm of M is denoted

$$\|M\| = \max_i \sum_{j=1}^{p} |M_{ij}|.$$

Note that $\|M + N\| \le \|M\| + \|N\|$ and that $\|MN\| \le \|M\|\|N\|$. The trace of M is denoted $tr\{M\}$. The eigenvalues of M are the solutions to the equation

$$|\lambda I - M| = 0.$$

It is well known that the equation has p solutions $\lambda_1, \ldots, \lambda_p$, which may be complex. There are not necessarily p linearly independent eigenvectors. As an example the matrix

$$\begin{bmatrix} 1 & 1 \\ 0 & 1 \end{bmatrix},$$

has two eigenvalues of 1 but only 1 eigenvector. The Jordan canonical form represents the matrix as

$$M = AJA^{-1},$$

where A is $p \times p$ of full rank and J is $p \times p$ and block diagonal with a typical block of the form

$$J_1(\lambda) = [\lambda], \quad J_2(\lambda) = \begin{bmatrix} \lambda & 1 \\ 0 & \lambda \end{bmatrix}, \quad J_3(\lambda) = \begin{bmatrix} \lambda & 1 & 0 \\ 0 & \lambda & 1 \\ 0 & 0 & \lambda \end{bmatrix}, \ldots$$

where λ is an eigenvalue of M. If M is symmetric then the eigenvalues are real, all the blocks are 1×1, and the columns of A are the eigenvectors. Moreover A is orthonormal such that $A^{-1} = A'$, see Lemma A.3.

LEMMA A.1 *Let M be $p \times p$ with eigenvalues $\lambda_1, \ldots, \lambda_p$. Then there exists a polynomial $P_{p-1}(.)$ of degree at most $p-1$, such that*

$$\|M^n\| \leq \max_{1 \leq i \leq p} |\lambda_i|^n P_{p-1}(n). \tag{A.1}$$

PROOF The Jordan representation is

$$M = AJA^{-1},$$

which implies

$$M^n = AJ^n A^{-1}.$$

For a typical Jordan block of size 3×3, say, we find

$$J_3(\lambda)^n = \begin{bmatrix} \lambda^n & n\lambda^{n-1} & \frac{1}{2}n(n-1)\lambda^{n-2} \\ 0 & \lambda^n & n\lambda^{n-1} \\ 0 & 0 & \lambda^n \end{bmatrix},$$

for which the norm is bounded by $|\lambda|^n$ times a polynomial of degree at most 2. A similar argument can be given for a Jordan block of any size, hence the result holds for M^n.   □

COROLLARY A.2 *If the eigenvalues of M are inside the unit disk then, for $|\lambda| = \max_i |\lambda_i|$, it holds for some $c > 0$*

$$\|M^n\| \leq c|\lambda|^{\frac{1}{2}n} \to 0, \quad n \to \infty. \tag{A.2}$$

Moreover

$$\sum_{i=0}^{\infty} M^i = (I - M)^{-1}, \tag{A.3}$$

and for any $p \times p$ matrix Ω

$$\|\sum_{i=0}^{\infty} M^i \Omega M'^i\| < \infty. \tag{A.4}$$

PROOF From the inequality

$$\|M^n\| \leq |\lambda|^n P_{p-1}(n) \leq |\lambda|^{\frac{1}{2}n} \sup_n |\lambda|^{\frac{1}{2}n} P_{p-1}(n) \leq c|\lambda|^{\frac{1}{2}n},$$

we find the first statement. It follows, since $\lambda_i \neq 1$, that we have

$$\sum_{i=0}^{n} M^i = \left(I - M^{n+1}\right)(I - M)^{-1},$$

which converges towards
$$(I - M)^{-1},$$
since $M^n \to 0$. Finally we evaluate the sum (A.4) by
$$\| \sum_{i=0}^{\infty} M^i \Omega M'^i \| \le c^2 \|\Omega\| \sum_{i=0}^{\infty} |\lambda|^i = c^2 \|\Omega\| (1 - |\lambda|)^{-1}.$$

$\square$

Now let M be symmetric and positive semi-definite, that is, $M = M'$ and $x'Mx \ge 0$. In this case the following well-known spectral decomposition of a symmetric matrix holds.

LEMMA A.3 *The equation*

$$|\lambda I - M| = 0,$$

has p solutions $\lambda_1 \ge \lambda_2 \ge \cdots \ge \lambda_p \ge 0$, the eigenvalues, with corresponding eigenvectors $v_1, \ldots, v_p$ satisfying

$$\lambda_i v_i = M v_i, \quad i = 1, \ldots, p,$$

and

$$v_i' v_j = 1 \ if \ i = j \ and \ 0 \ otherwise.$$

In matrix notation we let

$$V = (v_1, \ldots, v_p),$$

$$\Lambda = \mathrm{diag}\,(\lambda_1, \ldots, \lambda_p),$$

then $V\Lambda = MV$, $V\Lambda V' = M$, $V'MV = \Lambda$, $V'V = I = VV'$.

If the eigenvalues are different and positive then any invariant subspace $L \subset R^p$ (i.e. such that $y \in L$ implies $My \in L$) has the property that it is spanned by a subset of the eigenvectors.

PROOF The proofs of these results will not be given, since they can be found in most textbooks on matrices. The last result deserves a comment, however. If L is invariant, then also $L_\perp$, the orthogonal complement, is invariant. To see this take $y \in L_\perp$, such that $y'x = 0$ for all $x \in L$. Then also $y'Mx = 0$, since $Mx \in L$. But $y'Mx = (My)'x = 0$, shows that $My \in L_\perp$, and hence that $L_\perp$ is invariant.

Next we show that if L_1 is a one-dimensional linear subspace, then either $L_1 \subset L$, or $L_1 \subset L_\perp$. Thus take $x \in L_1$ and decompose $x = x_1 + x_2$, where $x_1 \in L$ and $x_2 \in L_\perp$. Then $Mx = Mx_1 + Mx_2$, but $Mx = \lambda x$ for some $\lambda > 0$, which shows that $Mx_1 + Mx_2 = Mx = \lambda x = \lambda x_1 + \lambda x_2$.

Since the decomposition of λx is unique, it follows that $Mx_1 = \lambda x_1$, and $Mx_2 = \lambda x_2$. This shows that x_1 and x_2 are both in L_1, since the eigenvalues are different, and hence that one of them must be zero, which proves that either $L_1 \subset L$ or $L_1 \subset L_\perp$. If L and $L_\perp$ have dimensions m and $p - m$ respectively, then if $L_1 \subset L$ we have $L = L_1 + L \cap L_{1\perp}$, where $L \cap L_{1\perp}$ has dimension $m - 1$, or else a similar decomposition is possible for $L_\perp$. In both cases we can peel away a linear subspace, a process that will terminate after p steps.   □

DEFINITION A.4 *We define* $M^{\frac{1}{2}} = V\Lambda^{\frac{1}{2}}V'$, *and if* M *is positive definite then* $M^{-\frac{1}{2}} = V\Lambda^{-\frac{1}{2}}V'$.

LEMMA A.5 *Let* M *and* N *be symmetric such that* M *is positive semi-definite and* N *is positive definite, then the equation*

$$|\lambda N - M| = 0, \tag{A.5}$$

has p *eigenvalues* $\lambda_1 \geq \lambda_2 \geq \cdots \geq \lambda_p \geq 0$, *with corresponding eigenvectors* $v_1, \ldots, v_p$, *such that*

$$N\lambda_i v_i = Mv_i, \quad i = 1, \ldots, p, \tag{A.6}$$

or in matrix notation

$$NV\Lambda = MV, \tag{A.7}$$
$$V'NV = I, \tag{A.8}$$
$$V'MV = \Lambda. \tag{A.9}$$

PROOF Define $A = N^{-\frac{1}{2}}MN^{-\frac{1}{2}}$, then A is positive semi-definite and symmetric, and
$$|\lambda N - M| = |N||\lambda I - A| = 0$$
has solutions $\lambda_1 \geq \lambda_2 \geq \cdots \geq \lambda_p \geq 0$ with corresponding eigenvectors $E = (e_1, \ldots, e_p)$, such that $E\Lambda = AE$ and $E'E = I$, see Lemma A.3. Now define $V = N^{-\frac{1}{2}}E$, then $NV\Lambda = MV$, $V'MV = \Lambda$ and $V'NV = I$.   □

Note that V is not orthogonal, and that $N^{-1}M$ is not symmetric, so that although λ is a solution to $|\lambda I - N^{-1}M| = 0$, this formulation does not guarantee that λ is real. We shall refer to the problem solved in Lemma A.5 as the basic eigenvalue problem. These eigenvalue results solve a number of extremum problems, of which we shall now give a few.

LEMMA A.6 *Let* M *be symmetric and positive semi-definite and* N *symmetric and positive definite. The function*

$$f(M) = tr\{N^{-1}M\} - \log |N^{-1}M|$$

is minimized by $M = N$, *and the minimum value is* p.

PROOF We decompose M with respect to N by solving (A.5) and find from (A.7) and (A.8)

$$M = V^{-1\prime}\Lambda V^{-1},$$

$$N^{-1} = VV',$$

such that

$$N^{-1}M = VV'V'^{-1}\Lambda V^{-1} = V\Lambda V^{-1},$$

$$|N^{-1}M| = |\Lambda| = \prod_{i=1}^{p}\lambda_i,$$

$$tr\{N^{-1}M\} = tr\{\Lambda\} = \sum_{i=1}^{p}\lambda_i.$$

Hence

$$f(M) = tr\{\Lambda\} - \log|\Lambda| = \sum_{i=1}^{p}(\lambda_i - \log\lambda_i),$$

which is minimized by the choice $\hat{\lambda}_i = 1$, $i = 1, \ldots, p$, and therefore by $N^{-1}M = VV^{-1} = I$ or $M = N$. □

LEMMA A.7 *Let M be symmetric and positive semi-definite and N symmetric and positive definite. The function*

$$f(x) = x'Mx/x'Nx$$

is maximized among all vectors $x \in R^p$ by $\hat{x} = v_1$ and the maximal value of f is λ_1, where λ_1 and v_1 are the maximal eigenvalue and the corresponding eigenvector in the equation

$$|\lambda N - M| = 0.$$

PROOF We apply Lemma A.5 and define y by $x = Vy$, then

$$x'Mx/x'Nx = y'\Lambda y/y'y = \sum_{i=1}^{p}\lambda_i y_i^2 / \sum_{i=1}^{p}y_i^2,$$

which is clearly bounded above by the maximal eigenvalue λ_1, and equality holds if $y_1 = 1$, $y_2 = \cdots = y_p = 0$. This choice of y implies that $\hat{x} = v_1$ the first column of V. Note that the maximizing value of x is not uniquely defined. One can always multiply by a constant different from zero and, if $\lambda_1 = \lambda_2$, one can even choose $\hat{x} = v_2$ or some linear combination of v_1 and v_2. □

This result is now generalized:

LEMMA A.8 *Let M be symmetric and positive definite and N symmetric and positive definite. The function*

$$f(x) = |x'Mx|/|x'Nx|$$

is maximized among all $p \times r$ matrices by $\hat{x} = (v_1, \ldots, v_r)$, and the maximal value is $\prod_{i=1}^{r} \lambda_i$, where again λ_i and v_i are solutions to the eigenvalue problem

$$|\lambda N - M| = 0, \tag{A.10}$$

where we assume that $\lambda_1 > \cdots > \lambda_p > 0$. We can also choose $\hat{x}$ times any non-singular $r \times r$ matrix as the maximizing argument.

An expansion of $\log f(x + h)$ around $\hat{x}$ is given by

$$\begin{aligned}
\log f(\hat{x} + h) = {} & \log f(\hat{x}) \\
& + tr\{(\hat{x}'M\hat{x})^{-1} h'(M - M\hat{x}(\hat{x}'M\hat{x})^{-1}\hat{x}'M)h\} \\
& - tr\{(\hat{x}'N\hat{x})^{-1} h'(N - N\hat{x}(\hat{x}'N\hat{x})^{-1}\hat{x}'N)h\} \\
& + O\left(\|h\|^3\right).
\end{aligned} \tag{A.11}$$

PROOF We first expand the determinant

$$|I + h|$$

$$= \left| \begin{bmatrix} 1+h_{11} & h_{12} & \cdots & h_{1p} \\ h_{21} & 1+h_{22} & \cdots & h_{2p} \\ \vdots & \vdots & & \vdots \\ h_{p1} & h_{p2} & \cdots & 1+h_{pp} \end{bmatrix} \right|$$

$$= 1 + \sum_{i=1}^{p} h_{ii} + \sum_{1 \leq i < j \leq p} h_{ii}h_{jj} - \sum_{1 \leq i < j \leq p} h_{ij}h_{ji} + O(\|h\|^3)$$

$$= 1 + \sum_{i=1}^{p} h_{ii} + \frac{1}{2}\sum_{i=1}^{p}\sum_{j=1}^{p} h_{ii}h_{jj} - \frac{1}{2}\sum_{i=1}^{p}\sum_{j=1}^{p} h_{ij}h_{ji} + O(\|h\|^3)$$

$$= 1 + tr(h) + \frac{1}{2}tr^2(h) - \frac{1}{2}tr(h^2) + O(\|h\|^3).$$

Here $\|h\| = \max_i \sum_{j=1}^{p} |h_{ij}|$. Taking logarithms we find

$$\log(|I + h|) = tr(h) - \frac{1}{2}tr(h^2) + O(\|h\|^3).$$

Next we expand the function

$$\log \left| (x + h)' M (x + h) \right|$$

$$= \log |x'Mx| + \log |I + (x'Mx)^{-1} (x'Mh + h'Mx + h'Mh)|$$

$$= \log |x'Mx| + 2tr\{(x'Mx)^{-1} (x'Mh)\} + tr\{(x'Mx)^{-1} (h'Mh)\} \quad \text{(A.12)}$$

$$- \tfrac{1}{2} tr\{(x'Mx)^{-1} (x'Mh + h'Mx)(x'Mx)^{-1} (x'Mh + h'Mx)\}$$

$$+ O\left(\|h\|^3\right),$$

where the last term simplifies to

$$-tr\{(x'Mx)^{-1} x'Mh (x'Mx)^{-1} x'Mh\}$$

$$-tr\{(x'Mx)^{-1} h'Mx (x'Mx)^{-1} x'Mh\}.$$

The function $\log f(x)$ has a stationary point $\hat{x}$ if the derivative at $\hat{x}$ in the direction h is zero for all h, hence the first order condition

$$M\hat{x} (\hat{x}'M\hat{x})^{-1} = N\hat{x} (\hat{x}'N\hat{x})^{-1}. \quad \text{(A.13)}$$

This is easier to interpret if we let $y = N^{\frac{1}{2}}\hat{x}$ and $A = N^{-\frac{1}{2}}MN^{-\frac{1}{2}}$, since then the result is that $Ay (y'Ay)^{-1} = y (y'y)^{-1}$. This means that Ay is in the space spanned by y, and hence that the space $sp(y)$ is invariant under the linear mapping A and therefore a union of invariant one-dimensional subspaces spanned by the eigenvectors e_i of A, see Lemma A.3. Thus $sp(y) = sp(e_{i_1}, \ldots, e_{i_r})$ for some choice of $i_1, \ldots, i_r$. This gives $sp(\hat{x}) = sp(v_{i_1}, \ldots, v_{i_r})$ and the value of the function $f(\hat{x}) = \prod_{k=1}^r \lambda_{i_k}$, which is clearly maximal if we choose $i_1 = 1, \ldots, i_r = r$, corresponding to the largest r eigenvalues of A, which gives the first result, since the eigenvalues of A can be found from (A.10).

From (A.12) we find the expansion of $\log f(\hat{x} + h)$. Note that when considering

$$\log |(\hat{x} + h)' M (\hat{x} + h)| - \log |(\hat{x} + h)' N (\hat{x} + h)|,$$

the first order terms vanish, but so do the second order terms involving

$$(\hat{x}'M\hat{x})^{-1} \hat{x}'Mh = (\hat{x}'N\hat{x})^{-1} \hat{x}'Nh,$$

which holds at the maximum point, see (A.13). The non-vanishing second order term is

$$-tr\{(\hat{x}'M\hat{x})^{-1} h'(M - M\hat{x}(\hat{x}'M\hat{x})^{-1}\hat{x}'M)h\}$$

$$-tr\{(\hat{x}'N\hat{x})^{-1} h'(N - N\hat{x}(\hat{x}'N\hat{x})^{-1}\hat{x}'N)h\},$$

which gives the required result, see (A.10).   □

LEMMA A.9 *Let the symmetric matrices M $(p_1 \times p_1)$ and N $(p_2 \times p_2)$ be positive definite and let A $(p_1 \times p_2)$ be such that the matrix*

$$\begin{bmatrix} M & A \\ A' & N \end{bmatrix}$$

is positive semi-definite. Assume that $p_1 \geq p_2 \geq r$. Then the function

$$f(x,y) = |x'Ayy'A'x|/|x'Mx||y'Ny|$$

is maximized among $p_1 \times r$ matrices x and $p_2 \times r$ matrices y as follows:
  First solve

$$|\lambda M - AN^{-1}A'| = 0, \qquad\qquad (A.14)$$

giving $\lambda_1 \geq \cdots \geq \lambda_{p_1} \geq 0$ and eigenvectors $V = (v_1, \ldots, v_{p_1})$ normalized as $V'MV = I$. Next solve

$$|\lambda N - A'M^{-1}A| = 0, \qquad\qquad (A.15)$$

giving $\lambda_1 \geq \cdots \geq \lambda_{p_2} \geq 0$ and eigenvectors $W = (w_1, \ldots, w_{p_2})$ normalized as $W'NW = I$. Note that (A.14) and (A.15) have the same positive eigenvalues.
  Then the maximum of $f(x,y)$ is attained for $\hat{x} = (v_1, \ldots, v_r)$ and $\hat{y} = (w_1, \ldots, w_r)$ and the maximal value is $\prod_{i=1}^{r} \lambda_i$. The solutions can be chosen such that $v_i = \lambda_i^{-\frac{1}{2}} M^{-1} A w_i$, $i = 1, \ldots, r$.

PROOF Let us first maximize for fixed value of y. The function

$$g_y(x) = |x'(Ayy'A')x|/|x'Mx|$$

is maximized by Lemma A.8. The corresponding eigenvalue problem is

$$|\lambda M - Ayy'A'| = 0.$$

Now the rank of the matrix $Ayy'A'$ is at most r, which shows that at most r eigenvalues $\Lambda = \text{diag}(\lambda_1, \ldots, \lambda_r)$ are positive. The corresponding eigenvectors $V_r = (v_1, \ldots, v_r)$ satisfy

$$MV_r\Lambda = Ayy'A'V_r,$$

which shows that V_r has the form $M^{-1}Ay\varphi$ for some $r \times r$ matrix $\varphi = y'A'V_r\Lambda^{-1}$. Inserting this we find

$$\max_x f(x, y) = |y'A'M^{-1}Ay|/|y'Ny|.$$

Again this is maximized by Lemma A.8 by solving (A.15). Note that if y_i is an eigenvector for the problem (A.15) with $\lambda_i > 0$, then $x_i = \lambda_i^{-\frac{1}{2}} M^{-1} A y_i$ is an eigenvector, properly normalized, for the same eigenvalue but for the dual problem (A.14). Thus we really only have to solve one of the eigenvalue problems. The maximum value is found by inserting the normalized eigenvalues $x = M^{-1} A y \Lambda^{-\frac{1}{2}}$ in the expression for $f(x, y)$.

That (A.14) and (A.15) have the same positive solutions follows from the matrix relation, see (A.26)

$$\begin{vmatrix} \rho M & A \\ A' & \rho N \end{vmatrix} = |\rho M| |\rho N - A'(\rho M)^{-1} A| = \rho^{p_1 - p_2} |M| |\rho^2 N - A'(M)^{-1} A|$$

$$= |\rho N| |\rho M - A(\rho N)^{-1} A'| = \rho^{p_2 - p_1} |N| |\rho^2 M - A(N)^{-1} A'|.$$

$$\square$$

LEMMA A.10 *Let now both M and N be positive semi-definite symmetric matrices of dimension $p \times p$ such that $Nx = 0$ implies $Mx = 0$. Let $rank(M) = m$ and $rank(N) = n$. Let x be $p \times r$, $r \leq n$. The function*

$$f(x) = |x'Mx|/|x'Nx|, \quad |x'Nx| \neq 0,$$

is maximized as follows: first solve $|\rho I - N| = 0$ for $\rho_1 \geq \cdots \geq \rho_n > \rho_{n+1} = \cdots = \rho_p = 0$ and eigenvectors $w_1, \ldots, w_p$, and define the matrix

$$C = (w_1, \ldots, w_n) \operatorname{diag} \left(\rho_1^{-\frac{1}{2}}, \ldots, \rho_n^{-\frac{1}{2}} \right),$$

such that $C'NC = I\,(n \times n)$. Next solve the eigenvalue problem $|\lambda I - C'MC| = 0$ for eigenvalues $\lambda_1 \geq \cdots \geq \lambda_n \geq 0$ and eigenvectors $v_1, \ldots, v_n$. The solution of the maximization problem is $\hat{x} = C(v_1, \ldots, v_r)$ and the maximum value is $f(\hat{x}) = \prod_{i=1}^{r} \lambda_i$. The solution $\hat{x}$ is orthogonal to the null space for N.

PROOF Since

$$N = W' \operatorname{diag}(\rho_1, \ldots, \rho_p) W$$

$$= (w_1, \ldots, w_n)' \operatorname{diag}(\rho_1, \ldots, \rho_n)(w_1, \ldots, w_n),$$

it is seen that the null space of N is spanned by $(w_{n+1}, \ldots, w_p)$, and that

$$x'Nx = x'(w_1, \ldots, w_n)' \operatorname{diag}(\rho_1, \ldots, \rho_n)(w_1, \ldots, w_n) x$$

only depends on x through the projection onto the orthogonal complement to the null space of N as spanned by $W_n = (w_1, \ldots, w_n)$. Since $x'N = 0$

implies that $x'M = 0$ it is seen that in order to maximize $f(x)$ it is enough to consider $f(x)$ only on the space spanned by W_n or C. For $x = Cy$ we find

$$f(x) = |y'C'MCy|/|y'y|,$$

which is maximized as indicated by Lemma A.8. $\qquad\qquad\square$

A.2 The Binomial Formula for Matrices

Let A and B be $p \times p$ matrices. The binomial formula states that

$$(A + B)^n$$

$$= \sum_{r=0}^{n} \sum_{i_1+i_2+\cdots+i_{r+1}=n-r} A^{i_1} B A^{i_2} B \cdots A^{i_r} B A^{i_{r+1}}$$

$$= A^n + \sum_{i+j=n-1} A^i B A^j + \sum_{i+j+k=n-2} A^i B A^j B A^k + \cdots + B^n.$$

The number of terms in the rth summand is $\binom{n}{r}$, and if A and B commute then

$$(A + B)^n = \sum_{r=0}^{n} \binom{n}{r} A^r B^{n-r}.$$

The exponential function is given by the expansion

$$\exp(A) = \sum_{r=0}^{\infty} A^r/r!.$$

The basic relation between the binomial formula and the exponential function is given in the classical result.

THEOREM A.11 *Let A be a square matrix, then for $T \to \infty$ it holds that*

$$\left(I + T^{-1}A\right)^T \to \exp(A).$$

PROOF   The binomial formula gives

$$\left(I + T^{-1}A\right)^T = \sum_{r=0}^{T} T^{(r)} A^r/T^r r! = \sum_{r=0}^{T} A^r/r! + \sum_{r=0}^{T} (T^{(r)}/T^r - 1) A^r/r!$$

$$= \sum_{r=0}^{T} A^r/r! + \sum_{r=0}^{N} (T^{(r)}/T^r - 1) A^r/r! + \sum_{r=N+1}^{T} (T^{(r)}/T^r - 1) A^r/r!.$$

The norm of the last term is bounded by $\sum_{r=N+1}^{\infty} \|A\|^r/r!$, independently of T. Hence we can first choose N such that the last term is small, and then T so large that the first term is close to $\exp(A)$ and the second term is small, since it only has finitely many terms. $\qquad\square$

In the following we shall give various refinements of this result using the binomial formula. These results resemble the well-known inequalities for the exponential function

$$e^x - 1 \leq x e^x, \quad x > 0,$$

$$e^x - 1 - x \leq \tfrac{1}{2}x^2 e^x, \, x > 0.$$

PROPOSITION A.12 *If* $T\|B_T\|$ *is bounded then for some constant* c *the following inequalities hold*

$$\| (I + B_T)^T \| \leq c, \tag{A.16}$$

$$\| (I + B_T)^T - I \| \leq T\|B_T\|c, \tag{A.17}$$

$$\| (I + B_T)^T - I - TB_T \| \leq \frac{1}{2}T^2\|B_T\|^2 c. \tag{A.18}$$

PROOF   The binomial formula gives

$$\| (I + B_T)^T \| = \| \sum_{r=0}^{T} \binom{T}{r} B_T^r \| \leq \sum_{r=0}^{T} T^r \|B_T\|^r / r! \leq \exp{(T\|B_T\|)},$$

which is bounded by the assumption on $\|B_T\|$. Next we get

$$\| (I + B_T)^T - I \| = \| \sum_{r=1}^{T} \binom{T}{r} B_T^r \| \leq \sum_{r=1}^{T} T^r \|B_T\|^r / r!$$

$$\leq \exp{(T\|B_T\|)} - 1 \leq T\|B_T\| \exp{(T\|B_T\|)} \leq T\|B_T\|c,$$

by the inequality $e^x - 1 \leq x e^x$ and the boundedness of $T\|B_T\|$. Finally we find

$$\| (I + B_T)^T - I - TB_T \| = \| \sum_{r=2}^{T} \binom{T}{r} B_T^r \| \leq \sum_{r=2}^{T} T^r \|B_T\|^r / r!$$

$$\leq \exp{(T\|B_T\|)} - 1 - T\|B_T\| \leq \tfrac{1}{2}T^2\|B_T\|^2 \exp{(T\|B_T\|)},$$

by the inequality $e^x - 1 - x \leq \tfrac{1}{2}x^2 e^x$.   □

In the following we consider equations of the form

$$\Delta X_t = (\alpha\beta' + B_T) X_{t-1} + \epsilon_t,$$

where the solution is given by

$$X_t - (I + \alpha\beta' + B_T)^t X_0 = \sum_{i=0}^{t-1} (I + \alpha\beta' + B_T)^i \epsilon_{t-i}. \tag{A.19}$$

LEMMA A.13 *Let $A = I + \alpha\beta'$, α and β ($p \times r$), and assume that the eigen-
values of $I + \beta'\alpha$ are less than 1 in absolute value, such that $\| (I + \beta'\alpha)^t \| \leq
c\lambda^t$ for some $\lambda < 1$ and all t, see (A.2). Assume also that $\|TB_T\|$ is bounded.
Then*

$$\lim_{t\to\infty} A^t = \beta_\perp (\alpha'_\perp \beta_\perp)^{-1} \alpha'_\perp, \qquad (A.20)$$

and for $t = 0, \ldots, T$ and some constant c

$$\| (A + B_T)^t \| \leq c, \qquad (A.21)$$
$$\|\beta' (A + B_T)^t - \beta' A^t\| \leq c\|B_T\|, \qquad (A.22)$$
$$\|\alpha'_\perp (A + B_T)^t - (I + \alpha'_\perp B_T \beta_\perp (\alpha'_\perp \beta_\perp)^{-1})^t \alpha'_\perp\| \leq c\|B_T\|T. \quad (A.23)$$

PROOF of (A.20): the binomial formula gives

$$A^T = (I + \alpha\beta')^T = \sum_{r=0}^T \binom{T}{r} (\alpha\beta')^r$$

$$= I + \alpha (\beta'\alpha)^{-1} \sum_{r=1}^T \binom{T}{r} (\beta'\alpha)^r \beta'$$

$$= I + \alpha(\beta'\alpha)^{-1}((I + \beta'\alpha)^T - I)\beta'$$

$$\to I - \alpha(\beta'\alpha)^{-1}\beta' = \beta_\perp(\alpha'_\perp\beta_\perp)^{-1}\alpha'_\perp,$$

by $(A.2)$.   □

PROOF of (A.21): again the binomial formula gives

$$(A + B_T)^t = \sum_{r=0}^t \sum_{i_1+i_2+\cdots+i_{r+1}=t-r} A^{i_1} B_T A^{i_2} B_T \cdots A^{i_r} B_T A^{i_{r+1}},$$

and hence from (A.20), we have $\|A^i\| \leq c_A$

$$\| (A + B_T)^t \| \leq \sum_{r=0}^t c_A^{r+1} \|B_T\|^r \binom{t}{r} \leq c_A \sum_{r=0}^t (c_A\|B_T\|t)^r /r!$$

$$\leq c_A \exp (c_A\|B_T\|t) \leq c_A \exp (c_A T\|B_T\|),$$

which is assumed bounded.   □

PROOF of (A.22): from the identity

$$(A + B_T)^{i+1} = (A + B_T) (A + B_T)^i \qquad (A.24)$$

we find since $\beta'(I + \alpha\beta') = (I + \beta'\alpha)\beta'$, that

$$\beta' (A + B_T)^{i+1} = \beta' (I + \alpha\beta' + B_T) (A + B_T)^i$$

$$= (I + \beta'\alpha) \beta' (A + B_T)^i + \beta' B_T (A + B_T)^i,$$

which by (A.19) has the solution

$$\beta' \left(A + B_T\right)^t - \left(I + \beta'\alpha\right)^t \beta' = \sum_{i=0}^{t-1} \left(I + \beta'\alpha\right)^i \beta' B_T \left(A + B_T\right)^{t-i},$$

hence

$$\|\beta' \left(A + B_T\right)^t - \left(I + \beta'\alpha\right)^t \beta'\| \leq \sum_{i=0}^{t-1} c\lambda^i \|\beta'\|\|B_T\|c_1 \leq c_2\|B_T\|,$$

since λ^i is summable. $\square$

PROOF of (A.23): from (A.24) we also find, since

$$\alpha \left(\beta'\alpha\right)^{-1} \beta' + \beta_\perp \left(\alpha'_\perp\beta_\perp\right)^{-1} \alpha'_\perp = I,$$

that

$$\alpha'_\perp \left(A + B_T\right)^{i+1}$$

$$= \alpha'_\perp \left(I + \alpha\beta' + B_T\right) \left[\alpha \left(\beta'\alpha\right)^{-1} \beta' + \beta_\perp \left(\alpha'_\perp\beta_\perp\right)^{-1} \alpha'_\perp\right] \left(A + B_T\right)^i$$

$$= \left(I + \alpha'_\perp B_T \beta_\perp \left(\alpha'_\perp\beta_\perp\right)^{-1}\right)\alpha'_\perp \left(A + B_T\right)^i + \alpha'_\perp B_T \alpha \left(\beta'\alpha\right)^{-1} \beta' \left(A + B_T\right)^i,$$

which by (A.19) can be solved as

$$\alpha'_\perp \left(A + B_T\right)^t - \left(I + \alpha'_\perp B_T \beta_\perp \left(\alpha'_\perp\beta_\perp\right)^{-1}\right)^t\alpha'_\perp$$

$$= \sum_{i=0}^{t-1}\left(I + \alpha'_\perp B_T \beta_\perp \left(\alpha'_\perp\beta_\perp\right)^{-1}\right)^i\alpha'_\perp B_T \alpha \left(\beta'\alpha\right)^{-1} \beta' \left(A + B_T\right)^{t-i},$$

and hence

$$\|\alpha'_\perp \left(A + B_T\right)^t - \left(I + \alpha'_\perp B_T \beta_\perp \left(\alpha'_\perp\beta_\perp\right)^{-1}\right)^t\alpha'_\perp\|$$

$$\leq \sum_{i=0}^{t-1} \|\left(I + \alpha'_\perp B_T \beta_\perp \left(\alpha'_\perp\beta_\perp\right)^{-1}\right)^i\|\|\alpha'_\perp B_T \alpha \left(\beta'\alpha\right)^{-1} \|\|\beta' \left(A + B_T\right)^{t-i} \|.$$

Now by (A.16) we have $\|\left(I + \alpha'_\perp B_T \beta_\perp \left(\alpha'_\perp\beta_\perp\right)^{-1}\right)^i\| \leq c_3$, and since

$$\|\alpha'_\perp B_T \alpha \left(\beta'\alpha\right)^{-1} \| \leq \|\alpha'_\perp\|\|B_T\|\|\alpha \left(\beta'\alpha\right)^{-1} \|,$$

we only have to show that $\sum_{i=0}^{t-1} \|\beta' \left(A + B_T\right)^{t-i} \|$ is bounded. We then apply the identities

$$\beta'A = \beta'(I + \alpha\beta') = (I + \beta'\alpha)\beta',$$

$$\beta'A^i = (I + \beta'\alpha)\beta' A^{i-1} = (I + \beta'\alpha)^i\beta'.$$

From these results we find

$$\sum_{i=0}^{t-1} \| \beta' (A + B_T)^{t-i} \|$$

$$\leq \sum_{i=0}^{t-1} \| \beta' (A + B_T)^{t-i} - \beta' A^{t-i} \| + \sum_{i=0}^{t-1} \| \beta' A^{t-i} \|$$

$$\leq T \max_{i \leq T} \| \beta' (A + B_T)^i - \beta' A^i \| + \sum_{i=0}^{T} \| (I_r + \beta' \alpha)^i \beta' \|.$$

The first term is by (A.22) bounded by $cT \| B_T \|$ and hence bounded, and the second term is bounded by $c \| \beta' \| \sum_{i=0}^{T} \lambda^i$, which completes the proof.
□

THEOREM A.14   *If the eigenvalues of $I + \beta' \alpha$ are less than 1 then*

$$\left(I + \alpha \beta' + T^{-1} B \right)^T \rightarrow C \exp (BC) = \exp (CB) C$$

where $C = \beta_\perp (\alpha'_\perp \beta_\perp)^{-1} \beta'_\perp$.

PROOF   First note that from (A.22) it follows that

$$\beta' \left(I + \alpha \beta' + T^{-1} B \right)^T - \beta' A^T \rightarrow 0, \ T \rightarrow \infty,$$

hence $\beta' \left(I + \alpha \beta' + T^{-1} B \right)^T = \beta' (A + B_T)^T$ has the same limit as

$$\beta' A^T = (I + \beta' \alpha)^T \beta',$$

which tends to zero by the assumption on the eigenvalues. Next consider

$$\alpha'_\perp \left(I + \alpha \beta' + T^{-1} B \right)^T,$$

which by (A.22) has the same limit as

$$(I + T^{-1} \alpha'_\perp B \beta_\perp (\alpha'_\perp \beta_\perp)^{-1})^T \alpha'_\perp \rightarrow \exp(\alpha'_\perp B \beta_\perp (\alpha'_\perp \beta_\perp)^{-1}) \alpha'_\perp.$$

Combining the results we find

$$\left(I + \alpha \beta' + T^{-1} B \right)^T$$

$$= (\alpha (\beta' \alpha)^{-1} \beta' + \beta_\perp (\alpha'_\perp \beta_\perp)^{-1} \alpha'_\perp) \left(I + \alpha \beta' + T^{-1} B \right)^T$$

$$\rightarrow \beta_\perp (\alpha'_\perp \beta_\perp)^{-1} \exp(\alpha'_\perp B \beta_\perp (\alpha'_\perp \beta_\perp)^{-1}) \alpha'_\perp = C \exp (BC) = \exp (CB) C.$$

□

A.3   The Multivariate Gaussian Distribution

We let X denote a p-dimensional Gaussian random variable with mean ξ and non-singular variance matrix Ω. The distribution is denoted by $N_p(\xi, \Omega)$, and the density is given by

$$(2\pi)^{-\frac{1}{2}p} |\Omega|^{-\frac{1}{2}} \exp\{-\tfrac{1}{2}(X - \xi)' \Omega^{-1}(X - \xi)\}$$

$$= (2\pi)^{-\frac{1}{2}p} |\Omega|^{-\frac{1}{2}} \exp\{-\tfrac{1}{2}tr\{\Omega^{-1}(X - \xi)(X - \xi)'\}\}. \tag{A.25}$$

If X is decomposed into X_1 and X_2 of dimension p_1 and p_2 $(p_1 + p_2 = p)$ and if ξ and Ω are decomposed similarly

$$\xi = \begin{bmatrix} \xi_1 \\ \xi_2 \end{bmatrix}, \ \Omega = \begin{bmatrix} \Omega_{11} & \Omega_{12} \\ \Omega_{21} & \Omega_{22} \end{bmatrix},$$

then the distribution of X_1 is Gaussian in p_1 dimensions with mean ξ_1 and variance Ω_{11}, whereas the distribution of X_2 given X_1 is Gaussian with mean $\xi_2 + \Omega_{21}\Omega_{11}^{-1}(X_1 - \xi_1)$ and variance $\Omega_{22.1} = \Omega_{22} - \Omega_{21}\Omega_{11}^{-1}\Omega_{12}$.

It is an important result of the multivariate Gaussian distribution, see Barndorff-Nielsen (1978), that we can parametrize the statistical model defined by letting (ξ, Ω) vary freely, either by (ξ, Ω) or by the parameters of the marginal distribution

$$\phi = \phi(\xi, \Omega) = (\xi_1, \Omega_{11}),$$

and the parameters of the conditional distribution

$$\psi = \psi(\xi, \Omega) = \left(\xi_2 - \Omega_{21}\Omega_{11}^{-1}\xi_1, \ \Omega_{21}\Omega_{11}^{-1}, \ \Omega_{22} - \Omega_{21}\Omega_{11}^{-1}\Omega_{12}\right),$$

when these two sets of parameters vary freely in their respective domains

$$(\phi, \psi) \in A \times B.$$

This is seen by solving for $\xi = \xi(\phi, \psi)$ and $\Omega = \Omega(\phi, \psi)$ for any value of (ϕ, ψ) in the domain of definition.

The important relation

$$|\Omega| = |\Omega_{11}||\Omega_{22} - \Omega_{21}\Omega_{11}^{-1}\Omega_{12}| \tag{A.26}$$

is most easily interpreted by noting that the left hand side is the normalizing constant in the density of X, whereas the right hand side is the product of the normalizing constants in the marginal distribution of X_1 and the conditional distribution of X_2 given X_1 respectively.

The interpretation of Ω as the variance of X is paralleled by the interpretation of Ω^{-1} as the precision or information in X. The basic 'duality' between marginal distributions and conditional distributions is nicely displayed in the result that the *variance* in the *marginal* distribution is found by restricting the variance matrix Ω to Ω_{11}, whereas the *precision* in the *conditional* distribution of X_2 given X_1 is found by restricting the precision Ω^{-1} to $\left(\Omega^{-1}\right)_{22} = \Omega^{22}$. This is seen from the well-known result

$$\left(\Omega^{22}\right)^{-1} = \Omega_{22} - \Omega_{21}\Omega_{11}^{-1}\Omega_{12}.$$

The basic estimation problem is that of finding estimates of ξ and Ω when we have T independent identically distributed observations from (A.25).

LEMMA A.15 *Let $X_1, \ldots, X_T$ be independent identically distributed Gaussian variables with mean ξ and variance Ω then*

$$\hat{\xi} = T^{-1}\sum_{i=1}^{T} X_i = \bar{X},$$

$$\hat{\Omega} = T^{-1}\sum_{t=1}^{T}\left(X_t - \bar{X}\right)\left(X_t - \bar{X}\right)',$$

and the maximized likelihood function is given by

$$L_{\max}^{-2/T} = (2\pi e)^p |\hat{\Omega}|. \tag{A.27}$$

PROOF The likelihood function is

$$L\left(\xi, \Omega\right) = \prod_{t=1}^{T}\left(2\pi\right)^{-\frac{1}{2}p}|\Omega|^{-\frac{1}{2}}\exp\{-\frac{1}{2}tr\{\Omega^{-1}\left(X_t - \xi\right)\left(X_t - \xi\right)'\}, \tag{A.28}$$

or, with $c = Tp\log(2\pi)$,

$$-2\log L\left(\xi, \Omega\right) = c + T\log|\Omega| + tr\{\Omega^{-1}\sum_{t=1}^{T}\left(X_t - \xi\right)\left(X_t - \xi\right)'\}. \tag{A.29}$$

The parameter ξ enters only in the last expression which can be simplified as follows

$$tr\{\Omega^{-1}\sum_{t=1}^{T}\left(X_t - \xi\right)\left(X_t - \xi\right)'\}$$

$$= tr\{\Omega^{-1}\sum_{t=1}^{T}\left(X_t - \bar{X}\right)\left(X_t - \bar{X}\right)'\} + T tr\{\Omega^{-1}\left(\bar{X} - \xi\right)\left(\bar{X} - \xi\right)'\}. \tag{A.30}$$

The last quantity is non-negative and only zero if $\xi = \bar{X}$, which shows that the maximum likelihood estimator of ξ is $\bar{X}$. Inserting this and applying the notation $\hat{\Omega} = T^{-1}\sum_{t=1}^{T}\left(X_t - \bar{X}\right)\left(X_t - \bar{X}\right)'$ we find

$$-2\log L(\xi, \Omega) \geq -2\log L(\bar{X}, \Omega)$$

$$= c + T\log|\Omega| + T tr\{\Omega^{-1}\hat{\Omega}\}$$

$$= c + T\log|\hat{\Omega}| + T(tr\{\Omega^{-1}\hat{\Omega}\} - \log|\Omega^{-1}\hat{\Omega}|).$$

By Lemma A.6 this is minimized by $\Omega = \hat{\Omega}$. This shows that the maximum likelihood estimators are as indicated. Inserting these in the likelihood function we find

$$-2\log L(\bar{X}, \hat{\Omega}) = c + T\log|\hat{\Omega}| + pT,$$

which shows (A.27). □

The basic regression problem is solved similarly.

LEMMA A.16 *Let* $X_t = \beta'v_t + \epsilon_t$, $t = 1, \dots, T$, *where* v_t *are deterministic regressors and* ϵ_t *are independent Gaussian variables with mean zero and variance* Ω. *The estimates of* β *and* Ω *are given by*

$$\hat{\beta} = (\textstyle\sum_{t=1}^{T} v_t v_t')^{-1} \sum_{t=1}^{T} v_t X_t' = S_{vv}^{-1} S_{vx}.$$
$$\hat{\Omega} = T^{-1} \textstyle\sum_{t=1}^{T} R_{xt} R_{xt}' = S_{xx} - S_{xv} S_{vv}^{-1} S_{vx},$$

with

$$R_{xt} = X_t - \hat{\beta}'v_t = X_t - S_{xv} S_{vv}^{-1} v_t.$$

PROOF   The likelihood function is found from (A.28)

$$-2\log L(\beta, \Omega) = c + T\log|\Omega| + tr\{\Omega^{-1} \sum_{t=1}^{T} (X_t - \beta'v_t)(X_t - \beta'v_t)'\}.$$

$$\tag{A.31}$$

We apply the same trick as in (A.30) and find

$$tr\{\Omega^{-1} \textstyle\sum_{t=1}^{T} (X_t - \beta'v_t)(X_t - \beta'v_t)'\}$$

$$= tr\{\Omega^{-1} \textstyle\sum_{t=1}^{T} (X_t - \hat{\beta}'v_t)(X_t - \hat{\beta}'v_t)'\}$$

$$+ tr\{\Omega^{-1}(\hat{\beta} - \beta)' \textstyle\sum_{t=1}^{T} v_t v_t'(\hat{\beta} - \beta)\}.$$

The last expression is non-negative and equal to zero only if $\beta = \hat{\beta}$. Thus the maximum likelihood estimator is $\hat{\beta}$, and the estimate of Ω is found as before. □

In regression it is often convenient to perform the estimation in a two-step procedure, and we show here how this is done.

LEMMA A.17 *Let* $X_t = \alpha' u_t + \beta' v_t + \epsilon_t$, *where* u_t *and* v_t *are deterministic regressors, and* ϵ_t *are independent Gaussian variables with mean zero and variance* Ω. *The estimator of* α *can be calculated in two steps as follows:*

1. *First regress* X_t *and* u_t *on* v_t *giving residuals* R_{xt} *and* R_{ut}, *that is, correct* X_t *and* u_t *for* v_t.

2. *The maximum likelihood estimator of* α *can be found by regressing* R_{xt} *on* R_{ut}.

PROOF   The likelihood function is found from (A.29) and is given by

$$-2 \log L (\alpha, \beta, \Omega)$$

$$= c + T \log |\Omega| + tr\{\Omega^{-1} \sum_{t=1}^{T} (X_t - \alpha' u_t - \beta' v_t)(X_t - \alpha' u_t - \beta' v_t)'\}.$$

Minimizing with respect to β gives the equation

$$\sum_{t=1}^{T} (X_t - \alpha' u_t - \beta' v_t) v_t' = 0,$$

or

$$S_{xv} - \alpha' S_{uv} = \hat{\beta}' S_{vv}.$$

Inserting the solution for β we find

$$X_t - \alpha' u_t - \hat{\beta}' v_t = X_t - \alpha' u_t - (S_{xv} - \alpha' S_{uv}) S_{vv}^{-1} v_t$$

$$= R_{xt} - \alpha' R_{ut},$$

with $R_{xt} = X_t - S_{xv} S_{vv}^{-1} v_t$ and $R_{ut} = u_t - S_{uv} S_{vv}^{-1} v_t$. Thus the concentrated likelihood function is

$$-2 \log L (\alpha, \beta, \Omega) = c + T \log |\Omega| + tr\{\Omega^{-1} \sum_{t=1}^{T} (R_{xt} - \alpha' R_{ut})(R_{xt} - \alpha' R_{ut})'\},$$

$$\text{(A.32)}$$

which shows, see (A.31), that the estimate of α is found by regression of R_{xt} on R_{ut}.   □

This result is of course closely related to the interpretation of α as the effect of u_t on X_t corrected for v_t, which is the *ceteris paribus* assumption usually made in econometrics.

LEMMA A.18 *Let*

$$X_{1t} = \alpha_1' v_t + \alpha_2' u_t + \epsilon_{1t},$$

$$X_{2t} = \beta' u_t + \epsilon_{2t},$$

where $(\epsilon_{1t}, \epsilon_{2t})$ *are independent Gaussian variables with mean zero and variance matrix*

$$\Omega = \begin{bmatrix} \Omega_{11} & \Omega_{12} \\ \Omega_{21} & \Omega_{22} \end{bmatrix}.$$

Here u_t and v_t are deterministic regressors. Then

$$E(X_{1t}|X_{2t}) = \alpha_1' v_t + (\alpha_2' - \Omega_{12}\Omega_{22}^{-1}\beta')u_t + \Omega_{12}\Omega_{22}^{-1}X_{2t},$$

$$\mathrm{Var}(X_{1t}|X_{2t}) = \Omega_{11} - \Omega_{12}\Omega_{22}^{-1}\Omega_{21} = \Omega_{11.2},$$

$$E(X_{2t}) \qquad = \beta' u_t,$$

$$\mathrm{Var}(X_{2t}) \qquad = \Omega_{22}.$$

The parameters $(\alpha_1', (\alpha_2' - \Omega_{12}\Omega_{22}^{-1}\beta'), \Omega_{12}\Omega_{22}^{-1}, \Omega_{11.2})$ vary independently of the parameters (β, Ω_{11}). This shows that estimates of α and β can be found as follows

1. Regress X_{2t} on u_t to determine $\hat{\beta}$ and $\hat{\Omega}_{22}$.

2. Regress X_{1t} on v_t, u_t, and X_{2t} giving regression estimates $\hat{\alpha}_1$, $\hat{a}_1$, $\hat{a}_2$, and $\hat{\Omega}_{11.2}$.

3. Calculate $\hat{\Omega}_{12} = \hat{a}_2\hat{\Omega}_{22}$, $\hat{\alpha}_2 = \hat{a}_1 + \hat{\beta}\hat{a}_2$, $\hat{\Omega}_{11} = \hat{\Omega}_{11.2} + \hat{\Omega}_{12}\hat{\Omega}_{22}^{-1}\hat{\Omega}_{21}$.

PROOF   This follows from the properties of the Gaussian distribution.
□

The reason that the simple regression solution exists to this problem is that although the two equations do not have the same regressors, it still holds that the regressors for X_{2t} are a subset of the regressors for X_{1t}. This is the structure that allows a simple solution.

A.4   Principal Components and Canonical Correlations

Let again X be Gaussian $N_p(\xi, \Omega)$. Let (Λ, V) solve the eigenvalue problem

$$|\lambda I - \Omega| = 0,$$

such that $V'\Omega V = \Lambda$. The variables $Y = V'X$ are distributed as

$$N_p(V'\xi, V'\Omega V) = N_p(V'\xi, \Lambda)$$

which shows that the components of Y are independent and that the variance of Y_i is λ_i. These linear combinations are called the *principal components* of X. By the results about eigenvectors and eigenvalues they can be characterized as follows.

Let $\mu \in R^p$ and consider the function

$$f(\mu) = \mathrm{Var}(\mu'X)/\mu'\mu = \mu'\Omega\mu/\mu'\mu.$$

From Lemma A.7 it follows that the direction μ which maximizes the variance of $\mu'X$ is given by the eigenvector v_1 and the maximal variance obtainable is λ_1.

Similarly it is seen that the function $f(\mu)$ is maximized among all directions μ orthogonal to v_1 by the eigenvector v_2, and that this restricted maximum value is λ_2. To see this note that if $\mu'\Omega v_1 = 0$, then $\mu \in sp(v_2, \ldots, v_p)$ such that $\mu = (v_2, \ldots, v_p)\xi$. Then

$$f(\mu) = \xi'(v_2, \ldots, v_p)'\Omega(v_2, \ldots, v_p)\xi/\xi'(v_2, \ldots, v_p)'\Omega(v_2, \ldots, v_p)\xi$$

$$= \xi'\text{diag}(\lambda_2, \ldots, \lambda_p)\xi/\xi'\xi$$

which is maximized by $\xi' = (1, 0, \ldots, 0)$, giving the maximal value λ_2.

Next let X_1 and X_2 be p-dimensional Gaussian variables with mean zero and variance matrix

$$\Omega = \begin{bmatrix} \Omega_{11} & \Omega_{12} \\ \Omega_{21} & \Omega_{22} \end{bmatrix}.$$

We can, as before, find the principal components of X_1 and X_2 by solving the eigenvalue problems $|\lambda I - \Omega_{11}| = 0$ and $|\lambda I - \Omega_{22}| = 0$ respectively, but we shall here consider the relations between the variables and consider the function

$$\rho(\mu, \nu)^2 = \text{Cor}(\mu'X_1, \nu'X_2)^2 = (\mu'\Omega_{12}\nu)^2 / (\mu'\Omega_{11}\mu)(\nu'\Omega_{22}\nu).$$

We want to find directions μ and ν in which this (squared) correlation is maximal. Lemma A.9 shows how one can solve this maximization problem, by solving the 'dual' eigenvalue problems

$$|\rho^2\Omega_{11} - \Omega_{12}\Omega_{22}^{-1}\Omega_{21}| = 0, \tag{A.33}$$

$$|\rho^2\Omega_{22} - \Omega_{21}\Omega_{11}^{-1}\Omega_{12}| = 0. \tag{A.34}$$

Let the eigenvectors for (A.33) be V_1 and the eigenvectors for (A.34) be V_2. The eigenvectors v_{1i} and v_{2i} are called the canonical variates, and ρ is the canonical correlation. Note that if we define new variables $U_i = V_i'X_i$ then U_i is Gaussian $N_p(0, I)$, and the covariance is given by

$$\text{Cov}(U_1, U_2) = V_1'\Omega_{12}V_2 = \text{diag}(\rho_1, \ldots, \rho_p).$$

Weak Convergence of Probability Measures on R^p and C[0,1]

THE purpose of this appendix is to explain the concept of weak convergence on $C[0,1]$, the space of continuous functions on the unit interval $[0,1]$, and hence explain what is behind the formulae involving Brownian motion, which appear in the discussion of the limit distributions in cointegration theory. The principal reference is Billingsley (1968).

The main conclusion is that apart from weak convergence of finite-dimensional distributions, which can be proved by applying the central limit theorem on R^p, we need to be able to bound the oscillations of the stochastic process. Hence apart from some general arguments involving compactness, separability, and other notions from functional analysis we need to make a genuine probabilistic argument in order to prove an inequality for the maximal fluctuation of the stochastic process in question.

Once weak convergence is understood, we can use it for two purposes, first to show the existence of stochastic processes on $C[0,1]$ like Brownian motion, and next to find distributions of suitable functionals of Brownian motion. The continuous mapping theorem immediately gives the limit distribution of functionals that are continuous on $C[0,1]$, and Donsker's invariance principle then shows that we can calculate limit distributions by choosing a suitable measure that converges weakly. This is also what is used for simulating the limit distributions. In many ways a more convenient tool is convergence on $D[0,1]$, that is, the space of functions that are right continuous and have left limits. It is, however, a bit more complicated to explain, so we focus on $C[0,1]$, even though some of the results are more naturally formulated for $D[0,1]$.

B.1   Weak Convergence on R^p

It will be assumed that the reader is familiar with the notion of weak convergence on R and R^p, and that the central limit theorem is well known, but for the sake of completeness let us just state the basic definitions and results in the following form:

Let P and P_n, $n = 1, 2, \ldots$ be probability measures on the Borel sets of R^p.

DEFINITION B.1 *The sequence P_n converges weakly to P if*

$$\int f dP_n \to \int f dP, \ n \to \infty,$$

for all bounded real valued continuous functions on R^p.

This definition is easy to formulate but is difficult to work with in specific examples, and it is convenient to have criteria for convergence which do not involve so many functions. It is enough to consider functions that are not only continuous, but also continuously differentiable with a bounded derivative. It is also enough to consider the special functions

$$f(x) = e^{it'x}, t \in R^p.$$

This gives rise to a discussion of the characteristic function. If instead of the continuous functions we consider functions of the form

$$f(x) = I\{x_1 \le a_1, \ldots, x_p \le a_p\},$$

we get the well-known definition of weak convergence that states that we have weak convergence if the distribution functions converge in points of continuity for the limit distribution. All these results are proved by showing that the particular class of functions, that we restrict attention to, can be used to approximate continuous functions. All definitions and results about weak convergence of probability measures can be given an equivalent formulation in terms of random variables. Thus the basic definition of weak convergence can be formulated as follows.

The sequence of p-dimensional random variables X_n converge weakly with P as their limit distribution if the distribution P_n of X_n converges weakly towards P. Convergence in probability of X_n to X requires that both variables are defined on the same probability probability space and is defined by $P|X_n - X| \ge \delta \xrightarrow{P} 0, \ n \to \infty$ for all $\delta > 0$.

The basic result that we need in all asymptotic analysis is the central limit theorem which in a simple form states

THEOREM B.2 *(The central limit theorem.) Let X_n be a sequence of independent identically distributed p-dimensional random variables with mean ξ and variance Σ, and let $S_n = X_1 + \cdots + X_n$, then*

$$n^{-\frac{1}{2}}(S_n - n\xi) \xrightarrow{w} N_p(0, \Sigma), \ n \to \infty.$$

The central limit theorem for martingales generalizes this result to hold for a much larger class of random variables allowing different distributions and dependence between the variables, and we give this below.

Let $X_{T.t}, t = 1, \ldots, T$ and $T = 1, 2, \ldots$ be an array of vector valued stochastic variables. Let $\mathcal{F}_{T.t}$ be an array of σ-fields such that $\mathcal{F}_{T.t-1} \subset \mathcal{F}_{T.t}$, and such that $X_{T.t}$ is measurable with respect to $\mathcal{F}_{T.t}$.

THEOREM B.3 *Under the assumptions that*

$$E(X_{T.t}|\mathcal{F}_{T.t-1}) = 0, \qquad \text{(B.1)}$$

$$\sum_{t=1}^{T} E(|X_{T.t}|^2 I\{|X_{T.t}| > \delta\}|\mathcal{F}_{T.t-1}) \xrightarrow{P} 0, \ for \ all \ \delta > 0, \qquad \text{(B.2)}$$

$$\sum_{t=1}^{T} \mathrm{Var}(X_{T.t}|F_{T.t-1}) \xrightarrow{P} I, \qquad \text{(B.3)}$$

it holds that $S_T = \sum_{t=1}^{T} X_{T.t} \xrightarrow{w} N(0, I)$.

The first condition states that the finite sequence $X_{T.1}, \ldots, X_{T.T}$ is a martingale difference sequence with respect to the increasing sequence of σ-fields $\mathcal{F}_{T.1}, \ldots, \mathcal{F}_{T.T}$. The second condition is the analogue of the classical Lindeberg condition, which can be replaced by

$$\sum_{t=1}^{T} E|X_{T.t}|^3 \to 0.$$

The last condition requires that we have normalized the variables properly. This version of the central limit theorem is taken from Helland (1982), see also Hall and Heyde (1980).

B.2   Weak Convergence on $C[0, 1]$

We now turn to weak convergence for measures defined on the space of continuous functions on the unit interval: $C[0, 1]$. The basic stochastic process, Brownian motion, is defined as follows:

DEFINITION B.4 *The Brownian motion $W(t)$, $t \in [0, 1]$ with variance Ω is defined as a stochastic process with the following properties*

$$W(0) = 0. \qquad \text{(B.4)}$$
$$W(t) \ is \ N_p(0, t\Omega). \qquad \text{(B.5)}$$
$$The \ process \ has \ independent \ increments. \qquad \text{(B.6)}$$
$$The \ process \ is \ continuous \ as \ a \ function \ of \ t. \qquad \text{(B.7)}$$

If $\Omega = I$ the process is called standard Brownian motion.

If W is a Brownian motion defined on some probability space we can find the distribution of the process by mapping the probability measure into the space $C[0, 1]$ by the mapping

$$\omega \to W(\cdot).$$

That is, to each ω we consider the sample path $t \to W(t)$ which by definition is a continuous function. For this to make sense one must of course first define a σ-field on $C[0,1]$. We therefore define the σ-field C generated by the open balls

$$B(x_0, \delta) = \{x \in C[0,1] : \sup_t |x(t) - x_0(t)| < \delta\}.$$

Here $B(x_0, \delta)$ is the ball around the function x_0 with radius δ, that is, the set of all functions which deviate less than δ from the given function x_0, or in other words, all functions lying in a 2δ band around the function x_0. Thus we consider the uniform norm on $C[0,1]$.

On $C[0,1]$ there is also a notion of convergence that is important

$$x_n \to x \text{ if } \sup_t |x_n(t) - x(t)| \to 0, \ n \to \infty,$$

that is, convergence of a sequence of functions x_n means uniform convergence on the unit interval.

Various functionals defined on $C[0,1]$ are continuous with respect to this notion of convergence. Consider for instance the evaluation functional L_s which to any function x associates the value of x at the point s, that is

$$L_s(x) = x(s).$$

It is clear that if $x_n \to x$ (uniformly) then it also converges at any given point, and hence that L_s is continuous and hence measurable with respect to the σ-field C. This shows that sets of the form

$$\{x : x(s_i) \le a_i, \ i = 1, \ldots, n\},$$

are measurable, and hence that we can discuss the distribution of the process at a finite number of points, the so-called finite-dimensional distributions.

Another continuous function that will be considered is the functional

$$x \to \int_0^1 x(t)dt,$$

which to any continuous function associates the integral of the function. To see that this is continuous, let $x_n \to x$, and evaluate

$$\left| \int_0^1 (x_n(t) - x(t))dt \right| \le \int_0^1 |x_n(t) - x(t)| \, dt \le \sup_t |x_n(t) - x(t)|.$$

Since convergence of x_n to x is defined such that x_n converges uniformly to x, we see that also the integrals converge. The functional $x \to \int_0^1 x(u)^2 du$

is also continuous by the above since the mapping from $C[0,1]$ to $C[0,1]$:
$x \to x^2$ is continuous. Consider finally the functional from $C[0,1]$ to $C[0,1]$
defined by

$$L(x)(t) = \int_0^t x(u)du.$$

This is also continuous, since

$$\sup_t |L(x)(t) - L(y)(t)| \le \sup_t |x(t) - y(t)|.$$

The definition of weak convergence on $C[0,1]$ is then given by Definition
B.1, which has to hold for all bounded real continuous functionals defined
on $C[0,1]$.

THEOREM B.5 *(The continuous mapping theorem) If $X_n \overset{w}{\to} X$ on $C[0,1]$,
and if L is any continuous functional on $C[0,1]$ with values in R^p or $C[0,1]$,
then $L(X_n) \overset{w}{\to} L(X)$.*

PROOF This is one of the results where the definition used for weak convergence is easily applied, since what we want to prove is that for any
bounded continuous function $f : R^p \to R$, or $C[0,1] \to R$ it holds that

$$E(f(L(X_n))) \to E(f(L(X))).$$

This is obvious since the mapping

$$x \to f(L(x))$$

is a composition of continuous mappings and hence continuous, and bounded
because f is bounded.   □

COROLLARY B.6 *If $X_n \overset{w}{\to} X$ then also $\int_0^1 X_n(t)dt \overset{w}{\to} \int_0^1 X(t)dt$ on R and*

$$\int_0^\cdot X_n(t)dt \overset{w}{\to} \int_0^\cdot X(t)dt \text{ on } C[0,1].$$

PROOF This follows since the mappings $x \to \int_0^1 x(t)dt$ and $x \to \int_0^\cdot x(u)du$
are continuous.   □

COROLLARY B.7 *If $X_n \overset{w}{\to} X$, then also the finite-dimensional distributions
converge.*

PROOF This follows since the mappings

$$x \to (x(s_1), x(s_2), \ldots, x(s_k))$$

of $C[0,1]$ into R^k are continuous.   □

Thus if we have weak convergence to, for instance, Brownian motion, we can immediately get weak convergence of a number of interesting functionals like the integral, which is the one we need.

B.3   Construction of Measures on $C[0,1]$

How then do we construct measures on the space $C[0,1]$, and how can we prove weak convergence ? There is a simple way of constructing a sequence of measures on $C[0,1]$ which will now be discussed.

Consider the random variables $Y_1, \ldots, Y_n$ with values in R. We form the partial sums $S_n = Y_1 + \cdots + Y_n$ and construct the continuous random function $X_n(t)$ by the definition

$$X_n(t) = n^{-\frac{1}{2}} S_{[nt]} + n^{-\frac{1}{2}}(nt - [nt])Y_{[nt]+1}. \qquad (B.8)$$

Note that if $nt = k$, k an integer, then

$$X_n(t) = n^{-\frac{1}{2}} S_k.$$

The continuous function $t \to X_n(t)$ interpolates linearly between the values at the points k/n. Thus $X_n(t)$ is a continuous function which is 0 at $t = 0$. The mapping from the probability space of the random variables X_n into $C[0,1]$ given by (B.8) induces a probability measure P_n on $C[0,1]$. One should of course check that this mapping is measurable. Thus we can construct measures on $C[0,1]$ which have all their mass on some rather simple functions, namely the piecewise linear functions. As $n \to \infty$ these functions become very jagged, and under suitable conditions on the random variables one can show that P_n converges weakly. In this way one can actually construct the Brownian motion as a limit of random walks.

Let us therefore start by assuming that Y_n is a sequence of independent identically distributed binary variables taking the values 1 and -1 with equal probability, such that S_n is a random walk. Note that $E(Y_n) = 0$, and $\text{Var}(Y_n) = 1$, and denote the probability measure on R^n induced by $Y_1, \ldots, Y_n$ by Q_n.

From the central limit theorem it follows that for any fixed t, the limit distribution of $X_n(t)$ is Gaussian with mean zero and variance t. This is seen since

$$n^{-\frac{1}{2}} S_{[nt]} \xrightarrow{w} N(0, t),$$

and the extra term from the expression for $X_n(t)$, see (B.8), is bounded in norm by

$$n^{-\frac{1}{2}} \max_{k \le n} |Y_k|, \qquad (B.9)$$

which tends to zero in probability by Chebychev's inequality:

$$Q_n\{n^{-\frac{1}{2}}\max_{k\le n}|Y_k| \ge \delta\} \le nQ_n\{n^{-\frac{1}{2}}|Y_1| \ge \delta\}$$

$$\le \delta^{-2}EY_1^2 I\{n^{-\frac{1}{2}}|Y_1| \ge \delta\} \to 0.$$

Similarly we can see that for any finite number of points $t_1, \ldots, t_k$ the joint distribution of $X_n(t_1), \ldots, X_n(t_k)$ converges to the joint distribution derived from standard Brownian motion. This joint distribution is most easily expressed by saying that the increments are independent and Gaussian with a variance equal to the length of the time interval.

We saw above that if there is weak convergence we must necessarily have that the finite-dimensional distributions converge, but unfortunately this condition is not enough to ensure weak convergence, and this chapter is an attempt to explain the nature of the extra argument that is needed to prove weak convergence.

B.4 Tightness and Prohorov's Theorem

In order to discuss this we must define and discuss the notion of tightness of a family of probability measures.

On R^p it is well known that for any probability measure P it holds that for all $\delta > 0$ there exists a compact set

$$[-a, a] = \{x \in R^p : |x_i| \le a_i, \, i = 1, \ldots, p\},$$

such that $P[-a, a] \ge 1 - \delta$.

Similarly for any sequence of probability measures that converges weakly on R^p there exists a compact set $[-a, a]$ such that for all n it holds that $P_n[-a, a] \ge 1 - \epsilon$. The general definition on $C[0, 1]$ is

DEFINITION B.8 *A family of probability measures $\mathcal{P}$ on $C[0, 1]$ is called tight if for all $\delta > 0$ there exists a compact set K for which*

$$P(K) \ge 1 - \delta, \quad \text{for all } P \in \mathcal{P}.$$

Informally one can say that if there is weak convergence the probability mass cannot 'escape to infinity', and it is this property that is called tightness. This property is what is needed apart from the convergence of the finite-dimensional distributions to ensure weak convergence on function spaces.

We now formulate Prohorov's theorem for $C[0, 1]$

THEOREM B.9 *(Prohorov's theorem.) Let $\mathcal{P}$ be the family of probability measures on $C[0, 1]$. Then $\mathcal{P}$ is tight if and only if any sequence in $\mathcal{P}$ has a convergent subsequence.*

In order to apply this result to the random walk considered above, assume for a moment that we have proved that the sequence of probability measures P_n induced by the functions $X_n(t)$ given in (B.8) were indeed tight. Then we could extract a convergent subsequence $P_{(n')}$, say. Let the limit probability measure be denoted P_∞, such that $P_{(n')} \xrightarrow{w} P_\infty$. Since weak convergence implies that finite-dimensional distributions converge we must have that P_∞ has the finite-dimensional distribution of the standard Brownian motion. It is not difficult to see that two probability measures are equal if they have the same finite-dimensional distributions. The basic argument behind this is that we can approximate the ball $B(x_0, \delta)$ by the finite dimensional sets

$$\{x \in C[0,1] : |x(i/n) - x_0(i/n)| \le \delta, i = 0, 1, \ldots, n\}.$$

Thus the finite dimensional sets are a determining class since they determine the probability measure uniquely, but not a convergence-determining class since an extra condition is needed to ensure convergence. It follows that P_∞ is standard Brownian motion, and since the limit is the same for any convergent subsequence the sequence itself must be convergent to standard Brownian motion. Note that the result actually defines the Brownian motion as the process on $C[0,1]$ with finite-dimensional distributions as defined by the properties (B.4), (B.5), (B.6), and (B.7). Thus if we can prove that P_n is tight then we can use Prohorov's theorem to show the existence of Brownian motion. The following quote is from Billingsley (1968:20).

The finite-dimensional sets are thus a determining class in $C[0,1]$ but not a convergence-determining class. The difficulty, interest, and usefulness of weak convergence in $C[0,1]$ all spring from the fact that it involves considerations going beyond those of finite-dimensional sets.

The proof of Prohorov's theorem involves general arguments from topology and functional analysis, and will not be discussed here. The main importance is to link the notion of weak convergence of probability measures with the notion of compactness in the space $C[0,1]$. This raises the important issue what such sets look like. For a function in $C[0,1]$ we define the modulus of continuity as follows

$$w_x(\delta) = \sup_{|s-t|<\delta} |x(s) - x(t)|.$$

A function x is uniformly continuous if $w_x(\delta) \to 0$ for $\delta \to 0$, and a set of functions A is equi-continuous if $\sup_{x\epsilon A} w_x(\delta) \to 0$ for $\delta \to 0$.

THEOREM B.10 *(Arzéla–Ascoli) The set A in $C[0,1]$ has compact closure if*

$$\sup_{x\epsilon A} |x(0)| < \infty, \; and \sup_{x\epsilon A} w_x(\delta) \to 0 \; for \; \delta \to 0.$$

Thus a compact subset of $C[0,1]$ is a closed set of functions which is equi-continuous.

B.5   Construction of Brownian Motion

We can now give the basic theorem that can be applied to prove tightness of a sequence of probability measures for the situations that we consider.

THEOREM B.11 *The sequence P_n is tight if the following two conditions are satisfied:*
For each positive η, there exists an a such that

$$P_n\{x : |x(0)| \geq a\} \leq \eta, \ n \geq 1.$$

For each positive ϵ and η, there exists a δ, with $0 < \delta < 1$ and an integer n_0 such that

$$\delta^{-1} P_n\{x : \sup_{t \leq s \leq t+\delta} |x(s) - x(t)| \geq \epsilon\} \leq \eta, \tag{B.10}$$

for all $0 \leq t \leq 1 - \delta$ and all $n \geq n_0$.

The reason for giving this theorem and the story behind it is to see that the type of condition that is needed to prove weak convergence is a condition that bounds the local oscillation of the stochastic process, and it is useful to collect the important inequalities in probability that allow one to evaluate the fluctuations of stochastic processes, like the maximal ergodic lemma, the martingale inequality, Kolmogorov's inequality etc., see Billingsley (1979). In the present context we need to show that a suitable compact set has large measure. For the space $C[0,1]$ the compact sets are defined by the property that the modulus of continuity should be uniformly small, and condition (B.10) above shows that if the stochastic process allows a suitable bound upon its fluctuations as measured by the modulus of continuity, then the probability measures are tight and allow weak convergence.

As an example of the type of calculation that is needed to prove (B.10) consider the random walk S_n and the continuous process $X_n(t)$ defined in (B.8). Let Q_n denote the probability on the space where $Y_1, \ldots, Y_n$ are defined and let P_n denote the distribution of $X_n(\cdot)$ on $C[0,1]$.

In order to show that for the random walk S_n condition (B.10) is satisfied we note that

$$\{\sup_{t \leq s \leq t+\delta} |X_n(t) - X_n(s)| \geq \epsilon\},$$

for large values of n, is roughly the same as

$$\{\max_{1\leq k\leq[n\delta]}|S_k|\geq\epsilon n^{\frac{1}{2}}\}.$$

The probability of this can be evaluated by

$$2Q_n\{\max_{1\leq k\leq[n\delta]}S_k\geq\epsilon n^{\frac{1}{2}}\}.$$

In order to bound this we apply the basic reflection principle, see Feller (1971), to the symmetric random walk and find for $x\leq a$

$$Q_m\{\max_{1\leq k\leq m}S_k\geq a,\ S_m=x\}=Q_m\{S_m=2a-x\},$$

such that

$$Q_m\{\max_{1\leq k\leq m}S_k\geq a\}$$

$$=\sum_{x=-m}^{a-1}Q_m\{\max_{1\leq k\leq m}S_k\geq a,\ S_m=x\}+Q_m\{S_m\geq a\}$$

$$=\sum_{x=-m}^{a-1}Q_m\{S_m=2a-x\}+Q_m\{S_m\geq a\}\leq 2Q_m\{S_m\geq a\}.$$

Hence we can evaluate for $\epsilon>0$

$$Q_n\{\max_{1\leq k\leq[n\delta]}S_k\geq\epsilon n^{\frac{1}{2}}\}\leq 2Q_n\{S_{[n\delta]}\geq\epsilon n^{\frac{1}{2}}\}.$$

By the central limit theorem this can be approximated by the tail of a Gaussian distribution $2(1-\Phi(\epsilon\delta^{-\frac{1}{2}}))$ which by Chebychev's inequality for the fourth moment is bounded by $6\delta^2\epsilon^{-4}$, hence

$$\delta^{-1}Q_n\{\max_{1\leq k\leq[n\delta]}S_k\geq\epsilon n^{\frac{1}{2}}\}\leq 2\delta^{-1}[Q_n\{S_{[n\delta]}\geq\epsilon n^{\frac{1}{2}}\}-(1-\Phi(\epsilon\delta^{-\frac{1}{2}}))]+6\delta\epsilon^{-4}.$$

This shows that for any ϵ and η we can choose a δ such that condition (B.10) is satisfied for n sufficiently large and hence that the process X_n is tight.

This completes our 'proof' that the measures P_n constructed on $C[0,1]$ from the random walks converge weakly to Brownian motion. Using Prohorov's theorem we have actually proved the existence of Brownian motion.

B.6 Stochastic Integrals with Respect to Brownian Motion

If F is a distribution function on $[0,1]$ and f is a continuous bounded function, we define the integral of f with respect to F by the limit

$$\int_0^1 f(u)dF(u)=\lim\sum_{i=0}^{n-1}f(u_i)(F(u_{i+1})-F(u_i)),$$

where the limit is taken over all partitions of the unit interval

$$0 = u_0 < u_1 < \cdots < u_n = 1,$$

as $\max_{0 \le i \le n-1} |u_{i+1} - u_i| \to 0$.

This defines the Riemann–Stieltjes integral. We can replace F by a function of bounded variation, that is, a function for which

$$\sum_{i=0}^{n-1} |F(u_{i+1}) - F(u_i)| \le c < \infty \text{ for all partitions.}$$

If we replace F by Brownian motion then in order for the limit to make sense we need another definition of the limit since Brownian motion does not have bounded variation.

Let therefore $X(u)$ be a stochastic process with continuous sample paths and $W(u)$ Brownian motion. Assume that they are both measurable with respect to an increasing family of σ–fields $\mathcal{F}_u$, $u \in [0, 1]$.

We then define the stochastic integral $\int_0^1 X(dW)$ as the L_2 limit of

$$\sum_{i=0}^{n-1} X(u_i)(W(u_{i+1}) - W(u_i)) \tag{B.11}$$

where the limit is taken over all partitions as $\max_{0 \le i \le n-1} |u_{i+1} - u_i| \to 0$.

Thus it is part of the definition that

$$\text{Var}\left[\int_0^1 X(dW)' - \sum_{i=0}^{n-1} X(u_i)(W(u_{i+1}) - W(u_i)) \right] \to 0.$$

The existence of this limit is not at all obvious and requires a detailed study, see Karatzas and Shreve (1988). If F has bounded variation, then it holds that

$$\int_0^1 F(dW) = F(1)W(1) - \int_0^1 W(u)dF(u),$$

such that in this special case the stochastic integral can be calculated as a Lebesgue–Stieltjes integral. Note that

$$\sum_{i=0}^{n-1} F(t_i)(W(t_{i+1} - W(t_i))$$

is distributed as

$$N(0, \sum_{i=0}^{n-1} F(t_i)^2(t_{i+1} - t_i)\sigma^2),$$

which converges weakly to

$$N(0, \int_0^1 F(u)^2 du\sigma^2).$$

Hence $\int_0^1 F(dW)$ is distributed as $N(0, \int_0^1 F(u)^2 du\sigma^2)$. The main application of the theory of stochastic integrals is in stochastic calculus, but this is not what we need it for. What we need to observe is that various product moments like (B.11) converge, and we apply this fact to express various limit distributions in terms of stochastic integrals.

Once these expressions are found the distribution is simulated using expressions similar to (B.11) for a sufficiently fine partition.

B.7   Some Useful Results for Linear Processes

We summarize some useful results about sums and product moments for multivariate i.i.d. processes ϵ_t with mean zero and variance matrix Ω, and apply them to linear processes.

THEOREM B.12 *For a sequence of p-dimensional independent identically distributed variables with mean zero and variance Ω it holds that*

$$T^{-\frac{1}{2}} \sum_{i=1}^{[Tu]} \epsilon_i \overset{w}{\to} W(u), \tag{B.12}$$

$$T^{-2} \sum_{t=1}^{T} (\sum_{i=1}^{t} \epsilon_i)(\sum_{i=1}^{t} \epsilon_i)' \overset{w}{\to} \int_0^1 W(u)W(u)' du, \tag{B.13}$$

$$T^{-1} \sum_{t=1}^{T} (\sum_{i=1}^{t-1} \epsilon_i)\epsilon_t' \overset{w}{\to} \int_0^1 W(dW)'. \tag{B.14}$$

If $F_T(t)$ is a sequence of deterministic functions defined for $t = 1, \ldots, T$, which converge to a function F defined on $[0, 1]$, such that $F_T([Tu]) \to F(u)$, then

$$T^{-\frac{1}{2}} \sum_{t=1}^{T} \epsilon_t F_T(t)' \overset{w}{\to} \int_0^1 (dW)F' = W(1)F(1)' - \int_0^1 W(u)dF(u)' \tag{B.15}$$

$$T^{-3/2} \sum_{t=1}^{T} \sum_{i=1}^{t} \epsilon_i F_T(t)' \overset{w}{\to} \int_0^1 W(u)F(u)' du. \tag{B.16}$$

The result (B.12) is Donsker's invariance principle for convergence in the space $C[0, 1]$ (or $D[0, 1]$), see Billingsley (1968), and the second follows from the continuous mapping theorem applied to the continuous functional $x \rightarrow \int_0^1 x(u)x(u)'du$. The result (B.14) and (B.15) are proved in the paper by Chan and Wei (1988) applying the Skorohod representation that replaces weak convergence by almost sure convergence. Finally (B.16) can be proved like (B.13) by applying the joint weak convergence of the processes $F_T([Tu]) \overset{w}{\rightarrow} F(u)$ and $T^{-\frac{1}{2}}\Sigma_{t=1}^{[Tu]}\epsilon_t \overset{w}{\rightarrow} W(u)$, and the continuous mapping $(x,y) \rightarrow \int_0^1 x(u)y(u)'du$.

In the analysis of the autoregressive model we meet many processes generated by linear combinations of the ϵ and we need the results from Theorem B.12 for such linear processes, see Phillips and Solo (1992). We therefore define the linear processes

$$U_t = \sum_{i=0}^{\infty} \vartheta_i \epsilon_{t-i}, \; V_t = \sum_{i=0}^{\infty} \psi_i \epsilon_{t-i},$$

where we assume that the coefficients ϑ_i and ψ_i decrease exponentially fast such that $\vartheta(z) = \sum_{i=0}^{\infty} \vartheta_i z^i$ and $\psi(z) = \sum_{i=0}^{\infty} \psi_i z^i$ are convergent for $|z| \leq 1 + \delta$ for some $\delta > 0$. This guarantees the existence of the processes U_t and V_t in the sense of almost sure convergence and gives the formula

$$\gamma_{uv}(h) = \text{Cov}(U_t, V_{t+h}) = \sum_{i=0}^{\infty} \vartheta_i \Omega \psi'_{i+h}.$$

THEOREM B.13 *Under the above assumptions on the processes U_t and V_t it holds that*

$$T^{-\frac{1}{2}} \max_{1 \leq t \leq T} |U_t| \overset{P}{\rightarrow} 0, \tag{B.17}$$

$$T^{-\frac{1}{2}} \sum_{t=1}^{[Tu]} \begin{bmatrix} U_t \\ V_t \end{bmatrix} \overset{w}{\rightarrow} \begin{bmatrix} \vartheta(1) \\ \psi(1) \end{bmatrix} W(u), \tag{B.18}$$

where $W(u)$ is Brownian motion. Further we have

$$T^{-2} \sum_{t=1}^{T} (\sum_{i=1}^{t} U_i)(\sum_{i=1}^{t} V_i)' \overset{w}{\rightarrow} \vartheta(1) \int_0^1 W(u)W(u)'du\psi(1)', \tag{B.19}$$

$$T^{-1} \sum_{t=1}^{T} (\sum_{i=1}^{t-1} U_i)V_t' \overset{w}{\rightarrow} \vartheta(1) \int_0^1 W(dW)'\psi(1)' + \sum_{h=1}^{\infty} \gamma_{uv}(h) \tag{B.20}$$

$$T^{-\frac{1}{2}} \sum_{t=1}^{T} \epsilon_t V'_{t-1} \overset{w}{\rightarrow} N(0, \Omega \otimes \psi(1)\Omega\psi(1)'). \tag{B.21}$$

If $F_T([Tu])$ is a sequence of deterministic functions that converges to a function $F(u)$ then

$$T^{-3/2} \sum_{t=1}^{T} (\sum_{i=1}^{t} U_i) F_T(t)' \xrightarrow{w} \vartheta(1) \int_0^1 W(u) F(u)' du, \qquad (B.22)$$

and

$$T^{-\frac{1}{2}} \sum_{t=1}^{T} U_t F_T(t)' \xrightarrow{w} \vartheta(1) \int_0^1 (dW) F' = \vartheta(1)[W(1)F(1)' - \int_0^1 W(u) dF(u)'].$$
$$(B.23)$$

PROOF The result (B.17) follows from the inequality

$$P\{\max_{1 \le t \le T} |U_t| \ge \epsilon T^{\frac{1}{2}}\} \le \sum_{t=1}^{T} P\{|U_t| \ge \epsilon T^{\frac{1}{2}}\}$$

$$\le \epsilon^{-2} E(|U_1|^2 1\{|U_1| \ge \epsilon T^{\frac{1}{2}}\} \to 0.$$

This result shows that the continuous process we find by interpolating linearly between the values of $T^{-\frac{1}{2}} U_t$ converges in probability, and hence weakly, to zero on $C[0, 1]$.

The proof of the remaining relations consists in reducing the results to the corresponding results given for i.i.d. variables in Theorem B.12. We expand the function $\vartheta(z)$ at the point $z = 1$, see Lemma 4.1, and find

$$\vartheta(z) = \vartheta(1) + (1 - z)\vartheta^*(z),$$

where for $z \ne 1$ and $|z - 1| < \delta$ we have the expansion

$$\vartheta^*(z) = (\vartheta(z) - \vartheta(1))/(1 - z) = -\sum_{i=0}^{\infty} z^i (\sum_{j=i+1}^{\infty} \vartheta_j) = -\sum_{i=0}^{\infty} z^i \vartheta_i^*.$$

This gives the representations

$$U_t = \vartheta(1)\epsilon_t + \Delta U_t^*, \ V_t = \psi(1)\epsilon_t + \Delta V_t^*,$$

where

$$U_t^* = \sum_{i=0}^{\infty} \vartheta_i^* \epsilon_{t-i}, \ V_t^* = \sum_{i=0}^{\infty} \psi_i^* \epsilon_{t-i},$$

such that

$$\sum_{i=1}^{t} U_i = \vartheta(1) \sum_{i=1}^{t} \epsilon_i + U_t^* - U_0^*. \qquad (B.24)$$

Normalizing by $T^{-\frac{1}{2}}$ we find from (B.17) that (B.18) follows from (B.12). The continuous mapping theorem applied to the process $T^{-\frac{1}{2}} \sum_{i=1}^{[Tu]} \epsilon_i$ and the functional $x \to \int_0^1 x(u) x(u)' du$ shows (B.19).

We next insert (B.24) and a similar expression for V_t into (B.20) and get

$$T^{-1} \sum_{t=1}^{T} (\sum_{i=1}^{t-1} U_i) V_t'$$

$$= T^{-1} \sum_{t=1}^{T} (\vartheta(1) \sum_{i=1}^{t-1} \epsilon_i + U_{t-1}^* - U_0^*)(\psi(1)\epsilon_t + \Delta V_t^*)'$$

$$= \vartheta(1)(T^{-1} \sum_{t=1}^{T} \sum_{i=1}^{t-1} \epsilon_i \epsilon_t')\psi(1)' + \vartheta(1)T^{-1} \sum_{t=1}^{T} (\sum_{i=1}^{t-1} \epsilon_i)\Delta V_t^{*\prime}$$

$$+ T^{-1} \sum_{t=1}^{T} (U_{t-1}^* - U_0^*) V_t'.$$

From (B.14) it follows that the first term converges towards

$$\vartheta(1) \int_0^1 W(dW)' \psi(1)',$$

and we next find the limit of the remaining terms. From the partial summation

$$\sum_{t=1}^{T} (\sum_{i=1}^{t-1} \epsilon_i)\Delta V_t^{*\prime} = (\sum_{t=1}^{T} \epsilon_t) V_T^{*\prime} - \sum_{t=1}^{T} \epsilon_t V_t^{*\prime},$$

we find by dividing by T that the law of large numbers implies

$$\vartheta(1) T^{-1} \sum_{t=1}^{T} (\sum_{i=1}^{t-1} \epsilon_i)\Delta V_t^{*\prime} \xrightarrow{P} -\vartheta(1)E(\epsilon_t V_t^{*\prime}) = (\sum_{i=0}^{\infty} \vartheta_i)\Omega(\sum_{i=1}^{\infty} \psi_i').$$

Finally the third term gives the limit

$$T^{-1} \sum_{t=1}^{T} (U_{t-1}^* - U_0^*) V_t' \xrightarrow{P} E(U_{t-1}^* V_t') = -\sum_{j=1}^{\infty} \sum_{i=j}^{\infty} \vartheta_i \Omega \psi_j'.$$

It remains to check that

$$\sum_{i=0}^{\infty} \vartheta_i \Omega \sum_{i=1}^{\infty} \psi_i' - \sum_{j=1}^{\infty} \sum_{i=j}^{\infty} \vartheta_i \Omega \psi_j' = \sum_{i=0}^{\infty} \vartheta_i \Omega \sum_{j=i+1}^{\infty} \psi_j' = \sum_{h=1}^{\infty} \gamma_{uv}(h).$$

To prove (B.21) we apply the central limit theorem for martingales (Theorem B.3) and define the σ-fields $\mathcal{F}_{T.t} = \sigma(\epsilon_1, \ldots, \epsilon_t)$ and

$$\tilde{\epsilon}_t = \Omega^{-\frac{1}{2}} \epsilon_t,$$

$$\tilde{V}_t = (\psi(1)\Omega\psi(1)')^{-\frac{1}{2}} V_t,$$

$$X_{T.t} = T^{-\frac{1}{2}} \tilde{\epsilon}_t \tilde{V}_{t-1}'.$$

Since V_{t-1} is measurable with respect to $\mathcal{F}_{T.t-1}$ it follows that $X_{T.t}$ is a martingale difference sequence, that is, condition (B.1) is satisfied. We calculate the sum of the conditional covariances in (B.3).

$$\sum_{t=1}^{T} \text{Var}\{X_{T.t}|\mathcal{F}_{T.t-1}\} = I \otimes T^{-1} \sum_{t=1}^{T} \tilde{V}_{t-1}\tilde{V}'_{t-1} \xrightarrow{P} I.$$

Finally we apply the stationarity of the processes to see that the Lindeberg condition is satisfied

$$\sum_{t=1}^{T} E(\|X_{T.t}\|^2 I\{\|X_{T.t}\| \geq \delta\} = E\|\tilde{\epsilon}_t \tilde{V}'_{t-1}\|^2 I\{\|\tilde{\epsilon}_t \tilde{V}'_{t-1}\| \geq T^{\frac{1}{2}}\delta\} \to 0.$$

This clearly implies condition (B.2). Thus the central limit theorem applies and the proof of (B.21) is complete. Finally (B.22) and (B.23) are proved from (B.15) and (B.16) using the representation (B.24).   □

References

AHN, S. K., and REINSEL, G. C. (1990), 'Estimation for partially non-stationary multivariate autoregressive models', *Journal of the American Statistical Association*, 85: 813–23.

ANDERSON, T. W. (1951), 'Estimating linear restrictions on regression coefficients for multivariate normal distributions', *Annals of Mathematical Statistics*, 22: 327–51.

—— (1971), *The Statistical Analysis of Time Series*. John Wiley, New York.

—— (1984), *An Introduction to Multivariate Statistical Analysis*, John Wiley, New York.

BABA, Y., HENDRY, D. F., and STARR, R. M. (1922), 'The demand for M1 in the U.S.A., 1960-1988', *Review of Economic Studies*, 59: 25–61.

BANERJEE, A., DOLADO, J. J., GALBRAITH, J. W., and HENDRY, D. F. (1993), *Co-Integration, Error Correction and the Econometric Analysis of Non-stationary Data*, Oxford University Press, Oxford.

—— and HENDRY, D. F. (eds.) (1992), 'Testing integration and cointegration', *Oxford Bulletin of Economics and Statistics*, 54: 225-480.

BARNDORFF-NIELSEN, O. E. (1978), *Information and Exponential Families in Statistical Theory*, John Wiley, New York.

BERGER, R. L., and SINCLAIR, D. F. (1984), 'Testing hypotheses concerning unions of linear subspaces', *Journal of the American Statistical Association*, 79: 158–63.

BILLINGSLEY, P. (1968), *Convergence of Probability Measures*, John Wiley, New York.

—— (1979), *Probability and Measures*, John Wiley, New York.

BOSWIJK, H. P. (1992), *Cointegration, Identification and Exogeneity: Inference in Structural Error Correction Models*, Thesis Publisher Tinbergen Institute, Amsterdam.

—— (1993), 'Testing for an unstable root in conditional and structural error correction models', *Journal of Econometrics*, 63: 37–60.

—— (1995), 'Testing identifiability of cointegration vectors', forthcoming in *Journal of Business and Economic Statistics*.

BREIMAN, L. (1992), *Probability*. Addison Wesley Pub. Co, Reading, Mass.

CHAN, N. H., and WEI, C. Z. (1988), 'Limiting distributions of least squares estimates of unstable autoregressive processes', *Annals of Mathematical Statistics*, 16: 367–410.

DOORNIK, J. A., and HANSEN, H. (1994), 'A practical test for univariate and multivariate normality', Discussion paper, Nuffield College.

—— and HENDRY, D. F. (1994), *PcFiml 8.0. Interactive Econometric Modelling of Dynamic Systems*, International Thomson Publishing, London.

ENGLE, R. F., HENDRY D. F., and RICHARD J. -F. (1983), 'Exogeneity', *Econometrica*, 51: 277–304.

——and GRANGER, C. W. J. (1987), 'Co-integration and Error Correction: Representation, Estimation and Testing', *Econometrica*, 55: 251–76.

————(1991), *Long-run Economic Relations: Readings in Cointegration*, Oxford University Press, Oxford.

——and YOO, S. B. (1991), 'Cointegrated economic time series: an overview with new results', in Engle and Granger (eds.), *Long-run Economic Relations: Readings in Cointegration*, 237–66, Oxford University Press, Oxford.

ERICSSON, N. R. (ed.) (1992), 'Cointegration, exogeneity and policy analysis, Part I and Part II', *Journal of Policy Modelling*, 14: 251–560.

FELLER, W. (1971), *An Introduction to Probability Theory and its Applications*, John Wiley, New York.

FISHER, F. M. (1966), *The Identification Problem in Econometrics*, McGraw-Hill, New York.

FULLER W. (1976), *Introduction to Statistical Time Series*, John Wiley, New York.

GODFREY, L. G. (1988), *Misspecification tests in Econometrics*, Cambridge University Press, Cambridge.

GONZALO, J., and GRANGER, C. W. J. (1995), 'Estimation of common long memory components in cointegrated systems', *Journal of Business and Economic Statistics*, 13: 27–36.

GRANGER, C. W. J. (1981), 'Some Properties of Time Series Data and their use in Econometric Model Specification', *Journal of Econometrics*, 16: 121–30.

——(1983), 'Cointegrated Variables and Error Correction Models', Discussion paper, University of California, San Diego.

——and KONISHI, T. (1993), 'Separation in cointegrating systems', Discussion paper, University of California, San Diego.

——and LEE, T. -H. (1989), 'Multicointegration', *Advances in Econometrics*, 8: 71–84.

GREGOIR, S., and LAROQUE, G. (1993), 'Multivariate integrated time series: A polynomial error correction representation theorem', *Econometric Theory*, 9: 329–42.

HALL, P., and HEYDE, C. C. (1980), *Martingale Limit Theory and its Applications*, Academic Press, New York.

HAMILTON, J. D. (1994), *Time Series Analysis*, Princeton University Press, Princeton.

HANSEN, H., and JUSELIUS, K. (1995), *CATS in RATS: Cointegration Analysis of Time Series*, Estima, Evanston.

HARBO, I., JOHANSEN, S., NIELSEN, B. G., and RAHBEK, A. C. (1995), 'Test for cointegrating rank in partial systems' Submitted to *Journal of Business Economics and Statistics*.

HELLAND, I. (1982), 'Central limit theorems for martingales with discrete or continuous time', *Scandinavian Journal of Statistics*, 9: 79–94.

HENDRY, D. F. (1995), *Dynamic Econometrics*, Oxford University Press, Oxford.

HYLLEBERG, S., ENGLE R. F., GRANGER, C. W. J., and YOO, S. B. (1990), 'Seasonal integration and cointegration', *Journal of Econometrics*, 44: 215–38.

JOHANSEN, S. (1988a), 'The mathematical structure of error correction models', *Contemporary Mathematics*, 80: 359–86.

—— (1988b), 'Statistical analysis of cointegration vectors', *Journal of Economic Dynamics and Control*, 12: 231–54.

—— (1989), *'Likelihood Based Inference on Cointegration. Theory and Applications'*, Lecture notes, Centro Interuniversitario di Econometria, Bologna.

—— (1991a), 'The power function of the likelihood ratio test for cointegration', in J. Gruber (ed.), *Econometric Decision Models: New Methods of Modelling and Applications*, 323–35. Springer Verlag, New York.

—— (1991b), 'Estimation and hypothesis testing of cointegration vectors in Gaussian vector autoregressive models', *Econometrica*, 59: 1551–80.

—— (1992a), 'A representation of vector autoregressive processes integrated of order 2', *Econometric Theory*, 8: 188–202.

—— (1992b), 'Determination of cointegration rank in the presence of a linear trend', *Oxford Bulletin of Economics and Statistics*, 54: 383–97.

—— (1992c), 'An $I(2)$ cointegration analysis of the purchasing power parity between Australia and USA', in C. Hargreaves (ed.), *Macroeconomic Modelling of the Long Run*, 229–48. Edward Elgar, London.

—— (1992d), 'Testing weak exogeneity and the order of cointegration in UK money demand data', *Journal of Policy Modelling*, 14: 313–35.

—— (1992e), 'Cointegration in partial systems and the efficiency of single equation analysis', *Journal of Econometrics*, 52: 389–402.

—— (1994), 'The role of the constant and linear terms in cointegration analysis of non-stationary variables', *Econometric Reviews*, 13: 205–29.

—— (1995a), 'A statistical analysis of cointegration for $I(2)$ variables', *Econometric Theory*, 11: 25–59.

—— (1995b), 'Identifying restrictions of linear equations: with applications to simultaneous equations and cointegration', *Journal of Econometrics*, 69: 111–32.

—— (1995c), 'The role of ancillarity in inference for non-stationary variables', *Economic Journal*, 105: 302–20.

—— (1996), 'A likelihood analysis of the $I(2)$ model', Submitted to *Scandinavian Journal of Statistics*.

—— and JUSELIUS, K. (1990), 'Maximum likelihood estimation and inference on cointegration: with applications to the demand for money', *Oxford Bulletin of Economics and Statistics*, 52: 169–210.

—— (1992), 'Testing structural hypotheses in a multivariate cointegration analysis of the PPP and UIP for UK', *Journal of Econometrics*, 53: 211–44.

—— (1994), 'Identification of the long-run and the short-run structure: an application to the ISLM model', *Journal of Econometrics*, 63: 7–36.

—— and NIELSEN, B. G. (1994), 'Asymptotics for tests for cointegrating rank in the presence of intervention dummies: manual for the simulation program DisCo', Program and manual at http://www.math.ku.dk/~sjo

—— and SCHAUMBURG, E. (1996), 'Inference for seasonally cointegrated autoregressive processes', Discussion paper, University of Copenhagen

—— and SWENSEN, A. R. (1994), 'Testing rational expectations in vector autoregressive models', Discussion Paper, University of Copenhagen.

JUSELIUS, K. (1992), 'Domestic and foreign effects on prices in an open economy: the case of Denmark', *Journal of Policy Modelling*, 14: 401–28.

—— (1994), 'On the duality between long-run relations and common trends in the $I(1)$ versus $I(2)$ model. An application to aggregate money holdings', *Econometric Reviews*, 13: 157–78.

—— (1995), 'Do purchasing power parity and uncovered interest rate parity hold in the long run? An example of likelihood inference in a multivariate time series model', *Journal of Econometrics*, 69: 211–40.

KAC, M. (1969), 'Some mathematical models in science', *Science*, 166: 695-9.

KARATZAS, I., and SHREVE, S. E. (1988), *Brownian Motion and Stochastic Calculus*, Springer Verlag, New York.

LEE, H. S. (1992), 'Maximum likelihood inferences on cointegration and seasonal cointegration', *Journal of Econometrics*, 54: 1–47.

LÜTKEPOHL, H. (1991), *Introduction to Multiple Time Series Analysis*, Springer-Verlag, New York.

—— (1994), 'Interpretation of cointegrating relations', *Econometric Reviews*, 13: 391–4.

MAGNUS, J. R. and NEUDECKER H. (1988), *Matrix Differential Calculus with Applications in Statistics and Econometrics*, John Wiley, New York.

MIZON, G. E., and RICHARD, J. -F. (1986), 'The encompassing principle and its application to non-nested hypothesis tests', *Econometrica*, 54: 657–78.

MOSCONI, R. (1993), 'Analysis of deterministic trends in cointegrated systems', Discussion Paper, Dep. Econ. e Prod. Politecnico di Milano.

—— and GIANNINI, C. (1992), 'Non-causality in cointegrated systems: representation, estimation and testing', *Oxford Bulletin of Economics and Statistics*, 54: 399–417.

PANTULA, S. G. (1989), 'Testing for unit roots in time series data', *Econometric Theory*, 5: 256–71.

PARK, J. Y. (1992), 'Canonical cointegrating regressions', *Econometrica*, 60: 119–43.

PARUOLO, P. (1995*a*), 'Asymptotic inference on the moving average impact matrix in cointegrated $I(1)$ VAR systems', forthcoming in *Econometric Theory*.

—— (1995b), 'Asymptotic efficiency of the 2 step estimator in $I(2)$ VAR systems', forthcoming in *Econometric Theory*,

—— (1996), 'On the determination of integration indices in $I(2)$ systems', *Journal of Econometrics*, 72: 313-56.

PERRON, P. and CAMPBELL, J. Y. (1993), 'A note on Johansen's cointegration procedure when trends are present', *Empirical Economics*, 18: 777-89.

PHILLIPS, P. C. B. (1988), 'Regression theory for near integrated time series', *Econometrica*, 56: 1021-44.

—— (1991), 'Optimal inference in cointegrated systems', *Econometrica*, 59: 283-306.

—— and SOLO, V. (1992), 'Asymptotics of linear processes', *Annals of Statistics*, 20: 971-1001.

RAHBEK, A. C. (1994), 'The power of some multivariate cointegration tests', forthcoming in *Econometric Theory*.

REIMARS, H. -E. (1992), 'Comparisons of tests for multivariate cointegration', *Statistical Papers*, 33: 335-59.

REINSEL, G. C. (1991), *Elements of Multivariate Time Series Analysis*, Springer-Verlag, New York.

REINSEL, G. C., and AHN, S. K. (1992), 'Vector autoregressive models with unit roots and reduced rank structure: estimation, likelihood ratio test, and forecasting', *Journal of Time Series Analysis*, 13: 353-75.

SAIKKONEN, P. (1995), 'Problems with the asymptotic theory of maximum likelihood estimation in integrated and cointegrated systems', *Econometric Theory*, 11: 888-911.

SHENTON, L. R., and BOWMAN, K. O. (1977), 'A bivariate model for the distribution of $\sqrt{b_1}$ and b_2', *Journal of the American Statistical Association*, 72: 206-11.

SIMS, C. A., STOCK, J. H., and WATSON, M. W. (1990), 'Inference in linear time series models with some unit roots', *Econometrica*, 58: 113-44.

STOCK, J. H. (1987), 'Asymptotic properties of least squares estimates of cointegration vectors', *Econometrica*, 55: 1035-56.

—— and WATSON, M. W. (1988), 'Testing for common trends', *Journal of the American Statistical Association*, 83: 1097-107.

—— —— (1993), 'A simple estimator of cointegrating vectors in higher order integrated systems', *Econometrica*, 61: 783-820.

STRANG, G. (1976), *Linear Algebra and its Applications*, Academic Press, New York.

TERÄSVIRTA, T., and MELLIN, I. (1986), 'Model selection criteria and model selection tests in regression models', *Scandinavian Journal of Statistics*, 13: 159-71.

URBAIN, J. P. (1992), 'On weak exogeneity in error correction models', *Oxford Bulletin of Economics and Statistics*, 52: 187-202.

WARNE, A. (1993), 'A common trends model: identification, estimation and inference', Discussion Paper, University of Stockholm.

VELU, R. P., and REINSEL, G. C. (1987), 'Reduced rank regression with autoregressive errors', *Journal of Econometrics,* 35: 317–35.

Subject Index

Author Index

LaVergne, TN USA
25 May 2010
183894LV00001B/30/P